Solid phase peptide synthesis

a practical approach

TITLES PUBLISHED IN THE PRACTICAL APPROACH SERIES

Series editors:

Dr D Rickwood
Department of Biology, University of Essex
Wivenhoe Park, Colchester, Essex CO4 3SQ, UK

Dr B D Hames
Department of Biochemistry, University of Leeds
Leeds LS2 9JT, UK

Affinity chromatography
Animal cell culture
Antibodies I & II
Biochemical toxicology
Biological membranes
Carbohydrate analysis
Cell growth and division
Centrifugation (2nd Edition)
Computers in microbiology
DNA cloning I, II & III
Drosophila
Electron microscopy in molecular biology
Gel electrophoresis of nucleic acids
Gel electrophoresis of proteins
Genome analysis
HPLC of small molecules
HPLC of macromolecules
Human cytogenetics
Human genetic diseases
Immobilised cells and enzymes
Iodinated density gradient media
Light microscopy in biology
Lymphocytes
Lymphokines and interferons
Mammalian development
Medical bacteriology
Medical mycology
Microcomputers in biology
Microcomputers in physiology
Mitochondria
Mutagenicity testing
Neurochemistry
Nucleic acid and protein sequence analysis
Nucleic acid hybridisation
Oligonucleotide synthesis
Photosynthesis: energy transduction
Plant cell culture
Plant molecular biology
Plasmids
Prostaglandins and related substances
Protein function
Protein purification methods
Protein sequencing
Protein structure
Proteolytic enzymes
Solid phase peptide synthesis
Spectrophotometry and spectrofluorimetry
Steroid hormones
Teratocarcinomas and embryonic stem cells
Transcription and translation
Virology
Yeast

Solid phase peptide synthesis

a practical approach

E Atherton

Cambridge Research Biochemicals,
Harston,
Cambridge CB2 5NX, UK

R C Sheppard

Medical Research Council Laboratory of Molecular Biology,
Hills Road, Cambridge CB2 2QH, UK

OXFORD UNIVERSITY PRESS
Oxford New York Tokyo

IRL Press
Eynsham
Oxford
England

First published 1989

British Library Cataloguing in Publication Data

Atherton E.
Solid phase peptide synthesis.
1. Peptides. Solid state, synthesis
I. Title II. Sheppard, R.C.
547.7′56

ISBN 0 19-963066-6
ISBN 0 19-963067-4(Pbk)

Previously announced as:

ISBN 1 85221 133 4 (hardbound)
ISBN 1 85221 134 2 (softbound)

Typeset and printed by Information Press Ltd, Oxford, England.

Preface

Like other volumes in this series, *Solid Phase Peptide Synthesis* concentrates on the practical aspects of the subject. It has its origins in a series of publications, laboratory notebooks, reports, and other experience accumulated in the Medical Research Council Laboratory of Molecular Biology, Cambridge from about 1972 onwards when a peptide chemistry research group was first established here. Its experimental content necessarily reflects the special techniques for peptide synthesis which were subsequently developed in this laboratory. This point should be made immediately because concentration on the one particular technique of fluorenylmethoxycarbonyl-(Fmoc)-polyamide solid phase synthesis implies no disrespect for the many others who have contributed valuably to the field. In particular, the authors are indebted beyond measure to the original inspiration by Bruce Merrifield who conceived and implemented the solid phase principle some ten years before our own work commenced. Appropriately, the publishers requested us to include a chapter on the Merrifield technique. This we have done with pleasure, though limitations in our personal experience have not allowed us to write with the authority we would have liked, nor to include details of recommended experimental procedures. This volume is not intended as a guide to Merrifield-style solid phase synthesis, though we hope that its practitioners will find much of interest and some of value, especially, for example, the sections dealing with the use of Fmoc-amino acids and their derivatives.

Development of the Fmoc-polyamide solid phase peptide synthesis has continued actively while this handbook has been in preparation, and there have been significant new results.* It has been necessary to establish a cut-off point for inclusion to avoid delaying publication excessively. This we have been obliged to do because of the increasingly widespread use of commercial synthesizers dedicated to continuous-flow Fmoc-polyamide chemistry. With the exception of the new work referred to above, the handbook is up to date at the time of writing, and includes results which have only been published in the scientific literature in preliminary form.

The authors thank most warmly the many colleagues past and present in the MRC Laboratory of Molecular Biology who have contributed to the experimental realization of the Fmoc-polyamide technique. It would be invidious to name them selectively. They are listed in the references, and all credit and thanks are due to them for their pains-taking work.

E.Atherton
R.C.Sheppard

*See, for example, 'A Solubilisable Support for Solid Phase Peptide Synthesis and for Inoculation of Experimental Animals' (*1*).

Contents

1. PEPTIDE SYNTHESIS—AN INTRODUCTION **1**
1.1 Protecting groups 2
1.1.1 Amino-protecting groups 3
1.1.2 Carboxy-protecting groups 4
1.1.3 Side-chain-protecting groups 5
1.2 Formation of the peptide bond 8
1.2.1 Anhydrides 9
1.2.2 Activated esters 9
1.2.3 Coupling agents 9
1.3 Racemization 11

2. SOLID PHASE SYNTHESIS—THE MERRIFIELD TECHNIQUE **13**
2.1 Historical introduction 13
2.2 The solid phase principle 14
2.3 Solid supports 16
2.4 α-Amino group protection 16
2.5 The reversible peptide–resin linkage 17
2.6 Side-chain-protecting groups 19
2.7 Formation of the peptide bond 20
2.8 The synthetic cycle 21
2.9 Cleavage from the resin support 22
2.10 Summary and conclusions 23

3. FLUORENYLMETHOXYCARBONYL-POLYAMIDE SOLID PHASE PEPTIDE SYNTHESIS—GENERAL PRINCIPLES AND DEVELOPMENT **25**
3.1 Historical introduction 25
3.2 General principles 26
3.3 Development 28
3.3.1 Optimization of reaction conditions. The importance of solvation 28
3.3.2 Mildening of reaction conditions. New protecting group combinations 31
3.3.3 Coupling reactions 32
3.3.4 Analytical control, reaction monitoring, and technology 33
3.4 Practical considerations. Reagent purification 34

4. THE SOLID SUPPORT **39**
4.1 Beaded gel resins 39
4.2 Physically supported gel resins 44
4.3 Note added in proof 45

5. **FLUORENYLMETHOXYCARBONYL-AMINO ACIDS** **47**
5.1 Preparation of Fmoc-amino acids 47
5.1.1 Amino acids not requiring side-chain protection 48
5.1.2 Amino acids with *t*-butyl-protected side chains 52
5.1.3 Amino acids with special side-chain-protecting groups 53

6. **PEPTIDE–RESIN LINKAGE AGENTS** **63**

7. **ACTIVATION PROCEDURES** **75**
7.1 Symmetric anhydrides of Fmoc-amino acids 75
7.2 Activated esters of Fmoc-amino acids 76
7.2.1 Pentafluorophenyl esters of Fmoc-amino acids 77
7.2.2 Fmoc-amino acid 3,4-dihydro-4-oxobenzotriazin--3-yl (Dhbt) esters 78
7.2.3 Esters of Fmoc-amino acids with 2,5-diphenyl-2,3-dihydro-4-hydroxy-3-oxo-thiophen-1,1-dioxide 82
7.3 Other potential activation procedures for use in Fmoc-polyamide synthesis 84

8. **INSTRUMENTATION FOR FMOC-POLYAMIDE SOLID PHASE SYNTHESIS** **87**
8.1 Manual instrumentation for use with beaded gel resins 87
8.2 Automatic equipment for use with beaded gel resins 89
8.3 Manually operated equipment for continuous-flow synthesis 90
8.4 Semi-automatic and automatic equipment for continuous-flow synthesis 93

9. **ANALYTICAL AND MONITORING TECHNIQUES** **107**
9.1 Qualitative colour tests 108
9.2 Quantitative amino acid analysis 109
9.3 Hplc examination of partially protected intermediate peptides 111
9.4 Spectrometric monitoring of the reagent stream in continuous-flow synthesis 112
9.4.1 The spectrometric record as verification of correct procedures and synthesizer function 114
9.4.2 Spectrometric monitoring of deprotection reactions 115
9.4.3 Spectrometric monitoring of acylation reactions using Fmoc-amino acid anhydrides 117
9.5 Spectrometric monitoring of the solid phase using Fmoc-amino Dhbt esters 122

10. **REACTION PROCEDURES AND OPERATING TECHNIQUES** **131**
10.1 Resin functionalization 132
10.2 Attachment of the first amino acid 134
10.3 Assembly of the peptide chain 137

10.3.1 Synthesis using beaded gel polydimethylacrylamide resin 137
10.3.2 Continuous-flow synthesis using polydimethylacrylamide gel supported in macroporous Kieselguhr 140

11. RESIN CLEAVAGE AND PURIFICATION **149**
11.1 Cleavage of the peptide from the solid support 149
11.1.1 Cleavage by nucleophiles 152
11.1.2 Cleavage from the alkoxybenzyl ester linkage by acids. Formation of free peptides 154
11.1.3 Cleavage from the benzhydrylamine linkage by acids. Formation of peptide amides 155
11.1.4 Cleavage from the very acid labile linkage by dilute acids. Formation of fully protected peptide fragments 155
11.2 Peptide purification 156
11.2.1 Ion-exchange chromatography 158
11.2.2 Preparative reverse-phase high-performance liquid chromatography 160

12. ILLUSTRATIVE SYNTHESES **163**
12.1 Synthesis of a dodecapeptide containing carboxy-terminal tryptophan 163
12.2 Synthesis of a heptadecapeptide amide containing an amino-terminal pyroglutamyl residue 168
12.3 Synthesis of a peptide amide using a benzhydrylamine linkage 174
12.4 Synthesis of a complex natural peptide containing a difficult combination of amino acids 176
12.5 Synthesis of an N-terminal and side-chain-protected octapeptide 183
12.6 Synthesis of 9-, 16-, 23- and 30-residue peptides using pentafluorophenyl and Dhbt esters in a commercial continuous-flow synthesizer 186

REFERENCES **191**

APPENDIX **195**

INDEX **201**

CHAPTER 1

Peptide synthesis—an introduction

The synthesis of peptides has been a challenge to organic chemists since the turn of the century. The early endeavours—notably those of Emil Fischer and his colleagues—were stimulated by the emerging theories of protein structure (*2*). By the middle of the century, however, the realization that other biologically important molecules had simpler amino acid sequences increased the stimulus and reduced the dimension of peptide synthesis to attainable proportions. The isolation, structure, and synthesis (*3*) of the lactogenic nonapeptide amide hormone oxytocin by du Vigneaud and his co-workers in the early 1950s initiated a new era in both biology and chemistry. New biologically active peptides were isolated apace, requiring new and improved methods for their synthesis. Pharmacological studies required synthesis not only of the often hard-to-isolate natural peptides, but also of numerous analogues, thus permitting investigation of the relationship between chemical structure and biological activity.

The classical methods of solution peptide synthesis were hard pressed to meet this explosive increase in demand. The total number of steps in synthesis of moderately sized peptides is substantial, and many of these are consecutive even if a segment condensation strategy (*Figure 1a*) is adopted in preference to stepwise elongation from the amino (*b*) or carboxy terminus (*c*). Even in skilful hands, yields in peptide bond-forming reactions were often only modest, giving low overall yields and contamination with side products. With the exception of the sometimes cumbersome technique of countercurrent distribution, purification methods for these often intractable mixtures were inadequately developed at this time. In short, although very substantial success was achieved using classical solution techniques, they were highly labour-intensive and needed much skill and experience. This was the background for the search in the 1950s

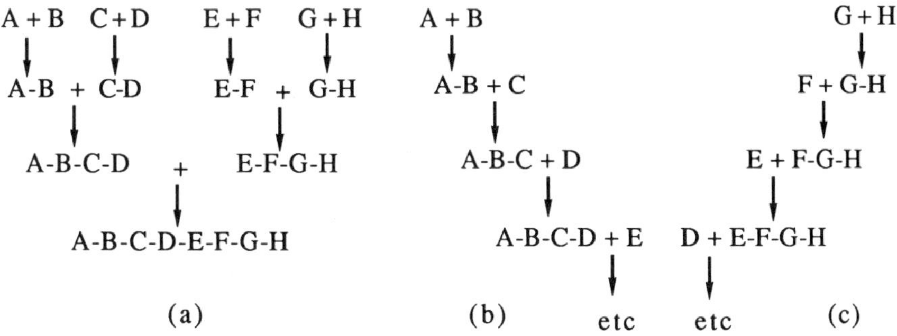

Figure 1. A, B, C, etc. represent individual amino acids. The amino terminus of an amino acid or peptide is conventionally written on the left and the carboxy terminus on the right. (a) Synthesis by regular segment condensation. (b) Stepwise synthesis by extension of the peptide chain from the amino terminus towards the carboxy terminus. (c) Stepwise synthesis from the carboxy terminus towards the amino terminus.

for workable accelerated procedures, of which solid phase synthesis has proved by far the most successful.

In this introductory chapter we shall merely sketch the principles and practice of modern solution synthesis insofar as they are also relevant to solid phase methods. Special attention will be paid to outstanding problems, with later discussion of how they have been ameliorated (or worsened) by solid phase techniques. This section is not fully referenced, and attention is drawn to the list of general sources given in the bibliography (*4*).

1.1 Protecting groups

Unambiguous formation of a peptide bond between two structurally similar amino acids requires that the amino group of one and the carboxy group of the other be prevented from participating in the coupling reaction. The protecting groups also have the important role of destroying the dipolar or zwitterionic character of amino acids and peptides:

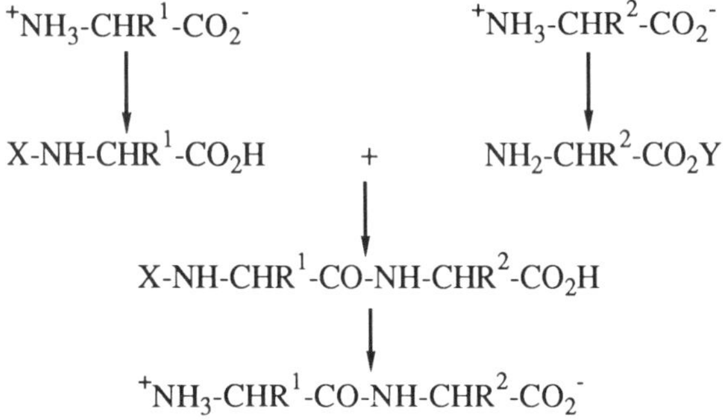

Since chemically reactive groupings are often also present in the side chains of naturally occurring amino acids, additional protecting groups may also be required for these.

Protecting groups have to be chosen so as to be easily introduced, to be chemically stable under the conditions of peptide synthesis, to reduce the reactivity of the amino or carboxy functions adequately, and to protect the adjacent chiral centre (in amino acids other than glycine) from racemization. Finally, they must be easily removable under mild conditions at the end or at intermediate phases in the synthesis. Some compromise has frequently been necessary in attempting to meet these stringent demands.

Protecting groups which are retained until assembly of the peptide chain is complete are known as 'permanent'; those which are removed at intermediate stages are 'temporary'. Clearly the permanent protecting groups require greater stability to the synthesis reaction conditions than those whose required lifespan is shorter. The choice of protecting group combinations depends very much on the synthetic strategy to be adopted. Stepwise elaboration of the peptide chain from the amino terminus (*Figure 1b*) (Nature's way) assigns, in the laboratory, a permanent protecting group to the amino function of the first amino acid and temporary protection to the carboxy groups of the series of residues to be added. For reasons to be discussed later, this strategy is usually not very efficient in the laboratory, and more commonly a strategy involving elongation from the carboxy terminus (*Figure 1c*) is chosen. In this case a permanent protecting group is attached to the carboxyl of the first residue, and temporary amino protection is used for the subsequently added residues. This is the technique almost universally employed in solid phase synthesis. The third alternative, the segment condensation approach (*Figure 1a*), is attractive in terms of minimization of the number of consecutive reaction steps and potentially in ease of purification of the final product, but may be less efficient because of unpredictable solubility and generally lower yields in coupling steps. It clearly requires careful choice of protecting groups. In all three cases permanent protection is usually also required for reactive side chain groupings.

1.1.1 *Amino-protecting groups*

Early in the history of peptide synthesis it was realized that urethane derivatives were particularly suitable for amino protection. Thus from 1932 when they were first introduced by Bergmann and Zervas (*5*), benzyloxycarbonylamino acids (**1**) (Z-amino acids) have been key intermediates in solution peptide synthesis. To a large extent they satisfied the criteria given above for protecting group design. They were easily prepared and chemically stable. The urethane nitrogen atom is usually inert to the subsequent peptide synthesis reaction conditions. Most importantly, the benzyloxycarbonyl group was easily cleaved by catalytic hydrogenolysis, a very mild chemical procedure which left newly formed peptide bonds unaffected. This facile cleavage made the benzyloxycarbonyl function ideal for temporary protection. Subsequently the group was also found to be cleavable under rather strong acidic conditions, notably by hydrogen bromide in acetic acid and later again by liquid hydrogen fluoride. These procedures for final deprotection enabled benzyloxycarbonyl groups (and benzyl ester derivatives in general) to be used in different strategies for more permanent protection. Finally it was found that benzyloxycarbonylamino acids possessed a high degree of optical stability. Racemization of chiral centres adjacent to benzyloxycarbonylamino functions was usually inhibited. This is now known to be a property of urethane protecting groups in general, and is an important factor favouring their widespread adoption.

The concept of temporary and permanent protecting groups requires at least two complementary types. *t*-Butoxycarbonylamino acids (*6*) (**2**) have properties which are substantially complementary to those of benzyloxycarbonyl derivatives. Thus *t*-butoxycarbonyl (Boc) derivatives are unaffected by catalytic hydrogenation, but are cleaved completely under relatively mild acidic conditions (for example trifluoroacetic acid at room temperature) where benzyloxycarbonyl groups are essentially inert. Thus selective cleavage of one in the presence of the other is usually possible. These properties are those of benzyl and *t*-butyl esters, and are shown again in the choice of these esters for carboxy group protection (Section 1.1.2). Benzyloxycarbonyl- and *t*-butoxycarbonyl-protecting groups dominated peptide synthesis strategies for many years. Very many others have been devised but found relatively slight application in solution techniques. Of these may be mentioned a number of ring-substituted benzyl urethanes with modified acid lability; other acid-labile urethanes, for example adamantyloxycarbonyl (**3**); biphenylisopropoxycarbonyl (**4**) (the latter is quite exceptionally labile and may be cleaved selectively in the presence of *t*-butoxycarbonyl); one notable base-labile urethane, the fluorenylmethoxycarbonyl group(*7*) (**5**); and a variety of non-urethane derivatives including *p*-toluene sulphonyl (**6**) and triphenylmethyl (**7**). All have application in specific strategies and will be referred to later.

(**1**) C_6H_5–CH_2-OCO-NH-CHR-CO_2H

(**2**) Me_3C-OCO-NH-CHR-CO_2H

(**3**) (1-adamantyl)–OCO-NH-CHR-CO_2H

(**4**) (4-biphenylyl)–CMe_2-OCO-NH-CHR-CO_2H

(**5**) (9-fluorenyl)–CH-CH_2-OCO-NH-CHR-CO_2H

(**6**) Me–C_6H_4–SO_2-NH-CHR-CO_2H

(**7**) $(C_6H_5)_3$C-NH-CHR-CO_2H

1.1.2 *Carboxy-protecting groups*

Initially, simple methyl (**8**) or ethyl (**9**) ester groups were used for masking carboxy functions, though their cleavage by aqueous alkaline hydrolysis was not always trouble-free. When satisfactory preparative procedures were developed for amino acid benzyl (**10**) and *t*-butyl (**11**) esters, these rapidly gained in popularity. They are cleaved under conditions (hydrogenolysis or acid treatment) analogously to the corresponding urethanes used for amino protection. Thus *t*-butyl esters may be used in a complementary fashion with benzyloxycarbonyl derivatives, and benzyl esters with *t*-butoxycarbonyl. The latter combination is the basis of the Merrifield solid phase technique. A number of variants with special applications have been devised, notably ring-substituted benzyl esters with modified stability. Of these, the *p*-alkoxy ester (**12**) with enhanced acid lability comparable to that of a *t*-butyl ester may be mentioned. Similar structures are used for linkage of the first amino acid to the resin in variants of the basic solid phase procedure.

(**8**)	$-CO_2Me$
(**9**)	$-CO_2C_2H_5$
(**10**)	$-CO_2CH_2C_6H_5$
(**11**)	$-CO_2CMe_3$
(**12**)	$-CO_2CH_2C_6H_4OMe$

1.1.3 *Side-chain-protecting groups*

More than half the amino acids commonly encountered in proteins contain functional side chains. These include acidic carboxy groups (aspartic, glutamic acids); basic residues (lysine, arginine, histidine); hydroxyamino acids (serine, threonine, tyrosine); sulphur-containing amino acids (cysteine, methionine); and finally the heterocyclic indole ring of tryptophan. Not all of these side chains are sufficiently reactive to require protection on every occasion. In solution synthesis, 'minimal' as well as 'global' side-chain protection strategies are followed. The former often poses fewer solubility problems but greater problems of reactant selectivity. Clearly the need for side-chain protection depends upon the severity of reaction conditions to be employed. Unfortunately, in solid phase synthesis reaction conditions tend to be rather severe (large excesses of reagents, extended reaction times, even elevated temperatures on occasions), and nearly complete side-chain protection is almost invariable used.

For those amino acids carrying amino or carboxy groups in their side chains, the same permanent protecting groups can often be employed for these and for the corresponding chain termini. It is worth noting, however, that the reactivities of functional groups present in amino acid side chains may differ significantly from superficially similar groups at peptide chain termini, whether protected or not. Thus the amino group in the side chain of lysine, for example, differs substantially in reactivity from that of a peptide-chain amino terminus. Its increased basicity (pK_a *c.* 10.5 as opposed to *c.* 8.9 for a peptide α-amino group of the same amino acid) is reflected in lowered stability to acid of the protected benzyloxycarbonyl derivative. Thus completely selective cleavage of temporary *t*-butoxycarbonyl groups may not be obtained in the presence of permanent side-chain benzyloxycarbonyl-protected lysine residues.

In this case, ring-modified benzyl derivatives with increased acid stability (for example the 2,6-dichloro derivative, **13**) may be suitable. Similar considerations apply to side-chain carboxy groups, though here the difference is not only of acid strength but also of steric relationship to the peptide chain. Thus side-chain esters of aspartyl residues (**14**) are excellently placed to interact with the nitrogen atom of the adjacent residue to form a succinimide derivative (**15**). Sterically hindered esters (*t*-butyl, cyclohexyl) which minimize this interaction may be preferred. A side-chain ester of glutamic acid (**16**) is similarly well placed to interact with its own nitrogen atom, forming a pyrrolidone carbonyl (pyroglutamyl) derivative (**17**).

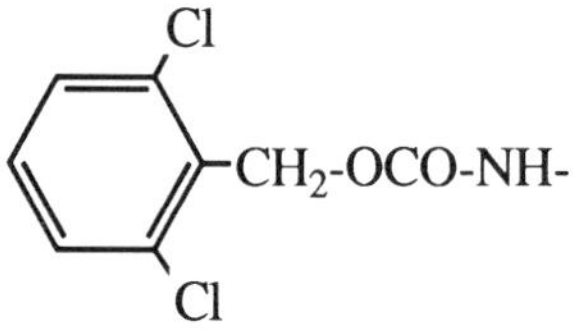

Cl

CH_2-OCO-NH-

Cl

(**13**)

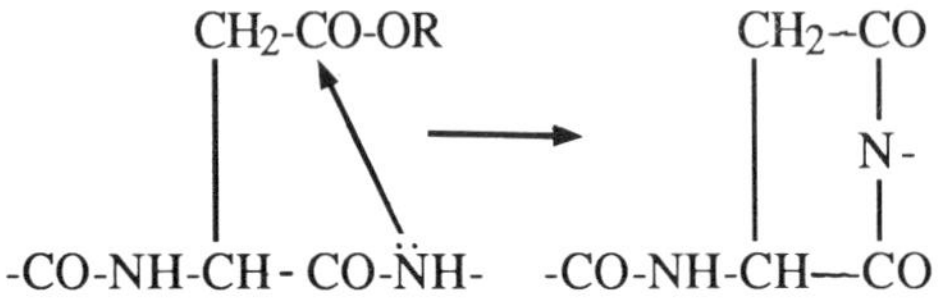

CH_2-CO-OR

-CO-NH-CH- CO-NH-

(**14**)

CH_2–CO

N-

-CO-NH-CH—CO

(**15**)

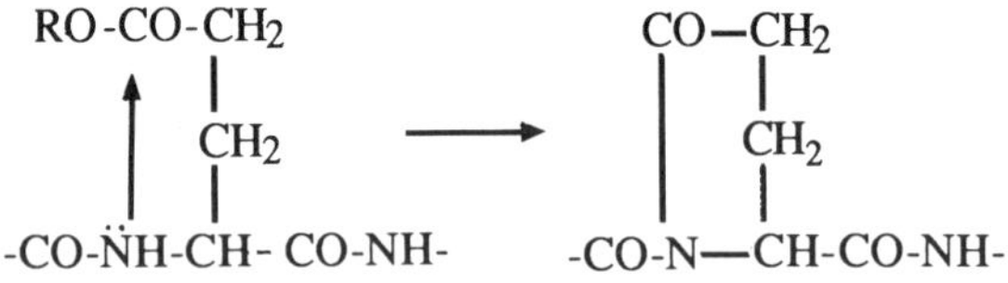

RO-CO-CH_2

CH_2

-CO-NH-CH- CO-NH-

(**16**)

CO—CH_2

CH_2

-CO-N—CH-CO-NH-

(**17**)

These potential side reactions are typical of the problems caused in peptide synthesis by reactive side chains. Much effort and ingenuity has been expended in the development of suitable protecting groups, though completely satisfactory solutions have not always been found.

The guanidino group of arginine presents a special case because of its exceptionally high basicity (pK_a *c.* 12.5). In applications where subsequent acylating conditions are relatively mild, adequate protection may sometimes be provided by simple protonation. Side-chain monoacyl derivatives (benzyloxycarbonyl, *t*-butoxycarbonyl, for example **18**, where the acyl group is arbitrarily assigned to the ω-nitrogen) are often inadequately protected and may be unstable. Nucleophilicity of the guanidine group is incompletley suppressed, and cyclization reactions between the acivated carboxyl group and the side-chain-affording lactams (**19**) may compete substantially with peptide bond formation. Diacyl derivatives of the guanidine group may be better in this respect, or stronger electron-withdrawing groups such as *p*-toluene sulphonyl or nitro may be employed to reduce its nucleophilicity. A number of ring-substituted arylsulphonyl derivatives, such as the methoxytrimethyl derivative (**20**), have recently been introduced and are cleavable under acceptably mild acidic conditions.

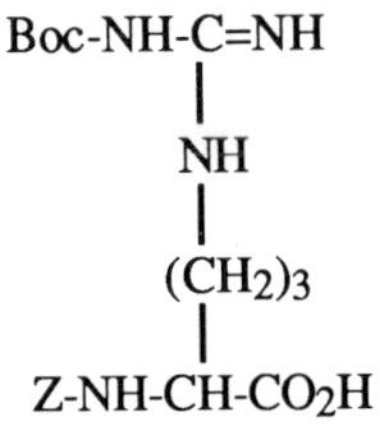

Boc-NH-C=NH
NH
$(CH_2)_3$
Z-NH-CH-CO_2H

(**18**)

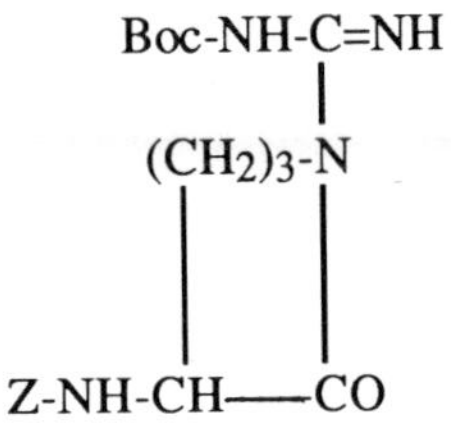

Boc-NH-C=NH
$(CH_2)_3$-N
Z-NH-CH——CO

(**19**)

Me Me
MeO– –SO_2-NH-C=NH
Me
NH
$(CH_2)_3$
Z-NHCHCO_2H

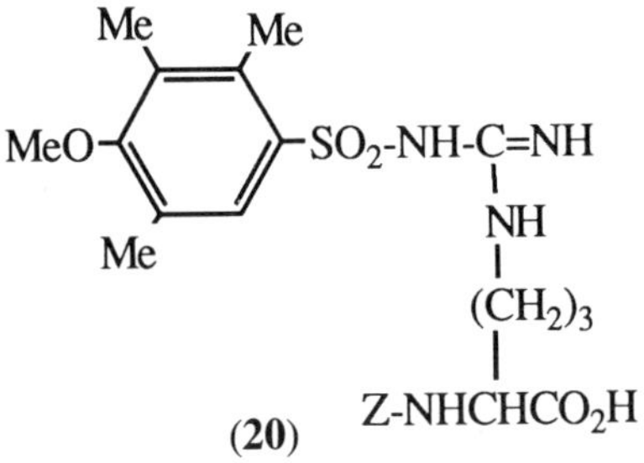

(**20**)

The amino acid histidine also presents special problems. The imidazole ring is itself readily acylated, and acyl imidazoles can promote acyl transfer side reactions. Additionally, the imidazole ring is a powerful catalyst for racemization of chiral α-carbon atoms, particularly that in carboxy-activated histidine itself. This potential for self-racemization is not eliminated in blocked but still basic N_{im}-alkyl derivatives (such as **21**) unless the alkyl group is located specifically on the π-nitrogen atom nearer to the asymmetric α-carbon, as in **22**. In most N_{im}-acyl derivatives the basicity of the imidazole ring is effectively suppressed, and location of the acyl-protecting group on one or other of the ring nitrogens is less important.

Simple side-chain hydroxy groups present little problem and are adequately protected as acid-labile benzyl or *t*-butyl ether derivatives. The thiol group of cysteine is a special

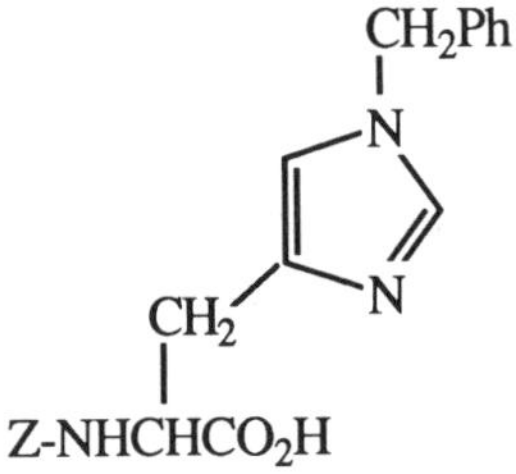

CH_2Ph
N
N
CH_2
Z-NHCHCO_2H

(**21**)

N
N
CH_2
CH_2Ph
Z-NHCHCO_2H

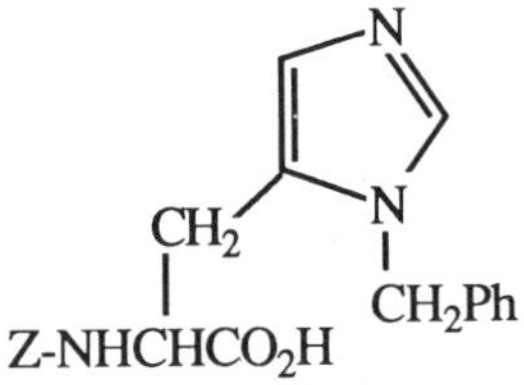

(**22**)

case. Thioethers (such as **23,24**), mixed disulphide (such as **25**), and the S-acetamidomethyl derivative (**26**) all provide adequate protection for the nucleophilic sulphur atom, though the first of these (**23**) requires vigorous conditions (sodium in liquid ammonia reduction, liquid hydrogen fluoride) for its cleavage. The S-*t*-butyl sulphide (**24**) is remarkably stable to acidic reagents, though the corresponding trityl (triphenylmethyl) derivative is usefully acid-labile. S-*t*-butyl compounds are cleaved by mercuric ion, as is the S-acetamidomethyl derivative (**26**). The disulphide (**25**) is deprotected under mildly reducing conditions.

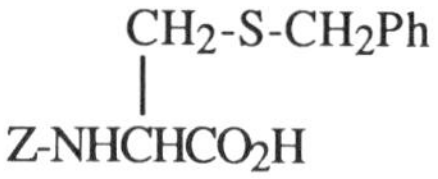

$$\begin{array}{c}CH_2\text{-}S\text{-}CH_2Ph\\ |\\ Z\text{-}NHCHCO_2H\end{array}$$

(**23**)

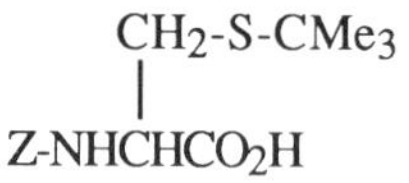

$$\begin{array}{c}CH_2\text{-}S\text{-}CMe_3\\ |\\ Z\text{-}NHCHCO_2H\end{array}$$

(**24**)

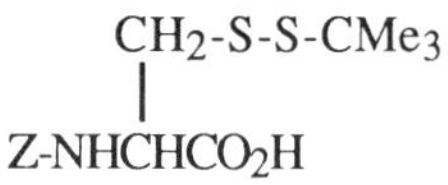

$$\begin{array}{c}CH_2\text{-}S\text{-}S\text{-}CMe_3\\ |\\ Z\text{-}NHCHCO_2H\end{array}$$

(**25**)

$$\begin{array}{c}CH_2\text{-}S\text{-}CH_2NHCOCH_3\\ |\\ Z\text{-}NHCHCO_2H\end{array}$$

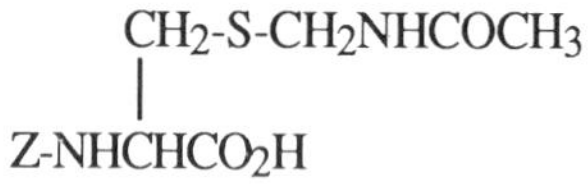

(**26**)

1.2 **Formation of the peptide bond**

The process of peptide bond formation under mild reaction conditions generally requires activation of the carboxy group. Acylating reagents established in more general organic chemistry, for example acyl halides, are commonly too reactive (overactivated) and prone to side reactions to be useful in peptide synthesis. Freedom from side reactions is of exceptional importance in the peptide series insofar as the synthetic products are often intractable and difficult to purify. Thus there has been a protracted search for mild activating procedures which nevertheless effect rapid and clean acylation of amines. Only a few examples which have been found particularly useful will be considered here.

It is convenient to distinguish activated amino acid derivatives (for example *p*-nitrophenyl esters of Boc-amino acids) which may be pre-prepared, stored, and used as required, from coupling agents, for example dicyclohexylcarbodiimide, which are added to the acylamino acid (sometimes in the presence of the amino component) achieving *in-situ* activation immediately prior to or at the time of coupling. Catalysts, such as hydroxybenzotriazole, are commonly added in both procedures.

1.2.1 *Anhydrides*

Mixed anhydrides between acylamino acids and a variety of other carboxylic (and sometimes inorganic) acids were early introduced into peptide synthesis. Of these, the most popular have been anhydrides with carbonic acid derivatives, for example with monoethyl carbonate as in the Boc-amino acid derivative (**27**). The mixed anhydride (**27**) contains two potentially reactive carbonyl groups. Selective acylation by the protected aminoacyl component in (**27**) is strongly favoured by the deactivating effect (electron-donating) of the alkoxy group, and more weakly by the activating (electron-withdrawing) effect of the acylamino substituent. Mixed carboxylic–carbonic anhydrides are not stable over long periods, and are usually prepared at low temperature immediately prior to coupling, using reagents such as ethyl or isobutyl chlorocarbonate. Selectivity in the reaction of mixed anhydrides with amines can also be induced by steric factors, as in the anhydride with bulky pivalic (trimethylacetic) acid (**28**). Symmetrical anhydrides of acylamino acids (for example **29**) are commonly employed, especially in solid phase synthesis. There is no ambiguity concerning which carbonyl is attacked by the incoming amino group, and they thus react exceptionally cleanly and in high yield (relative to the amino component). The yield relative to carboxylic acid can of course reach only a maximum of 50%. Symmetric anhydrides are more stable and have been stored for long periods, but commonly are prepared immediately prior to use with a reagent such as dicyclohexylcarbodiimide (Section 1.2.3)

(**27**) Boc-NHCHRCO-O-CO-OEt

(**28**) Boc-NHCHRCO-O-COCMe$_3$

(**29**) (Boc-NHCHRCO)$_2$O

1.2.2 *Activated esters*

Simple alkyl esters of protected amino acids undergo aminolysis at too slow a rate to be generally useful for peptide bond synthesis. Phenyl esters are more reactive, and when electronegative substituents are present in the aromatic ring may ammonolyse at rates approaching those of anhydrides. Noteworthy examples are *p*-nitrophenyl esters (for example **30**), 2,4,5-trichlorophenyl esters (**31**), and pentafluorophenyl esters (**32**) (*8*). Acylamino-acid derivatives of all three types are usually easily prepared and are stable crystalline solids which may be stored for long periods without decomposition. More recently, a series of esters of N-hydroxylamine derivatives have been found particularly useful. Typical examples are the N-hydroxysuccinimide ester (**33**) and the analogous N-hydroxy-oxo-dihydrobenzotriazine derivative (*9*) (**34**)). Related 1-hydroxybenzotriazole (*10*) is commonly used as a catalyst in acylation reactions involving other activated esters. Its rate-accelerating effect is almost certainly due to formation of the intermediate benzotriazolyl ester (**35**).

1.2.3 *Coupling reagents*

Although a substantial number of reagents have been devised for activating acylamino acids immediately prior to peptide bond formation, only one need be mentioned here, since its importance is overwhelming. Dicyclohexylcarbodiimide (**36**) was introduced into peptide synthesis in the 1950s (*11*). It reacts with acylamino acids to form the initial adduct (**37**). This O-acylurea has never been isolated, but reacts further depending upon the particular reaction conditions. In the absence of added nucleophile (amino component or excess carboxylate), (**37**) slowly rearranges to the N-acylurea (**38**). In the presence of excess carboxylate, that is, when say 1 equivalent of carbodiimide is added to 2 equivalents of acylamino acid), the adduct (**37**) is attacked by carboxylic acid or carboxylate anion, forming the anhydride (**39**) with displacement of dicyclohexylurea

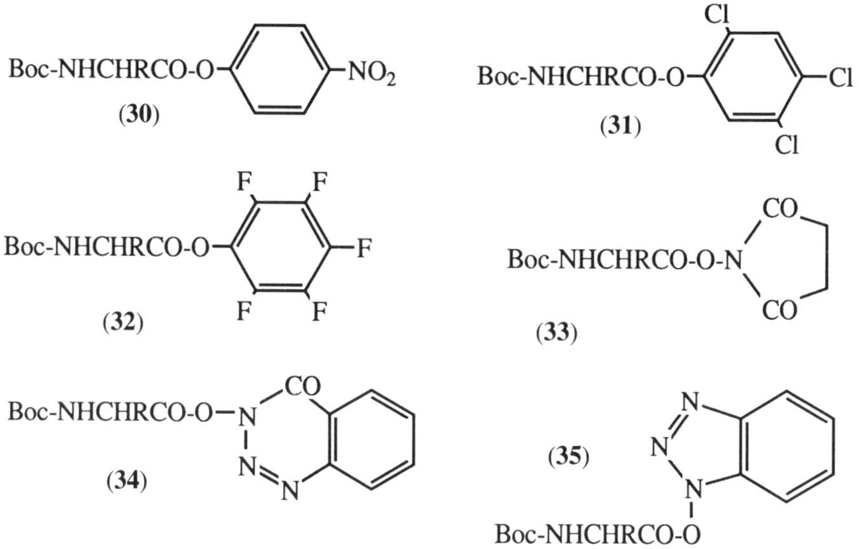

(30) Boc-NHCHRCO-O-C6H4-NO2

(31) Boc-NHCHRCO-O-C6H2Cl3

(32) Boc-NHCHRCO-O-C6F5

(33) Boc-NHCHRCO-O-N(CO)2

(34) Boc-NHCHRCO-O-N (benzotriazinone)

(35) Boc-NHCHRCO-O (benzotriazole)

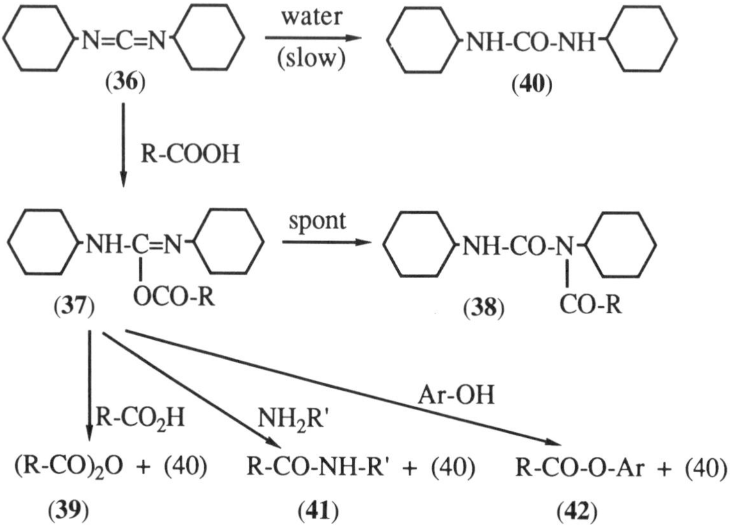

(**40**), the hydration product of carbodiimide. This is the standard method for preparation of acylamino acid anhydrides in peptide chemistry. In the presence of amino component (that is, when carbodiimide is added to a mixture of acylamino acid and amine), the initial adduct (**37**) reacts with amine to form the peptide derivative (**41**) and again dicyclohexylurea is eliminated. Of course, amine acylation may be partly through the anhydride intermediate depending on relative reaction rates. This 'one-pot' procedure (addition of carbodiimide to a mixture of amine and carboxylic acid) is the standard use of dicyclohexylcarbodiimide as a coupling agent. In the presence of phenols or other reactive hydroxy compounds, adduct (**37**) forms ester derivatives (**42**). These may be isolated as such, as in the preparation of acylamino acid *p*-nitrophenyl esters for instance, or if the amino component is also present in the reaction mixture, this in turn will be acylated. This is a common coupling procedure with hydroxybenzotriazole used as the catalytic hydroxy component.

Carbodiimides are thus versatile reagents in peptide chemistry. The particular carbodiimide used can be chosen to simplify isolation of the desired product. Thus dicyclohexylcarbodiimide (the most popular) gives as co-product the highly insoluble urea (**40**) which can often be separated almost quantitatively from soluble peptide derivatives by simple filtration. Diisopropylcarbodiimide gives a much more soluble diisopropylurea and finds application in some solid phase techniques where separation of totally insoluble resin-bound peptide derivative from soluble reagents is not a problem. Carbodiimides bearing tertiary amine or quaternary ammonium groups are used in solution peptide synthesis because of the ease of elimination of the corresponding acid or water-soluble ureas.

1.3 **Racemization**

Nineteen of the 20 common amino acids (those commonly present in proteins) are optically active, possessing chiral (asymmetric) centres at their α-carbon atoms. Two, isoleucine and threonine, have second chiral centres in their side chains. In the proteins and in most naturally occurring peptides, the α-carbon atoms all possess the same relative (L) configurations. Their physical and especially their biological properties are critically dependent upon the integrity of these chiral centres.

All 19 optically active amino acids have hydrogen atoms as one of the substituents at their asymmetric α-carbons. Removal (ionization) and reattachment of this hydrogen atom therefore constitutes a potentially facile mechanism for racemization. The enhanced carbonyl reactivity of the adjacent carboxyl group when activated for a coupling reaction provides a simple mechanism (enolization) whereby this hydrogen atom may be removed. Thus there is risk of racemization by direct ionization of the α-hydrogen during activation and coupling procedures.

In practice it seems that direct ionization of this α-hydrogen is not usually a major source of racemization during peptide synthesis. A second mechanism—formation, racemization, and ring opening of oxazolones—is potentially much more serious:

R NH-C H -NH-CHR-C O CO-X (**43**) → R N—C H -NH-CHR-C O CO (**44a**) ⇌ H N—C R -NH-CHR-C O CO (**44b**)

In this process, the activated carbonyl group effectively acylates the acylamino group (peptide bond) preceding it in the peptide chain (**43**). The resulting oxazolone (**44a**) may racemize much more readily (**44a** ⇌ **44b**), possibly due to some pseudo-aromatic character in the derived anion. Furthermore, the oxazolone, racemized or not, can react with the amino component, acylating it just as its precursor can (**43**). This then provides an alternative, more important mechanism for incorporation of racemic amino acid residues during peptide synthesis. Oxazolones of type (**44**) are generally reactive species, prone to other side reactions and generally lowering the yield and purity of the synthetic peptide. It is probably for these reasons that synthetic strategies based on chain extension from the amino terminus (*Figure 1b*), which provides opportunity for oxazolone formation at every stage, are relatively inefficient in the laboratory. Nature does not find this a problem. Caution is obviously also necessary in the choice of coupling procedures in the segment condensation strategy (*Figure 1a*). When possible, segments should be joined at glycine residues where racemization is not a problem, or at the secondary amino-acid proline, where the oxazolone mechanism seemingly does not apply. It is a fortunate fact of chemistry that when the amide group in **43** is part of a urethane structure, as in Boc- and Fmoc-amino acids and the like, the tendency to oxazolone formation is apparently much reduced. Furthermore, the oxazolone if formed is more resistant to racemization. Thus the stepwise peptide synthesis from the carboxy terminus (*Figure 1c*), using urethane-protected amino acids at every stage, is relatively free from racemization and other side reactions attending oxazolone formation, accounting for the efficiency and popularity of this procedure, particularly in solid phase synthesis.

CHAPTER 2

Solid phase synthesis—the Merrifield technique

2.1 Historical introduction

Solid phase peptide synthesis has an interesting history. The procedure was first proposed (*12*) by R.B.Merrifield in 1962, with a full paper (*13*) published in 1963. In the latter, Merrifield described the preparation of the tetrapeptide leucylalanylglycylvaline by successive addition of benzyloxycarbonylamino acids to a polystyrene resin. To enable cleavage of the benzyloxycarbonyl protecting groups without concomitant detachment of the peptide from the resin support, the latter was nitrated, the nitrobenzyl ester linking groups being more resistant to acids. The synthesis was undoubtedly successful, but perhaps did not augur well for extended applications because the coupling and/or deprotection reaction were not brought to completion and the target tetrapeptide was contaminated with shorter peptides. Thus extension to longer sequences with increased purification problems was unpromising. Within a year, however, the situation had changed dramatically. A third paper (*14*) by Merrifield, published in 1964, described substantial changes in technique, particularly replacement of benzyloxycarbonyl-protected amino acids by the much more acid-labile *t*-butoxycarbonyl derivatives. This and other changes resulted in greatly improved chemical efficiency and permitted synthesis of the naturally occurring nonapeptide bradykinin in highly purified form. This synthesis was a landmark in peptide chemistry. It took just a few days to complete singlehanded (it could have taken as many weeks using classical techniques), and offered immediate promise of a solution to the fast-growing demands for peptides in pharmacology and other biological sciences.

Wide, rapid and often successful application of the method ensued. Not all workers were over-enthusiastic, however, and some peptide chemists (as opposed to biologists) were critical. Their training and experience indicated that strictly quantitative reactions were rare in organic chemistry, especially in fields as complex as that of peptide chemistry. Yet because of the absence of purification of resin-bound peptide after each chemical reaction, quantitative yields were essential in solid phase synthesis if pure products were to be obtained. Failing this, it was felt that solid phase synthesis could only be applicable up to the limited level where purification of the expected complex mixtures was possible. High-performance chromatographic methods had yet to be developed. It may be that many chemists underrated the skill of biochemists in the separation of mixtures of water-soluble substances. On the other hand, biochemists and others may have been unaware of the chemical pitfalls which attend any long sequence of reactions in organic chemistry, and of the need for rigorous characterization of synthetic products produced by a technique which was operated essentially blind.

These early years of solid phase peptide synthesis were characterized by rapid exploitation of solid phase synthesis in biological applications. There was relatively little input of new chemistry after Merrifield's outstanding 1964 paper, and for many years the technique was widely practised unchanged. Full credit must be given to Bruce Merrifield, both for the original conception and for implementing it so quickly in a form which in careful hands was evidently both effective and practical.

Attention is drawn to a number of review articles and books by Merrifield (*15,16*) and others (*17*) which discuss the Merrifield technique at various stages in its development. No attempt is made in this chapter to review in detail the many hundreds, possibly thousands of individual papers which have developed or applied the Merrifield technique.

2.2 **The solid phase principle**

The principle of all solid phase synthesis is simple enough. The growing chain, be it peptide, oligonucleotide (*18*) or other suitable oligomer, is elaborated while it is attached to a stable, solid particle. It usually remains attached to this particle throughout all the synthetic steps and is separated from soluble reagents and solvents by simple filtration and washing. Finally, the desired product is detached from the solid support, and purification and characterization is carried out in free solution.

There are a number of immediate consequences. The separation processes are quick and simple, and can be machine-aided. There is an enormous time and labour advantage over the corresponding operations in solution chemistry which commonly involve techniques of solvent extraction, filtration, evaporation, and crystalization. These often result in substantial losses of material, so that solid phase synthesis may be much more effective in this sense also. Retention of the resin-bound peptide in the same reaction vessel at all times also minimizes physical losses. Because soluble reagents can be so easily removed by filtration, large excesses can be used, encouraging high efficiency in the various chemical steps.

It would be remarkable if such great simplification were not attended by some inbuilt disadvantages. Pre-eminent amongst these is the need for very high reaction efficiencies if useful, purifiable products are to be reliably obtained. Although soluble reagents and by-products are easily removed, insoluble by-products, notably those attached to the resin support, are retained throughout and accumulate to contaminate the final synthetic peptide. Amongst these insoluble by-products will be products of incomplete reaction. The problem is undoubtedly reduced by the ability to use large excesses of reagents which help to drive slow bimolecular or higher-order reactions towards completion, but all who have carried out solid phase synthesis in an analytical way will know that incomplete reactions do occur, and that the circumstances leading to them are not always predictable. Products of chemical attrition of the growing peptide chain also accumulate, their formation being encouraged by the tendency to harshness in the reaction conditions commonly employed. These harsh reaction conditions are again a consequence of the need to drive possibly recalcitrant reactions towards completion, together with the need for very stable permanent protecting groups (including the peptide–resin linkage) which have to survive many synthetic cycles before being cleaved themselves. Finally, the solid phase nature of the system renders inappropriate or insensitive many of the anlaytical procedures which are normally used by chemists to follow the progress and

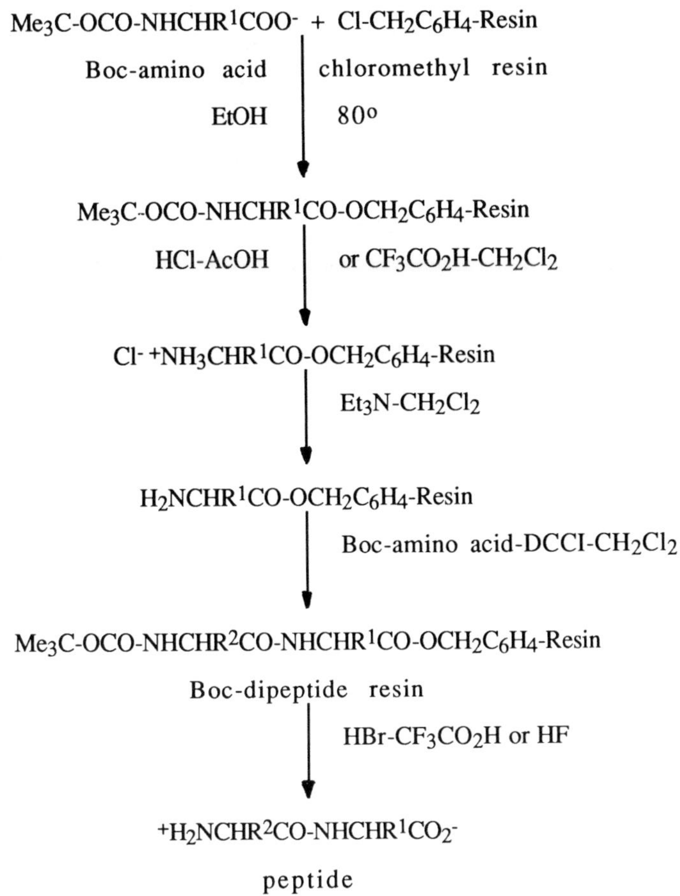

Figure 2. Standard experimental scheme for solid phase peptide synthesis. Synthesis of a dipeptide.

characterize the products of organic synthesis. Most spectroscopic techniques are of very limited value, and amino-acid analysis is usually too slow to be useful in controlling the synthesis. Recourse has commonly been had to simple qualitative colour tests for assessing completion of reactions. Not uncommonly, solid phase peptide synthesis has been carried out completely blind. This approach, which the authors believe should be strongly deprecated, has been encouraged by the rapid development of machinery capable of carrying out automatically operations such as reagent measurement, addition, agitation and filtration, without the need for human intervention or even presence.

Time has shown how the advantages of solid phase synthesis have clearly outweighed these disadvantages.

The original chemistry (*14*) of the Merrifield system is illustrated for synthesis of a simple dipeptide in *Figure 2*. It may be noted that some early beliefs regarding solid phase synthesis must now be recognized as requiring modification. Thus solubility problems which so bedevil extended solution syntheses, and for which solid phase synthesis was initially welcomed as a total solution, are not eliminated in the solid phase method. The symptoms simply reappear in different form. This particular problem is discussed later (Section 3.3.1).

2.3 **Solid supports**

The solid support is the unique feature which distinguishes solid phase synthesis from all other techniques. The general requirements for a useful support have been set out by Erickson and Merrifield (*15*):

> It must contain reactive sites at which the peptide chain can be attached and later removed, and yet it must be stable to the physical and chemical conditions of the synthesis. The support must allow rapid unhindered contact between the growing peptide chain and the reagents. It must be readily separable from the liquid phase at every stage of the synthesis and be physically stable during these operations. In addition, the support must provide enough points of attachment to give a useful yield of peptide per unit volume and must minimize the interactions between bound peptide chains, although the limits of these requirements are not yet clear.

Not all of these requirements are easily met, and there is some conflict. Thus unhindered contact between the support-bound peptide chain and dissolved reagents is seemingly most easily achieved in a lightly cross-linked gelatinous system freely permeated by liquid media. The traditional polystyrene supports are of this type. On the other hand, minimization of interactions between bound peptide chains might better be achieved in a more rigid system functionalized on a solid surface. Surface functionalized silica has been investigated in this connection, though the capacity may be low. Intermediate between these extremes lie a number of actual or potential solid phase systems which have been variously described as popcorn, macroporous, macroreticular, and graft copolymer. In practice, it has been found that simple gelatinous supports have thus far offered the best combination of properties.

Merrifield selected gelatinous polystyrene beads for his system, and this choice has stood the test of time. The lowest cross-linking consistent with total insolubility and physical strength was considered desirable for maximum reagent accessibility. Commonly this is achieved by including 1% of divinylbenzene in the polymerization mixture, though Birr has employed much softer 0.5% divinylbenzene–styrene copolymers in a special reactor (*19*). Lightly cross-linked polystyrene beads typically used in the Merrifield technique swell to volumes of 6–8 ml g^{-1} in relatively non-polar organic solvents such as dichloromethane, so that, relative to solvent, the actual polymer matrix contributes only a small fraction of the interior of the beads.

Gelatinous polymers other than polystyrene have been suggested and employed in solid phase synthesis from time to time. Of these, perhaps the most significant have been a series of polar polyamide resins. These are discussed later (Chapter 4).

2.4 α-**Amino group protection**

The vast majority of solid phase peptide syntheses have employed *t*-butoxycarbonyl-(Boc-) amino acids exclusively. Indeed the name 'Merrifield technique' is synonymous with the *t*-butoxycarbonyl-polystyrene implementation of the solid phase principle. From time to time alternative acid-labile amino-protecting groups, such as biphenylisopropoxycarbonyl (**4**), α,α-dimethyl-3,5-dimethoxybenzyloxycarbonyl-(3,5-di-

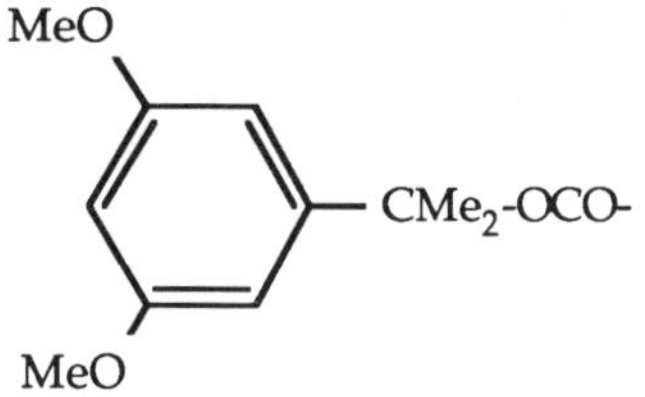

MeO
CMe_2-OCO-
MeO

(45)

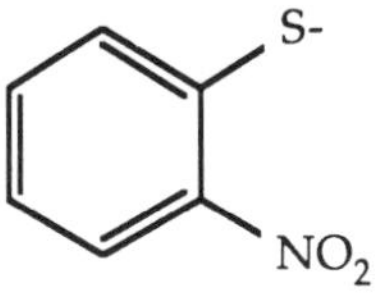

S-
NO_2

(46)

$CHCH_2$-OCO-

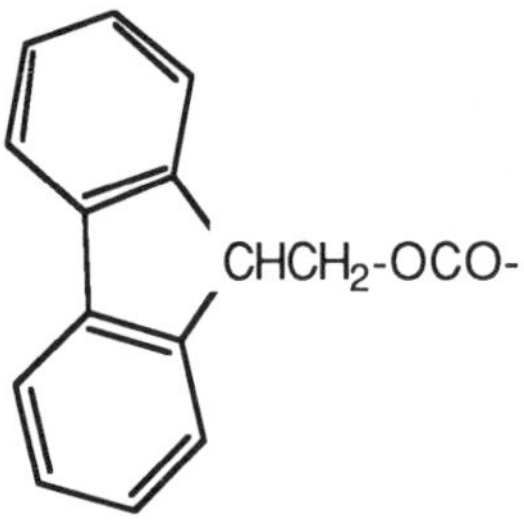

(47)

methoxyphenylisopropoxycarbonyl-) (**45**), and *o*-nitrophenylsulphenyl (**46**), have been suggested and used in special applications, but have not had major impact. However, the appearance of base-labile protecting groups, notably fluorenylmethoxycarbonyl (Fmoc) derivatives (**47**), is having an impact on polystyrene-based synthesis. Since these derivatives also form the basis of the Fmoc–polyamide technique, they are discussed in detail later (Chapter 5).

t-Butoxycarbonyl derivatives are easily cleaved by anhydrous mineral or strong organic acids; trifluoroacetic acid is currently the most popular. Some side reactions may occur during deprotection steps, notably reaction of the newly generated *t*-butyl cations with nucleophilic side chains. Unprotected side chains of tryptophan, tyrosine, methionine, and histidine are potentially at risk in this connection, and scavenging reagents for reactive cations are commonly added to the deprotection reagent.

2.5 The reversible peptide–resin linkage

Benzyl ester linkages have been almost universally used for attachment of the first amino acid to the polymer support. In part, this choice must originally have been influenced by the prior selection of polystyrene as the carrier, providing as it did a relatively straightforward means for generating the benzyl ester system through partial chloromethylation and reaction of the aryl chloromethyl derivative with the triethylammonium salt of a carboxylic acid (*Figure 3*). Caesium salts have also achieved popularity in this last step. In later years, however, chloromethylation of polystyrene was recognized as a potentially troublesome reaction giving rise to other contaminating functional groups attached to the polymer. Additional cross-linking within the resin matrix was also a possibility. The common reagent, chloromethyl methyl ester, has also been recognized as a potential carcinogen. Chloromethylation of polystyrene and reaction of chloromethyl

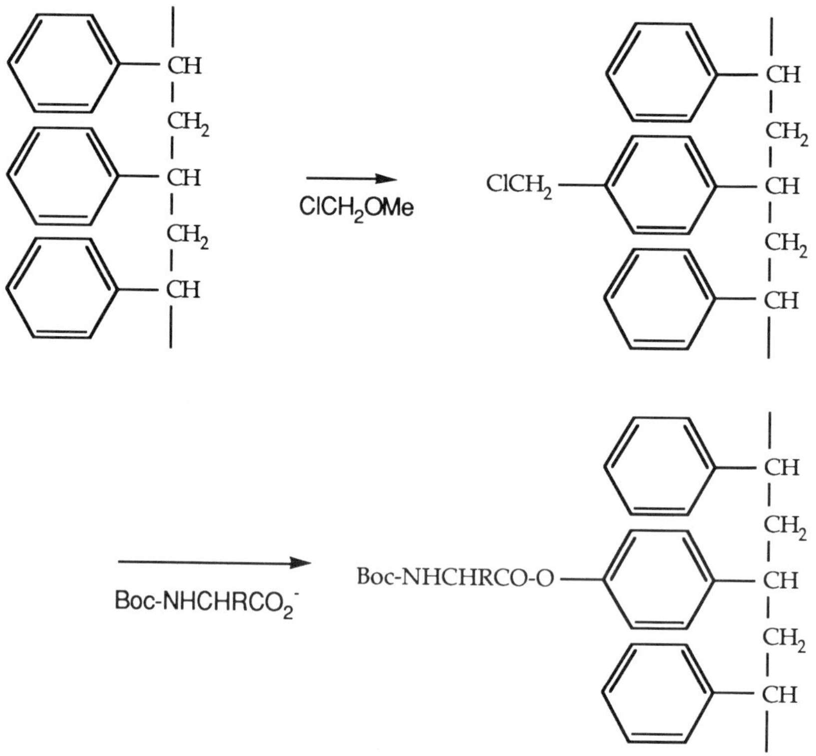

Figure 3. Functionalization and linkage of first amino acid to polystyrene.

derivative with a suitable salt of the first N-protected amino acid has therefore waned in popularity for attachment of the first amino acid, commonly being replaced by use of individual peptide–resin linkage agents (see also Chapter 6). Foremost amongst these in the Merrifield polystyrene series is *p*-hydroxymethylphenylacetic acid (**48**), which, combined with aminomethylpolystyrene, gives the so-called PAM–resin (**49**). It may be that the favoured qualities of this resin are a consequence not just of the increased stability of the benzyl ester conferred by the electron-withdrawing *p*-carboxamidomethyl substituent (the original reason for its introduction), but to its preparation by a route not involving chloromethylation or other Friedel–Crafts-type reactions.

When individual linkage agents are employed (as opposed to direct chloromethylation and reaction of the solid support), two procedures are available for attachment of the C-terminal amino acid. In the first, the linkage agent is attached to the suitably modified polymer (as indicated above for the PAM–polystyrene resin), and the protected amino acid derivative esterified to the resulting resin-bound hydroxyl group. In the second, the C-terminal protected amino acid is esterified to the linkage agent in solution, and the composite then attached to the suitable functionalized resin. The general linkage agent approach is used exclusively in the Fmoc-polyamide system, usually following the first of these procedures.

The peptide–resin linkage must of course remain intact throughout the various stages

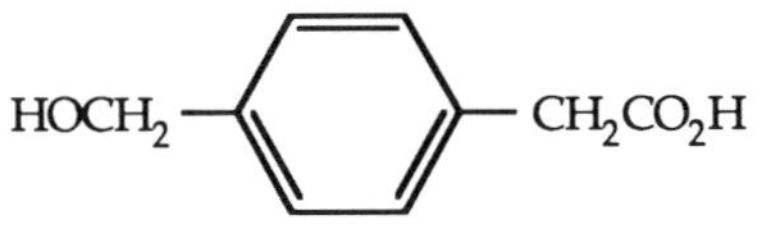

$HOCH_2-C_6H_4-CH_2CO_2H$

(48)

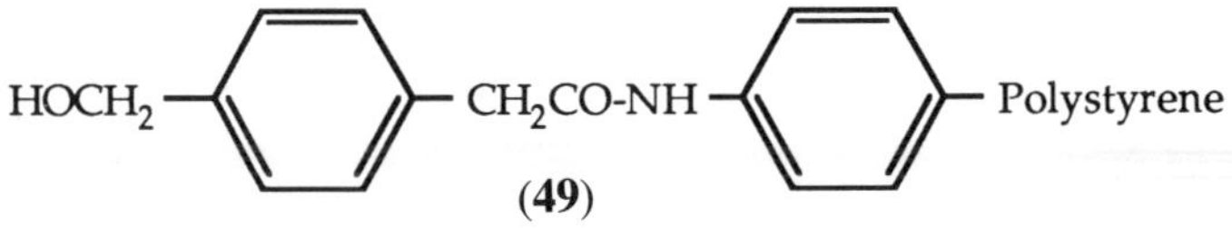

$HOCH_2-C_6H_4-CH_2CO\text{-}NH-C_6H_4-$Polystyrene

(49)

$HOCH_2-C_6H_4-OCH_2-C_6H_4-$Polystyrene

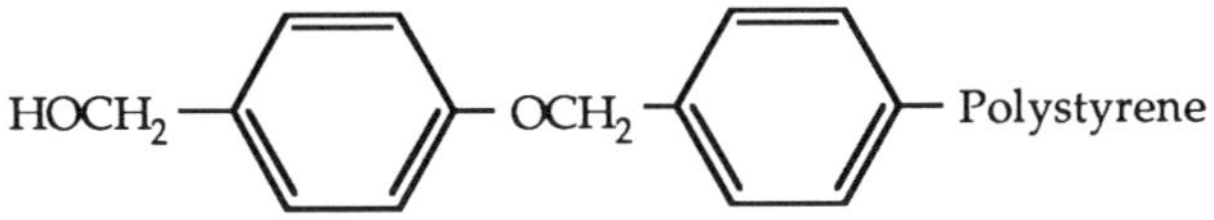

(50)

of chain elongation and temporary protecting group cleavage. The choice of *t*-butoxycarbonylamino-acids (Section 2.4) for chain extension afforded the possibility of selective temporary α-amino-protecting group cleavage using relatively mild acidic reagents, with ultimate cleavage of the more resistant peptide–resin benzyl ester linkage by stronger acids such as hydrogen bromide–trifluoroacetic acid mixture or liquid hydrogen fluoride. This combination has served well, though steady loss of peptide from the resin through partial cleavage of the C-terminal benzyl ester as the synthesis proceeds is sometimes observed. This loss may be of the order of 1–2% per cycle, which is significant for longer syntheses. Bleeding of peptide from the resin is much reduced with the modified PAM linkage mentioned above. In special strategies, for example using Fmoc-amino acids (see Chapter 5 *et seq.*), more acid-labile peptide–resin linkages may be of value. The *p*-alkoxybenzyl alcohol resin (**50**) of Wang (*20*) is noteworthy in this respect.

2.6 Side-chain-protecting groups

It is convenient in solid phase peptide synthesis if the majority or all of the permanent protecting groups (those attached to amino-acid side chains and the carboxy-terminal resin linkage) are cleaved simultaneously in a single step at the end of the synthesis. Thus choice of a benzyl ester function for the peptide resin linkage strongly favours similar protection of amino-acid side chains. This has generally been followed, benzyl ether, thioether, ester, and urethane derivatives being used for side chain hydroxyl, thiol, carboxyl, and amino functions. Not all of the simple benzyl derivatives have adequate stability to acid *vis-à-vis* *t*-butoxycarbonyl. On the other hand, some are too stable to permit easy cleavage at the end of the synthesis. Fortunately their reactivities can usually be adjusted by appropriate nuclear substitution of the benzylic ring. Thus, for example, the more stable 2,6-dichlorobenzyloxycarbonyl (**51**) and 2-bromobenzyl (**52**) derivatives have been used for side-chain protection of lysine and tyrosine residues, and the less acid-stablc *p*-methyl- (**53**) and *p*-methoxybenzyl (**54**) derivatives for cysteine.

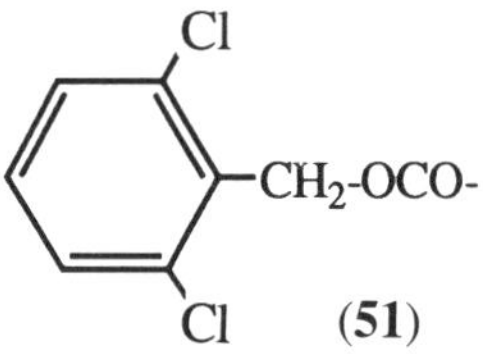

Cl
$-CH_2-OCO-$
Cl (**51**)

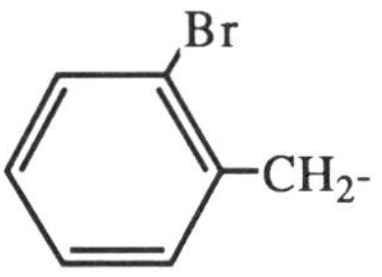

Br
$-CH_2-$
(**52**)

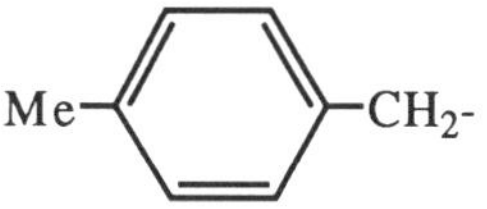

Me– –CH_2- (**53**)

MeO– –CH_2- (**54**)

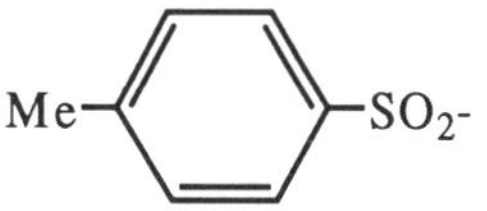

Me– –SO_2- (**55**)

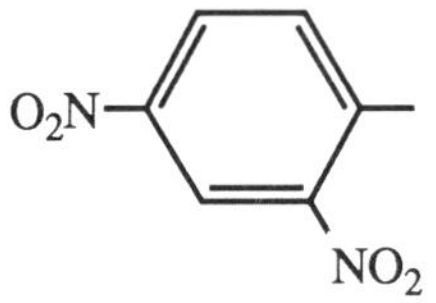

O_2N– NO_2 (**56**)

Acid-labile groups of different type have been necessary for arginine [nitro, tosyl (**55**)], and the *im*-dinitrophenyl (**56**) derivative (cleaved by thiolysis) continues to find application for histidine.

2.7 **Formation of the peptide bond**

From the beginning, polystyrene-based solid phase synthesis has used dicyclohexylcarbodiimide as the near-universal peptide-bond-forming reagent. The chemistry of dicyclohexylcarbodiimide-mediated coupling reactions has been discussed previously (Section 1.2.3). Most syntheses have used the reagent in the conventional manner: it is added to the mixture of amino resin and protected amino acid in amount equivalent to the latter and in a non-polar solvent (dichloromethane). The mechanism of such an activation and acylation process may be complex (see p. 11), but whether the major part of the acylation reaction proceeds through an O-acylurea (**37**) or an *in-situ*-produced symmetric anhydride intermediate (**39**) is unimportant for the present discussion. The same peptide reaction product and co-product, dicyclohexylurea (**40**), are formed in both cases. Dicyclohexylurea is only sparingly soluble, but sufficiently so for it to be eliminated from the reaction vessel during the following extensive washing procedures. Carbodiimides giving more soluble urea derivatives, for example the diisopropyl analogue, have also been recommended. A common side-product of dicyclohexylcarbodiimide coupling reactions, the N-acylurea (**38**), formation of which may cause significant isolation problems in solution chemistry, is relatively unimportant in solid phase synthesis, and is similarly eliminated from the reaction vessel by thorough washing.

Very recently there has been a swing towards prior activation of the protected amino acid before addition to the amino resin. Thus if two equivalents of carboxylic acid are used relative to carbodiimide, again preferably in a non-polar solvent, the relatively stable symmetric anhydride is formed very rapidly and may be separated from dicyclohexylurea at this stage. This procedure has the advantage that the amino resin does not come into contact with other chemical species which might cause yield-lowering side reactions, paricularly with the very reactive carbodiimide itself. On the other hand it is expensive: twice as much protected amino acid is required to maintain the same concentration of acylating agent. This pre-formed anhydride procedure was part of the original Fmoc-polyamide technique, and is discussed further in Chapter 7. It has come into prominence in Boc-polystyrene chemistry more recently, largely because of the availability of equipment for automatically preparing Boc-amino acid anhydrides outside of the main peptide synthesis reaction vessel.

There are some circumstances in which carbodiimide activation of protected amino acids is disadvantageous, regardless of whether the *in-situ* activation–acylation or preformed anhydride techniques are used. These are when there is a risk of side-chain modification by the reagent, the modified amino-acid residues then being incorporated into the synthetic peptide chain. For the amino acids asparagine and glutamine, this problem was recognized early in the study of carbodiimides in peptide chemistry. The activated O-acylurea of asparagine (**57**), for example, may decompose partly with formation of N-protected β-cyanoalanine (**58**). This side reaction may be minimized or possibly even eliminated* by addition of hydroxybenzotriazole to the activation mixture, but a safer procedure involves the use of pre-prepared activated esters of asparagine and glutamine which have been freed of cyano derivatives by careful purification.

CH_2-$CONH_2$ (side chain); Me_3C-OCO-NHCHCO-O-C(=N-cyclohexyl)-NH-cyclohexyl (**57**) → Me_3C-OCO-NHCHCO-OH with side chain CH_2-CN (**58**)

2.8 **The synthetic cycle**

After the first amino acid has been reversibly linked to the solid support, all the following steps save the last constitute a repeated cycle of deprotection, neutralisation, and acylation reactions (see *Figure 2*). A typical basic experimental protocol is given in *Table 1*.

The precise reaction conditions involved in each of these processes has varied over the years and from laboratory to laboratory, but not dramatically so. In the most recent publication from Merrifield's laboratory (*21*) to hand, the deprotection, neutralization, and acylation steps were carried out on 0.8 mmol of Boc-alanyl-PAM–resin using (i) 50% trifluoroacetic acid/dichloromethane for 20 min (cleavage of the terminal *t*-butoxy-carbonyl group); (ii) 5% diisopropylethylamine/dichloromethane (time unspecified, neutralization of the amine trifluoroacetate salt); and (iii) double coupling with preformed symmetrical anhydrides (3.6 mmol, 3 eq of the Boc-amino acid) for 1 h each in dichloromethane and then in dimethylformamide. (Presumably the numerical values

*Formation of β-cyanoalanine may also be masked and rendered unimportant by reversion to asparagine during final cleavage of the peptide-resin with liquid hydrogen fluoride.

Table 1. Reaction protocol for the basic Merrifield procedure (1969).

Operation	*Rpts*	*Time (min)*
1. Dichloromethane wash	2	2
2. Trifluoroacetic acid in dichloromethane (1:1)		2
3. Trifluoroacetic acid in dichloromethane (1:1)		21
4. Dichloromethane wash	5	2
5. Chloroform wash	3	2
6. Triethylamine in chloroform (1:10)		7
7. Chloroform wash	3	2
8. Dichloromethane wash	3	2
9. Boc-amino acid (3 eq.) in dichloromethane		7
10. DCCI (3 eq.) in dichloromethane		300
11. Dichloromethane wash	2	2
12. Ethanol wash	3	2

quoted in (iii) are incorrect; it seems likely that 2 aliquots of 3 equiv each of anhydride were used in successive acylation reactions.) A third coupling of symmetrical anhydride in N-methylpyrrolidinone at 50°C for 2 h was used when necessary to give greater than 99.8% completion as determined by a quantitative ninhydrin assay.

This example illustrates how the paramount need for very high reaction efficiencies can require the use of vigorous reaction conditions. Two successive coupling reactions and even a third at elevated temperature were found necessary before the desired yields were obtained in this ambitious, 50-residue synthesis. Total exposure to trifluoroacetic acid of the growing peptide chain exceeded 8 h.

2.9 Cleavage from the resin support

In conventional polystyrene-based synthesis, the first (C-terminal) amino acid is linked to the support through a benzyl ester-type linkage. Essentially the same linkage is involved in PAM-polystyrene syntheses, though the benzyl ester now bears a *p*-carboxamidomethyl substituent rather than the usual direct attachment to the polyethylene chain. The electron-withdrawing character of the carboxamido group increases the stability of the ester function towards acidic reagents, and reduces premature loss of peptide during intermediate deprotection cycles. It also reduces the rate of peptide detachment during the final acidic cleavage reaction.

Strongly acidic reagents are required for benzyl ester cleavage. Two reagents have found wide application—anhydrous hydrogen bromide in trifluoroacetic acid, and liquid hydrogen fluoride. The former avoids the need for special equipment for handling volatile and highly toxic hydrogen fluoride, but the latter is probably more effective and widely used. Destruction of acid-sensitive tryptophan residues may be less. A recent variant in the hydrogen fluoride technique (the so-called low−high HF method) utilizes an initial treatment of the peptide resin with hydrogen fluoride in the presence of a relatively large amount of dimethylsulphide, followed by evaporation of the latter and then a second treatment with hydrogen fluoride. Most benzyl groups are thought to be removed by a second-order, SN2 reaction in the first step, minimizing side reactions involving benzyl cations. More resistant protecting groups are then cleaved by the higher concentration of hydrogen fluoride. Another recent introduction is use of the strongly acidic reagent trifluoromethane sulphonic acid for final cleavage of benzyl derivatives. In all cases, electrophile scavengers (for example anisole, divalent sulphur compounds) are commonly added to the reaction mixture to reduce attack of nitronium ions or *t*-butyl or benzyl cations on sensitive amino acids, for example tryptophan, tyrosine, and methionine.

2.10 Summary and conclusions

The Merrifield solid phase synthesis technique has proved of inestimable value. It has made possible the economic synthesis of many thousands of peptides which in turn have contributed very substantially to knowledge in other fields, notably in biology. The Merrifield implementation is simple and quick to operate, and the commercial availability of both reagents and instrumentation has brought peptide synthesis into many non-chemically-oriented laboratories.

It is difficult to assess the global success rate for solid phase peptide synthesis. Unsuccessful syntheses are rarely published, and indeed detailed publication of syntheses now regarded by many as routine is becoming infrequent in the absence of a special chemical research element. Failures do occur, both for technical reasons and because of problems which are intrinsic to the chemistry of the method and the amino-acid sequence. The causes for failure are commonly undetermined, and indeed sometimes the occurrence of the failure itself is unnoticed, especially where syntheses are carried out with inadequate analytical control. This is encouraged by the availability of commercial peptide synthesizers which operate overnight and without the need for human presence.

There are some operator inconveniences and some areas of chemistry where increasing knowledge has indicated possible further development. The former includes the hazards and difficulty of handling liquid hydrogen fluoride; some of the latter are discussed below. Their existence in no way denies the indubitable success of the Merrifield technique.

CHAPTER 3

Fluorenylmethoxycarbonyl-polyamide solid phase peptide synthesis—general principles and development

3.1 Historical introduction

As indicated in Chapter 2, some classically oriented peptide chemists were initially inhibited from using solid phase methods because of what were perceived as significant inbuilt weaknesses. Amongst these were the inability to purify and characterize intermediates, the need for near-quantitative conversions in acylation and deprotection reactions, the general vigour of reaction conditions, and the lack of sensitive analytical techniques for following the progress of solid phase chemistry. Of these, the first is a true feature of the method and cannot easily be changed without losing the major speed, simplicity, and efficiency advantages of the solid phase technique.* The second, the need for near quantitative yields, is an inevitable consequence of the first. Quantitative reactions are regrettably rare in general organic chemistry. Their achievement usually requires careful optimization of reaction conditions in each individual case. Quantitative conversion of starting materials is nullified if over-vigorous conditions designed to ensure this induce side reactions of the product. Finally, no chemist likes to be kept in the dark about the progress of a long series of reactions until the very end, when it is likely to be too late for any remedial action which might have been necessary.

Considerations of this sort prompted our re-investigation of solid phase peptide synthesis in the early 1970s. We accepted entirely that Merrifield's solid phase principle (Section 2.2) provided a valuable framework for peptide synthesis, and that the speed and simplification it offered were likely to be necessary if the expanding demands of modern biology were to be satisfied. On the other hand, it seemed that implementation of this principle could be achieved in ways other than that chosen by Merrifield and his colleagues some 10 years earlier, and that other implementations might reduce the supposed weaknesses. We therefore elected to study in turn several aspects of solid phase synthesis relevant to the above. We were concerned first with optimization of reaction conditions in order to improve the prospect of near-quantitative yields. Our previous experience in peptide synthesis carried out in solution had suggested that solvation of the growing peptide chain and of the polymer backbone might be significant in determining reaction rates and yields in Merrifield synthesis.

Our first thoughts were presented at a meeting of the Eleventh European Peptide Symposium held in Vienna in 1971 (*22*). There we suggested that the growing peptide-

*Purification of intermediate peptides is possible in principle in assemblies using solid phase fragment condensation techniques, but problems of insolubility and purification have largely prevented development of such techniques to a reliable and useful stage.

polymer system might be considered as analogous to a graft copolymer system composed of chains of different type. This led immediately to the concept of polar polyamide supports well solvated by polar aprotic media suitable also for the various reactions involved in peptide synthesis (Section 3.3.1). Experience using these supports in combination with *t*-butoxycarbonyl- (Boc-) amino acid anhydrides and hydrogen-fluoride-cleaved linkages led to the search for new protecting group combinations, new activated species, and to the concept of variable peptide-resin linkage agents (Section 3.3.2). From these emerged the chemistry of the current Fmoc-polyamide system. Concurrently new continuous flow technology was being developed, taking advantage of the properties of the Fmoc group for reaction monitoring and providing a particularly simple machine-aided system.

The results of these investigations have been published in papers presented at European and American Peptide Symposia, in a series of articles in the *Journal of the Chemical Society* (Perkin I and Chemical Communication sections), and in some other journals. These are referred to in the following text. Many of the experimental procedures described are set in context in these publications. An early progress review has also appeared (*23*), as well as specific discussion of the role of the solid support in solid phase synthesis (*24*).

3.2 General principles

The guiding principles governing development of the Fmoc-polyamide solid phase synthesis are straightforward. Accepting that stepwise addition of amino acids to polymer support leads to accumulation of the products of incomplete reaction and to the products of undesired side reactions, the immediate objective must be to establish a system optimized in chemistry so that reactions proceed with maximum efficiency and yet mild enough so that undesired degradative reactions are minimized. Optimization of reaction conditions is to be achieved by careful choice of reactants and solvents. Ambiguous reactions, for example the potential two-way opening of mixed anhydrides, are to be avoided or subjected to careful evaluation before use. Likewise, differential reactivity in the selective cleavage of protecting groups is to be avoided if possible. Minimization of side reactions requires that synthesis and deprotection steps are carried out under chemically mild conditions, and that no other reactive species are present or inadvertently introduced into the system which might participate in side reactions. This last requirement underlines the need for highly purified reactants and solvents. Amongst the reactants must be considered the polymer support itself. Purity of polymers is difficult to establish. Chemical manipulation of the polymer support should therefore be minimized to reduce the risk of accumulation of unknown reactive groups prior to peptide synthesis. Flexibility should be a feature of any new solid phase system. It should, for example, be readily adaptable to the synthesis of side-chain-protected as well as free peptides and peptide amides, and if possible to the assembly of protected peptides in a solid phase fragment condensation approach to the synthesis of large peptides. Finally, opportunity should be taken wherever possible to facilitate analytical control of solid phase synthesis, particularly by real-time quantitative monitoring of both acylation and deprotection reactions. It was envisaged that this might require major changes in the current technology of solid phase synthesis.

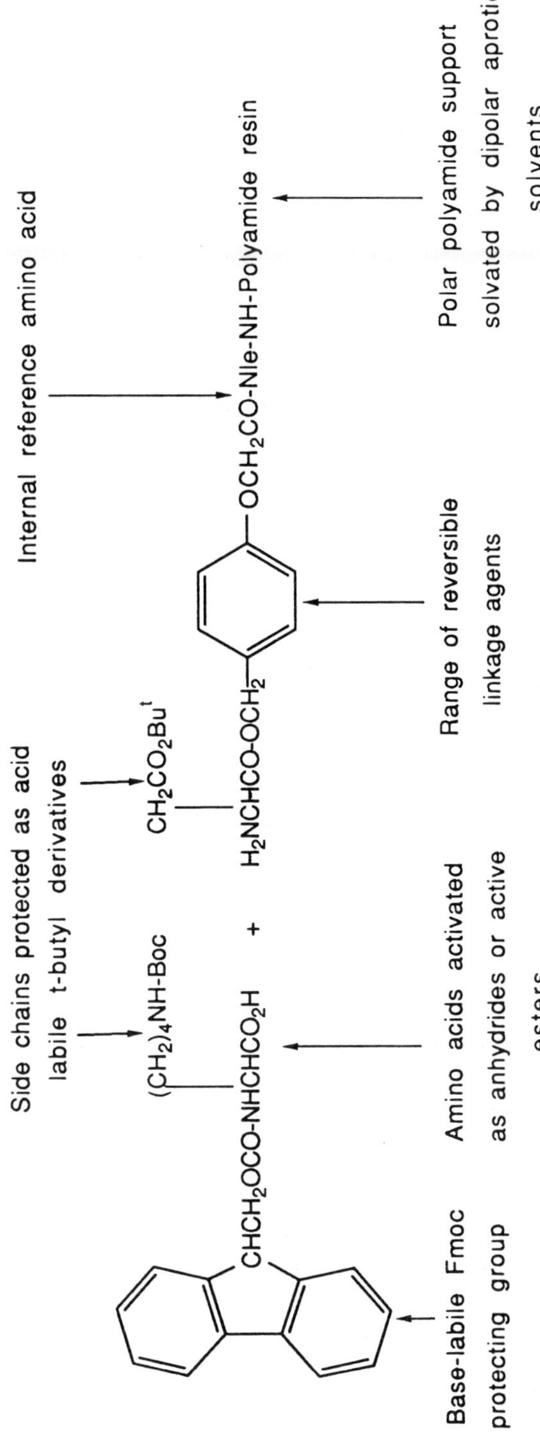

Figure 4. The chemistry of Fmoc-polyamide synthesis illustrated by the carboxy and amino components for a simple dipeptide coupling.

These are all desirable principles. Inevitably some compromises have been necessary as development of the Fmoc-polyamide technique has proceeded.

3.3 **Development**

The chemical features of the current Fmoc-polyamide peptide synthesis are summarised in *Figure 4*. The stages in development leading to this chemistry are discussed in the following sections.

3.3.1 *Optimization of reaction conditions. The importance of solvation*

Optimization of reaction conditions is a matter of organic chemistry. While unimolecular reactions are concentration-independent, bimolecular and higher-order reactions proceed faster at higher concentration. Thus coupling reactions which must involve at least two reacting species are best carried out at maximum concentration when they are favoured relative to unimolecular decompositions. On the other hand, high concentrations encourage aggregation. In free solution, aggregation may lead to precipitation. In the solid (gel) phase, aggregation is not necessarily prevented by the polymeric nature of the system but is manifested differently. It may cause marked hindrance of reaction. Thus solvation of the entire polymeric system may be crucial for efficient solid phase synthesis.

Three solvation states (*Figure* 5a–c) of the peptide–polymer combination were initially envisaged (*22*) and a fourth (*Figure* 5d) added later.

In situation (a), the carrier polymer is depicted in an extended, fully solvated state, as are the shorter pendant peptide chains. Reactive centres, the terminal amino groups in peptide synthesis, are well separated and mobile. In (b), the carrier polymer is again well solvated but the peptide chains have now collapsed, minimizing contact with the dispersing medium which for them now has poor solvating power. The terminal amino

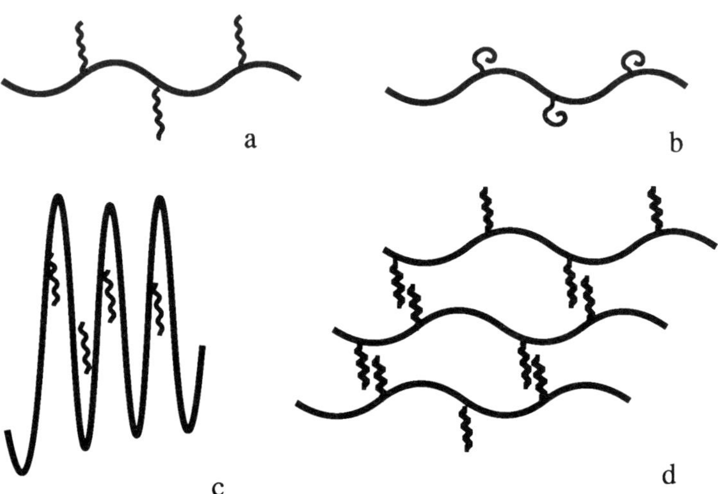

Figure 5. Simplified representation of possible conformational states of a graft copolymer system.

groups may now be buried and subject to massive steric hindrance. Situation (d) is similar, but contact of the peptide chains with the solvent is now minimized through interchain, as opposed to intrachain, aggregation. Individual side chains such as those of asparagine and glutamine may contribute to this aggregation, which may also be regarded as intervention of additional cross-linking in the polymer support system. In situation (d), hindrance of reaction is again to be anticipated. Finally in (c), solvation of the polymer backbone is poor. It undergoes internal collapse with entrainment and again hindrance of the peptide chains.

These are four hypothetical states which may exist in actual peptide synthesis. Experience has indicated that structural transitions do indeed take place as the nature of the system changes. Thus we have frequently observed that a resin-bound peptide which was initially highly swollen in the dispersing medium and thus highly solvated suddenly shrinks at a particular chemical operation. In the Boc-amino acid series, this may be the case when the protecting group is cleaved by hydrogen chloride in acetic acid and the peptide chain acquires a positive charge. During chain elongation in the Boc or Fmoc system, shrinkage may occur at a certain chain length or sequence (*25*). In either case, shrinkage is most easily interpreted as due to intervention of one or other of the internally aggregated states, especially *c* or *d*, with exclusion of solvent.

Evidence has been provided (*26*) in an unrelated polymer system for the existence of structures *a*–*c*. Thus a graft copolymer of natural rubber (polyisoprene) and methyl methacrylate dissolved in benzene to give a clear solution in which both the apolar hydrocarbon and more polar methacrylate chains were believed to be extended, as in *a*. Addition of methanol to this solution causes formation of colloidal particles in which the hydrocarbon chains have collapsed (cf. situation *c*), whereas addition of petroleum ether to the benzene solution is believed to produce the complementary situation analogous to *b*.

In actual solid phase peptide synthesis, the situation is a dynamic one because of the changing nature of the peptide chain as elongation proceeds, and also because of the alternation between protected, positively charged (in the Boc-series), and neutral end groups. Certainly at all times the desired situation is that depicted in *Figure* 5a in which both the support and the growing peptide are extended, mobile, and unhindered. Incursion of one or other of states *b*–*d* is likely to be deleterious, and may be the explanation of the sudden onset of disastrously low or variable amino-acid incorporations which have been reported in the literature from time to time (see for example *27*–*30*). Thus optimization of solid phase synthesis requires that the dispersing medium be a good solvating agent for both the polymer support and the protected peptide. It must also, of course, constitute a good reaction medium for the various chemical steps involved.

Experience from peptide synthesis in solution suggests that dipolar aprotic solvents of the dimethylformamide type are most likely to satisfy these requirements. Long, side-chain-protected peptides are frequently only sparingly soluble in organic solvents, but, of those available, dimethylformamide has been by far the most widely and successfully used. Many simple acylation reactions are faster in dimethylformamide than in less polar media such as dichloromethane or chloroform. Thus in a study of the reaction of benzyloxycarbonylglycine *p*-nitrophenyl ester with ethyl glycinate, Kemp and his colleagues (*31,32*) found that the reaction in dimethylformamide was some 4500 times faster than in chloroform. Intermediate rates were measured for reactions in acetonitrile, dioxan, and toluene; only dimethylsulphoxide provided a faster reaction with enhancement by a further factor of three.

Dimethylacetamide has also been used successfully in Fmoc-polyamide solid phase synthesis. At one time it was favoured over dimethylformamide because the potential acidic impurity (acetic acid) was judged less deleterious than formic acid. Fmoc-amino acids also have marginally greater long-term stability in dimethylacetamide. Its use was discontinued when it was found that some acylation reactions were significantly slower in dimethylacetamide. A third solvent in the same series, N-methylpyrrolidone, was initially discounted when it was discovered that Fmoc derivatives were cleaved at a possibly significant rate just on contact with the solvent (*62*), but may merit reconsideration for use under carefully controlled conditions.

The situation is less clear regarding solvation of the polymer support. Merrifield's cross-linked polystyrene resin swells maximally in relatively apolar solvents. This is presumably the principal reason for the widespread adoption of dichloromethane in solid phase synthesis. Dichloromethane is unlikely to provide the best solvation of protected peptide chains, nor the best acylation medium, though it may be advantageous in the dicyclohexylcarbodiimide activation of acylamino acids. In dimethylformamide, cross-linked polystyrene swells some two-fold less (*33*). Initially we took the view that the use of dimethylformamide was unlikely to be advantageous in polystyrene-based solid phase synthesis because of this reduced solvation. Incursion of collapsed states such as *c* in *Figure 5* seemed possible. This is apparently not the case,* and a recent study has shown that use of dimethylformamide is effective in overcoming problems encountered in polystyrene-supported synthesis using dichloromethane (*34*). Evidently the improved peptide solvation and kinetic properties conveyed by the polar solvent more than outweigh the reduced solvation of the apolar polymer support.

A clearer picture is presented by consideration of polymer supports other than polystyrene. Full solvation of the peptide–polymer system by dimethylformamide might be easily achieved if the polymer were itself of a polar nature. It could possibly even be structurally related to the solvent and/or the peptide chain. Polyamides were obvious possibilities. Disappointingly, commercial polyacrylamide gel proved quite unsuitable (cf. ref. *35*). It failed to swell appreciably in dimethylformamide or in any other organic solvent which might realistically be considered for solid phase peptide synthesis. We ascribed this to the existence of strong internal hydrogen bonding which was disrupted only by powerful donor–acceptor molecules such as water. In agreement, chemical modification of polyacrylamide to replace most of the primary amide groups by tertiary amides provided a new gel support which swelled substantially in a wide range of organic media (*36*). This first polydimethylacrylamide support proved suitable for peptide synthesis. It enabled assembly of a decapeptide test sequence which had not been previously attainable by standard solid phase techniques (*36*), and provided the first validation of our views concerning the importance of full solvation of the whole peptide–polymer system. It encouraged more controlled direct synthesis of various

*Possibly this is due to a specific complexing effect between the polystyrene aromatic rings and dimethylformamide. Benzene itself forms a spectroscopically detectable complex with dimethylformamide.

cross-linked polydimethylacrylamides and their evaluation. These flexible new solid supports with their functional similarity to dispersing dimethylformamide may be considered 'transparent' to soluble reactants. They form the basis of current Fmoc-polyamide chemistry and are described in detail in Chapter 4.

3.3.2 *Mildening of reaction conditions. New protecting group combinations*

In any solid phase synthesis, the starting resin and the progressively extended synthetic chain are subjected to many treatments with chemical reagents without intermediate purification. In the cleavage of Boc groups, for example, the total exposure to trifluoroacetic acid may exceed 7 h in the synthesis of a 20-residue peptide. Total exposure to acylating conditions may exceed 20 h. During all this time, the existing polypeptide chain as well as the permanent protecting groups must remain unaffected. This last requirement has led to the use of very stable side-chain-protected derivatives which will themselves ultimately require vigorous conditions for their cleavage.

There is thus clear need for exceptionally mild and specific reagents to achieve repetitive α-amino-protecting-group cleavage, acylation, and final side-chain deprotection and detachment from the resin. The first and last of these are commonly interrelated. In the Merrifield system, employment of acid-labile derivatives for both temporary and permanent protection means that the latter will require exceptionally strongly acidic treatment for their removal at the end of the synthesis. Thus attempts to devise milder reaction conditions essentially require reconsideration of the protecting group and resin linkage system as a whole. Mildening of acylation conditions requires consideration of the reagents involved, but, equally importantly, the removal of polymer- and solvent-induced steric and kinetic restraints as discussed above. Thus the time of exposure to acylating conditions may be reduced, and especially the need for repeated couplings avoided.

In our reconsideration of overall protecting group strategy, we examined new combinations which did not require differential cleavage by the same reagent type. The limiting requirement is that the permanent side-chain-protecting groups and perhaps simultaneously the peptide–resin linkage should be cleaved under acceptably mild conditions. A cleavage reagent safer and more experimentally convenient than liquid hydrogen fluoride was also desirable. *t*-Butyl derivatives have an accepted reputation for both amino and carboxy protection in solution peptide synthesis (Section 1.1). They are cleaved rapidly and efficiently by acidic reagents (trifluoroacetic acid, anhydrous hydrogen chloride) in acceptably short times (5–20 min). In the Merrifield system, *t*-butyl derivatives are used in the form of Boc groups for amino protection, but in a repetitive sense so that total exposure to acid is long. We felt that *t*-butyl derivatives were well suited to side-chain protection which would require only a single acid treatment in deprotection. The acid lability of *t*-butyl groups is approximately equalled by that of similar *p*-alkoxybenzyl derivatives. The latter constitute convenient alternative acid-labile structures, very suitable for the construction of peptide–resin linkage agents. Use of individual peptide–resin linkage agents rather than direct linkage to the resin confers considerable advantage and flexibility to the Fmoc-polyamide technique.

A number of base-labile protecting groups were considered for α-amino protection (*37*). Of these, the 9-fluorenylmethoxycarbonyl (Fmoc) derivatives of Carpino and Han (*7*) proved particularly suitable. They were cleaved cleanly and rapidly by solutions

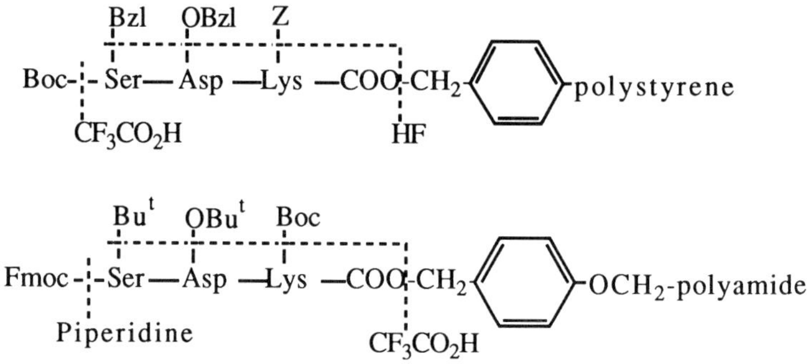

Bzl OBzl Z

Boc- Ser—Asp —Lys —COO-CH_2-⟨C_6H_4⟩-polystyrene

CF_3CO_2H HF

Bu^t OBu^t Boc

Fmoc - Ser—Asp —Lys —COO-CH_2-⟨C_6H_4⟩-OCH_2-polyamide

Piperidine CF_3CO_2H

Figure 6. Protecting group combinations for the Boc-benzyl-polystyrene (upper) and Fmoc-*t*-butyl-polyamide (lower) strategies of solid phase synthesis. In the Boc-benzyl technique, benzyl derivatives variously substituted in the aromatic ring to modify their acid stability may be used. Note that the benzyl ester linkage in the Fmoc-polyamide system similarly has a *p*-alkoxy substituent, greatly enhancing acid lability of the ester bond.

of secondary bases in dimethylformamide, conditions which as far as could be discerned left even particularly sensitive *t*-butyl derivatives entirely unaffected. Thus seemingly complete selectivity between α-amino and side-chain deprotection reactions was easily obtained (*37*). The overall protecting group strategies of the Fmoc-*t*-butyl and Boc-benzyl systems are illustrated in *Figure 6*. The preparation and properties of Fmoc-amino acids are covered in detail in Chapter 5, and linkage agents in Chapter 6.

3.3.3 *Coupling reactions*

Efficiency and freedom from side reactions are the overriding requirements in peptide bond formation. In place of the usual *in-situ* activation of the acylamino acid by dicyclohexylcarbodiimide, we chose to employ preformed activated derivatives. This reduces the risk of side reactions of the resin-bound peptide induced by contact with the activating agent. Thus activation by dicyclohexylcarbodiimide was performed outside the main reaction vessel and the product separated from co-product dicyclohexylurea before addition to the resin. The ratio of acylamino acid to carbodiimide was chosen to encourage formation of the anhydride (*39*) rather than the O-acylurea (*37*) (Section 1.2.3). Use of a slight deficiency of carbodiimide ensured that it was fully consumed before contact with the amino resin.

Similar minimization of side reactions was achieved by use of previously prepared and purified activated ester derivatives. Traditional activated esters, notably those derived from *p*-nitro- or 2,4,5-trichlorophenol, may be used in solid phase synthesis under kinetically appropriate conditions; acylation reactions are nevertheless usually slow. Reaction rates may be accelerated by addition of acylation catalysts such as 1-hydroxybenzotriazole. We found, however, that esters of pentafluorophenol (**59**) originally introduced into solution peptide synthesis by Kisfaludy (*8*) were exceptionally reactive and, in the presence of catalyst hydroxybenzotriazole, approached that of symmetrical anhydrides. The strength of the carbon−fluorine bond and the absence of other reactive centres encouraged the belief that their use would be exceptionally free of side reactions. This proved to be the case. On the other hand, esters of N-hydroxysuccinimide (**60**) which might also have had the desired reactivity were

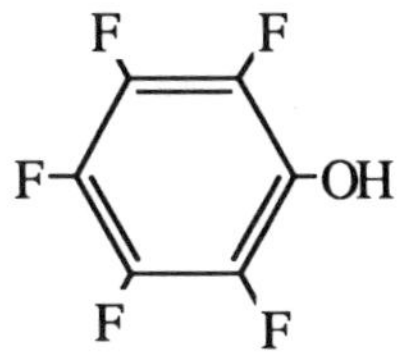

(59)

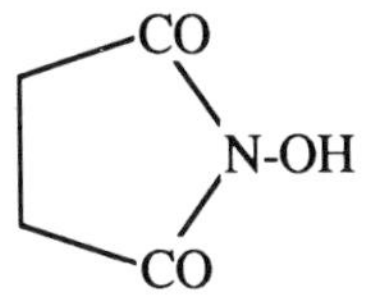

(60)

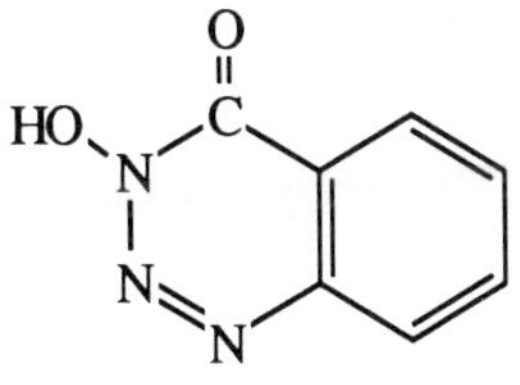

(61)

unsuitable in our experience, presumably because the presence of multiple carbonyl groups provided alternative reaction paths. Esters of 3,4-dihydro-1-hydroxy-3-oxo-benzotriazine (**61**) might also have fallen into this category, but a careful study (*39*) showed that the alternative reaction at the ring carbonyl was unlikely to be a significant source of contaminant in solid phase synthesis. All of these activated derivatives of Fmoc-amino acids are discussed in Chapter 7.

3.3.4 *Analytical control, reaction monitoring, and technology*

The difficulty of analytical control of solid phase synthesis has been one of its major drawbacks. Most usual spectroscopic techniques are inapplicable. Amino acid analysis is slow and the results for resin-bound peptides often distinctly less precise than with isolated peptides. A useful early advance in this respect was the concept of internal reference amino acids. An amino acid residue usually not itself present in the peptide sequence being synthesized, was interposed between the reversible linkage agent and the polyamide resin (*Figure 4*). It is thus permanently bound to the resin during the synthetic steps, and provides a fixed reference point for the interpretation of amino acid analysis data.

Techniques as diverse as electrometric titration, nuclear magnetic resonance spectroscopy, binding of coloured reagents to the resin and subsequent elution, amongst others, have been suggested from time to time for monitoring solid phase reactions quantitatively. None, however, have provided a method useful and simple enough to become a regular part of day-to-day solid phase synthesis. A possible exception is the simle qualitative colour test with ninhydrin for residual unreacted amino groups carried out under conditions suggested by Kaiser and Colescott (*42*). This provides a sensitive indication of completion of the acylation reaction, though it requires to be carried out manually and therefore is often ignored in machine-aided synthesis. The ninhydrin reaction on amino polystyrene resins has also been quantitated (*43*), but usually provides only a post-synthesis measure of acylation.

The replacement of *t*-butoxycarbonylamino acids by fluorenylmethoxycarbonyl derivatives introduced the possibility of direct spectrometric monitoring of solid phase synthesis. The fluorenyl group has strong absorbance in the ultraviolet region, and its uptake from solution on to the solid phase in acylation and release from the solid phase into solution in deprotection provides opportunity for real-time quantitation. On the other hand, measurements in solution are not easily carried out in a shaken or stirred reaction vessel containing an insoluble resin suspension. This provided further motivation for the development of a practical solid phase system using pumped liquid flow through a stationary resin bed. The additional advantages of economy, efficiency, and simplicity afforded by flow techniques in solid phase peptide synthesis had been recognised earlier (*44,45*), but implementation had evidently not been satisfactory using available solid supports. For the Fmoc-polyamide technique, a novel solution to the problems of pumped flow through gelatinous supports was found by polymerizing the gel within the pores of an inert, rigid macroporous carrier (*47*). Accessibility of reagents to the enclosed gel was retained while the physically rigid carrier permitted free solvent flow without the generation of high pressures. The mechanics of this continuous-flow solid phase technique (*48,49*) are described in Chapter 8. It is rapidly gaining in popularity over earier procedures (*37,41*) using an agitated resin bed, especially since commercial equipment using flow principles has become available. The continuous spectrometric monitoring which flow techniques permit are discussed in Chapter 9.

More recently an entirely different approach to monitoring the acylation reaction has been developed (*98,99*). During a study of the applicability of activated Fmoc-amino acid esters of (**61**) to solid phase synthesis, it was observed that a transient yellow colour developed on the resin during the coupling reaction and faded as the reaction progressed. This yellow coloration was attributed to ionization of the liberated hydroxybenzotriazine by residual, resin-bound amino groups. It provided an immediate visual indication of completion of the acylation step. In the continuous-flow technique, the stationary resin bed allowed direct measurement of colour intensity. Thus it was possible for the first time to develop a fully automated system in which feedback control enabled automatic termination of the acylation reaction when it was measured as complete. This technique is described in Chapter 10.

3.4 **Practical considerations. Reagent purification**

It is appropriate in a chapter devoted to 'general principles' to consider those rather practical considerations which have important bearing on successful outcome of solid phase peptide synthesis. Foremost amongst these must be the question of reagent purity. The importance of minimization of side reactions has already been stressed. An obvious source of side reactions is contaminants present in any one of the chemical reagents involved—the polymer support, the protected amino acids, activating and deprotecting reagents, and the dispersing solvent. Reagent purity is perhaps more important in solid phase synthesis than in any other synthetic technique. This is not only because of the very restricted opportunities for elimination of accumulated impurities, but also because high reaction yields are commonly ensured by use of large reagent excesses. Thus relatively small proportions of contaminants may be very significant.

The reagent in largest excess is clearly the solvent which is used both as reaction medium and for extensive washing. A typical synthesis using 1 g of gel resin may involve contact with up to 300 ml of solvent per cycle (considerably less in the continuous-flow technique). One per cent (w/v) of contaminant in that solvent would total 3 times the weight of resin. In conventional solid phase synthesis, 0.0365 g of hydrogen chloride present in the dichloromethane could inhibit entirely acylation of 1 mequiv of amino groups, contained in say 1 – 10 g of resin depending on initial loading. In Fmoc synthesis using polystyrene or polyamide resins, a proportion of free dimethylamine in the dimethylformamide could cause significant loss of Fmoc protecting groups. If this occurred during the acylation step, then double insertion of amino acids might be the consequence. Thus thorough purification of seemingly innocuous solvents is of prime importance.

We give here details of purification procedures which have been used successfully in our laboratory for many years. Doubtless there are equally effective alternatives in many cases, but these are not in our experience. For example, prolonged contact with molecular sieves has been suggested for removal of dimethylamine from dimethylformamide.

Safety considerations should not be overlooked. One of the motivating objectives in developing the Fmoc-polyamide technique was to provide a safer technique, particularly one which did not use extremely hazardous reagents such as liquid hydrogen fluoride. This objective has been achieved, but almost all organic reagents have a degree of toxicity or other hazard associated with them and need careful handling. Many chemical techniques, such as distillation, can be intrinsically dangerous when carried out inexpertly. It is beyond the scope of this book to give detailed descriptions of standard chemical techniques, but less experienced users are recommended to consult a standard practical text, for example Vogel's *Textbook of Practical Organic Chemistry*, before proceeding with steps such as reagent purification. All distillations, and especially distillations *in vacuo*, should be carried out behind a glass screen and preferably in a fume cupboard. Safety spectacles should be worn at all times.

Dimethylformamide (DMF)

Analar grade DMF is fractionally redistilled at approximately 15 mm Hg pressure and *c*. 50 °C through a 12-in fractionation column packed with Fenske steel gauze or glass helices. The apparatus used is illustrated in *Figure 7*. The stopcock controlling the reflux – collection ratio has small grooves allowing precise regulation. When the DMF starts to reflux, the stopcock controlling collection is set to collect about one in every fourth drop from the condenser. Approximately 50 – 70 ml is collected in this way from a total of 1.5 – 2 litres, and then the stopcock fully opened. If any change in temperature is observed when changing from partial to full collection, indicative of a temperature gradient on the column, this process is repeated after collecting a further 10 – 15 ml. Repetition of this process is carried out until no temperature change is observed. A fresh collecting flask is introduced while keeping the boiling DMF under vacuum, the receiver evacuated and DMF collected with minimum reflux.

Distillation of DMF is carried out continuously as the solid phase assembly proceeds, ensuring that fresh DMF is always available.

Dichloromethane

Dichloromethane is distilled from phosphorus pentoxide (10 g l^{-1}) through a 12-in fractionating column containing glass helices, b.p. 38 – 41 °C.

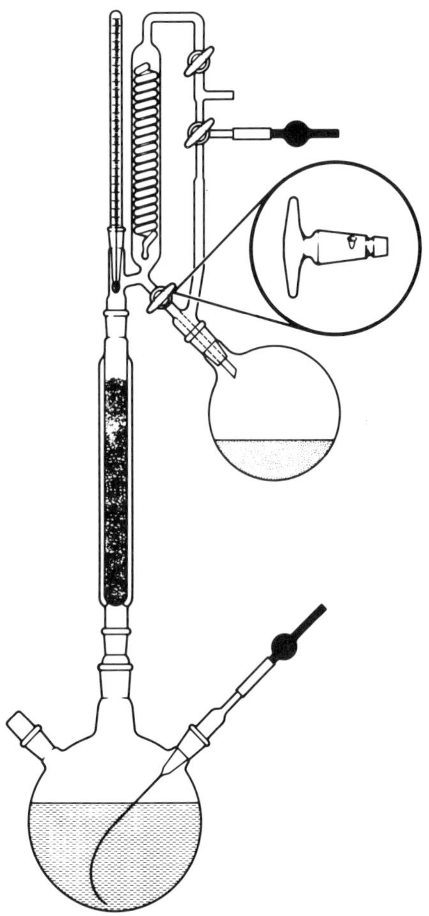

Figure 7. Vacuum distillation apparatus used for the convenient purification of dimethylformamide. Note the small 'V' marks filed into both sides of the distillation control tap facillitating precise control of distillation rate. The two upper vacuum taps allow the receiving vessel to be changed without lowering the vacuum in the main distillation flask. Air is admitted to the system only through silica gel drying tubes, and a similarly filled Dreschel bottle is interposed between the still and water pump.

Dichloroethane

This is distilled in a similar manner to dichloromethane, b.p. 82–84°C.

Acetic acid (AcOH)

Acetic acid is heated under reflux with chromium trioxide (20 g l^{-1}) for 1 h. Use anti-bumping chips. The condenser is then repositioned for collection and an anti-splash head fitted. Great care should be exercised to avoid superheating, as sudden nucleation can cause very vigorous boiling. *A safety shield must be used*. A forerun of about 5% of the volume being distilled is discarded before collection of the main fraction, b.p. 116–118°C.

t-Amyl alcohol (t-AmOH)

t-Amyl alcohol is distilled from potassium carbonate (5 g l^{-1}) through a 12-in fractionating column containing glass helices, b.p. 100−103°C.

Diisopropylethylamine (DIEA)

Diisopropylethylamine is initially distilled from ninhydrin (1−2 g l^{-1}) and then redistilled from potassium hydroxide pellets (5−10 g l^{-1}) under nitrogen, discarding a small forerun, b.p. 125−127°C. It is used as a 10% v/v solution in DMF. Small volumes only should be prepared because of the instability of the mixture.

Piperidine

Piperidine is distilled under nitrogen from potassium hydroxide pellets (10−20 g l^{-1}). The initial distillate, approximately 5% of the total, is discarded, and then the main fraction, b.p. 106°C, collected. For cleavage of Fmoc derivatives, a 20% v/v solution in DMF is used.

Trifluoroacetic acid (TFA)

Trifluoroacetic acid is distilled cautiously with slow heating at atmospheric pressure, b.p. 72°C. Rapid heating gives anomalous boiling points. Trifluoroacetic acid is toxic and corrosive, and should be handled with care in a fume cupboard.

Ethylene diamine

Ethylene diamine is heated under reflux with sodium metal (10−15 g l^{-1}) and then distilled under nitrogen, rejecting the first 5% of the distillate, b.p. 117°C.

1-Hydroxybenzotriazole (HOBt)

1-Hydroxybenzotriazole is recrystallized from water and used as the hydrate.

4-Dimethylaminopyridine (DMAP)

4-Dimethylaminopyridine is recrystallized from ether containing decolorizing charcoal. It is obtained as a white crystalline solid, m.p. 100−112°C.

N,N′-Dicyclohexylcarbodiimide (DCCI)

N,N′-Dicyclohexylcarbodiimide is distilled cautiously in high vacuum under nitrogen using an air condenser; b.p. is 126°C at 0.7 mm Hg. DCCI is toxic and a skin irritant to which some individuals become very sensitive. The distillation must be carried out in a fume hood, and rubber gloves must be used when weighing the reagent.

CHAPTER 4

The solid support

4.1 Beaded gel resins

In the previous chapter, reasons were given favouring the choice of polar supports for solid phase synthesis. In particular, supports freely permeated and solvated by polar aprotic media which at the same time were good reaction media for the reactions of peptide synthesis were indicated. Internal hydrogen bonding within the support should be minimized. The polymeric system chosen consisted of polydimethylacrylamide insolubilized by cross-linking with an appropriate bisacryloylamide (*40,41*). Bisacryloylethylene diamine conveniently filled this last role. More recently a number of structural variants have been described by others, of which polyacryloylpyrrolidine (*50*) and polyacryloylmorpholine (*51*) may be mentioned.

To minimize chemical manipulation of the formed polymer, it was originally envisaged that appropriate functionality for attachment of the growing peptide chain might be co-polymerized into the system from the outset. Thus the first synthetic polyamide resin was obtained (*40*) from a monomer mixture comprising dimethylacrylamide (**62**), bisacryloylethylene diamine (**63**), and the unsymmetrical diacylamine derivative (**64**). This last provided an ethylenic acryloyl group for the polymerization reaction, a six-carbon spacer chain separating the functionality from the polymer backbone, an internal reference amino acid (β-alanine) useful in analytical control of synthesis, and a functional amino group (protected as its Boc derivative) providing a starting point for peptide chain growth. The resulting resin (**66a**) was useful to peptide synthesis but had disadvantages. Regular bead formation was difficult to obtain and some polymerizations gave largely amorphous polymer which was difficult to handle. This was probably due to the complex derivative (**64**) which had very different solubility and phase distribution properties to those of the other monomers. It was also difficult to prepare.

Replacement of (**64**) by acryloylsarcosine methyl ester (**65**) solved these problems. This functionalizing agent is much more closely related to the basic monomer (**62**), and the procedures given below generate nicely beaded polymer without difficulty. Additionally, the similar structures of (**62**) and (**65**) suggest that they will polymerize at comparable rates, increasing the likelihood of uniform distribution of functional groups throughout the resin matrix. This second resin (**66b**) carries carbomethoxy groups rather than (protected) amine, and a post-polymerization chemical step is necessary to convert it into the amino-polymer (**66c**).

The beaded gel functionalized with methoxycarbonyl groups ('Pepsyn') is manufactured commercially in the United Kingdom and is presently distributed by Milligen (see Appendix).

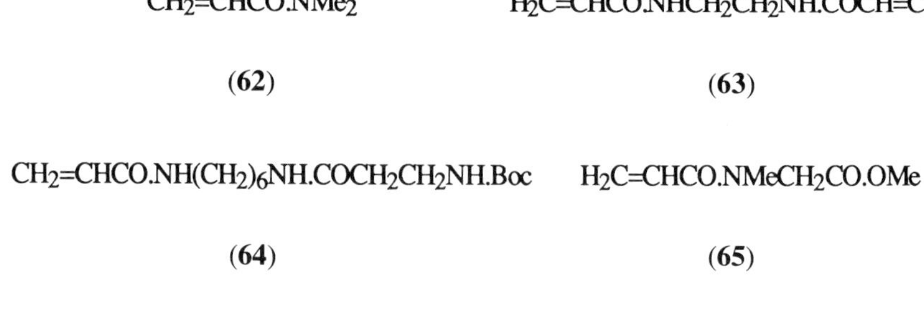

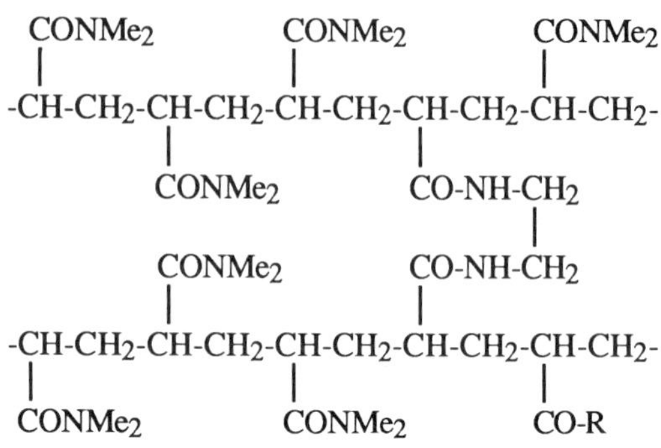

(**66a**) R = -NH$(CH_2)_6$NH-CO$(CH_2)_2$NH-Boc

(**b**) R = -NMeCH_2CO-OMe

(**c**) R = -NMeCH_2CO-NH$(CH_2)_2NH_2$

N,N-Dimethylacrylamide

Acryloyl chloride (20 g, 0.22 mol) was dissolved in anhydrous ether (200 ml) and cooled to −60°C in acetone−dry ice. To the stirred solution was added dropwise over 30 min a cooled solution of dimethylamine (20 g, 0.44 mol) in ether (80 ml). After 30 min, the mixture was allowed to warm to 10°C, hydroquinone (300 mg) was added and the mixture allowed to stand overnight. The mixture was filtered and ether removed by rotary evaporation. The resultant oil was distilled under reduced pressure into a flask containing hydroquinone (5 mg) and stored at 5°C, b.p. 71−72°C at 12 mm Hg.

N,N'-Bisacryloylethylenediamine (41)

Anhydrous sodium acetate (217 g, 2.6 mol) and 1,2-diaminoethane (72 g, 1.2 mol) were added to anhydrous chloroform (1.2 litres) and cooled to 0°C in an ice-bath. Distilled acryloyl chloride (218 g, 2.4 mol) was added dropwise during 1 h to the stirred mixture which was then allowed to warm to 10°C. Hydroquinone (2 g) was added, and the mixture heated under reflux for 1 h and filtered hot. The filtrate was allowed to cool and the crystalline product collected, dissolved in hot chloroform (2 litres) and filtered. On cooling, the product crystallized, and was collected, dried over calcium chloride, and stored in the dark. Yield 162 g (80%), m.p. 141–143°C. A sample (40 g) recrystallized from chloroform gave 31 g, m.p. 143–144°C (lit., m.p., 144–145°C); tlc (silica) in ethyl acetate–acetone (1:1), R_f 0.25 (single spot).

Alternative preparation of N-N′-bisacryloylethylenediamine

Ethylene diamine (6.8 ml, 100 mmol) dissolved in acetonitrile (400 ml) was added dropwise over 1 h to a cooled (0°C) and stirred solution of distilled acryloyl chloride (8.94 ml, 110.0 mmol) in acetonitrile (600 ml). The ice-bath was removed and the reaction mixture stirred for 3.5 h at room temperature. The precipitated salt was filtered and the filtrate concentrated *in vacuo* until crystallization started. The product was collected after standing overnight in the refrigerator and dried *in vacuo* giving 3.86 g, m.p. 144–145°C.

Sarcosine methyl ester hydrochloride (41)

Methanol (400 ml) was cooled and stirred in an ice–salt bath, and thionyl chloride (32.2 ml) added dropwise, followed by sarcosine (36 g, 0.4 mol) over 15 min. The mixture was stirred in the cold for 20 min, allowed to warm to room temperature during 2 h, and then heated under reflux for 2 h. The cooled solution was evaporated and the residue recrystallized from methanol–ether to give the hygroscopic methyl ester hydrochloride (51 g, 90%), m.p. 121.5–122.5°C. Tlc always indicated the presence of traces of sarcosine.

Acryloylsarcosine methyl ester (41)

Sarcosine methyl ester hydrochloride (30.9 g, 0.22 mol) was dissolved in chloroform (280 ml) and cooled with stirring in an ice–salt bath. Triethylamine (61.9 ml, 44.75 g, 0.44 mol) was added dropwise during 10 min followed by a solution of acryloyl chloride (18.0 ml, 19.9 g, 0.22 mol) in chloroform (150 ml) during 1.5 h. The cooling bath was then removed and the reaction mixture stirred overnight. Evaporation of the chloroform gave a white solid which was triturated with ether (400 ml) and filtered. Hydroquinone (*c.* 10 mg) was added to the filtrate which was then evaporated and the residual oil distilled *in vacuo* into a receiving flask containing a further 10 mg of hydroquinone. Acryloylsarcosine methyl ester (23 g, 66%) had b.p. 96°C at 0.4 mm Hg; nmr 3.18 and 3.32 (asymmetrical doublet, 3 H, -CONMe- showing *cis–trans* isomerism), 3.84 (s, 3 H, $-CO_2Me$), 4.38 (s, 2 H, $-CH_2-$), and 5.8–7.2 (m, 3 H, $CH_2{=}CHCO-$).

The suspension polymerization of the monomers is best carried out with a specially designed paddle stirrer and reaction vessel (*52*) (*Figure 8*) which, under the conditions described, gives the beaded polymer. A propeller stirrer or vibromixer in a round-

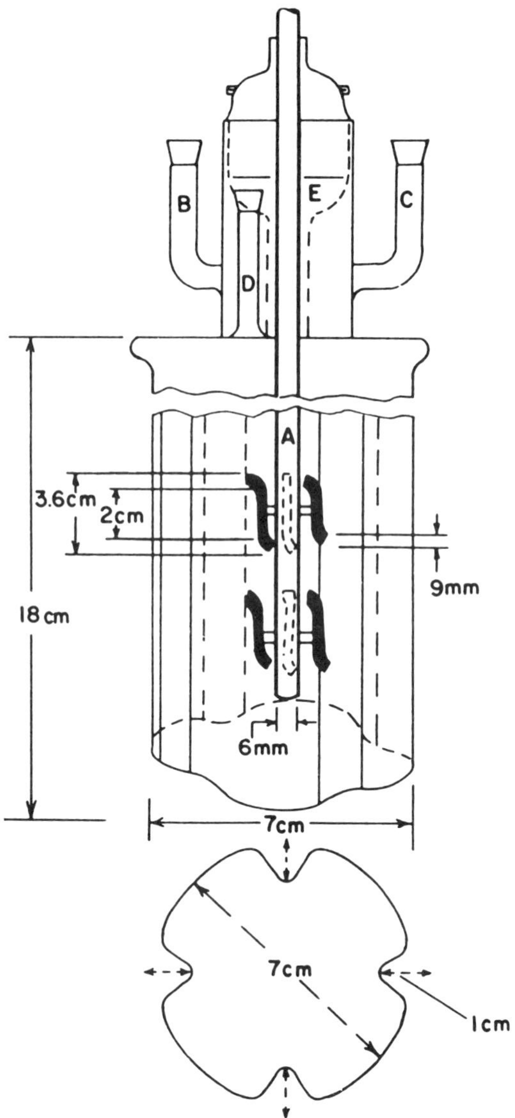

Figure 8. Polymerization vessel for the production of beaded gel polymers (*52*).

bottomed flask has also given adequate results once optimization of the mixing had been established. This is of the utmost importance, since different mixing techniques or stirring speeds give varying sizes of beads. The acryloyl derivatives must be free of oligomers. In the case of acryloylsarcosine methyl ester, partial polymerization beforehand could result in undesirable clumping of functional groups in the final resin. The two liquid monomers, dimethylacrylamide and acryloylsarcosine methyl ester, should therefore be freshly distilled into flasks containing a few mg of hydroquinone.

Exclusion of oxygen and thorough purging with nitrogen of all polymerization solutions is necessary. Two resin preparations are described, one giving resin with nominal functionality (sarcosine content) of 0.30–0.35 mmol g^{-1} and the other of 1.10 to 1.20 mmol g^{-1}. Usually not all the incorporated sarcosine is available for peptide chain growth.

Copoly(dimethylacrylamide-bisacryloylethylenediamine-acryloylsarcosine methyl ester)

Typically, cellulose acetate butyrate (12.5 g) was completely dissolved in dichloroethane (300 ml) and placed in a cylindrical fluted polymerization vessel (*Figure 8*) fitted with a stirrer and nitrogen inlet and maintained at 50 ± 1°C in a thermostatically controlled water-bath. The solution was stirred at 450 ± 20 rpm (counter or stroboscope) and flushed with nitrogen for 10 min before the monomer mixture, consisting of dimethylacrylamide (15 g, 0.152 mol), acryloylsarcosine methyl ester (1.25 g, 7.96 mmol), and bisacryloylethylenediamine (1.75 g, 10.4 mmol), diluted with cooled (5°C) DMF–water (1:2, 150 ml) and mixed well with ammonium persulphate (2.25 g), was added. Polymerization was allowed to continue under a very slow stream of nitrogen for *c*. 15 h when the mixture was cooled, diluted with acetone–water (1:1), stirred until a homogeneous suspension was obtained, and filtered. The recovered polymer was washed and fine particles removed by stirring and decantation using acetone–water (1:2) (3 × 1 litre) and then acetone (3 or 4 × 500 ml). The polymer was finally washed with ether (2 × 500 ml), collected by filtration, and dried (P_2O_5) *in vacuo*; yield *c*. 15 g of completely beaded resin (found: Sar, 0.35 mmol g^{-1}). The average bead size is between 50 and 100 μm.

High-loading beaded copoly(dimethylacrylamide-bisacryloylethylenediamine-acryloylsarcosine methyl ester) gel

Cellulose acetate butyrate (7.5 g) was dissolved in freshly distilled dichloroethane (225 ml) at 49°C under a stream of nitrogen in the polymerization vessel with stirring. The temperature was controlled by placing the reaction vessel in a thermostatically controlled water bath and the stirring speed adjusted to 450 rpm. The monomer mixture consisting of dimethylacrylamide (11.25 g, 113.6 mmol), acryloylsarcosine methyl ester (3.75 g, 23.73 mmol) and bisacryloylethylenediamine (1.65 g, 9.82 mmol) was dissolved in DMF–water (1:2, 75 ml) which had been cooled in a refrigerator beforehand. Ammonium persulphate (2.08 g) dissolved in DMF–water (1:2, 32 ml) was then added to the monomer mixture, which was immediately poured into the polymerization vessel. Stirring speed, nitrogen flow and temperature were kept constant throughout the polymerization period (18 h). The polymerization mixture was then poured on to a large sintered glass funnel and washed thoroughly with dichloroethane without suction. Washing on the funnel was continued with DMF, DMF–water (1:1) and DMF. The resin was then transferred to a large glass cylinder, and fines were removed by decantation (2× with DMF). The resin was filtered, washed with acetone and ether, and then dried under high vacuum over phosphorus pentoxide to constant weight, yield 12 g. (Found: Sar, 1.19 mmol g^{-1}).

Both resins swell substantially in a wide range of solvents. One gram (dry volume *c.* 2.2 ml) typically swells to 20–21 ml in water, dimethylformamide, dichloromethane, pyridine, or methanol. In dioxan the swollen volume is only 10 ml. In the swollen state the resins are physically stable and withstand gentle agitation in a Merrifield-style (*53,102*) synthesis reaction vessel for many days. We have not used them in stirred vessels, but nitrogen agitation has been satisfactory elsewhere (see Section 8.1) (*55*).

4.2 **Physically supported gel resins**

The beaded gels were found to be too soft and easily deformed for convenient use in pumped-flow equipment. Early experiments using polydimethylacrylamide gels in packed glass columns gave indications of excessive compression of the resin and generation of high liquid pressures. This is evidently also the case for other beaded gel polymers. Hplc-type stainless steel columns and pumping equipment were used elsewhere in a series of exploratory flow experiments using beaded polystyrene (*44*), and, in another investigation, pressures up to 10 000 psi have been mentioned (*45*). Large-cross-section steel columns were chosen by Meienhofer and his colleagues (*46*) to reduce these pressures. High-pressure systems are inconvenient from the practical point of view, but, more seriously, any collapse of the internal open matrix character of the resin support and the consequent reduction in internal volume must reduce reactant accessibility and increase the steric crowding of the attached peptide chains (*48*).

The problems are simply solved by polymerizing the gel resin within a rigid macroporous framework, chosen so as to maintain channels for solvent flow while at the same time allowing rapid diffusion of reactants into and out of the physically supported gel. A number of framework materials can be envisaged for this purpose. Thus far we have found inorganic particles prepared by sintering the powdered mineral in the presence of an organic binder the most suitable. Macroporous Kieselguhr was originally obtained from the UK Atomic Energy Research Establishment, Harwell (*54*), but is now available commercially under the name 'Macrosorb' from Sterling Organics (see Appendix). This highly absorbent material has a pore size many thousands of Å in diameter (*54*) and an accessible pore volume about one-third of the total dry volume. Its rigidity, mechanical strength, and large pore size make it a near-ideal carrier for gel resins. Preparation of the supported gel is simpler than for the beaded resins above, since particle size is set by the Kieselguhr element and a stable liquid–liquid suspension is not required.

Physically supported copoly(dimethylacrylamide-bisacryloylethylenediamine-acryloylsarcosine methyl ester) (*47,49*)

N,N-Dimethylacrylamide (33.3 g, 336 mmol) and then acryloylsarcosine methyl ester (2.83 g, 18 mmol) were added to a solution of bisacryloylethylenediamine (3.90 g, 23.2 mmol) in water–dimethylformamide (3.1:2 v/v; 137 ml). Aqueous ammonium persulphate (10%, 25 ml) was added and the mixture immediately poured on to the Kieselguhr support (335 – 500 μm, 100 g) and stirred thoroughly with a glass rod. The polymerization mixture was put into a desiccator and evacuated with a water pump vacuum for 2 min when vigorous degassing occurred. It was left *in vacuo* for 15 min, after which the vacuum was broken by the introduction of nitrogen and the mixture left for 2.5 h. After being washed thoroughly with water on a sintered glass filter, the Kieselguhr-polymer was passed through a 700 μm sieve, which released excess of surface polymer, and was then washed on a sintered funnel by back-flowing with water. The support was then washed four times by decantation before being filtered, washed with acetone and then ether, and dried under high vacuum over P_2O_5; yield 125.5 g (found: Sar, 0.108 mequiv g^{-1}).

The physically supported gel resin forms a free-flowing powder which packs well into glass columns. Negligible pressure is generated at moderate liquid flow rates. The resin is physically rigid, but the Kieselguhr element is friable. It can be crushed easily, and generates fines when subjected to abrasion. Pressure build-up is usually associated with fine particles blocking the supporting filters. The resin should not be stirred mechanically or with a spatula, and should especially not be subjected to the grinding action of stirring with a magnetic bead.

The polydimethylacrylamide-Kieselguhr resin is manufactured by Sterling Organics under the name Macrosorb SPR, and is currently distributed by Pharmacia-LKB as Ultrasyn and by Milligen as Pepsyn K (see Appendix). Resin with capacity 0.25 meq g^{-1} as well as the regular 0.1 meq g^{-1} is now available.

4.3 Note added in Proof

The increasing popularity of continuous flow methods of solid phase synthesis is now encouraging the development of suitable supports elsewhere. Two new versions which have just appeared on the market should be mentioned. Polyhipe is a polydimethyl-acrylamide supported in (and chemically bonded to) macroporous polystyrene, and Rapp resin, a polyoxyethylene grafted onto polystyrene. Early reports on the use of both resins are encouraging.

CHAPTER 5

Fluorenylmethoxycarbonyl-amino acids

The fluorenylmethoxycarbonyl- (Fmoc-) *t*-butyl strategy (*37,58*) for solid phase synthesis has been outlined previously (Section 3.3.2), and contrasted with the conventional Boc-benzyl system. In this new strategy, *t*-butyl-based side-chain-protecting groups cleavable by a single mildly acidic treatment are chosen where possible. The peptide–resin linkage (Chapter 6) may also be acid-labile, but based on the enhanced sensitivity to acid of alkoxy-substituted benzyl esters. This combination of side-chain and carboxy-terminus (resin-linkage) permanent protecting groups requires temporary protection of the α-amino terminus with a group of entirely different lability. Base-labile Fmoc derivatives which had been suggested for solution peptide synthesis some years previously (*7*) were found to be nearly ideal. The same combination of base- and acid-labile protecting groups was conceived independently and simultaneously by Meienhofer and his colleagues (*56*) for polystyrene-based solid phase synthesis. It is gaining increasing acceptance in this technique also.

For a recent review of the Fmoc protecting group, see ref. *57*. This fully referenced article contains extensive tabulated data for Fmoc-amino acids and their side-chain-protected and activated derivatives, and is supplementary to the following brief discussion.

The Fmoc amino-protecting group (**67**) owes its base lability to the special characteristics of the dibenzocyclopentadiene structure. Resonance stabilization of the derived cyclopentadienide anion (**68**) imparts exceptional acidity to the 9-hydrogen atom of (**67**), enabling its removal by bases and initiation of the β-elimination reaction, (**68**) → (**69**) + (**70**). It is not known whether decarboxylation of (**70**) occurs immediately, but no special proton source needs to be added before the acylation step (*37*). The liberated dibenzofulvene usually reacts further with the basic reagent, forming (in the case of piperidine-induced deprotection reactions) the adduct (**71**).

5.1 Preparation of Fmoc-amino acids

Most users of Fmoc-amnino acids in solid phase peptide synthesis will purchase commercially synthesized derivatives which are now available from a number of suppliers (see Appendix) and are slowly decreasing in cost. Experience has shown the value of checking all such derivatives for identity and purity by melting point and optical rotation, and preferably by high-performance liquid chromatography or thin-layer chromatography where applicable at the time of purchase. This is especially important in the case of activated derivatives (pentafluorophenyl and dihydrooxobenzotriazinyl esters, Section 7.2.2) which are also available commercially.

In the laboratory, Fmoc-amino acids are usually prepared from the chloroformate (**72**) (*7*) or the derived hydroxysuccinimide ester (**73**) (*59–61*). The former is the original reagent introduced by Carpino and Han (*7*). It is itself easily prepared from

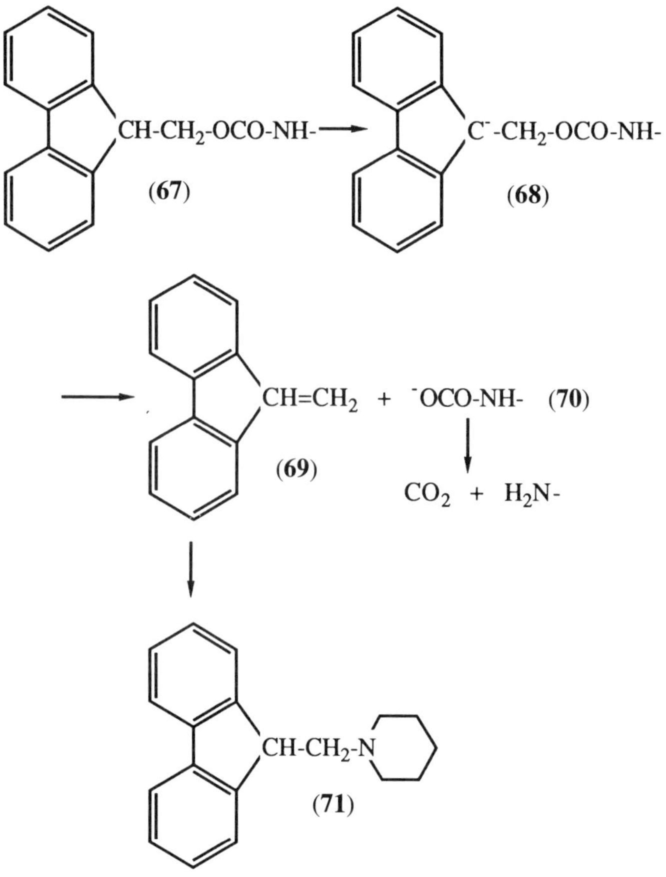

CH-CH_2-OCO-NH- → C^--CH_2-OCO-NH-

(67) **(68)**

→ CH=CH_2 + $^-$OCO-NH- **(70)**

(69) CO_2 + H_2N-

CH-CH_2-N

(71)

fluorenylmethanol and phosgene. It reacts rapidly with most simple amino acids in weakly alkaline media. Crude reaction products, especially from glycine, alanine, phenylalanine or N_ϵ-trifluoroacetyl-lysine (Section 5.1.3) are sometimes contaminated with the corresponding Fmoc-dipeptides which must be removed by careful recrystallization. The hydroxysuccinimide ester is a superior reagent in this respect and commonly gives cleaner reaction products. A number of other reagents employed for the preparation of Fmoc-amino acids have been listed (*57*).

The following sections give some illustrative preparations of Fmoc-amino acids. For trifunctional amino-acid derivatives which require additional side-chain protection, brief comment is made of the relative merits of alternative side-chain-protecting groups where appropriate.

5.1.1 *Amino acids not requiring side-chain protection*

These are usually straightforward to prepare, though solubility properties of starting amino acids and products vary. Crude products should always be examined by hplc

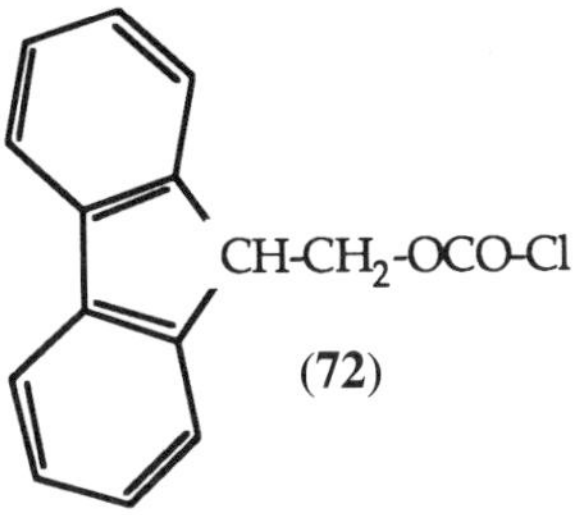

CH-CH$_2$-OCO-Cl

(72)

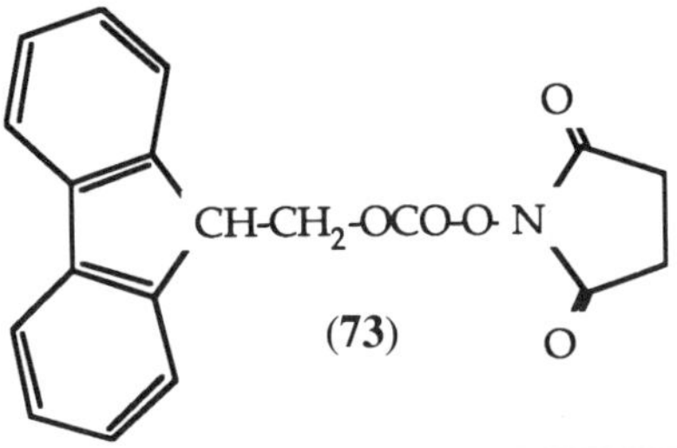

O

CH-CH$_2$-OCO-O-N

(73)

O

and/or tlc for the presence of contaminants (especially dipeptide derivatives), and recrystallized as necessary. Some illustrative examples are given below. Physical data are collected in *Table 2*.

N-Fmoc-L-valine

L-Valine (5.85 g, 50 mmol) was dissolved in a mixture of dioxan (50 ml) and 10% sodium carbonate (133 ml) and stirred vigorously at ice temperature. To this stirred solution fluorenylmethyl chloroformate (13.58 g, 52.5 mmol) disolved in dioxan (50 ml) was added dropwise over a 15-min period. The ice-bath was removed and the reaction mixture stirred for 1 h. Tlc in chloroform–methanol–acetic acid (85:10:5 v/v) followed by development with ninhydrin revealed only traces of unreacted valine. A small amount of the sodium salt of the product precipitated during reaction. Water (500 ml) was added to the reaction mixture and the clear solution extracted with ether (3 × 150 ml). The aqueous solution was then acidified cautiously with hydrochloric acid to pH 3 and the white precipitate formed was extracted into ethyl acetate (3 × 150 ml). The extracts were combined and washed with water (3 × 200 ml), dried over anhydrous sodium sulphate, filtered and evaporated. Crystallization from ethyl acetate–petroleum either gave 11.5 g (68%), m.p. 146–147°C, $[\alpha]_D$ −17.7° (c = 1 in DMF). (Found: C, 70.97; H, 6.48; N, 4.00. $C_{20}H_{21}O_4N$ requires C, 70.78; H, 6.24; N, 4.13%.)

N-Fmoc-L-asparagine

L-Asparagine (6.61 g, 50.0 mmol) was dissolved in a mixture of dioxan (50 ml) and 10% sodium carbonate (133 ml). Fluorenylmethyl chloroformate (13.5 g, 52.5 mmol) dissolved in dioxan (50 ml) was added dropwise to the briskly stirred solution over a period of 15 min at room temperature. The reaction mixture was stirred for 4 h at room temperature during which time a white solid precipitated. The solid was collected, washed thoroughly with water and then ether, and stirred with 10% citric acid (500 ml). The product was filtered, washed with water until the washings were neutral, and the remaining white solid dried *in vacuo* over phosphorus pentoxide. Yield 12 g. Recrystallization from methanol (in which the product dissolves only slowly on heating) gave 8.75 g (49%), m.p. 189–191°C, $[\alpha]_D$ −11.0° (c = 2 in DMF). (Found: C, 64.19; H, 5.21; N, 7,95. $C_{19}H_{18}O_5N_2$ requires C, 64.40; H, 5.12; N, 7.91%.)

Table 2. Fmoc-amino acids. Literature references are collected in ref. *57*.

Compound	Reagent	Yield (%)	m.p. (°C)	$[\alpha]_D$ (°)	Solvent conc.
Fmoc-Ala-OH	Fmoc-Cl	97	143–144	−18.6	DMF (1)
Fmoc-Ala-OH	Fmoc-OSu	96	142–143	−19.7	DMF (1)
Fmoc-DL-Ala-OH	Fmoc-Cl	88			
Fmoc-Ala-OMPA[(a)]	Fmoc-Cl	54[(b)]	144–145		
Fmoc-Arg-OH	Fmoc-Cl	89	145–160		
Fmoc-Arg(Adoc)$_2$-OH	Fmoc-Cl	80	152–154	+ 2.1[(c)]	CH_3OH (1.03)
Fmoc-Arg(Boc)-OH	Fmoc-Cl	24[(d)]	170–171	−11.5	DMF (1)
Fmoc-Arg(Mbs)-OH	Fmoc-Cl	56	Amorph.	− 6.6	DMF (0.74)
Fmoc-Arg(Mds)-OH	Fmoc-Cl	30	121–123		
Fmoc-Arg(Mtr)-OH	Fmoc-Cl	60	118–120	+ 7.9	CH_3OH (0.5)
Fmoc-Arg(Pme)-OH	Fmoc-Cl	73	125–127	+ 2.1	CH_3OH (0.5)
Fmoc-Asn-OH	Fmoc-Cl	98	185–186	−11.4	DMF (1)
Fmoc-Asn(Mbh)-OH	Fmoc-Cl	72	182–184	+ 0.84	DMF (1)
Fmoc-Asp(OBu^t)-OH	Fmoc-Cl	58	148–149	+ 9.1	EtOAc (1)
				−20.3	DMF (1)
Fmoc-Cys(Acm)-OH	Fmoc-Cl	75	150–154	−27.5	EtOAc (1)
Fmoc-Cys(Bu^t)-OH	Fmoc-Cl	61	135–136	− 1.9	EtOAc (1)
				−23.2	DMF (1)
Fmoc-Cys(S-Bu^t-OH	Fmoc-Cl	72	74–76	−84.6	EtOAc (1)
Fmoc-Cys(Trt)-OH	Fmoc-OSu	90	174–178	+20.6	Dmf (1)
Fmoc-Cys(Bzl)-OH	Fmoc-Cl	90	125–126	−40.6	CH_3OH (1)
Fmoc-Glu(OBu^t)-OH	Fmoc-Cl	71	76–77	+ 0.8	EtOAc (1)
Fmoc-Gln-OH	Fmoc-Cl	97	221–223	−17.0	DMF (1)
Fmoc-Gln(Mbn)-OH	Fmoc-Cl	59	177–178.5		
Fmoc-Gly-OH	Fmoc-Cl	88	173–176		
Fmoc-Gly-OH	Fmoc-OSu	68	175–176		
Fmoc-His(Boc)-OH[(e)]		62[(f)]	149–151	+15.2	DMF (1)
Fmoc-His(BocTf)-OH	Fmoc-Cl	10[(g)]	143–155	+14.7	EtOAc (1)
Fmoc-His(Fmoc)-OH	Fmoc-Cl	91[(h)]	161–163	− 6.8	DMF (1)
Fmoc-His(π-Bom)-OH	Fmoc-Cl	41	160	+ 1.8	CH_3OH (0.6)
Fmoc-His(π-Bum)-OH	Fmoc-Cl		175–176	− 7.5	AcOH (1)
Fmoc-His(Ppc)-OH		37[(f)]	114–116	− 2.5	CH_3OH (1)
Fmoc-Ile-OH	Fmoc-Cl	82	145–147	− 9.8	EtOAc (1)
				−11.9	DMF (1)
Fmoc-Leu-OH	Fmoc-Cl	91	153–154	− 6.9	EtOAc (1)
				−24.1	DMF (1)
Fmoc-Lys(Boc)-OH	Fmoc-Cl	99	123–124	+ 5.1	EtOAc (1)
				−11.7	DMF (1)
Fmoc-Lys(Tfa)-OH	Fmoc-Cl	67	140–141	− 2.5	CH_3OH (1)
Fmoc-Lys(Z)-OH	Fmoc-Cl	81	108–110	− 2.0	CH_3OH (1)
Fmoc-Met-OH	Fmoc-Cl	92	129–132	− 0.3	EtOAc (1)
				−28.3	DMF (1)
Fmoc-Met(O)-OH[(i)]		56	164–166	− 6.0	DMF (1)
Fmoc-Phe-OH	Fmoc-Cl	97	181–183	−37.6	DMF (1)
Fmoc-Phe-OH	Fmoc-OSu	91	178–179	−41.7	DMF (1)
Fmoc-D-Phe-OH	Fmoc-Cl	83	176–181.5	+37.5	DMF (0.87)
Fmoc-Pro-OH	Fmoc-Cl	92	114–115	−39.0	EtOAc (1)
Fmoc-Pro-OH	Fmoc-OSu	86	116–117	−33.2	DMF (1)
Fmoc-Ser-OH	Fmoc-Cl	89	86–88	+14.9	EtOAc (1)
Fmoc-Ser-OH	Fmoc-OSu	87	86–88	+14.8	EtOAc

Fmoc-Ser(Bu^t)-OH	Fmoc-Cl	90	126–129	+25.4	EtOAc (1)
				− 1.5	DMF (1)
Fmoc-Ser(Bzl)-OH	Fmoc-OSu	79	118–119	+25.1	EtOAc (1)
Fmoc-Thr-OH	Fmoc-Cl	62	Amorph.	− 4.8	CH_3OH (1)
				+15.5	EtOAc (1)
Fmoc-Thr-OH[(j)]	Fmoc-OSu	95	165	+ 9.8	DMF
Fmoc-Thr(Bu^t)-OH	Fmoc-Cl	84	129–132	+15.5	EtOAc (1)
				− 4.5	DMF (1)
Fmoc-Trp-OH	Fmoc-Cl	81	165–166	+10.0	EtOAc (1)
				−26.6	DMF (1)
Fmoc-D-Trp-OH	Fmoc-Cl	61	166.5	+26.8	DMF (1.08)
Fmoc-Tyr(Bu^t)-OH	Fmoc-Cl	58	150–151	+ 5.2	EtOAc (1)
				−27.6	DMF (1)
Fmoc-Tyr(Me)-OH	Fmoc-Cl		161–162	−28.5	DMF (1)
Fmoc-Val-OH	Fmoc-Cl	82	143–144	+ 4.8	EtOAc (1)
				−16.1	DMF (1)
Fmoc-Val-OH	Fmoc-OSu	87	142–143	−18.7	DMF (1)

Notes: [a]4-methylphenoxyacetic acid ester; [b]two-step synthesis; [c]variable; [d]three-step synthesis; [e]cyclohexylammonium salt; [f]from bis(Fmoc)-histidine; [g]yield from three-step synthesis; [h]very variable; [i]by oxidation of Fmoc-Met with hydrogen peroxide; [j]dicyclohexylammonium salt.

N-Fmoc-L-isoleucine

L-Isoleucine (66 g. 0.50 mol) and sodium carbonate (53 g) were dissolved in a mixture of water (650 ml) and acetone (650 ml). Fluorenylmethylsuccinimidyl carbonate (165 g, 0.49 M) was added over a period of 60 min to the briskly stirred solution while the pH was kept between 9 and 10 by the addition of 1 M sodium carbonate. After stirring overnight, ethyl acetate (2 litres) was added and the mixture acidified with 6 M hydrochloric cid. The ethyl acetate layer was separated and washed with water (4 × 1.5 litre), dried over anydrous magnesium sulphate, and evaporated to approximately 500 ml. The product crystallized on the addition of petroleum ether yielding 162 g (93%) m.p. 143°C, $[\alpha]_D$ −12.1° (c = 1 in DMF).

N-Fmoc-L-methionine

L-Methionine (74.5 g, 0.5 mol) was dissolved together with sodium carbonate (53.0 g) in water (650 ml). Fluorenylmethylsuccinimidyl carbonate (163.4 g, 0.49 M) dissolved in acetone (650 ml) was added in portions over a period of 60 min. The briskly stirred solution was kept at pH 9–10 by the addition of 1 M sodium carbonate. After stirring overnight the acetone was evaporated, ethyl acetate (1.5 litre) added and the mixture acidified with 2 M hydrochloric acid. The ethyl aetate layer was separated, washed with water (4 × 1.5 litre), dried over anhydrous magnesium sulphate, and evaporated to approximately one-third volume. The product crystallized on the addition of petroleum ether yielding 164 g (90%), m.p. 119–121° C, $[\alpha]_D$ −28.75° (c = 1 in DMF).

5.1.2 *Amino acids with t-butyl-protected side chains*

Fmoc derivatives of the *t*-butyl esters or ethers of aspartic acid, glutamic acid, serine, threonine and tyrosine have been prepared in two ways. The simplest, by far the most convenient, but frequently the most costly procedure is to convert the corresponding commercially available benzyloxycarbonyl derivatives. This is easily achieved through hydrogenolysis and then reacylation using (**72**) or (**73**). It is illustrated below for the preparation of Fmoc-glutamic acid *t*-butyl ester and, for the second stage, threonine *t*-butyl ether. It is similarly applicable to the other amino acids in this group and we have used this procedure routinely. The alternative procedure described (*63*) involves hydrogenolysis of Fmoc-amino acid α-benzyl esters. This route should be used with caution in view of the later-discovered cleavage of the Fmoc group itself by hydrogenolysis (*62,64*).

Some amino acids, notably lysine and histidine, naturally fall into this section insofar as the *t*-butyl-based side-chain-protected derivatives Fmoc-Lys(Boc)-OH and Fmoc-His(Boc)-OH are available, but the special chemistry of the side chains warrants more extensive discussion. These are included in Section 5.1.3.

N-Fmoc-L-glutamic acid γ-t-butyl ester

N-Benzyloxycarbonyl-L-glutamic acid γ-*t*-butyl ester (10 g, 29.6 mmol) was hydrogenolysed in the presence of palladium on carbon catalyst in methanol (150 ml) for 2.5 h when tlc indicated complete reaction. Some of the zwitterionic product precipitated and was redissolved by addition of a water–methanol mixture. The catalyst was filtered through prewashed celite and the filtrate evaporated. The residual glutamic acid γ-*t*-butyl ester (6.01 g, 29.6 mmol) was dried in high vacuum. This ester was dissolved in a mixture of 10% aqueous sodium carbonate (79 ml) and dioxan (30 ml) and cooled to ice temperature. Fluorenylmethyl chloroformate (8.04 g, 31.1 mmol) dissolved in dioxan (30 ml) was then added dropwise over 15 min with vigorous stirring, and the ice-bath removed. After 4 h stirring, tlc indicated the absence of starting material. The reaction mixture was poured into water, extracted with ether (3 × 200 ml), the aqueous solution acidified cautiously with solid citric acid and the resultant oil extracted with ethyl acetate (3 × 200 ml). The ethyl acetate extracts were combined, washed with water until neutral, dried over anhydrous sodium sulphate and evaporated to give an oil which was crystallized from ethyl acetate–heptane and 1 or 2 drops of water giving 7.82 g (62%), m.p. 79–83°C, $[\alpha]_D$ 0.85° (c = 1 in ethyl acetate). (Found: C, 67.52; H, 6.59; N, 3.16. $C_{24}H_{27}O_6N$ required C, 67.75; H, 6.40; N, 3.29%.)

N-Fmoc-L-threonine t-butyl ether

L-Threonine *t*-butyl ether (24.9 g, 0.14 mol) was dissolved together with sodium carbonate (15 g) in a mixture of water (250 ml) and acetone (250 ml). Fluorenylmethyl succinimidyl carbonate (45.8 g, 0.14 M) was added in portions over a 60 min period with vigorous stirring and maintenance of the pH at approximately 10 by the addition of 1 M sodium carbonate. After stirring overnight the acetone was evaporated, the mixture acidified to pH 2.0 by the addition of 1 M potassium hydrogen sulphate, and the product extracted into ethyl acetate (500 ml). The organic phase was separated and washed with water (3 × 500 ml) dried over anyhydrous magnesium carbonate, filtered, and evaporated to small volume. On addition of petroleum ether, the product crystallized. Yield 38.2 g (68.6%), m.p. 125–126°C, $[\alpha]_D$ −6.0° (c = 1 in DMF).

5.1.3 *Amino acids with special side-chain-protecting groups*

For some protein amino acids, side-chain-protecting groups based on acid-labile *t*-butyl derivatives do not exist or have not proved completely satisfactory. Arginine is the most notable example. For others, alternative protecting groups are also applicable in certain circumstances.

5.1.3.1 *Lysine*

Early experiences (*65*) using the symmetric anhydride of Fmoc·Lys(Boc)·OH were not always satisfactory. On occasions incomplete amino-acid incorporation was observed, even though the ninhydrin colour test had indicated that acrylation was complete. This problem was later resolved when it was discovered that activated ester derivatives of Fmoc·Lys(Boc)·OH coupled reliably, and the pentafluorophenyl and dihydrooxo-benzotriazinyl esters now provide excellent reagents. The protected amino-acid may be prepared from N_ϵ-Boc-lysine by the general procedures given in Section 5.1.1. In special situations, the N_ϵ-trifluoroacetyl derivative has also proved useful. It is incorporated successfully by the symmetric anhydride procedure. The N_ϵ-trifluoroacetyl group is unaffected by normal acidic deprotection conditions and by anhydrous piperidine, but is readily cleaved by mild alkaline treatment using aqueous piperidine. It thus provides special purification opportunities for lysine-containing peptides by ion-exchange chromatography before and after cleavage of the trifluoroacetyl group. Equally important, use of the more polar trifluoroacetyl side-chain derivative enables the hydrophobic character of some protected sequences to be lowered, reducing the risk of synthetic problems arising from internal aggregation (Section 3.3.1).

N_α-Fmoc-N_ϵ-trifluoracetyl-L-lysine

N_ϵ-Trifluoroacetyl-L-lysine (6 g, 24.8 mmol) (*118*) was suspended in a mixture of dioxan (23 ml) and 10% aqueous sodium carbonate (47 ml), cooled to ice temperature and stirred vigorously while a solution of fluorenylmethyl chloroformate (6.7 g, 26.0 mmol) in dioxan (35 ml) was added dropwise over a 15 min period. The ice-bath was removed and the reaction mixture stirred for 3 h at room temperature when tlc indicated that only trace amounts of the starting material remained. The mixture was poured into water (700 ml), extracted with ether (2 × 300 ml), cautiously acidified with hydrochloric acid, and the product extracted into ether (3 × 200 ml). These ether fractions were combined, washed with water, dried over sodium sulphate and evaporated to give an oil which crystallized on standing. Recrystallization from methanol–water gave after drying 8.45 g (73.3%), m.p. softening at 142°C, finally melting at 162°C. Tlc showed the presence of a slow-running contaminant.

Close control of the reaction by use of a pH-stat did not significantly alter the product purity. The material was subjected to purification on a Lobar C silica column eluted with chloroform–methanol–acetic acid (95:25:25) at a flow rate of 4 ml min^{-1}. Two-min fractions were collected, pure fractions by tlc were pooled and evaporated.

From 3 separate applications (6 g each) the pure products were combined and recrystallized from aqueous methanol giving 15.2 g of the pure trifluoroacetyl derivative, m.p. 140–141°C, $[\alpha]_D$ −2.5 (c = 1 in methanol). (Found: C, 59.59; H, 4.82; N, 6.08. $C_{23}H_{23}F_3N_2O_5$ required C, 59.48; H, 4.99; N, 6.03%.) The later-eluting compound from the silica column was collected and isolated. From an application of 6 g to the column, typically 250–300 mg of the impurity were isolated. It was identified as Fmoc.Lys(Tfa).Lys(Tfa).OH by nmr spectroscopy and, after cleavage of the protecting groups, by chromatographic comparison with an authentic sample of the dipeptide H.Lys.Lys.OH. (Found: C, 54.10, H, 5.12; N, 7.94. $C_{31}H_{34}F_6N_4O_7$ requires C, 54.07; H, 4.93; N, 8.14%.)

5.1.3.2 *Histidine*

Histidine presents special problems in peptide synthesis largely because of its particular ease of racemization (Section 1.3). *im*-Alkyl derivatives in which the imidazole ring retains its intrinsic basicity are particularly prone to racemization unless the alkyl substituent is located exclusively on the π-nitrogen atom as in (**74**),* as opposed to the τ-nitrogen more distant from the chiral centre as in (**75**). Few histidine derivatives have been prepared in which the *im*-protecting group is uniquely located in the π-position, but of these the acid-labile *t*-butoxymethyl compound (**76**) is potentially important in the Fmoc series (*67*). In our experience, this derivative is difficult to prepare, and in

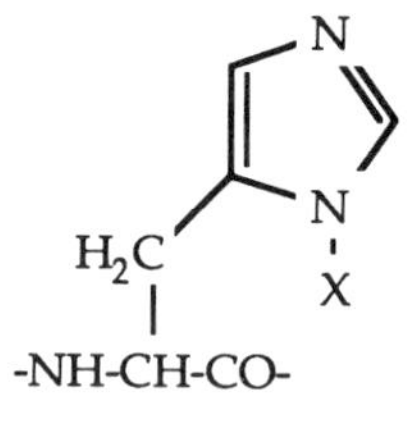

N
N
X
H_2C
-NH-CH-CO-

(**74**)

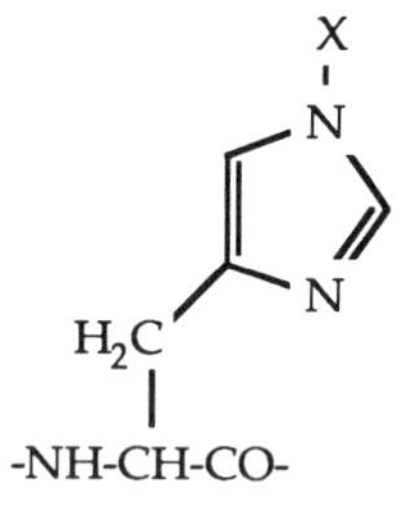

X
N
N
H_2C
-NH-CH-CO-

(**75**)

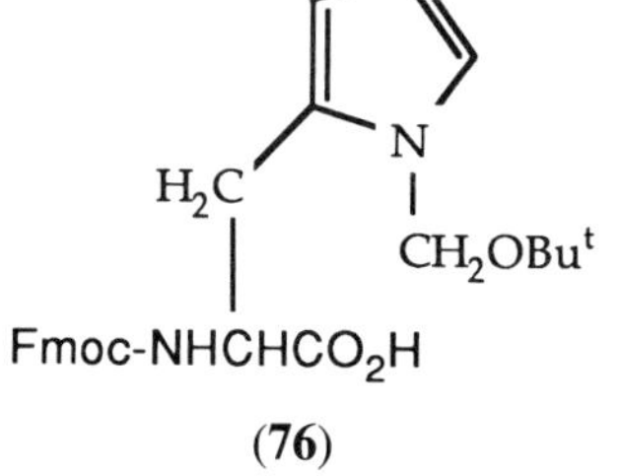

N
N
CH_2OBu^t
H_2C
Fmoc-NHCHCO$_2$H

(**76**)

Fmoc
N
N
H_2C
Fmoc-NHCHCO$_2$H

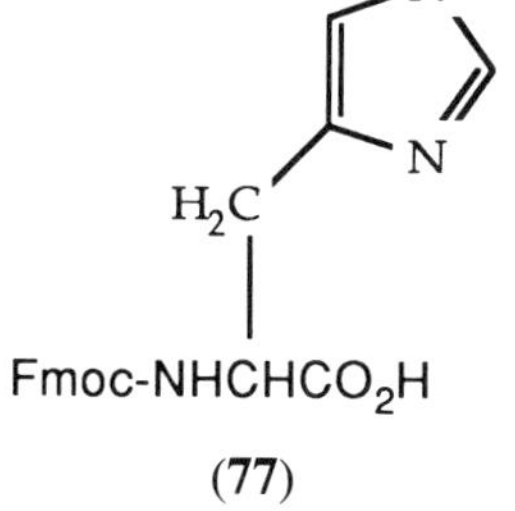

(**77**)

*A possible exception is the N_{im}-trityl derivative which under carefully controlled conditions has been coupled with less than 1% racemization (*68*). Racemization is still severe in esterification reactions, however (*68*).

other similarly basic N-alkyl histidines, anhydride formation has been slow (*66*). In our laboratory we have therefore preferred to use *im*-acyl derivatives for side-chain protection of Fmoc-histidine. In simple *im*-acyl histidines, the basicity and thus the racemization potential of the imidazole ring is effectively reduced, and the precise location of the acyl substitutent becomes less important.

The simplest and most readily accessible derivative is N_{α},N_{im}-bis(fluorenylmethoxy-carbonyl)-histidine (**77**)*. Its use in Fmoc-polyamide solid phase synthesis is akin to that of bis(Boc)-histidine in the Merrifield technqiue. As in this latter case, the imidazole protecting group is removed at the first deprotection step following its introduction.

Thereafter incoming amino acids acylate both the α- and *im*-nitrogen atoms. A second peptide chain is not developed on the histidine residue, however, since the aminoacylimidazole is itself cleaved at every cycle.

Although it couples well by the symmetrical anhydride technique (activated ester derivatives have not been evaluated), there are some disadvantages in the use of bis(Fmoc)-histidine. The protected amino acid is only sparingly soluble, and conversion of the anhydride has to be carried out in dimethylformamide solution. Acylation at the α-amino and imidazole groups by succeeding residues may also require use of larger excesses of costly reagents. Loss of the imidazole protecting group precludes use in segment condensation strategies. Finally, there is risk that the free imidazole ring may catalyse peptide chain growth at any residual hydroxyl groups present on the polymeric support, though this can be prevented by prior acetylation.

Fmoc-His(Boc)-OH can be prepared directly from the bis-Fmoc derivative by reaction with di-*t*-butyl dicarbonate (*66*), and is now our preferred intermediate. It is more soluble and can be coupled without racemization by conversion to the symmetric anhydride in the usual manner. Activated ester derivatives (pentafluorophenyl and dihydrooxo-benzotriazinyl esters) have also been prepared and used successfully. Their long-term stability has, however, yet to be established.

The *im*-Boc derivative offers the advantage that the protecting group appears to be substantially stable during subsequent deprotection and acylation reaction steps. This has been demonstrated most convincingly by quantitative monitoring of successive deprotection reactions (Fmoc groups release, Section 9.4.2); no increase was noted after incorporation of a His(Boc) residue into the peptide chain, as would be expected if following residues acylated both the α-amino and imidazole groups. This result conflicts with earlier indications (*69*), which suggested loss of the *im*-Boc group to the extent of 5% or more for each synthetic cycle. Dangers associated with unprotected basic imidazole rings are therefore largely avoided.

Bis-Fmoc-L-histidine

Histidine (4.56 g, 30 mmol) was vigorously stirred in water (120 ml) and the pH adjusted to 8.2 with 10% sodium carbonate. The solution was then cooled in an ice-

*In (**77**) and all other *im*-acyl derivatives discussed, the location of the *im*-substituent has not necessarily been defined, though it is expected to be predominantly on the τ-nitrogen atom as shown.

bath and Fmoc chloroformate (19.41 g, 75 mmol) dissolved in dioxan (200 ml) added dropwise over a 20–30 min period with vigorous stirring. The pH was maintained at 8.2 by further addition of 10% sodium carbonate. The reaction mixture was stirred for 3 h at room temperature, during which time a white solid precipitated, and was then added to water (1.5 litre). The aqueous phase was extracted with ether 3 times, then with ethyl acetate, and acidified with hydrochloric acid. The precipitated solid was collected, washed thoroughly with water and dried under high vacuum over phosphorous pentoxide. Yield 16.4 g (91%), m.p. 161–163°C, $[\alpha]_D$ −6.8° (c = 1 in DMF). A small sample was recrystallized from dimethylformamide–ether giving m.p. 163–165°C, $[\alpha]_D$ −6.7° (c = 1 in DMF). (Found: C, 72.18; H, 4.92: N, 7.34. $C_{36}H_{29}N_3O_6$ require C, 72.11; H, 4.88; N, 7.01%.)

This preparation is difficult and gives somewhat variable results, probably because of the sparing solubility of the sodium salt in the reaction mixture.

N_α-Fmoc-N_{im}-t-butoxycarbonyl-L-histidine (66)

Bis-Fmoc-L-histidine (10 g, 16.6 mmol) was suspended in DMF (100 ml) and diisopropylethylamine (5.38 g, 42 mmol) added with stirring. Di-*t*-butyl-dicarbonate (9.08 g, 42 mmol) was added and stirring continued until the reaction was complete (5.2 h, hplc). The solvent was removed at 0.1 mm Hg and 30°C and the residual syrup dissolved in ethyl acetate and washed with citric acid solution (10%, 200 and 100 ml) and then with water 4 × 50 ml). The organic layer was dried with sodium sulphate filtered and evaporated. The residual oil was dissolved in diethyl ether (75 ml) and added dropwise with stirring to petroleum ether (b.p. 80–100°C, 300 ml). The precipitate was filtered, washed with petroleum ether and dried *in vacuo* to give a crude solid (7.6 g). This was dissolved in ethyl acetate (5 ml) and warm diethyl ether (75 ml) and the mixture was added dropwise to stirred petroleum ether (b.p. 80–100°C, 300 ml). The product (5.6 g) was collected. Fmoc-His(Boc)-OH had m.p. 95–100°C, $[\alpha]_D$ −5.7° (c = 1 in DMF). Hplc showed it to be more than 97% pure. The cyclohexylammonium salt prepared by addition of cyclohexyamine to an ethereal solution of the free acid and recrystallization from methanol had m.p. 149–151°C, $[\alpha]_D$ + 15.2° (c = 1 in DMF). (Found: C, 66.71; H, 7.16; N, 9.65. $C_{32}H_{40}O_6N_4$ required C, 66.64; H, 6.99; N, 9.72%).

Caution should be exercised in deviating from the above procedure, as other preparations have been found to contain significant racemate.

5.1.3.3 *Arginine*

The guanidino side chain of arginine presents serious problems of protection. In some simple derivatives, such as N_α-Fmoc-N_G-*t*-butoxycarbonyl-arginine, the guanidino function appears to be inadequately protected, and difficulties are observed in coupling reactions. For others, such as N_α-Fmoc-N_G,N'_G-bis(adamantyloxycarbonyl)arginine, there are also serious preparative difficulties. The bis(adamantyloxycarbonyl) compound is also undesirably hydrophobic for ideal use in the polar polyamide system, and partial conversion to ornithine derivatives has been observed. The best results have been obtained thus far with various N_G-arylsulphonyl arginines, notably the 4-methoxy-2,3,6-trimethyl derivative (**78**) (*70*). This is the most acid-labile of a number of

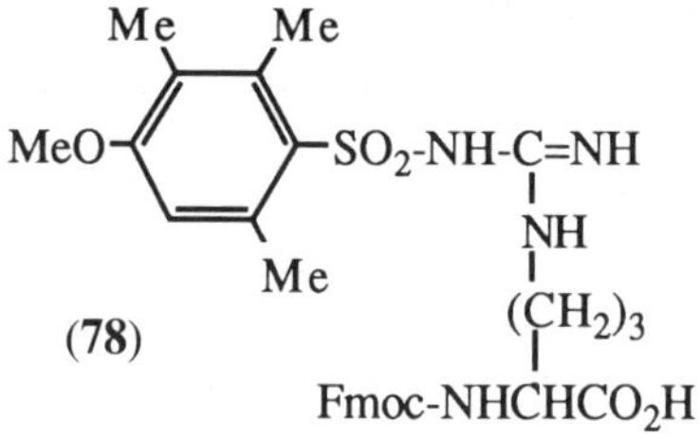

Me Me
MeO- -SO_2-NH-C=NH
NH
Me
(78) $(CH_2)_3$
Fmoc-NHCHCO_2H

Me Me
Me O SO_2-
Me Me
(79)

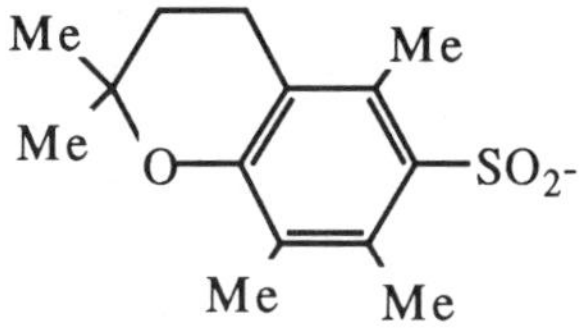

substituted arylsulphonyl compounds which we have thus far examined, though it requires variable and (for peptides containing multiple arginine residues) sometimes prolonged (up to 16 h or more) treatment with trifluoroacetic acid for complete cleavage. Cleavage by trifluoroactic acid in the presence of trimethylsilyl trifluoromethane sulphonate (*71*) has given variable results in our laboratory. Only in the special case of His-Arg- and Arg-His-containing sequences has partial conversion of arginine to ornithine been encountered using the Mtr protecting group.

A new arrival on the scene has been the further modified arylsulphonyl protecting group (**79**), designed to permit maximum stabilization of the presumed intermediate sulphonyl cation by the 4-oxygen substituent. Thus far only the N_α-benzyloxycarbonyl derivative has been described (*72*), although the Fmoc derivative is commercially available (Novabiochem; see Appendix). The protecting group is reportedly cleaved by trifluoracetic acid within 20 min at room temperature; extension to the Fmoc series therefore offers promise of a solution to the problem of arginine protection.

One significant side reaction has been detected using arylsulphonyl-protected arginine derivatives (*73,74*). In sequences containing both arginine and tryptophan, the cleaved arylsulphonyl residue may partially substitute into the indole nucleus, generating a contaminating *in*-arylsulphonyl peptide. Added scavengers appear to be relatively ineffective in inhibiting this.

N_α-Fmoc-N_G-4-methoxy-2,3,6-trimethylbenzenesulphonyl-L-arginine

(a) *Using fluorenylmethyl chloroformate.* N_G-4-methoxy-2,3,6-trimethyl-benzene-sulphonyl-L-arginine (*136*) (6.46 g, 16.71 mmol) was partially dissolved in chloroform (130 ml), cooled to ice temperature with vigorous stirring, and diisopropylethylamine (5.82 ml, 33.4 mmol) added. Fluorenylmethyl chloroformate (4.27 g, 16.71 mmol) was added in portions to the stirred mixture over a period of 10 min. The arginine derivative dissolved as reaction occurred. Reaction was almost complete after 7 min (tlc). After a further 50 min the chloroform was evaporated and the residue dissolved with vigorous shaking in a mixture of 10% aqueous sodium carbonate and ethyl acetate. The aqueous phase was washed with ethyl acetate (2 × 50 ml), acidified with solid citric acid and the product extracted into ethyl acetate (2 × 75 ml). The combined extracts were washed several times with water, dried over anhydrous sodium sulphate and evaporated, yielding 8.93 g of crude product. Tlc revealed impurities and the compound failed to crystallize. The material was purified by silica column chromatography on a Lobar C column, eluting with chloroform–methanol–acetic acid (95:2.5:2.5 v/v). A flow rate of 4 ml min^{-1} was employed and 3-min fractions collected. Fractions were asayed by tlc and those containing pure Fmoc.Arg(Mtr).OH were combined and evaporated, finally in high vacuum. The resultant solid was dissolved in ethyl acetate, washed thoroughly with water, dried over anhydrous sodium sulphate and evaporated to a small volume. This was added dropwise to vigorously stirred petroleum ether to precipitate the product, which was filtered and dried. This washing and precipitation technique is necessary to eliminate residual acetic acid which interferes in coupling reactions. Typically from 9.56 g of crude Fmoc.Arg(Mtr).OH applied to the Lobar column in two separate batches, 5.73 g (60%) of the pure derivative was obtained, m.p. 118–120°C (dec), $[\alpha]_D$ + 7.9° (c = 0.5 in methanol). (Found: C, 60.37; H, 6.02; N, 9.08. $C_{31}H_{36}N_4O_7S$ 0.5 H_2O requires C, 60.71; H, 6.02; N, 9.05%.)

(b) *Using fluorenylmethyl succinimidyl carbonate.* N_G-4-Methoxy-2,3,6-trimethylbenzenesulphonyl-L-arginine (10.8 g, 27.9 mmol) was stirred in chloroform (80 ml) at room temperature and diisopropylethylamine (4.9 ml, 28 mmol) added to give a clear solution. Fluorenylmethyl-succinimidyl carbonate (9.43 g, 28 mmol) was added and the mixture stirred overnight. The solvent was evaporated, the residue partitioned between ethyl acetate and 10% potassium hydrogen sulphate. The organic phase was separated, washed with 10% potassium hydrogen sulphate (2 × 20 ml), water (3 × 20 ml), dried over magnesium sulphate, filtered and evaporated to yield an oil, Dissolution in ethyl acetate followed by addition of petroleum ether gave a solid which was filtered off and dried to yield 16.9 g. (100%), $[\alpha]_D$ + 5.9° (c = 0.51 in methanol).

An alternative procedure for the synthesis of arginine-containing peptides is to use the N_G-unprotected amino acid. The zwitterionic N_α-Fmoc-arginine is straightward to prepare and couples well, using dicyclohexylcarbodiimide in the presence of excess 1-hydroxy-benzotriazole (*69*). The latter functions both as an acylation catalyst and as protonating acid for the basic guanidine function. Subsequent amino acids are best coupled as activated ester derivatives, again in the presence of excess hydroxybenzotriazole or dihydrohydroxyoxobenzotriazine, with acylation times kept to a minimum (*75*). In the absence of these weak acids, substantial conversion to ornithine occurs through acylation of the free guanidine group and subsequent decomposition. Side-chain-unprotected Fmoc-arginine is particularly suitable for the addition of a final N-terminal residue.

N_α-Fmoc-L-arginine

Arginine monohydrate (4.75 g, 0.025 mol) was dissolved in a mixture of dioxan (66 ml) and 10% sodium carbonate (50 ml), stirred and cooled to ice-bath temperature. Fmoc N-hydroxysuccinimide (8.74 g, 0.026 mol) dissolved in dioxan (100 ml) was added to the above solution dropwise over a period of 0.5 h. The ice-bath was taken away and the mixture stirred at room temperature for 2 h, during which time the product precipitated. On addition of water (0.5 litre), more product precipitated and was then filtered and washed thoroughly with water until the washings were pH 6.0. Drying in high vacuum over P_2O_5 yielded 8.73 g (89%), m.p. softening at 140°C, finally melting at 160°C.

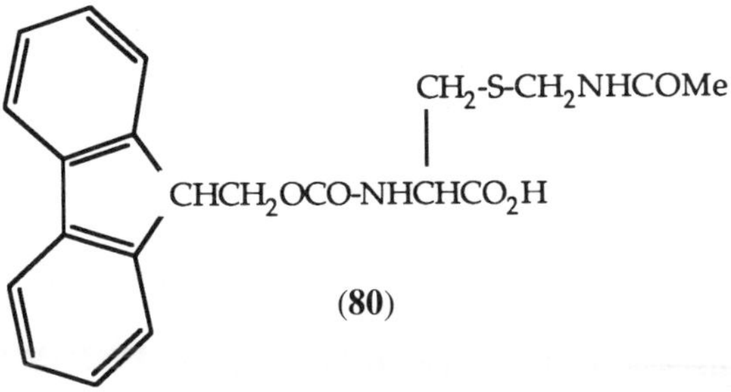

$$\text{Fmoc: } CHCH_2OCO\text{-}NHCHCO_2H \text{ with side chain } CH_2\text{-S-}CH_2NHCOMe$$

(80)

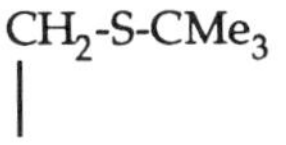

CH_2-S-CMe_3

(81)

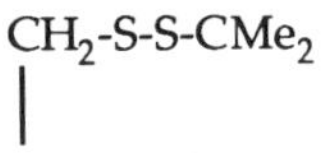

CH_2-S-S-CMe_2

(82)

CH_2-S-CPh_3

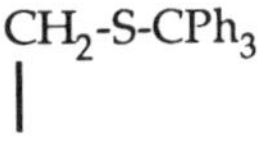

(83)

5.1.3.4 *Cysteine*

Several protecting groups (**80–83**) are available for the thiol group of cysteine derivatives (*76,77*). Only the S-trityl derivative (**83**) is sufficently acid-labile to be compatible with O-*t*-butyl derivatives (ethers, esters and urethanes) of other amino-acid side chains. Thus free thiol peptides are generated directly from peptide–resins containing S-trityl residues by treatment with trifluoroacetic acid in the presence of suitable scavengers (see Chapter 11). This is particularly useful for the synthesis of peptides which are subsequently to be coupled through the thiol group to carrier proteins for antibody production. Separate cleavage of the S-protecting groups (**80–82**) is required after completion of the synthesis. This may be considered advantageous in that it permits the purification of S-protected cysteine peptides without complication from oxidative disulphide formation. N-Fmoc-S-acetamidomethylcysteine (**80**) is the currently preferred reagent. In contrast to the S-trityl derivative, the acetamidomethyl group adds polar character to the protected peptide chain. This may be useful in sequences where aggregation problems are experienced during assembly. The S-protecting group is cleaved by mercuric salts (*78*), by thiols (*79*) and importantly by iodine (*80*) when disulphide formation to cystine derivatives occurs. The S-*t*-butyl derivative (**81**) is also cleaved by mercuric ion (*81*). The *t*-butyl disulphide (S-*t*-butylsulphenyl derivative) (**82**) has entirely different reactivity, being cleaved reductively by thiols (*82*). Thus these various derivatives used in combination enable differential protection of cysteine residues in polycysteinyl peptides, permitting selective formation of disulphide bridges (*83*).

The thiolate anion is a good leaving group, and all S-protected cysteine derivatives have the potential for base-catalysed β-elimination. This decompositon is not observed in normal peptide synthesis, but may be significant when the cysteine residue is carboxy-terminal, i.e. the α-hydrogen is adjacent to an activating ester carbonyl rather than to a carboxamido group. Racemization of carboxy-terminal cysteine residues is also a significant risk.

N-Fmoc-S-trityl-L-cysteine (77)

S-Trityl-L-cysteine (1100 g, 3.03 mol) was washed thoroughly with deionized water and then dissolved in a mixture of water (5 litres), acetone (4.4 litres) and sodium carbonate (660 g). Fluorenylmethyl succinimidyl carbonate (999.4 g, 2.96 mol) was then added followed by M aqueous sodium carbonate (*c*. 500 ml) to maintain the pH at about 8–9. After stirring overnight, ethyl acetate (11 litres) was added and the mixture cautiously acidified with M hydrochloric acid to pH 2. The organic phase was separated, washed successively with M, 0.5 M, and 0.25 M hydrochloric acid (3 litres, 2 times each), dried over $MgSO_4$, and evaporated. The product was recrystallized from ethyl actate–light petroleum yielding 1562 g (90%), m.p. 174–178°, $[\alpha]_D$ + 20.65° (c = 1 in DMF), (Found: C, 75.39; H, 5.41, N,2.35. $C_{37}H_{31}NO_4S$ requires C, 75.87; H, 5.33; N, 2.39%).

N-Fmoc-S-acetamidomethyl-L-cysteine (76)

S-Acetamidomethyl-L-cysteine monohydrate (3.15 g, 15.0 mmol) was dissolved in a mixture of 10% aqueous sodium carbonate (45 ml) and dioxane (20 ml). The solution was stirred and cooled to ice temperature and a solution of Fmoc chloride (4.41 g, 17.0 mmol) in dioxane (15 ml) was added dropwise during 30 min. The ice-bath was removed and the mixture was stirred for 1.5 h at room temperature, when tlc indicated almost complete reaction. After a further 1 h the reaction mixture was poured into water (400 ml), extracted with ether (3 × 100 ml), and acidified with 10% citric acid to pH 3. The resultant white crystalline solid was collected and freed from citric acid by partitioning between ethyl acetate and water, and the organic phase was washed several times with water before being dried (Na_2SO_4) and evaporated. After several unsuccessul attempts to crystallize the product, it was dissolved in propan-2-ol, and then water was added to cloud point. The mixture was cooled and the title product crystallized (4.5 g, 75%),m.p. 150–154°C, $[\alpha]_D$ –27.5° (c = 1 in ethyl acetate). (Found: C, 60.25; H, 5.4; N, 6.9. $C_{21}H_{22}N_2O_5S$ requires C, 60.86; H, 5.34; N, 7.76%.)

In other preparations the compound failed to crystallize in a pure form and was purified on a Lobar C silica column using chloroform–methanol–acetic acid (370:20:10 v/v/v) as elutant prior to recrystallization.

N-Fmoc-S-(t-butylsulphenyl)-L-cysteine (76)

S-(*t*-Butylsulphenyl)-L-cysteine (3.14 g, 15.0 mmol) was dissolved in water (27 ml) and the solution was treated dropwise with 1 M sodium hydroxide (14 ml). Sodium carbonate (1.69 g, 16.0 mmol) was added and the resulting solution was cooled in an ice-bath, water (10 ml) and dioxane (21 ml) were added, followed by a solution of Fmoc chloride (3.9 g, 15.07 mmol) in dioxane (39 ml) dropwise during 15 min. The mixture was stirred in the ice-bath for 2 h and then for 15 min at room temperature, after which time tlc indicated the presence of only trace amounts of the starting cysteine derivative. The mixture was poured into ice-water (450 ml), washed with ether (2 × 100 ml), then acidified to pH 2 and the product was extracted into ether. The ether layer was washed with water (4 × 100 ml), dried (Na_2SO_4), and evaporated to give a foam which was crystallized from dichloromethane-*n*-hexane to give the title compound (5.45 g, 84%), m.p. 74–76°C, $[\alpha]_D$ −87.0° (c = 1 in ethyl acetate), lit. (*63*) m.p. 74–76°C, $[\alpha]_D$ −84.6° (c = 1 in ethyl acetate).

N-Fmoc-S-t-butyl-L-cysteine (76)

S-(*t*-Butyl)-L-cysteine hydrochloride (3.2 g, 15.0 mmol) was dissolved in a mixture of 10% aqueous sodium carbonate (60 ml) and dioxane (30 ml). The solution was cooled in an ice-bath and stirred, and a solution of Fmoc chloride (4.41 g, 17.0 mmol) in dioxane (15 ml) was added dropwise during 15 min. The ice-bath was removed, and after the mixture had been stirred for 30 min, tlc indicated very little starting material remaining. After a further 30 min the mixture was poured into water (400 ml), extracted with ether (3 × 100 ml), the solution was acidified with solid citric acid, and the resultant oil was extracted into ether (3 × 100 ml). The latter ether extracts were combined, washed thoroughly with water, dried (Na_2SO_4), and evaporated to give a foam which was crystallized from dichloromethane–light petroleum to give the title compound as white needles (4.7 g, 79%), m.p. 135–136°C, $(\alpha]_D$ −24.0 (c = 1 in DMF), lit. (*63*) m.p. 135–136°C, $[\alpha]_D$ −23.2° (c = 1 in DMF).

CHAPTER 6

Peptide – resin linkage agents

The chemical linkage of the growing peptide chain to the resin support is crucial in solid phase synthesis. It has to be easily formed, stable to repeated cycles of acylation and deprotection reactions, and yet easily cleaved at the end of the synthesis without damage to newly formed peptide bonds. In the past, some compromise has been necessary in attempting to meet these conflicting requirements. Thus the simple benzyl ester linkage which has most commonly been used with polystyrene resins requires rather vigorous cleavage conditions, typically acidolysis by liquid hydrogen fluoride or trifluoromethane sulphonic acid. Although this implies substantial acid stability, slow cleavage also occurs during the repeated mild acid treatments required for removal of *t*-butoxycarbonylamino protecting groups.

The situation is very different in solid phase strategies which do not use reagents of the same type for both α-amino deprotection and detachment of the completed peptide from the resin. The lability of the peptide – resin linkage can be optimized without fear of premature cleavage. If it does occur, premature cleavage would involve a different chemical reaction mechanism, and this is more easily handled than situations involving differential reactivity to the same reagent type.

Because of this need for optimization and also to impart additional flexibility to the method, the new concept of individual reversible linkage agents was introduced (*40*). Small linker molecules, usually containing a free hydroxyl group, are constructed such that the derived esters have the desired stability and lability. Thus the original benzyl ester linkage of the Merrifield technique was initially mimicked in the Boc-polyamide variant by setting up the system shown below: (*40,41*)

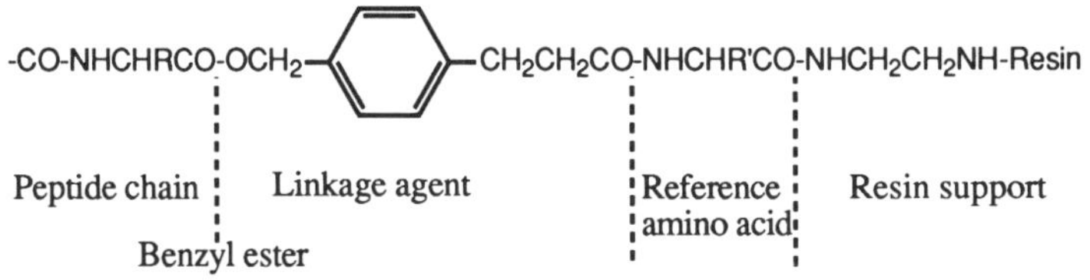

-CO-NHCHRCO-OCH$_2$-C_6H_4-CH$_2$CH$_2$CO-NHCHR'CO-NHCH$_2$CH$_2$NH-Resin

Peptide chain | Linkage agent | Reference amino acid | Resin support

Benzyl ester

The *p*-hydroxymethylphenypropionic acid unit was attached to the amino-resin by prior activation of the linkage agent carboxyl group (activated esters are commonly preferred but even anhydrides may be used without serious self-acylation), and the growing peptide chain, then attached through a benzyl ester with the new hydroxy group. An additional novel feature also introduced at this time was the concept of the internal reference amino acid. This was attached directly to the aminoethyl-polyamide resin, and provided a useful reference point for the interpretation of amino-acid analysis data. It does not form part of the peptide being synthesized and is usually chosen not to be amongst its constituent amino acids. A non-protein amino acid, commonly norleucine, is convenient. At the end of peptide synthesis by the Boc-polyamide technique, the benzyl ester is cleaved under the same conditions as in the Merrifield system.

This particular linkage agent system does not of itself convey particular advantage because it was designed to have ester lability close to that of the direct peptide–polystyrene linkage. It was the prototype of a series of benzyl alcohol linkage agents (*84*) in which the lability of derived benzyl esters towards acids and nucleophilic bases was adjusted by substitution in the aromatic ring. The reagents (**84–86**) have proved the most useful in combination with Fmoc-amino acids. Acid stability of the derived benzyl esters increases in the order **84**>**85**>**86**; the *p*-hydroxymethyl-phenylpropionyl system has stability intermediate between (**84**) and (**85**).

Esters of the benzyl alcohol (*84*) are essentially stable to anhydrous acids. They survive prolonged treatment with acids as strong as hydrogen fluoride. Conversely, these esters are exceptionally easily cleaved by nucleophilic reagents, including hydroxide and methoxide ions, ammonia, and hydrazine. This combination of properties renders (**84**) very suitable for the preparation of peptide amides and the like. The acid stability allows prior cleavage of all *t*-butyl derivatives (particularly side-chain esters of aspartic and glutamic acids)* while the peptide remains attached to the resin, and then detachment by, for example, methanolic ammonia to produce peptide amides. Carrying out the two deprotection steps in this order eliminates the risk of side chain ester ammonolysis and transpeptidation reactions. Although with linkage agent (**84**) and methanolic ammonia the peptide is detached from the resin quickly, ammonolysis is usually prolonged to ensure that the peptide methyl ester is not formed as a by-product. Slow cleavage and methyl ester formation may be a significant problem with peptides containing sterically hindered C-terminal residues (valine, isoleucine, threonine).

$HOCH_2-C_6H_4-CO_2H$ (**84**)

$HOCH_2-C_6H_4-OCH_2CO_2H$ (**85**)

$HOCH_2-C_6H_3(OMe)-OCH_2CO_2H$ (**86**)

$H_2NCHRCO-NHCHRCO-OCH_2-C_6H_4-CO-NH-$ (**87**)

*The stability towards acids of esters of (**84**) is such that even side-chain benzyl esters may be cleaved selectively.

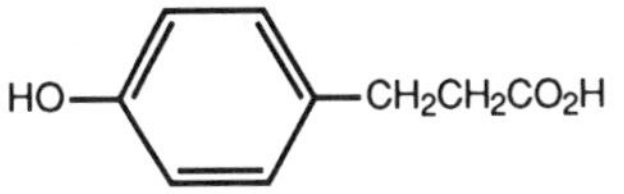

HO– C_6H_4 –$CH_2CH_2CO_2H$ **(88)**

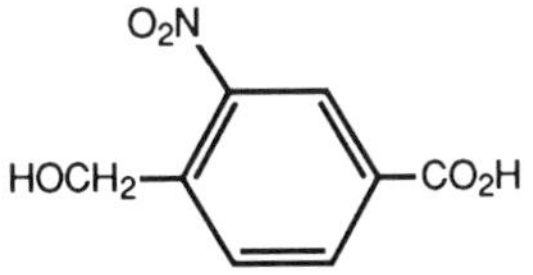

O_2N

$HOCH_2$– C_6H_3 –CO_2H **(89)**

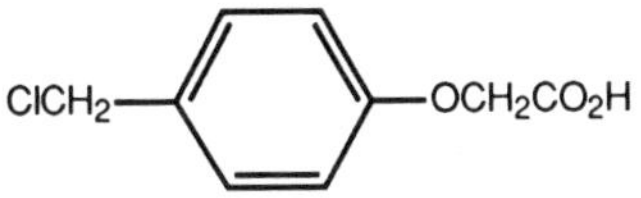

$ClCH_2$– C_6H_4 –OCH_2CO_2H **(90)**

Intramolecular aminolysis with loss of peptide from the resin (**87**, arrow) is a possible side reaction with any peptide–resin linkage in which the carbonyl group is susceptible to nucleophilic attack. It is potentially particularly serious in the Fmoc series because the basic deprotection conditions liberate the free amino terminus directly, and not in a protonated form as in techniques based on Boc-amino acids. As a general rule, deprotection reactions in the early stages of solid phase synthesis using Fmoc derivatives should not be carried out unless the following acylation reaction is to follow immediately. In practice, it is found that intramolecular aminolysis occurs at a serious rate in the case of linkage agent (**84**) only at the dipeptide level when the carboxy-terminal residue is proline or other secondary amino acid.* For linkage (**84**), this problem may sometimes be solved by using a Boc-amino acid derivative for addition of the second residue. The linkage agent (*91*) (see below) provides a general solution to the problem of C-terminal peptide amide synthesis. The phenolic derivative (**88**) provides a generally base-labile linkage with potential in special cases for peroxide-catalysed alkaline cleavage (*85*); the nitro derivative (**89**) has been investigated as a potential photolabile linkage agent (*86*).

Reagent (**85**) (*37,84*) is the standard peptide–resin linkage agent in the Fmoc-polyamide technique. The *p*-alkoxy substituent labilizes the derived benzyl ester towards acid, giving reactivity comparable to *t*-butyl derivatives. Thus peptides linked to the resin through esters of (**85**) may be cleaved by mild acid treatment (usually with trifluoroacetic acid) at the same time and under the same conditions as *t*-butyl side-chain protecting groups are removed. The reagent is commercially available, but its preparation (and of useful activated derivatives) is also given below. Cleavage conditions in relation to amino-acid composition are discussed in Chapter 11.

Increased lability to acid is conveyed by the second alkoxy group in linkage agent (**86**) (*84*). This reagent was prepared as part of an investigation into fragment condensation strategies in solid phase synthesis (*87*). This is a potentially attractive procedure, but one which has not yet become of general applicability because of the unpredictable and often unfavourable solubility properties of amino- and side-chain protected peptides. An example of the use of linkage (**86**) is given in Section 12.5.

*This problem has recently been discussed in the Fmoc-polystyrene series by Pedroso *et al.* (*89*).

The derived peptide benzyl esters are cleaved by dilute anhydrous trifluoroacetic acid under conditions which leave most *t*-butyl-based side chain protecting groups largely unaffected (*87*).

Esterification of the first amino acid to the hydroxyl group of the linkage agent may be affected before or after the latter has been attached to the resin support. Esterification before attachment was early recognized as having potential advantage (*40*), though it is not always easy to achieve experimentally. One approach is to 'protect' the carboxyl group of the linker agent by conversion to a moderately reactive activated ester. Trichlorophenyl esters have proved most suitable. They are sufficiently stable not to interfere with esterification of the free linker hydroxyl group to the first protected amino acid, while being sufficiently reactive to acylate the resin amino function subsequently. The details of linkage agent preparation given below include some early examples of prior amino acid attachment utilizing Boc-amino acids which may serve as models in the Fmoc series. Also included below is a description of the chloromethyl linkage (**90**), an intermediate in one synthesis of (**85**) which provides an alternative mechanism for attaching the first residue akin to that of the Merrifield technique (*Figure 3*). This has not been used extensively in our laboratory since the initial investigation (*88*). The general area of attachment of the first residue in solid phase synthesis is discussed fully in Section 10.2.

There have been recent developments in the design of amide-forming linkages in the polystyrene series which offer a solution to a number of the problems discussed above. Direct formation of amides by acidolysis of benzylamine-type polymers has long been established (*4*) but similar linkages with the degree of acid-lability appropriate to the Fmoc-*t*-butyl strategy have only recently become available (e.g. refs. *90,119–123*). Rink (*90*) has described the trialkoxybenzhydrylamine resin (**91**) which is cleaved by a mixture of trifluoroacetic acid and dichloromethane (1:1) within 15 min. Preparative details are given below the similarly conceived (*91*) linkage agent (**92**) suitable for use with Fmoc-*t*-butylpolyamide chemistry. For the preparation of peptide amides, this attachment to the resin circumvents entirely the occasional problems of ammonolysis (of **84**) and diketopiperazine formation discussed above. There are additional advantages regarding the ease of attachment of the first residue to a resin-bound amino group rather than hydroxyl. This is particularly significant in relation to the formation of peptide amides with 'difficult' carboxy-terminal residues at the C-terminus, especially asparagine and glutamine. Linkage through the side chains of the α-*t*-butyl esters of aspartic acid or glutamic acid offers a simple route to C-terminal asparagine and glutamine peptide acids (see Section 12.3).

3-(4-Chloromethylphenyl)propionic acid

A mixture of 3-phenylpropionic acid (120 g, 0.80 mol), anhydrous zinc chloride (19.8 g) and formalin (20.3 g) was stirred at 80°C (oil-bath) while anhydrous hydrogen chloride gas was bubbled through for 6 h. The reaction mixture was left to cool overnight, the solid collected by filtration and washed with a little water, then dissolved in dichloromethane, filtered and evaporated, giving 154 g of crude product contaminated with other isomers (nmr). Three recrystallizations from isopropanol gave the desired product free of other isomers 46 g (29%), m.p. 114–121°C foaming at 110°C, (lit. m.p. 118–119°C).

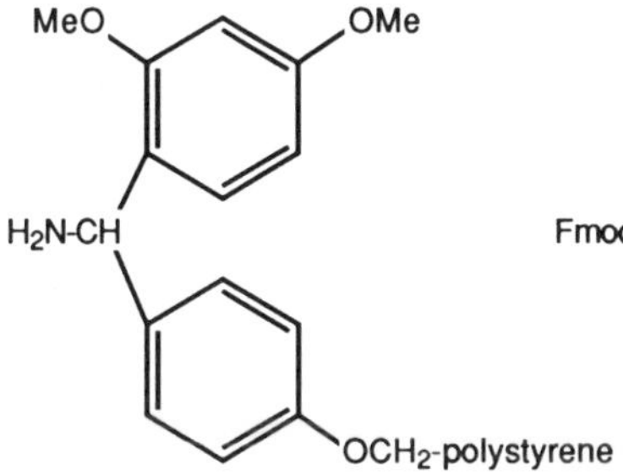

MeO OMe H2N-CH OCH2-polystyrene

(91)

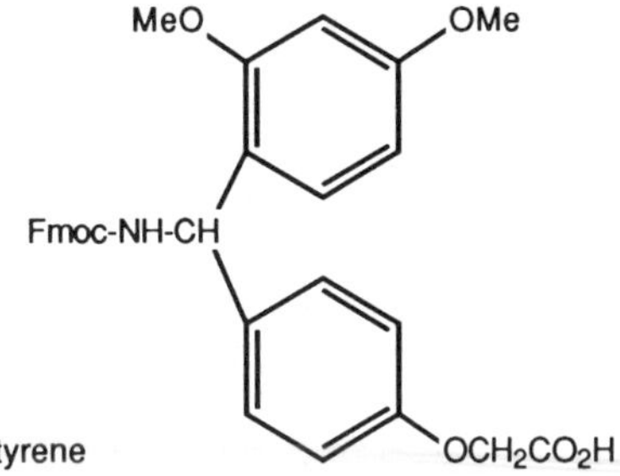

MeO OMe Fmoc-NH-CH OCH2CO2H

(92)

3-(4-Hydroxymethylphenyl)propionic acid (41)

3-(4-Chloromethylphenyl)propionic acid (28 g, 0.14 mol) was heated in boiling water (600 ml) containing sodium iodide (1.5 g) for 15 min. On cooling an oil formed, which crystallized on scratching. After standing for several hours at 5°C the hydroxymethyl derivative (21.5 g, 85%), m.p. 144–146°C, was collected. Recrystallization from water gave m.p. 148–150°C (softening at 130°C). (Found: C, 66.45; H, 6.75. $C_{10}H_{12}O_3$ requires C, 66.65; H, 6.71%.)

3-(4-Hydroxymethylphenyl)propionic acid 2,4,5-trichlorophenyl ester

DCCI (24 g, 0.116 mol) dissolved in DMF (20ml) was added dropwise during 10 min to a stirred and ice-cooled solution of the foregoing carboxylic acid (20 g, 0.11 mol) and 2,4,5-trichlorophenol (23 g, 0.12 mol) in DMF (60 ml). The mixture was allowed to warm to room temperature and stirred overnight. Dicyclohexylurea was removed by filtration and the filtrate evaporated to an oil which soon crystalized. Recrystallization from ethyl cetate–light petroleum gave the trichlorophenyl ester (25.7g, 65%), m.p. 85–89°C, raised to 94–96°C on recrystallization from propan-2-ol. (Found: C, 53.75; H, 3.7; Cl, 29.8. $C_{16}H_{13}Cl_3O_3$ requires C, 53.44; H, 3.64; Cl, 29.57%.)

4-Formylphenoxyacetic acid (84)

A mixture of 4-formylphenol (Aldrich, 15 g, 0.123 mol), water (40 ml), and sodium carbonate (18.6 g, 0.175 mol) was heated to 70°C with stirring and purged with nitrogen for 0.5 h. A solution of chloracetic acid (110 g, 1.16 mol) in water (160 mol) which had been adjusted to pH 9 with solid sodium carbonate was then added dropwise to the warm solution over 0.5 h. After a further 15 min, potassium iodide (1 g) was added and the mixture stirred under nitrogen atmosphere for 24 h at 70°C. The pH at this stage was *c*.4.5 and tlc indicated that the reaction was 70–80% complete. The solution was adjusted to pH 6 with sodium hydroxide and washed three times with ether. 4-Formylphenoxyacetic acid crystallized when the aqueous solution was acidified to pH 2, and was collected after standing for several hours at 5°C and washed well with water, yielding 14.8 g (67%), m.p. 193.5–195°C (lit. 198°C). It was used directly in the next stage without further purification.

4-Hydroxymethylphenoxyacetic acid (**85**) *(84)*

The foregoing formyl derivative (17 g, 0.094 mol), 1 N sodium hydroxide (94.4 ml), and methanol (90 ml) were stirred together, and solid sodium borohydride (3.6 g, 0.094 mol) added portionwise. After 1 h the reaction mixture was cooled in an ice-bath and acidified to pH 2–3. Solid sodium chloride was added, the solution extracted several times with ethyl acetate, and the combined extracts washed with brine, dried (Na_2SO_4), and evaporated. The crystalline residue was recrystallized from ethyl acetate yielding 11.9 g (69%), m.p. 114–116°C.

4-Hydroxymethylphenoxyacetic acid 2,4,5-trichlorophenyl ester

This ester was prepared from the foregoing acid (12.0 g, 65 mmol), 2,4,5-trichlorophenol (14.3 g, 72 mmol), and DCCI (13.6 g, 65 mmol) in ethyl acetate (80 ml) initially in an ice–salt bath and then overnight at room temperature. Recrystallization of the product from ethyl acetate–light petroleum (b.p. 60–80°C) gave 11.7 g (49%) m.p. 100–102°C. An analytical sample had m.p. 97–105°C. (Found: C, 49.85; H, 3.2, $C_{15}H_{11}Cl_3O_4$ requires C, 49.82; H, 3.07%.)

4-Hydroxymethylphenoxyacetic acid pentafluorophenyl ester (93)

4-Hydroxymethylphenoxyacetic acid 2.0 g, 10.98 mmol) was dissolved in dioxan (20 ml) and a solution of pentafluorophenol (2.22 g, 12.08 mmol) in dioxan (10 ml) added. The mixture was stirred, cooled in ice and dicyclohexylcarbodiimide (2.49 g, 12.08 mmol) dissolved in dioxan (10 ml) added. After 60 min stirring at ice temperature, the cooling bath was removed and the mixture allowed to warm to room temperature. After stirring for a total of 14 h, tlc indicated no unchanged acid remaining. After 24 h the reaction mixture was filtered, the dicyclohexylurea washed with dioxan and the total filtrate evaporated *in vacuo*. The resulting yellowish oil was stirred with *n*-hexane for 3 h and the solid obtained filtered and dried under high vacuum giving 3.7 g of crude product. This was recrystallized from hexane–ether to give 2.1 g (54%) m.p. 112–113°C. (Found: C, 51.71; H, 2.68; $C_{15}H_9O_4F_5$ requires C, 51.74; H, 2.61.)

4-Hydroxymethylphenoxyacetic acid Dhbt ester (39)

4-Hydroxymethylphenoxyacetic acid (6.0 g, 32.9 mmol) was dissolved in THF (60 ml) and the solution was cooled to −15°C. DCCI (6.79 g, 32.9 mmol) in THF (10 ml) was added with stirring. After 2 min Dhbt-OH (5.37 g, 32.9 mmol) was added and the mixture was stirred at −15°C for 30 min. After 16 h at 20°C the precipitate was removed by filtration and the filtrate concentrated *in vacuo*. The residual syrup was stirred with diethyl ether to afford 3,4-dihydro-4-oxo-1,2,3-benzotriazin-3-yl 4-hydroxymethylphenoxyacetate (10.1 g, 94%), m.p. 98–99°C. (Found: C, 58.65; H, 4.05; N, 12.6. $C_{16}H_{13}N_3O_5$ requires C, 58.71; H, 4.00; N, 12.84%.) The infrared spectrum had maxima at 1823 (C=O), and 1725cm^{-1} (C=O) and no absorption at 2100cm, indicating the absence of *o*-azidobenzoic acid Dhbt ester. 3,4-Dihydro-4-oxo-1,2,3-benzotriazin-3-yl 4-chloro-methylphenoxyacetate, and 3,4-dihydro-4-oxo-1,2,3-benzotriazin-3-yl 4-hydroxymethyl-3-methoxyphenoxy-acetate can be prepared by the same procedure (*39*).

3-Methoxy-4-formylphenol (84)

In a one-litre three-necked flask fitted with a dropping funnel, drying tube ($CaCl_2$), and mercury-sealed stirrer were placed redistilled 3-methoxyphenol (Aldrich, 140 ml, 1.28 mol) and freshly distilled phosphoryl chloride (200 ml, 2.15 mol). The solution was mechanically stirred at 0°C while DMF (redistilled, 150 ml, 1.94 mol) was added dropwise over 45 min and then at room temperature for 16 h. The pale yellow oil was poured onto crushed ice (2.5 litres) and after 10 min the cloudy solution washed twice with ether (1 litre and 400 ml). The aqueous layer was again cooled at 0°C and adjusted to pH 5–6 by careful addition of sodium hydroxide (77.7 g, 1.94 mmol) and then anhydrous sodium acetate (759 g, 9.25 mol). Water (150 ml) and ethyl acetate (750 ml) were added and after separation of the organic layer the aqueous phase was washed further with ethyl acetate (250 ml). The combined organic extracts were washed with water (250 ml) and saturated brine (250 ml), dried (Na_2SO_4), and evaporated. The residual oily solid was triturated with boiling petroleum ether (b.p. 60–80°C, 3 × 100 ml), and the crystalline 3-methoxy-4-formylphenol (38.4 g, 20%) collected with a mixture of petroleum ether (b.p. 60–80°C) and ether (1:1, 100 ml) m.p. 158.5–160°C (lit. m.p. 153°C). The product gave a single spot (R_f 0.55) on tlc in chloroform–methanol–acetic acid (85:10:5) (CMA) in which it was clearly distinguished from isomeric 3-methoxy-6-formylphenol (R_f 0.76). The nmr spectrum was consistent with the expected structure.

3-Methoxy-4-formylphenoxyacetic acid (84)

3-Methoxy-4-formylphenol (40 g, 0.263 mol) was added to molten chloroacetic acid (40 g, 0.423 mol) on a steam bath, producing a deep red solution. To this was added slowly with effervescence aqueous sodium hydroxide 50 ml, prepared by dissolved sodium hydroxide (100 g) in water (100 ml). The mixture solidified after 5 min. After 15 min further additions of chloroacetic acid (40 g, 0.423 mol) and water (30 ml) were made with hand-mixing, followed by further sodium hydroxide solution (30 ml). Further portions of sodium hydroxide (2 × 5 ml) were added when the pH had fallen to 8–9. After 60 min, water (400 ml) and sodium hydroxide solution (10 ml) were added and the mixture warmed until solution was obtained. Acidification with 6 N hydrochloric acid produced a copious precipitate which was collected after cooling to 0°C, washed with water, dried *in vacuo* (silica gel), and recrystallized from boiling 95% ethanol (1 litre). The 3-methoxy-4-formylphenoxyacetic acid (36.8 g, 66.5%) had m.p. 208.5–209°C, R_f 0.41 (CMA, see above). (Found: C, 56.80, H, 5.02. $C_{10}H_{10}O_5$ requires C, 57.12; H, 4.8%.)

3-Methoxy-4-hydroxymethylphenoxyacetic acid (**86**) *(84)*

The foregoing formyl derivative (4.2 g, 20 mmol) was dissolved in a mixture of 1 N aqueous sodium hydroxide (20 ml), water (40 ml), and methanol (20 ml). To the stirred solution at pH 11 was added solid sodium borohydride (0.756 g). After 4.5 h at room temperature, the solution was cooled at 0°C, water (100 ml) and solid sodium hydrogen sulphate was added to pH 2 followed by brine (100 ml). The solution was extracted with ethyl acetate (200 ml), the extract washed with brine (3 × 100 ml) and the washings re-extracted with ethyl acetate (100 ml). The combined extracts were dried (Na_2SO_4) and evaporated *in vacuo* at *c*. 20°C. Ethyl acetate (25 ml) was added to the residue and the crystalline product (2.51 g, 59%, m.p. 100–103°C) collected after standing overnight at −20°C and washed with ether. A second crop (0.53 g, 12.5%, m.p. 98–98.5°C) was obtained by evaporation of the filtrate and washings and dissolution in warm ethyl acetate (25 ml). Both crops gave a single spot on tlc, R_f 0.37 (CMA). Recrystallization of the total product from ethyl acetate–methanol gave 3-methoxy-4-hydroxymethylphenoxyacetic acid (1.92 g, 45%), m.p. 106–107°C. (Found: C, 56.39; H, 5.96; M^+ 212. $C_{10}H_{12}O_5$ requires C, 56.60; H, 5.70%, MW 212).

3-Methoxy-4-hydroxymethylphenoxyacetic acid pentafluorophenyl ester

3-Methoxy-4-hydroxymethylphenoxyacetic acid (2 g, 9.4 mmol) and pentafluorophenol (1.95 g, 10.4 mmol) were dissolved in dioxan (30 ml) with stirring and slight warming. The solution was then cooled in an ice-bath and DCCI (2.15 g, 10.4 mmol) was added in dioxan (10 ml). The mixture was stirred in ice for 1 h and then at room temperature for a further 2.75 h, after which time tlc indicated a faint trace of starting acid. After a total reaction period of 4.25 h the dicyclohexylurea was filtered and washed with a small volume of dioxan. The total filtrate was evaporated at a water pump and then the residual dioxan taken off under oil-pump vacuum. *n*-Hexane (250 ml) was added and the mixture stirred at room temperature for 2.5 h and the crystalline ester was filtered to give after drying 3.1 g (86.5%). This material was recrystallized from ether–*n*-hexane to give 2.13 g (59.5%), m.p. 115–116°C. An analytical sample melted at 116–118°C. (Found: C, 51.03; H, 3.00. $C_{16}H_{11}O_5F_5$ requires C, 50.80; H, 2.93%.)

4-Bromomethylbenzoic acid (37)

α-Bromo-*p*-toluonitrile (20 g, 0.102 mol) was heated with constant boiling hydrobromic acid (200 ml) for 5 h under reflux. After cooling the solid was collected, washed with water, and dried *in vacuo*. Recrystallization from ethyl acetate gave *p*-bromomethylbenzoic acid (12.5 g, 57%), m.p. 231–232°C. A second crop (4.5 g 20.5%) had m.p. 225–227°C (lit., 223–224°C).

4-Hydroxymethylbenzoic acid (**84**) *(37)*

4-Bromomethylbenzoic acid (12.5 g, 0.058 mol) was boiled in water (500 ml) for 1 h after dissolution. After cooling, the crystalline product was collected and recrystallized from water. *p*-Hydroxymethylbenzoic acid (7.8 g, 88%) had m.p. 181–183°C (lit. m.p. 179–181°C).

4-Hydroxymethylbenzoic acid 2,4,5-trichlorophenyl ester

A solution of 4-hydroxymethylbenzoic acid (4.5 g, 30 mmol) and 2,4,5-trichlorophenol (6.5 g, 33 mmol) in DMF (40 ml) was cooled to 0°C and a solution of DCCI (6.8 g, 33 mmol) in a minimum volume of DMF added dropwise with stirring. The reaction mixture was stirred and allowed to warm to room temperature overnight. The dicylohexylurea was filtered and the solution evaporated *in vacuo*. The residual oil was dissolved in ethyl acetate (50 ml), insoluble urea filtered, and light petroleum added. On cooling the trichlorophenyl ester (8.5 g, 86%) crystallized, m.p. 130–135°C. An analytical sample melted at 139.5–141°C. (Found: C, 50.85; H, 3.05. $C_{14}H_9Cl_3O_3$ requires C, 50.71; H, 2.74%.)

3-Nitro-4-bromomethylbenzoic acid

4-Bromomethylbenzoic acid (12 g, 55.8 mmol) was added over 0.5 h to stirred fuming nitric acid (100 ml) at −10°C and then stirred for a further 2 h at this temperature. The mixture was then poured onto crushed ice, the product filtered, washed with ice-water until the filtrate was neutral (litmus paper) and then dried *in vacuo* over P_2O_5 giving a pale yellow solid which was recrystallized from dichloromethane to give 10.3 g (71%), m.p. 132–136°C.

3-Nitro-4-hydroxymethylbenzoic acid (**89**)

A mixture of 3-nitro-4-bromomethylbenzoic acid (26 g, 100.0 mmol) and water (750 ml) was heated under reflux for 1 h, activated charcoal added, and heating continued for a further few minutes before filtration. On cooling, the product (11.7 g, 59%, m.p. 174–177°C) crystallized. (Found: C, 48.78; H, 3.74; N, 7.06. $C_8H_7NO_5$ requires C, 48.74; H, 3.58; B, 7.10.)

3-Nitro-4-hydroxymethylbenzoic acid 2,4,5-trichlorophenyl ester

3-Nitro-4-hydroxymethylbenzoic acid (1 g, 5.0 mmol) was dissolved in the minimum volume of ethyl acetate containing several drops of DMF, 2,4,5-trichlorophenol (1.05 g, 5.3 mmol) was added and the solution stirred on an ice bath. DCCI (1.09 g, 5.3 mmol) was then added dropwise in ethyl acetate (5 ml) and the reaction mixture covered to eliminate light. After 1 h stirring the reaction mixture was a solid mass and DMF was added until it became mobile. It was then stirred overnight allowing the ice to melt. Dicyclohexylurea was filtered, the filtrate evaporated and then recrystallized from 2-propanol, giving 1.04 g (55%). A second recrystallization gave 0.6 g (32%) m.p. 165–168°C. (Found: C, 44.95; H, 2.53; N, 3.78. $C_{14}H_8NO_5Cl_3$ requires C, 44.65; H, 2.14; N, 3.72).

3-4-(N-t-Butoxycarbonylglycyloxymethyl)phenylpropionic acid 2,4,5-trichlorophenyl ester

DCCI (3.0 gm, 14.5 mmol) dissolved in dichloromethane (15 ml) was added to a solution of *t*-butoxycarbonylglycine (5.25 g, 30 mmol) in dichloromethane (20 ml). The mixutre was stirred at room temperature for 15 min, filtered, and a solution of 3-(4-hydroxymethylphenyl)propionic acid trichlorophenyl ester (4.86 g, 13.5 mmol) in dichloromethane (40 ml), and then pyridine (1.23 ml), added to the filtrate. After 3 h at room temperature the reaction mixture was evaporated, the oily residue washed in ethyl acetate with 10% aqueous citric acid (2 ×), water (2 ×), ice-cold saturated aqueous sodium hydrogen carbonate (2 ×), water (2 ×), and brine, dried (Na_2SO_4, and concentrated to small volume. Precipitated dicyclohexylurea was filtered off and the filtrate evaporated to an oil which crystallized in trituration with light petroleum. The *t*-butoxycarbonylglycine derivative (5.6 g, 80%) had m.p. 106–107°C, raised to 106–108°C on recrystallization from ether–light petroleum. (Found: C, 53.45; H, 4.55; N, 1.6; Cl, 20.78. $C_{23}H_{24}Cl_3NO_6$ requires C, 53.45; H, 4.68; N, 2.71; Cl, 20.58%.)

3-(4-N-t-Butoxycarbonyl-L-alanyloxymethyl)phenylpropionic acid 2,4,5-trichlorophenyl ester

This alanine derivative (81%) was prepared in a similar manner to the foregoing and had m.p. 87–88°C (softening at 60°C), m.p. 87–88°C after recrystallization from propan-2-ol, $[\alpha]_D$ −23.75°C (c=1 in MeOH). (Found: C, 54.0; H, 4.95; N, 2.45. $C_{24}H_{26}Cl_3NO_6$ requires C, 54.30; H, 4.94; N, 2.64%.)

3-(4-N-t-Butoxycarbonyl-L-Phenylalanyloxymethyl)phenylpropionic acid 2,4,5-trichlorophenyl ester

The phenylalanine derivative (69%) had m.p. 73–75°, raised on recrystallization from propan-2-ol to 79–80°C, $[\alpha]_D$ −7.8° (c=1 in Dmf). (Found: C, 59.4; H, 4.9; N, 2.15; Cl, 17.5. $C_{30}H_{31}Cl_3NO_6$ requires C, 59.37; H, 4.98; N, 2.31; Cl, 17.52%.)

3-(4-N-t-Butoxycarbonyl-γ-benzyl-L-glutamyloxymethyl)-phenylpropionic acid 2,4,5-trichlorophenyl ester

The γ-benzyl glutamyl derivative (69%) had a m.p. 81–83°C raised to 84–85°C on recrystallization from ether–light petroleum. $[\alpha]_D$ −10.6° (c=1 in DMF). (Found: C, 58.7; H, 5.05; N, 2.05. $C_{33}H_{34}Cl_3NO_8$ requires C, 58.37; H, 5.05; N, 20.6.)

4-(α-Oxo-2'4'-dimethoxybenzyl)phenol (91)

To a stirred mixture of 1,3-dimethoxybenzene (221.1 g, 1.6 mol), 4-hydroxybenzoic acid (110.5 g, 0.80 mol) and zinc chloride (273 g, 2 mol) at 60°C in a flask fitted with a calcium chloride guard tube, phosphorus oxychloride (285 ml, 3.0 mol) was added dropwise over a period of 10 min. The reaction mixture was maintained at 60°C for 90 min and the resulting dark-red liquid poured onto 2.5 kg of ice contained in a 10 litre vessel and mixed vigorously. When the mixture had warmed to room temperature, sodium carbonate (610 g) was added with stirring to raise the pH of the aqueous phase to 3. Ethyl acetate (500 ml) was added and the mixture transferred to a 10 litre separating funnel together with a further 1000 ml of ethyl acetate. The aqueous phase was separated, extracted with a further 500 ml of ethyl acetate and the combined extracts washed with brine (2 × 1000 ml). The organic phase was dried ($MgSO_4$) and evaporated *in vacuo* at 40°C. The resulting dark-red solid was shaken with 60–80°C light petroleum (250 ml), filtered and washed with 60–80°C petroleum (500 ml). The product was recrystallized from hot methanol (150 ml) and washed with 1:1 methanol–water (3 × 100 ml) to yield 153 g (74%) of the phenol as a peach-coloured solid, m.p. 140–144°C. (Found: C, 70.05, H, 5.54; $C_{15}H_{14}O_4$ requires C, 69.76; H, 5.46%.)

4-(α-oxo-2'4'-dimethoxybenzyl)phenoxyacetic acid (91)

A stirred mixture of the foregoing phenol (153 g, 0.593 mol), sodium chloroacetate (630 g, 5.42 mol), potassium iodide (5 g) and water (1.1 litre) at 85°C was kept at pH 11–14 by the addition of 50% w/v aqueous sodium hydroxide until the reaction was complete [tlc $CHCl_3$–MeOH (5:2), R_f 0.85 (phenol) and 0.45 (phenoxyacetic acid)]. The reaction product was transferred while still hot to a 5 litre conical flask, cooled to 20°C, ethyl acetate (1 litre) added and the pH adjusted to 2 with concentrated hydrochloric acid. The copious precipitate was filtered, washed with water (4 × 500 ml) and dried *in vacuo* over P_2O_5 to yield 144 g (77%) of an off-white solid, m.p. 163–163.5°C.

A second crop was recovered by separating the organic phase of the filtrate, washing with brine (1000 ml), drying $MgSO_4$) and evaporating *in vacuo* at 40°C. The orange solid was shaken with ethyl acetate (100 ml), filtered and washed with diethyl ether (4 × 25 ml) to yield 30 g (16%), m.p. 162–163°C.

The two crops were dissolved together with hot methanol (800 ml) and water (360 ml) added. After standing overnight, the precipitate was collected, washed with methanol–water (1:1, 250 ml) and dried *in vacuo* to yield 155 g (83%) of the ketone, m.p. 165–166°C. (Found: C, 64.39; H, 5.11. $C_{17}H_{16}O_6$ requires C, 64.55; H, 5.10%.)

4-(α-Oximino-2',4'-dimethoxybenzyl)phenoxyacetic acid

A solution of the foregoing ketone (151 g, 0.48 mol) in water (500 ml) and methanol (100 ml) at 50°C was adjusted to pH 7 with 20% w/v aqueous sodium hydroxide. A slurry of hydroxylamine hydrochloride (403 g, 5.8 mol) in water (600 mol) was added, and the mixture heated at 80°C maintained at pH 5 until reaction was complete (hplc), typically 5 h. The solution was cooled to 15°C and the pH adjusted to 2 with concentrated hydrochloric acid. The precipitated pale-pink solid (128 g, 81%) was filtered, washed with water (2 × 250 ml) dried *in vacuo* over P_2O_5, and used in the following step without purification.

4-(α-Fmoc-amino-2',4'-dimethoxybenzyl)phenoxyacetic acid **(92)** *(91)*

A mixture of the foregoing oxime (2.5 g, 7.55 mmol), glacial acetic acid (35 ml), and zinc dust (7 g) was stirred overnight at room temperature and then at 60°C for 60 min when reaction was complete (hplc). The residual zinc was removed by filtration, washed with acetic acid (3 × 5 ml), and the filtrate and washings evaporated to yield 3.0 g of white solid (theory 2.4 g). This was dissolved in water (50 ml) and acetone (50 ml), and the pH adjusted to 10.5 with M aqueous sodium carbonate. This pH was maintained while a solution of Fmoc-oxysuccinimide (10% w/v in acetone) was added in portions until all the starting material had been consumed (hplc). The reaction mixture was cooled to 0°C, ethyl acetate (75 ml) added and the pH for the aqueous layer adjusted to 1.5 with M $KHSO_4$. The aqueous layer was separated, extracted further with ethyl acetate (50 ml), and the combined extracts washed with brine (100 ml), dried ($MgSO_4$), and evaporated *in vacuo* at 40°C. The residual oil solidified and was recrystallized from ethyl acetate–petroleum ether (b.p. 60–80°C) to yield 2.15 g (52%) of the Fmoc derivative, m.p. 180–181°C. (Found: C, 71.21; H, 5.66; N, 2.60; $C_{32}H_{29}NO_7$ requires C, 71.23; H, 5.42; N, 2.60%.)

Coupling of the foregoing linkage agents to polydimethylacrylamide gel and physically supported resins and attachment procedures for the first amino acid derivative are described in Sections 10.1 and 10.2.

Esters of the benzyl alcohol derivatives may undergo acidolysis with generation of intermediate benzyl cations. These latter are reactive species and, unless rapidly quenched, may undergo further reaction with electron-rich amino-acid side chains. Tyrosine, tryptophan, and methionine residues are particularly susceptible. The choice of scavenger reagents which minimize this further reaction is discussed in Chapter 11.

CHAPTER 7

Activation procedures

Efficient and unambiguous peptide bond formation requires chemical activation of either the amino or carboxy component, almost invariably the latter. The activating group or reaction has to be chosen with care in order to achieve the very high coupling efficiency required, and to avoid side reactions. The latter may arise in a number of ways. Inappropriately chosen acylating species may be ambiguous in their reactivity, providing more than one site for reaction. Mixed anhydrides (such as **93**, arrows) are obvious examples. Some acylating agents are over-reactive, attacking supposedly protected functions in addition to the terminal amino group, or undergoing decomposition reactions themselves. In *in-situ* activation, the activating reagent may react with the amino as well as carboxy component. Some acylating agents may just be impure, the impurities also reacting with the resin-bound peptide. Partially racemic activated derivatives are serious examples of this last type.

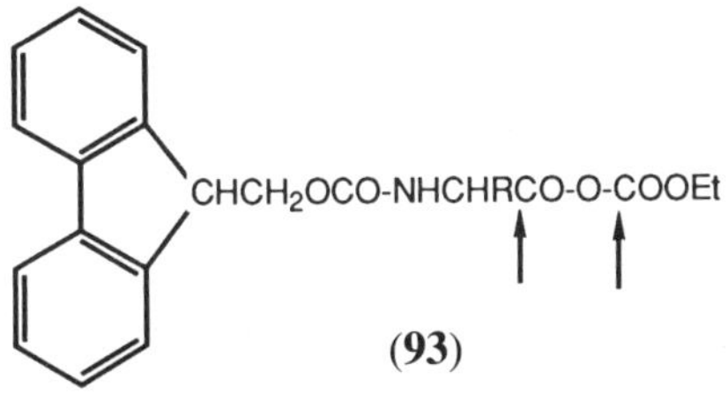

$CHCH_2OCO\text{-}NHCHRCO\text{-}O\text{-}COOEt$

(**93**)

The classical Merrifield solid phase procedure employed *in-situ* activation by dicyclohexylcarbodiimide (Section 2.7). This was a particularly appropriate choice for the apolar polystyrene environment. Reaction of acylamino acids with carbodiimides is fast in media such as dichloromethane (DCM) which are, at the same time, good swelling agents for polystyrene gel. In polar organic solvents such as dimethylformamide (DMF), the activation reaction is apparently much slower. In the early development of the Boc- (*40,41*) and Fmoc-polyamide (*37*) techniques, external activation of the acylamino acid was preferred, i.e. the protected amino acid and carbodiimide were mixed in the absence of the resin-bound amino component. This permitted rapid activation in a non-polar medium, and had the additional advantage that contact of the amino component with reactive carbodiimide or with the co-product urea was avoided. External activation is now also commonly employed in Boc-polystyrene solid phase synthesis.

7.1 Symmetric anhydrides of Fmoc-amino acids

Fmoc-amino acids react with 0.5 eq of dicyclohexylcarbodiimide in DCM solution to form the symmetrical anhydride (**94**) (Section 1.2.3). The two reactive carbonyl groups

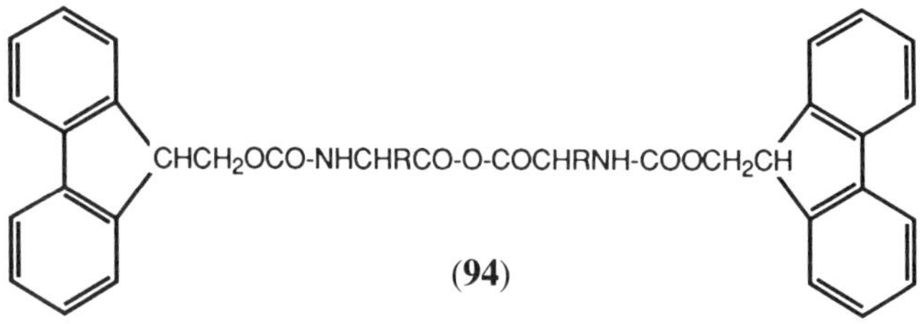

$CHCH_2OCO\text{-}NHCHRCO\text{-}O\text{-}COCHRNH\text{-}COOCH_2CH$

(94)

in symmetrical anhydrides are identical, the same acylated product being obtained through attack at either. A slight (up to 5%) deficiency of carbodiimide in the activating reaction ensures that little if any unreacted diimide remains which might later react with the amino resin.

Preparation of Fmoc-amino acid symmetrical anhydrides (49).
The Fmoc-amino acid (1 mmol) is dissolved in the minimum amount of freshly distilled DCM (less than 5 ml; a few drops of DMF may be added if necessary to ensure complete solution) in a 50 ml round-bottomed flask containing a small magnetic stirrer bead. A solution of dicyclohexylcarbodiimide (98 mg, 0.475 mmol) in DCM (1 ml) is added. Precipitation of dicyclohexylurea usually begins almost immediately. The mixture is stirred at room temperature for 10 min, filtered through a small sintered glass funnel, the solid washed with a little DCM, and the combined filtrate evaporated under reduced pressure (rotary evaporator). The frequently crystalline anhydride is dissolved in DMF (2 ml) and used immediately.

For some Fmoc-amino acids (for example norleucine, glycine, alanine, S-acetamido-methyl-cysteine, N_ϵ-trifluoroacetyl-lysine) the anhydride itself may precipitate from the DCM solution during preparation. Care should be taken if the precipitate appears unusually voluminous or unlike dicyclohexylurea. In cases of doubt, the precipitate may be washed quickly with ether, air-dried, and weighed. When precipitation does occur, the suspension is evaporated directly in the reaction flask without prior filtration, the residue swirled with the volume of DMF required in the acylation reaction, and the mixture filtered directly into the solid phase reaction vessel or sample container.

Heimer *et al.* (*96*) utilized water-soluble carbodiimide for the preparation of a number of simple Fmoc-amino acid anhydrides, the urea and any residual diimide being removed by aqueous washing. They report that the products purified by recrystallization were stable to storage for up to two years. Our preferred practice has always been to prepare anhydrides immediately before use. Physical data for purified anhydrides (*96*) are given in *Table 3*.

7.2 **Activated esters of Fmoc-amino acids**

Fmoc-amino acid anhydrides are excellent reagents for solid phase synthesis, but the need for preparation immediately before use makes them inconvenient. Instrumentation for automatic preparation of symmetrical anhydrides is necessarily complicated.

Table 3. Isolated symmetrical anhydrides of Fmoc-amino acids.

Anhydride	*Yield*	*m.p.* (°C)	$[\alpha]_D$ (°)	Solvent[a]
$(Fmoc\text{-}Ala)_2O$	84	125–126	−13.6	EtOAc
$(Fmoc\text{-}D\text{-}Ala)_2O$	70	125–126	+12.1	EtOAc
$(Fmoc\text{-}Gly)_2O$	50	165–166		
$(Fmoc\text{-}Phe)_2O$	70	152–153		
$[Fmoc\text{-}Tyr(Bu^t)]_2O$	93	94–96	−3.9	EtOAc
$(Fmoc\text{-}Val)_2O$	86	173–174	+2.8	CHCl3
$(Fmoc\text{-}D\text{-}Val)_2O$	86	173–174	−2.8	CHCl3

[a]Concentration is 1 in all cases.

$CHCH_2OCO\text{-}NHCHRCO\text{-}O\text{-}C_6F_5$

(**95**)

Symmetrical anhydrides also make inefficient use of the sometimes costly protected amino acids. Activated esters are frequently stable crystalline solids which may be prepared or purchased in bulk, stored at low temperature for extended periods, and dispensed as required. On the other hand, the *p*-nitrophenyl and trichlorophenyl esters most commonly used in classical solution methods react only sluggishly in solid phase synthesis, especially with sterically hindered amino acids which often require overnight reaction. Of the range of activated esters surveyed, pentafluorophenyl esters (**95**) (*8*) appeared to be the most reactive of the coventional type, and proved to be excellent reagents in Fmoc-polyamide synthesis. The derivatives (**96**) of 2,3-dihydro-3-hydroxy-4-oxo-benzotriazine have more recently also proved especially suitable (*39*).

7.2.1 *Pentafluorophenyl esters of Fmoc-amino acids (8,92,93)*

Pentafluorophenyl (Pfp) esters are efficient acylating agents and their chemical structures provide little opportunity for side reactions. They react somewhat more slowly than symmetric anhydrides, though this is increased significantly in the presence of hydroxybenzotriazole catalyst (*39*). Preparation using dicyclohexylcarbodiimide is usually straightforward, and of the common amino acids, only the very soluble derivatives of Fmoc-O-*t*-butyl serine and Fmoc-O-*t* butyl threonine fail to crystallize. The analogous esters of 3-hydroxy-4-oxodihydrobenzotriazine (Dhbt esters, see p. 78) provide suitable alternatives in these cases. Both Pfp and Dhbt esters of N_α-Fmoc-N_G-methoxytrimethylbenzene sulphonylarginine have been prepared. The Dhbt ester is more stable to lactam formation in DMF solution (*95*) but the pentafluorophenyl derivative is more easily prepared. The presence of small amounts of inert lactam does not interfere with peptide synthesis, and good results have been obtained with preparations of both esters.

Fmoc-L-leucine pentafluorophenyl ester (93).

Fmoc-L-leucine (10.6 g, 30 mmol) was dissolved in dioxan (40 ml) and a solution of pentafluorophenol (6.07 g, 33 mmol) in dioxan (10 ml) added. The solution was stirred and cooled in an ice-bath and dicyclohexylcarbodiimide (6.81 g, 33 mmol) in dioxan (15 ml) added. The mixture became very viscous and was diluted with further dioxan (55 ml). It was stirred for 60 min in the ice-bath and a further 3 h at room temperature. Thin-layer chromatography ($CHCl_3$−MeOH−AcOH, 85:10:5) indicated little Fmoc-leucine remaining at this time, and after a total of 4.5 h the reaction mixture was filtered and evaporated *in vacuo*. The pentafluorophenol ester crystallized on addition of *n*-hexane and was collected after standing overnight, yield 13.5 g (87%), m.p. 112−113°C, $[\alpha]_D$ −24.2°C (c = 1 in chloroform). Tlc revealed the presence of trace amounts of Fmoc-leucine and dicyclohexylurea as the only contaminants.

N_α-Fmoc-N_G-4-methoxy-2,3,6-trimethylbenzene sulphonyl-L-arginine pentafluorophenyl ester (77).

A solution of pentafluorophenol (127 g, 0.69 mol) in ethyl acetate (200 ml) was added to N_α-Fmoc-N_G-4-methoxy-2,3,6-trimethylbenzene sulphonyl-L-arginine (75 g, 0.12 mol) and rinsed in with further ethyl acetate (25 ml). The mixture was heated on a water-bath until complete solution was obtained, allowed to cool to room temperature and then to −10°C in an acetone−carbon dioxide bath. A precooled (−10°C) solution of dicyclohexylcarbodiimide (50.7 g, 0.25 mol) in ethyl acetate (75 ml) was added with vigorous stirring, the cooling bath replaced with ice-water and the mixture allowed to stand for 2−2.5 h until reaction was complete (tlc). Glacial acetic acid (7.2 ml) was added and after a further 10 min stirring precipitated dicyclohexylurea removed by filtration into a precooled flask. Diethyl ether (3 litres) and petroleum ether (5 litres) were added to the vigorously stirred filtrate and the precipitated product [82.7 g (89%), m.p. 119−121°C, $[\alpha]_D$ −6.4° (c = 1 in chloroform)] collected immediately and dried *in vacuo*. Hplc examination usually shows the presence of contaminating lactam (6−9%).

Fmoc-amino acid pentafluorophenyl esters are available from a number of commercial suppliers (see Appendix). Physical data are collected in *Table 4*.

7.2.2 *Fmoc-amino acid 3,4-dihydro-4-oxobenzotriazin-3-yl esters (Dhbt esters)*

These esters (**96**) (*9,97−99*) are efficient acylating agents reacting at rates similar to symmetric anhydrides without added catalyst (*39*). They possess the special property that the hydroxy component (**97**) liberated during the reaction forms a brightly coloured complex with resin-bound amino groups. They are thus self-indicating for completion of acylation (*9,39*). This aspect of their use is discussed in Chapter 9.

A comparison has been made of the use of Dhbt and Pfp esters in a polyamide synthesis of the dynorphin 1−8 sequence (H-Tyr-Gly-Gly-Phe-Leu-Arg-Arg-Ile-OH) starting from a common Fmoc-isoleucyl-resin preparation (*95*). The two assemblies gave similar yields

Table 4. Pentafluorophenyl esters of Fmoc-amino acids.

Compound	*Yield*	*m.p. (°C)*	$[\alpha]_D$ (°)	Solvent[a]
Fmoc-Ala-OPfp	93	171–173	−22.7	$CHCl_3$
Fmoc-Asn-OPfp	96	164–165	−13.1	Dioxan
Fmoc-Arg(Mtr)-OPfp	89	119–121[b]	−6.4[b]	$CHCl_3$
Fmoc-Asp(OBu^t-OPfp	89	98–100	−2.5	$CHCl_3$
Fmoc-Asp(OBzl)-OPfp	75	128–131	−14.0	EtOAc
Fmoc-Cys(Acm)-OPfp	78	157–158	−32.6	$CHCl_3$
Fmoc-Cys(Bzl)-OPfp	89	132–134	−31.0	$CHCl_3$
Fmoc-Gln-OPfp	97	151–153	−19.8	Dioxan
Fmoc-Glu(OBu^t)-OPfp	82	121–123	−25.2	$CHCl_3$
Fmoc-Gly-OPfp	99	160–161		
Fmoc-Ile-OPfp	78	96– 98	−13.4	$CHCl_3$
Fmoc-Leu-OPfp	96	114–116	−25.7	$CHCl_3$
Fmoc-Lys(Boc)-OPfp	85	89– 93	−14.2	$CHCl_3$
Fmoc-Lys(Z)-OPfp	93	106–108	−10.5	$CHCl_3$
Fmoc-Met-OPfp	93	102–104	−31.0	$CHCl_3$
Fmoc-Phe-OPfp	93	154–157	−20.3	$CHCl_3$
Fmoc-Pro-OPfp	82	127–129	−59.2	$CHCl_3$
Fmoc-Ser-OPfp	84	125–130	−21.3	$CHCl_3$
Fmoc-Thr-OPfp	77	126–128	−33.0	$CHCl_3$
Fmoc-Trp-OPfp	85	185–186	−42.1	$CHCl_3$
Fmoc-Tyr(Bu^t)-OPfp	61	76– 78	−12.7	$CHCl_3$
Fmoc-Val-OPfp	85	122–123	−21.9	$CHCl_3$

[a]Concentration 1; [b]impure (see text). Literature references are collected in ref. *57*.

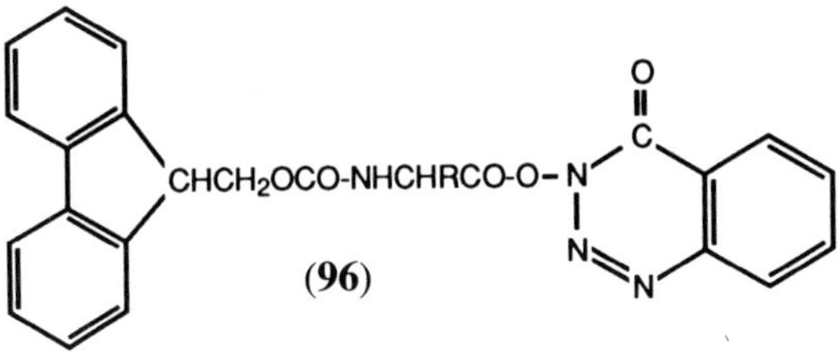

CHCH$_2$OCO-NHCHRCO-O-N

(96)

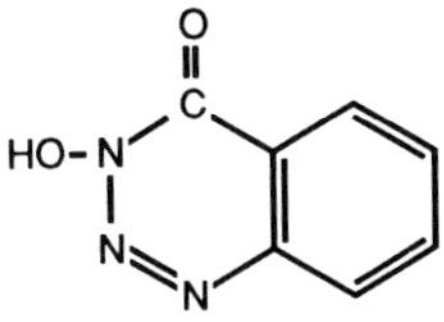

HO-N

(97)

CO-O

N_3

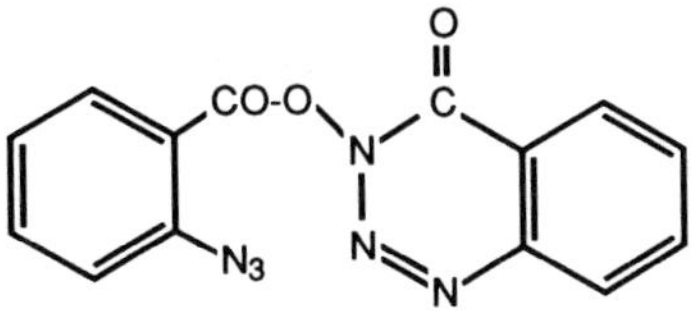

(98)

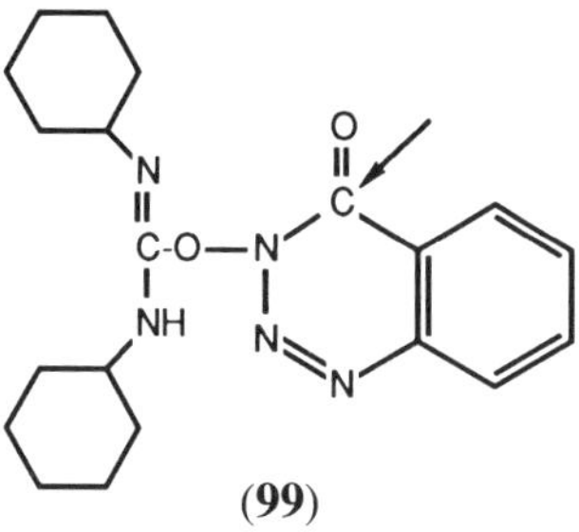

(**99**)

of the octapeptide and analytical hplc of of the crude product revealed the same minor impurity peaks (*95*).

Special care has to be exercised in the preparation and purification of Dhbt esters, since under inappropriate reaction conditions, small quantities of the by-product (**98**) may be formed (*9,39*). This is itself an activated ester derivative and may act as a chain-terminating agent in solid phase peptide synthesis. Its absence is easily established by hplc examination of the Fmoc-amino acid ester. Commercial samples should be checked similarly.

Formation of the azidobenzoate (**98**) clearly involves activation of the triazine (**97**) by reaction with carbodiimide yielding (**99**), which is in turn attacked at the ring carbonyl by a second molecule of (**97**). Thus formation of contaminating azidobenzoate during preparation of Fmoc-amino acid Dhbt esters is a consequence of initial competition between the carboxylic acid and triazine for carbodiimide (9). In agreement, we found (*39*) that when the preparative reaction was carried out by prior mixing of Fmoc-amino acid and carbodiimide at low temperature, and the triazine added subsequently, the formation of (**98**) was effectively abolished. Dhbt esters of Fmoc-amino acids are not yet widely commercially available, and their preparation is therefore illustrated below with both general and specific examples. In cases where functional amino-acid side chains are present which may interact with the initial carbodiimide adduct, prior reaction of the Fmoc-amino acid with carbodiimide is not recommended, and reactions are best carried out at very low temperatures.

General procedure for the preparation of Dhbt esters (39).

Example A. Fmoc-Gly-ODhbt

Fmoc-Gly-OH (1.78 g, 6 mmol) was dissolved in THF (20 ml) and the solution cooled to −15°C. Dicyclohexylcarbodiimide (DCCI) (1.24 g, 6 mmol) was added and the mixture was stirred at −15°C for 5 min. Solid HO-Dhbt (0.978 g, 6 mmol) was added and the mixture stirred at −10°C for 30 min and then at 0°C for 4 h. After standing overnight at 0°C, precipitated dicyclohexylurea was removed by filtration and the filtrate concentrated *in vacuo*. The resulting syrup was crystallized from diethyl ether. After drying over phosphorus pentoxide, the glycine ester (2.48 g, 93%) had m.p. 156−159°C.

Example B. Fmoc-Lys(Boc)-ODhbt

Fmoc-Lys(Boc)-OH (11.68 g, 25 mmol) was dissolved in dry THF (60 ml) and cooled to −15°C. DCCI (5.15 g, 25 mmol) dissolved in THF (6 ml) was added and after 5 min at −15°C, solid HO-Dhbt (4.0 g, 25 mmol) rinsed in with THF (5 ml). The mixture was stirred at −15°C for 20 min and then at 4°C (cold-room) for 3.5 h. The mixture was filtered and the solvent removed at reduced pressure. The residue was dissolved in ether (100 ml) and hexane (100 ml) added and the solution stored at 4°C overnight. The white solid was collected by filtration, washed with 40/60° petroleum ether and dried (silica) *in vacuo* to give the ester (14.5 g, 95%, m.p. 157−159°C).

Fmoc-Asn-ODhbt

Fmoc-Asn-OH (3.9 g, 11 mmol) was dissolved in DMF (43 ml) with gentle warming and the solution then cooled to −50°C. HO-Dhbt (1.97 g, 12 mmol), dissolved in DMF (7 ml) was added followed by solid DCCI (2.25 g, 10.9 mmol) and the mixture allowed to warm to 0°C over a period of 1 h. The mixture was stirred at 0°C for 1 h and left in the refrigerator overnight. The precipitate was removed by filtration and the DMF evaporated at 0.05 mm Hg and 15°C until the product started to crystallize. Dry diethyl ether (125 ml) was added and stirring was continued for 1 h at 0°C. The product was collected, washed with diethyl ether and hexane and dried *in vacuo* to give the crude ester (5.76 g). This material (5.00 g) was dissolved in dry DMF (25 ml) and filtered to remove residual dicyclohexylurea. Dry diethyl ether (300 ml) was added and the mixture was left overnight in the refrigerator to crystallize. The product was filtered off, washed with diethyl ether and dried to afford the triazinyl ester (4.07 g, 74%), m.p. 129−132°C. The analogous glutamine derivative was prepared in a similar way.

Fmoc-Arg(Mtr)-ODhbt

Fmoc-Arg(Mtr)-OH (4.87 g, 8 mmol) was dissolved in dry THF (10 ml) and the solution cooled to −30°C. DCCI (1.64 g, 8 mmol) dissolved in THF (5 ml) was added and the mixture stirred for 5 min at −30°C. Solid HO-Dhbt (1.30 g, 8 mmol) was added and washed in with THF (5 ml). The yellow suspension was stirred vigorously at −25°C for 1 h and then at −10°C to −5°C (ice−salt bath) for 4 h. The reaction mixture was filtered rapidly and evaporated at 25−30°C under high vacuum. Diethyl ether (150 ml) was added and the mixture kept overnight at −15°C. The yellowish solid was collected, washed with diethyl ether and dried (silica) to give the ester (6 g, 99.5%, m.p. 116−121°C) shown by hplc to be completely free of azide and lactam contaminants. An earlier preparation was carried out similarly except that the reaction temperature was higher (−15°C for 2.5 h and then overnight at 0°C). The crude product was dissolved in dichloromethane (5 ml) and added dropwise to petroleum ether with stirring. The mixture was stirred at 0°C for 2 h and the product filtered and dried *in vacuo* to afford Fmoc-Arg(Mtr)-O-Dhbt (1.90 g, 84%); m.p. 125−130°C; $[\alpha]_D$ 25−58.8° (c = 1 in DMF). Other preparations carried out at this temperature usually contained variable amounts of lactam by-product (hplc).

Fmoc-Cys(Acm)-ODhbt

The general procedure was followed except that Fmoc-Cys(Acm)-OH was dissolved in DMF (10 ml) prior to addition of THF. Crystallization from DMF and diethyl ether affording the triazinyl ester in 86% yield; m.p. 154–156°C; $[\alpha]_D$ −103.0°C (c = 1 in DMF).

Fmoc-His(Boc)-ODhbt

Fmoc-His(Boc)-OH (1.43 g, 3.0 mmol) was dissolved in THF (3 ml), cooled to −15°C and a solution of DCCI (618 mg, 3.00 mmol) in THF (2 ml) added with stirring. After 4 min solid HO-Dhbt (489 mg, 300 ml) was added and stirring continued for 3.5 h at −15°C and then at 0°C for 4 h. The mixture was filtered and the filtrate concentrated *in vacuo*. The resulting oil was dissolved in a mixture of THF and diethyl ether (1:4, 20 ml), filtered and the filtrate added dropwise to stirred petroleum ether (80–100°C, 100 ml). After 3 h at 0°C the solid product was collected, dried *in vacuo* over phosphorus pentoxide. Fmoc-His(Boc)-O-Dhbt (1.70 g, 91% yield), had m.p. 95–105°C; $[\alpha]_D$ −35.8°C (c = 1 in DMF).

A range of Fmoc-amino acid Dhbt esters is now listed in the catalogue of Novabiochem (see Appendix).

The structures (**96**) of the triazinyl esters are considerably more complex than, for example, those of the earlier pentafluorophenyl esters (**95**). Some caution is therefore appropriate in assuming that they will always react cleanly in peptide bond-forming reactions. The ring carbonyl in (**96**) provides a potential second site for nucleophilic attack by amines and has already been implicated in the conversion of (**99**) to (**98**). This possibility was studied for the worst-case example of Fmoc-isoleucine Dhbt ester reacting with glycyl resin (*39*). Attack at the ring carbonyl was estimated to be less than 0.1%. It is probable that side reactions of this type are responsible for poor product purity from other activated derivatives, notably from esters (**100**) of N-hydroxysuccinimide which were previously investigated.

Physical constants for a range of Dhbt esters of Fmoc-amino acids are collected in *Table 5*.

7.2.3 *Esters of Fmoc-amino acids with 2,3-dihydro-2,5-diphenyl-4-hydroxy-3-oxo-thiophen-1,1-dioxide (TDO esters)*

These esters (**101**) may be readily prepared by reaction between Fmoc-amino acids and the cyclic carbonate (**102**) in the presence of catalytic amounts of pyridine (*100*).

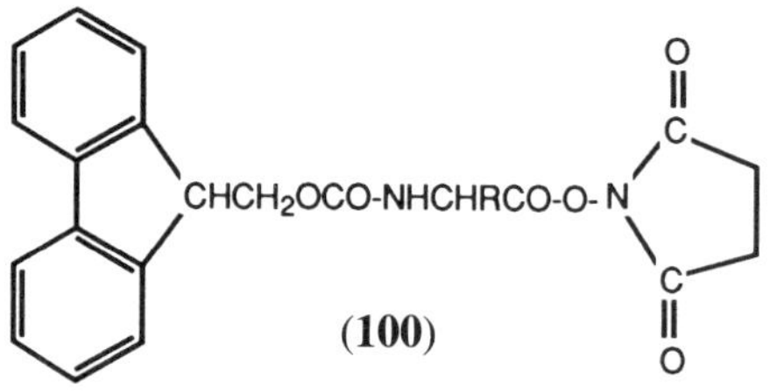

$CHCH_2OCO$-NHCHRCO-O-N

(**100**)

Table 5. Physical properties of Fmoc-amino acid Dhbt esters (100).

Compound	*Crystalln. solvent*[a]	*Yield (%)*	*m.p. (°C)*	$[\alpha]_D$[b] (°)
Fmoc-Ala-ODhbt	Dioxan–ether	91	156–158	–137
Fmoc-Arg(Mtr)-ODhbt	DCM–petrol	84	125–130	–58.8
Fmoc-Asn-ODhbt	DMF–ether	86	129–132	–57.4
Fmoc-Asp(OBu^t)-ODhbt	Ether–hexane	87	87–91	–77.7
Fmoc-Cys(Acm)-ODhbt	DMF–ether	86	154–156	–103.0
Fmoc-Gln-ODhbt	DMF–ether	75	110–120	–85.3
Fmoc-Glu(OBu^t)-ODhbt	Ether–hexane	89	103–107	–99.7
Fmoc-Gly-ODhbt	Ether	85	156–159	
Fmoc-His(Boc)-ODhbt	Ether–petrol	91	95–105	–35.8
Fmoc-Ile-ODhbt	Dioxan–ether	83	122–125	–111.0
Fmoc-Leu-ODhbt	Ether–hexane	80	83–84	–116.0
Fmoc-Lys(Boc)-ODhbt	Ether	89	158–162	–85.2
Fmoc-Met-ODhbt	Ether	95	136–138	–107.0
Fmoc-Phe-ODhbt	DCM–hexane	94	194–199	–110.9
Fmoc-Pro-ODhbt	Ether	94	167–169	–155.5
Fmoc-Ser(Bu^t)-ODhbt	Ether–hexane	96	65–75	–29.3
Fmoc-Thr(Bu^t)-ODhbt	Ether–hexane	96	65–73	–32.2
Fmoc-Trp-ODhbt	THF–ether	88	144–146	–79.6
Fmoc-Tyr(Bu^t)-ODhbt	Ether–hexane	97	91–96	–85.3
Fmoc-Val-ODhbt	Ether	80	116–118	–125.5

[a]Ether is diethyl ether; hexane is *n*-hexane; petrol is light petroleum, b.p. 60–80°C; DCM is dichloromethane. [b]In DMF.

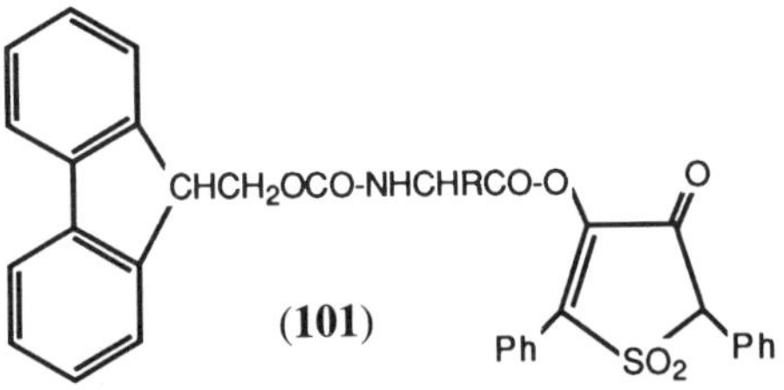

CHCH$_2$OCO-NHCHRCO-O

(101)

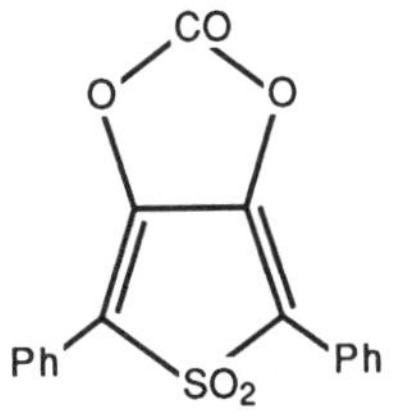

(102)

In the presence of base the ring ketone in (**101**) enolizes, providing a negatively charged oxygen atom well placed to act as a base catalyst in acyl transfer to amino (*100*) and hydroxyl (*101*) groups. Such internally catalysed reactions usually proceed best in relatively non-polar media, and acylation of amines is correspondingly faster in dichloromethane than in dimethylformamide. TDO esters may therefore have particular application for peptide bond formation in polystyrene or polyamide-based syntheses carried out in apolar media (*100*). Their present significance in Fmoc-polyamide synthesis stems from the observation (*101*) that transesterification to resin-bound hydroxyl groups is catalysed by simple tertiary bases under mild conditions. No perceptible cleavage of the Fmoc group occurs. Powerful catalysts such as 4-dimethylaminopyridine are not required and in the cases studied acylation proceeded without detectable racemization. This application is discussed further in Section 10.2.

General procedures for the preparation of TDO esters have been given by Steglich and his colleagues (*100*). The procedure is illustrated here with a single example from work in our own laboratory (*101*). It should be noted that the ester (**101**) contains an additional asymmetric centre, and that melting points, optical rotation, and some other physical characteristics may vary depending upon the diastereoisomer content (*100*). In our experience, the esters are best characterized by hplc.

γ-t-Butyl N_α-Fmoc-L-glutamate TDO ester

A mixture of γ-*t*-butyl Fmoc-glutamic acid (6.38 g, 15 mmol) and the cyclic carbonate (**102**) (5.38 g, 16.5 mmol) in pure dichloromethane (110 ml) was stirred in an ice-bath while pyridine (0.14 ml, 1.7 mmol) was added. A clear solution was obtained after about 20 min; after 1.5 h slight precipitation occurred and the mixture was kept in the refrigerator overnight. The mixture was then evaporated to about half volume and 50 ml of DCM–*n*-hexane (1:1) was added to the resulting slurry. After standing overnight in the refrigerator, the product (8.23 g, 77.5%) was collected. Hplc (Aquapore RP 300 column, solvent A: 0.1% trifluoroacetic acid, solvent B: 10% A, 90% acetonitrile, isocratic elution at 40% B for 1 min, sample injection then linear gradient of 40–80% B over 15 min and isocratic at 80% B for 4 min at 1.5 ml min^{-1}) showed only traces of free Fmoc γ-*t*-butyl glutamate (elution time 10.1 min) and hydroxysulphone (the hydrolysis product of **102**) in the crude TDO ester (elution time 16.6 min). The former was removed by a single recrystallization from DCM–*n*-hexane (yield 73% overall). Yields and melting points for Fmoc-amino acid TDO esters are collected in *Table 6* (*100*).

7.3 Other potential activation procedures for use in Fmoc-polyamide synthesis

The range of activation procedures which may be used in Fmoc-polyamide solid phase synthesis is not limited to the foregoing. Increasing usage of the technique elsewhere has led to the emergence of other reagents with clear potential. Foremost amongst these is probably the 'BOP' reagent, benzotriazolyloxy-trisdimethylaminophosphonium hexafluorophosphate (**103**), of Castro and colleagues (*125*), which is finding application in polystyrene and polyamide-based synthesis (*116,124*). The reagent reacts with N_α-protected amino acids in the presence of base to form hydroxybenzotriazolyl esters which may react with amines faster than do symmetrical anhydrides (*124*). In the continuous-flow Fmoc-polyamide synthesis of a 24-residue sequence, better results were obtained than with pentafluorophenyl esters (*116*). Although too much general reliance should not necessarily be placed on single comparisons, the BOP reagent is clearly

Table 6. Fmoc-amino acid TDO esters (*100*).

	Yield (*a*)	(*b*)	*Recryst. solvent*	*m.p. (°C)*	*Hplc time* Ester	Acid
Fmoc-Ala-OTDO	94	84	EA–P	177–181	14.7	6.6
Fmoc-Arg(Mtr)-OTDO	80			138–141	14.9	9
Fmoc-Asp(OBu^t)-OTDO	95	91	EA–P	178–179	16.2	9.6
Fmoc-Asn(Mbh)-OTDO	80	74	EA–P	174–176		
Fmoc-Cys(Acm)-OTDO	89			156–158	13.5	5.2
Fmoc-Cys(Bu^t)-OTDO	81			192–194	17.6	11.1
Fmoc-Cys(SBu^t)-OTDO	95	83	DCM–P	131–133	17.9	11.9
Fmoc-Cys(Trt)-OTDO	89			105–108	20.3	15.4
Fmoc-Gln(Mbh)-OTDO	88			165–167	15.6	10.0
Fmoc-Glu(OBu^t)-OTDO	93	78	DCM–P	166–168	16.5	10.2
Fmoc-Gly-OTDO	98			179–182	13.9	5.7
Fmoc-Ile-OTDO	68			203–207	16.1	9.2
Fmoc-Leu-OTDO	100	85	EA–P	183–186	16.7	9.7
Fmoc-Lys(Boc)-ODO	100	88	DCM–P	153–155	15.9	9.5
Fmoc-Met-OTDO	86			148–151	15.5	8.2
Fmoc-Nle-OTDO	96	92	EA–P	188–190	16.6	9.8
Fmoc-Orn(Boc)-OTDO	95	85	EA–P	173–175	16.2	9.9
Fmoc-Phe-OTDO	85			214–216	16.3	9.7
Fmoc-Pro-OTDO		81	DCM–P	153–154	14.7	6.8
Fmoc-Ser(Bu^t)-OTDO		92		184–186	16.2	9.5
Fmoc-Thr(Bu^t)-OTDO	90	77	EA–P	179–181	16.9	10.0
Fmoc-Trp-OTDO		77	EA–P	226–228	15.1	8.8
Fmoc-Tyr(Bu^t)-OTDO	95	90	EA–P	164–165	13.5[c]	8.7
Fmoc-Val-OTDO	93	83	EA–P	186–189	15.9	8.5

[a]Crude product; [b]after recrystallization from the solvent given (EA, ethyl acetate; DCM, dichloromethane; P, petroleum ether); [c]gradient 45–90% B over 15 min; otherwise see preceding text.

N-O-P(NMe$_2$)$_3$ PF_6^-

(**103**)

PF_6^- N–O–C^+(NMe$_2$)=NMe$_2$

(**104**)

a promising and relatively low-cost addition to the list of activating reagents suitable for solid phase synthesis.

Knorr and his colleagues (*117*) have recently recommended the related tetramethyluronium hexafluorophosphate derivative (*126,127*) (**104**) as an easily-prepared, low-cost reagent with high reactivity and without undesired side reactions. It has been used very successfully for the continuous-flow polyamide synthesis of a number of medium-length peptides (*117*).

CHAPTER 8

Instrumentation for Fmoc-polyamide solid phase synthesis

Solid phase peptide synthesis can be carried out completely without specialized equipment, or with dedicated, fully-automatic commercial synthesizers costing tens of thousands of pounds. This chapter surveys both laboratory-assembled and commercially available dedicated instrumentation which makes Fmoc-polyamide solid phase synthesis convenient and time-efficient. Emphasis is placed on continuous-flow technology which is presently unique to the Fmoc-polyamide method and which appears to have significant overall advantage. Sufficient detail is included in this chapter to enable construction of both manual and automatic synthesizers in laboratory workshops.

8.1 Manual instrumentation for use with beaded gel resin

Conventional solid phase reaction vessels, shakers and valving may be used for Fmoc-polyamide chemistry. Two systems have been used extensively with the soft, beaded gel resin. The first makes use of a simple adaptation of the original Merrifield-style reaction vessel (*53,102*) (*Figure 9*). The slightly conical shape above the lower sintered glass filter facilitates detachment of the swollen gel from the filter disc during filling, and the glass rod spanning the vessel at its mid-part encourages separation of the gel mass into its constituent particles. The upper filter (A) is present only to ensure that resin does not pass into the tubing during agitation or through overfilling. Any liquid which collects above the upper filter during agitation is returned to the cell during the emptying process. An alternative design (B) is of lower internal volume and has a direct capillary connection between the filter and outlet. Both permit agitation of the cell in a wrist-action shaker through more than 180°. The cell is thus totally internally wetted throughout. The dimensions shown are for a reaction cell capable of accommodating about 1 g of the highly swollen gel. Altex or other standard fittings of thick-walled, low-volume capillary glass permit connection of the cell to 1/16-in or 1/8-in o.d. polytetrafluoroethylene (ptfe) tubing.

The cell is conveniently attached to the two-valve system shown in *Figure 10*. The solvent-resistant valves are of a readily available rotary type (Anachem, see Appendix) connected by 0.125-in ptfe tubing. Valve A switches between FILL (solid line) and EMPTY((dotted line) configurations. In the FILL position, reagents or solvent selected by valve B enter the cell under controlled nitrogen pressure from a manifold. Only two reagent reservoirs are normally required to carry out Fmoc-polyamide chemistry. Valve B can also be used to select a nitrogen stream which purges the lines connecting the cell and may also be used to agitate the resin suspension. In the EMPTY configuration, the cell contents flow to waste, again under nitrogen pressure.

Vacuum may also be used to assist cell filling and drainage if preferred. For the reaction and wash periods when the cell is rotated in a wrist-action shaker, it is preferable

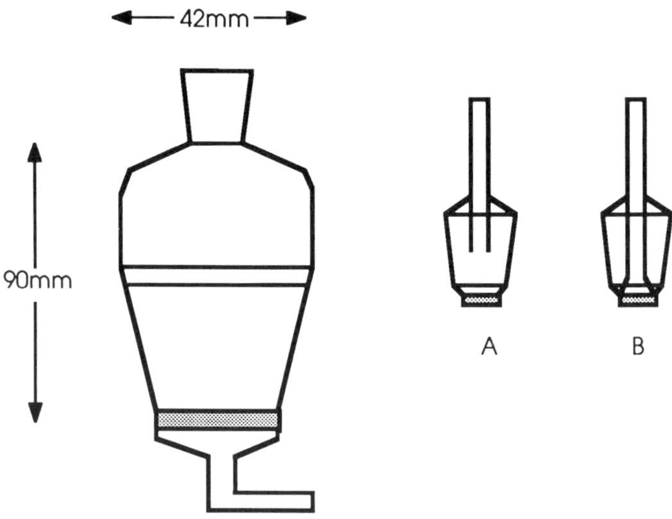

Figure 9. Glass reaction vessel for beaded gel resin.

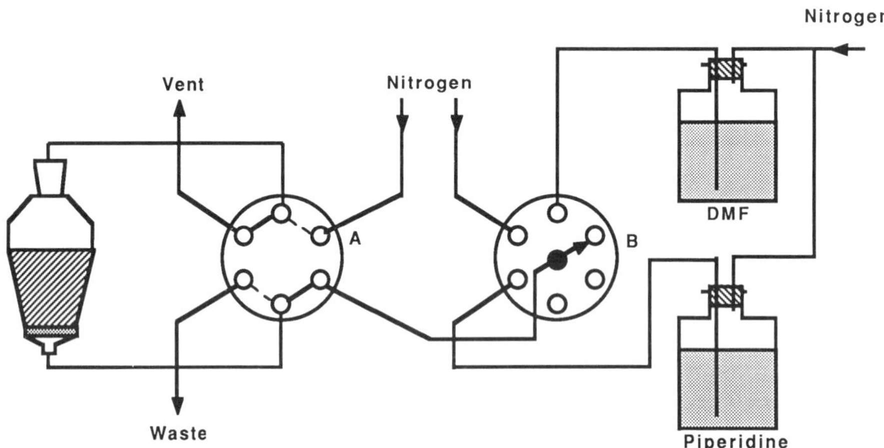

Figure 10. Simple manual equipment for using beaded gel resin.

to set valve A midway between the FILL and EMPTY positions. All the connections to the reaction vessel are then isolated.

The second system, which has been used extensively at Cambridge Research Biochemicals Ltd, employs a 'bubbler' reaction vessel (*103*) (*Figure 11*). The resin suspension is contained in a cylindrical reaction vessel and is agitated with nitrogen introduced through the three-way tap. Reagents are added manually from wash bottles, automatic pipettes, or measuring cylinders and drained from the resin into the lower reservoir under slight vacuum. Any resin particles which collect above the liquid level in the reaction vessel are washed down at each reagent addition. This is a particularly simple and low-cost system which has proved very effective in practice.

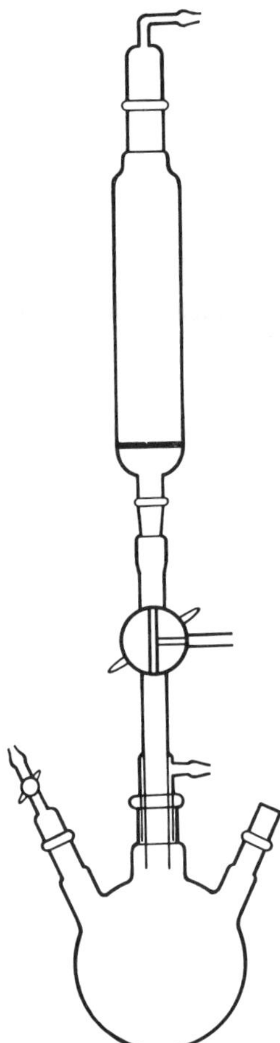

Figure 11. Bubbler system for manual synthesis.

8.2 Automatic equipment for use with beaded gel resins

It is probable that most commercially available solid phase peptide synthesizers of conventional design can be used successfully in the Fmoc-polyamide procedure. Our own experience has been limited to the Beckman Model 990 instrument. As designed, this uses a stirred ptfe or ptfe-lined glass reaction vessel with a large unwetted surface above the liquid level. Using the early Boc-polyamide technique (*41*) which, in common with the Merrifield procedure, used volatile acidic and basic reagents, a white crystalline deposit sometimes accumulated on this unwashed surface. The reaction cup was therefore replaced (*41*) by a conventional glass reaction vessel (*Figure 9*) which was totally wetted internally by rotation through an angle of about 180°. Some minor ancillary modifications to the synthesizer were also necessary to ensure complete and reliable filling of the new reaction vessel (*41*). It is not at all certain that these modifications are necessary for operation with the current Fmoc-polyamide technique. Probably the surface deposits initially observed consisted of the acetate or hydrochloride salt of the tertiary amine used in the neutralization step in the Boc deprotection procedure. Such deposits could not occur in the Fmoc technique, though the principle of avoiding unwashed surfaces where resin particles or droplets of liquid reagents may collect remains a sound one.

8.3 Manually operated equipment for continuous-flow synthesis

The continuous-flow system, which is of more recent introduction and is growing rapidly in popularity, is described in greater detail.

A typical manual system for continuous-flow synthesis is shown in *Figure 12* (*49*). Essentially, a reaction vessel in the form of a glass column equipped with sintered glass or ptfe filters at the top and bottom is required, together with a reciprocating pump* and provision for flowing solvent and reactants through the resin bed to waste, and for recirculation. As in the discontinuous manual system (Section 8.1), this can be accomplished with just two valves. Valve A switches between FLOW (solid line) and RECIRCULATE (dotted line) modes, and valve B selects reagents and solvents. Addition of activated Fmoc-amino acids may take place directly to the top of the column or, if valve B is a multiway rotary valve as shown, conveniently through a syringe barrel fitted with a glass or ptfe filter disc. Since under normal circumstances negligible pressure is generated in the system, thin flexible ptfe tubing may be used for connections within

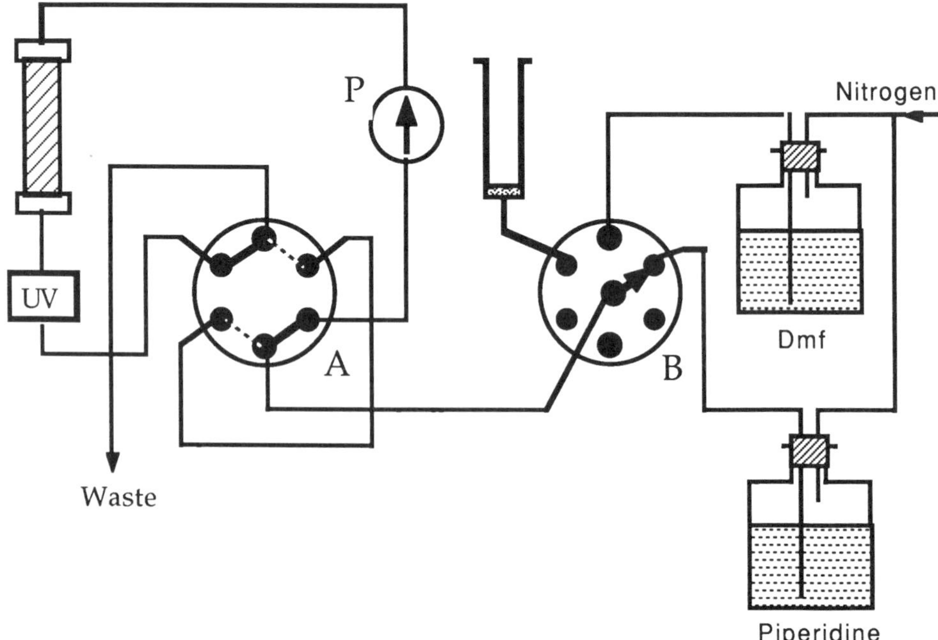

Figure 12. Simple manual system for continuous-flow synthesis.

*Others have suggested use of peristaltic-type pumps in this application, but we have preferred the more robust Milton – Roy-type metering pump. Most flexible plastic tubing wears and deforms rapidly when stressed in contact with DMF or piperidine, and constancy of flow rate is essential if advantage is to be taken of the monitoring potential of flow systems (Section 9.4.2).

the recirculation loop. This minimizes the total loop volume and hence the final dilution of the applied activated Fmoc-amino acid.

Other connections may be of larger-bore tubing without disadvantage. All glass reactor columns fitted with an upper Quickfit joint and the detachable filter top shown in *Figure 9b* were originally used, but commercial glass and ptfe solvent-resistant chromatographic columns are equally suitable. They are available from Omnifit (see Appendix) and other suppliers in a range of sizes and with adjustable endpieces. The upper and lower ptfe filters should be of coarse porosity (100 μm) to avoid unnecessary back pressure. The lower filter should be renewed at the start of each synthesis, and the upper one frequently. Usually there is no significant change in bed volume as the synthesis proceeds,* but the column should contain a small air space above the surface of the resin and liquid to help take up the pulsating action of the pump. If this air space diminishes (dissolves) with time, it is probably due to the generation of internal pressure through a blocked filter or other constriction in the system. Restricted flow on the inlet side of the pump may also encourage the entry of air bubbles during the suction part of the pump cycle.

The effluent liquid stream is passed through a silica ultraviolet absorption cell, located as in *Figure 12*. This permits continuous monitoring of reagent concentration and correct instrument function, and is discussed in the following chapter. A normal 1 mm thick cell appears optimal. Very narrow pathlength (0.1 mm) or low-volume micro-cells are not necessarily advantageous, and increase liquid pressure unnecessarily. The pump is an adjustable flow rate reciprocating type with stainless steel or saphire piston and check valves. The electrically controllable variable speed LCD/Milton–Roy pump (Appendix) now available is particularly convenient. Only ptfe and glass surfaces contact the solvent or reagent elsewhere. Care should be taken in the design of flow systems utilizing such pumps to minimize suction during the inlet cycle. Larger-bore tubing should be used to connect reagent bottles, and if necessary very slight nitrogen pressure applied. Excessive pressurization of the reagent bottles may override the metering action of the pump.

Equipment for manually operated continuous-flow solid phase synthesis

The original instrument (*49*) was assembled from Altex rotary valves types 243291 (three-way) and 243288 (Anachem, see Appendix) and a Dosapro Milton–Roy Minipump 'A' (Appendix). Later instruments used an LCD-Milton–Roy pump (Appendix). The flow rate was 3.3 ml min^{-1}. Connections utilized 1/16-in (within the recirculating loop) or 1/8-in o.d. ptfe tubing and Altex fittings (Anachem). The column was initially of all-glass construction, 15 mm i.d. with a sintered glass support and Altex or luer fitting at the lower end and a B14 Quickfit standard taper joint at the upper. A mating B14 cone was also fitted with a small sintered filter and Altex or luer connector. A column length of 44 mm between the upper and lower filters

*Remarkably this is not always the case when Pepsyn K is used for oligodeoxyribonucleotide synthesis when quite large changes in bed volume have been observed. It is possible that these effects may have been due in part to use of resin samples with substantial polydimethylacrylamide gel on the surface of the kieselguhr particles. The higher loading Pepsyn K resins now becoming commercially available have also been reported to swell significantly as peptide synthesis proceeds.

accommodates about 2.3 g of polydimethylacrylamide-Kieselguhr resin prepared as described in Section 4.2 (the commercial resin currently available is appreciably less dense and only about 1.5 g is accommodated in the above column reactor). Later, a commercial solvent resistant chromatographic column (Omnifit) with adjustable end pieces was used equally successfully. The sample chamber consisted of a 5 ml glass syringe barrel in which a coarse porosity sintered glass filter was fused or a porous ptfe filter retained with a circular stainless-steel wire clip at the bottom.

Simple laboratory-assembled equipment of this type has been in regular use and appears to be completely satisfactory. One similar instrument has been produced commercially. This, the Cambridge Research Biochemicals' PEPSYNthesiser (*Figure 13*), is essentially a cased version of the flow scheme shown in *Figure 12*, although the rotary valves may be of different type and with slight interconnection differences. Provision is made for mounting two reactor columns on the front panel for simultaneous synthesis of peptide analogues, and there is a manual injection port for sample addition.

LKB Biochrom (now Pharmacia LKB Biochrom) are marketing automatic and manual instruments. The latter, Model 4175 (*Figure 14*), is a more sophisticated manual instrument than that of *Figures 12* or *13* with nitrogen-driven slider valves controlled from a keypad which provides directly LOAD, RECYCLE, WASH and DEPROTECT configurations. The pump speed is electrically controlled and is displayed continuously.

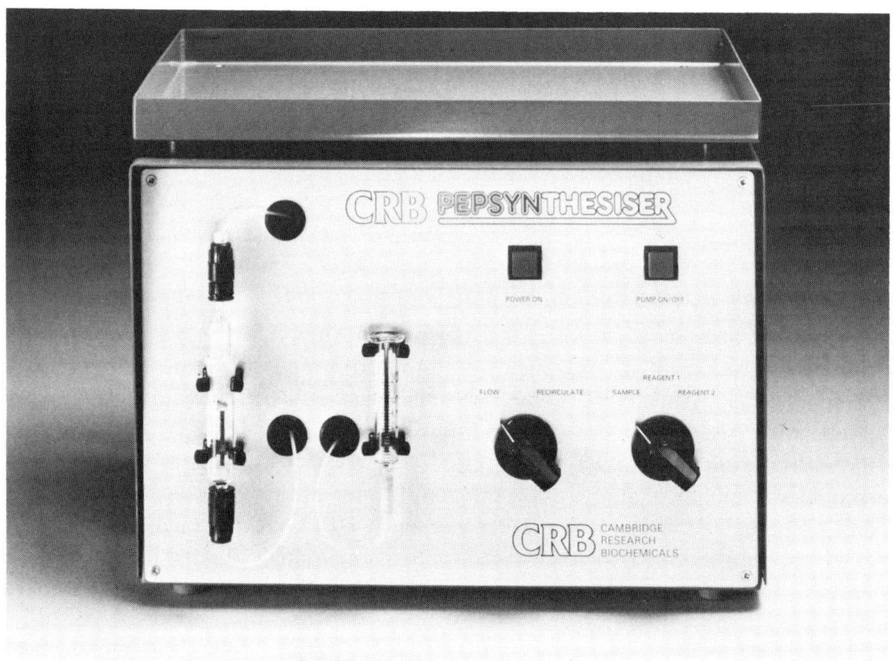

Figure 13. The CRB PEPSYNthesiser I. The first commercial instrument for manually operated continuous-flow solid phase synthesis.

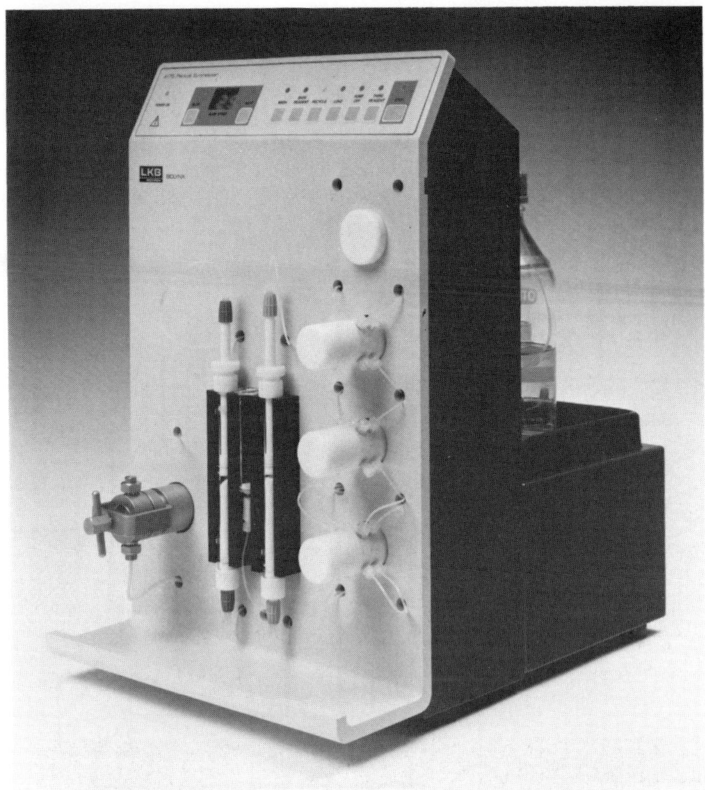

Figure 14. The Pharmacia-LKB Model 4175. A more sophisticated commercial instrument for manual synthesis.

Like the CRB instrument, the Model 4175 is equipped with two reactor columns and a sample injection port, and has provision for continuous spectrometric monitoring. The LKB instrument is potentially capable of computer control, bringing it into the semi-automatic category (see p. 97).

8.4 Semi-automatic and automatic equipment for continuous-flow synthesis

The chemical processes for deprotection (Fmoc group cleavage), washing and acylation (activated Fmoc-amino acid addition) are particularly easily mechanized and controlled using flow techniques. The flow scheme (*49*) of a simple computer-controlled semi-automatic instrument capable of unattended addition of a single amino acid residue is outlined in *Figure 15*. A laboratory instrument is illustrated in *Figure 16*. It is suitable for use with both manually prepared symmetrical anhydrides and with the subsequently introduced activated esters. Essentially the semi-automatic synthesizer consists of a pumped reagent selection, flow, recirculation and monitoring system as before, with additional facilities for reversing the direction of flow through the column (optional), activated sample introduction through a sample loop, and controlled nitrogen pressurization of the selected reagent bottle. A single pneumatically operated slide valve

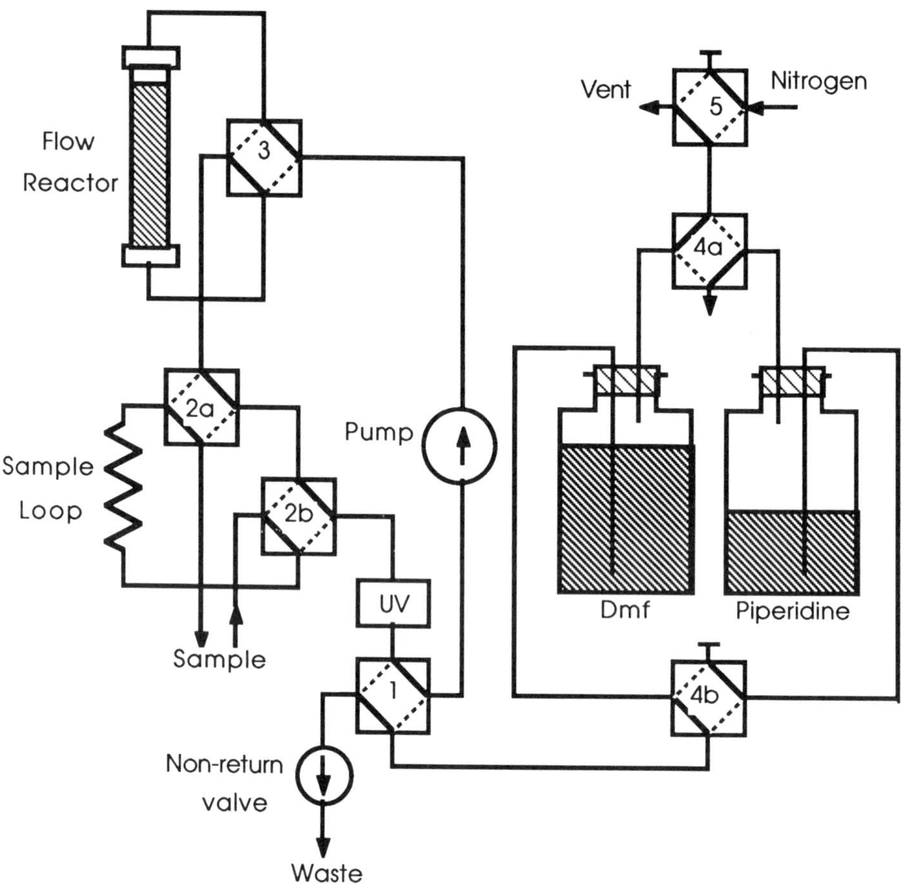

Figure 15. Semi-automatic (single residue addition) equipment for continuous-flow synthesis.

type is used throughout. Individual valves or ganged pairs (V2a,b; V4a,b) are operated through pneumatic actuators and return springs. In the implementation shown in *Figure 16*, each actuator has been modified by addition of an opto-electronic sensing mechanism (equivalent to a simple microswitch contact) enabling its status to be determined electronically. This is a valuable feature which enables the controlling computer to verify correct valve configuration at all times. Gas flow to each actuator is controlled by a simple low-voltage solenoid valve.

In *Figure 15*, all the valves are shown in their off or resting state. This is the fail-safe situation with V1 (flow/recirculate) in recirculate mode; V2 (ganged pair, loop in/out), loop out; V3 (reverse flow), flow down column; V4 (ganged pair, reagent and nitrogen selection), reagent 1 (DMF); and V5 (nitrogen on/off), off. Note that nitrogen pressurization of the reagent bottles is used only during the initial purging of the reagent lines and priming of the pump, and is not usually maintained during pumped flow of reagents. A non-return check valve in the drain outlet reduces the possibility of flowback of reagent into the (incorrect) reservoir, and the outlet itself is raised above the maximum

Figure 16. An early laboratory-constructed semi-automatic synthesizer. The valves and glass reactor column are mounted in an open panel for ease of accessibility, with the pump and reagent bottle behind. The flow scheme is essentially that of *Figure 15*.

liquid level in the reservoirs preventing siphoning to waste. An additional slider valve would have provided more positive control here.

The control system is outlined in *Figure 17.* The microcomputer originally chosen (Hewlett Packard HP85) provides in a single compact unit all the facilities depicted in the upper half of the figure, viz. microprocessor and keyboard, display screen, printer and program/data storage cassette. Other more modern microcomputers could equally easily be used; a larger memory than the 32 kilobytes of the early HP85 would be advantageous. Plug-in Hewlett Packard interface units provide serial (RS232) communication with single-beam digitized output ultraviolet monitor (LKB Ultrospec), and a second parallel (IEEE 488) interface particularly suitable for controlling laboratory instruments. This transmits control signals to relay assemblies which in turn operate the nitrogen solenoids. It also receives status signals from the valve actuators through a contact sensing assembly.

Three levels of control are provided on the laboratory instrument. Simple toggle switches with indicator lights actuate the solenoids directly and provide direct control

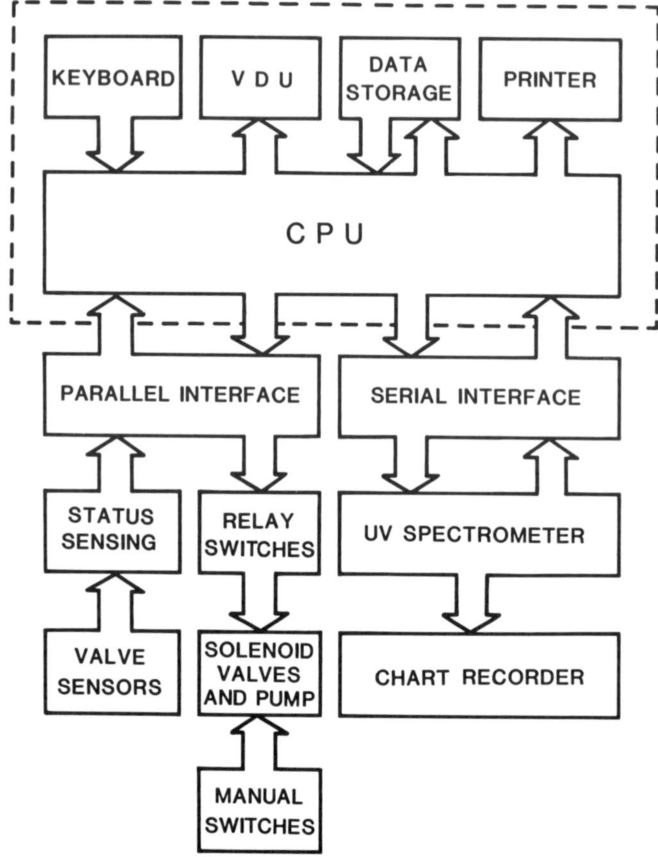

Figure 17. Microprocessor-based control system for semi-automatic and automatic synthesizers.

of individual valves and of the pump, even in the absence of the computer. At this level the instrument operates as a simple manual synthesizer without error checking or other refinement. A higher level of manual control is available through the computer keyboard, in this case through a series of software defined keys corresponding to control words such as FLOW, RECIRCULATE (see below). Each initiates a series of valve and/or pump operations appropriate to the named function, and then verifies correct status of all the valves. Alternate sets of software-defined functions facilitate procedures such as data collection by the spectrometer and data processing. In the third level of control, the same or similar control words are executed automatically in a stored sequence and at preselected time intervals. In this mode, provision is also made for manual intervention through HOLD, RESUME and ADVANCE functions, as well as reversion to fully manual control.

Specification of the laboratory semi-automatic instrument (*49*)

This was assembled using 4-way 0.031-in bore Altex slide valves type 243265 (Anachem), each fitted with one pneumatic actuator type 243270 and one return spring type 243271. Valves V2 and V4 (*Figure 15*) were assembled with two slider valves per actuator unit. All return spring units were modified by attachment of a small projecting blade at the rear which interrupted the beam of an opto-electronic sensor when the valve was actuated. An adjustable nitrogen supply of *c.* 90 psi controlled by 24 V DC solenoid air valves type 243629 (Anachem) was provided for the pneumatic actuators. A second nitrogen supply of *c.* 3 psi was provided for the reagent bottles. The pump and column assembly were initially as in the manual instrument described above, but a LDC/Milton–Roy variable speed pump and 1 cm diameter glass and ptfe chromatographic columns (Omnifit) were later used. A non-return valve type TCKA 6201070A (Lee Products) was included in the drain outlet. The sample loop was constructed of 1/8-in o.d. ptfe tubing and had a volume of 3.5 ml. It was filled by suction from a 5 ml glass syringe with the sample contained in a 5 ml syringe barrel fitted with a glass or ptfe sintered filter.

The microcontroller consisted of a Hewlett Packard HP85 microcomputer fitted with an additional 16K memory unit (minimum memory requirement is presently about 32K), I/O Rom, and serial (RS232) and parallel (HPIB) interfaces. The serial interface connects directly with an LKB Ultrospec 4050 uv monitor. The parallel interface connects with a Microlink IEEE 488 Interface Unit (Biodata Ltd, Appendix) containing two 4-way heavy-duty relay modules type HDR4, one 8-way contact sensor module type CC8, and bus control and power supply modules. A regulated 24 V 3 A supply for the solenoid valves is also provided in the Microlink Unit. In a separate unit, a series of toggle switches are connected in parallel with the relay contacts, enabling direct manual control of the solenoid valves and of the pump.

Control functions for semi-automatic synthesizer

The following sequences of control valve and pump operations were defined in the Basic software and initiated either by keyboard commands (manual operation) or during execution of the control program (automatic mode). REAGENT: Kbd entry 1, V4 OFF. kbd entry 2, V4 ON. Flow: V1 OFF, V5 ON, delay 3 sec (purge lines), V1 ON, Pump ON, V5 OFF. RECIRCULATE: V1 OFF, Pump ON. REVERSE: V3 toggles OFF/ON or ON/OFF. LOOP I/O: V2 toggles OFF/ON or ON/OFF. TIME: variable time delay before execution of next command (automatic mode) or warning tone (manual mode). PAUSE: (automatic mode only) PUMP OFF, cancelled by CONT(inue) key. MONITOR: displays alternate set of functions for control of data output from the uv spectrometer, data storage and recall, processing, printout and plotting.

The semi-automatic (single residue) instrument described above may be used for Fmoc-amino acid anhydrides or with the later-introduced activated ester derivatives. Two commercial instruments of this type have been produced. The Cambridge Research Biochemical's PEPSYNthesiser II is illustrated in *Figure 18*. This simple and compact instrument carries out all the operations of single residue addition and deprotection under microcomputer control. Liquid flow is controlled by an internal pump and electromagnetically operated valves. Individual amino acid derivatives are introduced by way of a manually filled syringe barrel mounted on the front panel. Two reaction columns

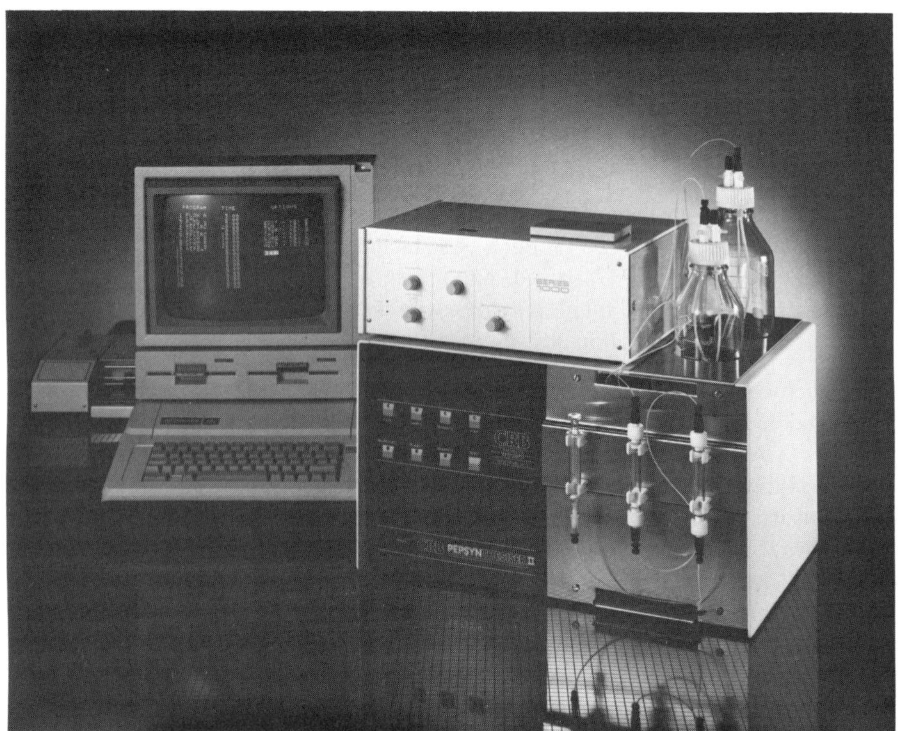

Figure 18. The Cambridge Research Biochemicals' PEPSYNthesiser II. A computer-controlled synthesizer capable of carrying out automatically all the functions required for single residue addition.

are provided, simplifying analogue production, and a similarly compact variable wavelength spectrometer continuously monitors the reagent stream.

Milligen/Biosearch manufacture the Milligen 9020 which has replaced the PEPSYNthesiser II. It is basically similar to that of the laboratory-assembled instrument (*Figure 15*) with additional valving to accommodate three reaction columns and four reagent bottles. The main liquid flow is controlled by a dual-headed Waters hplc pump capable of flow rates up to 45 ml min^{-1}, and a pressure-sensing device monitors the reagent stream. The high flow rate combined with the use of large sample loops filled manually via an injection port facilitate scaling up. Manual synthesis of up to 100 mmol of peptide is said to be feasible. All operations for one cycle of amino acid addition and deprotection are controlled by a computer built into the synthesizer unit, which also contains a uv spectrometer monitoring the reagent stream both before and after it enters the reaction column.

For the next stage of mechanization, automatic addition of a number of amino acid residues in sequence, a facility for introducing the activated derivatives in sequence has to be provided. It is possible to construct devices for generating N-protected amino acid anhydrides from the carboxylic acid and carbodiimide immediately before each acylation step and transferring them automatically into the reactor vessel or column, but they are complex. It is at this level of mechanization that the use of stable, pre-activated derivatives becomes particularly advantageous. Fully automatic continuous-flow synthesizers for use with Fmoc-amino acid pentafluorophenyl esters (*92*) or other pre-activated derivatives have now been constructed; the flow scheme for the first laboratory instrument (*94*) is shown in *Figure 19*, and the laboratory implementation in *Figure 20*.

This instrument was designed with a minimum component count in mind, and particularly to make use of a single reciprocating pump to effect all liquid transfers. These include sample dissolution and introduction, as well as the basic flow and recirculate functions. An alternative approach would have been to adapt the sample loop system of the earlier semi-automatic instrument (*Figure 15*) using now a motor-driven syringe and additional valving to dissolve and transfer the Fmoc-amino acid esters sequentially into the sample loop. This is the approach adopted in the current versions of the commercial instruments with a motor-driven syringe pump used for the sample handling operations.

Syringe barrels fitted with coarse porosity sintered glass or ptfe filters were used as sample chambers. These are ideally suited for solid sample dissolution by nitrogen agitation, completely prevent undissolved particles from entering the pump or valving system, and present negligible flow resistance during sample transfer when the reciprocating pump is operating in a relatively unfavourable suction mode.

The fully automatic instrument retains the flow/recirculate, reverse flow and reagent selection valves of the semi-automatic device (*Figure 15*), and adds additional valving and sample chambers enabling solid samples to be dissolved and introduced into the flowing scheme. The recirculating loop is now divided by valves 2a and 3 (*Figure 19*) so that the output stream from the pump passes either to the reactor column through valve 4 as before, or is diverted through valves 2b, 6, 5 and the rotary valve to the selected sample chamber.

Dissolution of the contained solid is effected by a nitrogen stream switched by valves

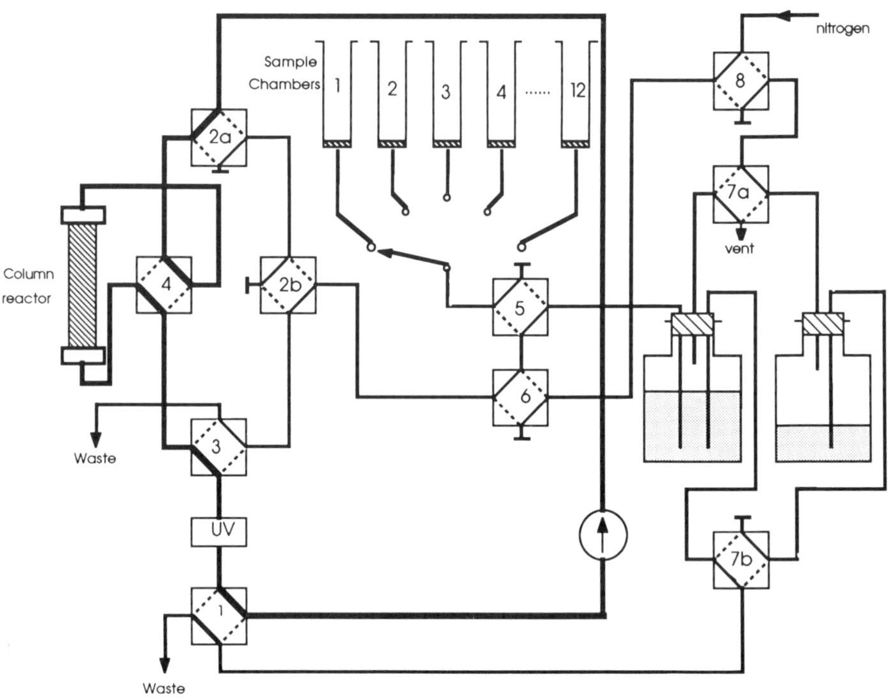

Figure 19. Fully automatic continuous-flow synthesizer. The main recirculation loop is shown in heavy line.

8, 6 and 5. The dissolved activated derivative is then introduced into the recirculation loop and reactor column through valves 5, 6, 2b and 3. As the complexity of these liquid flow systems increases, special care needs to be taken with 'housekeeping' operations in which valves and lines are rinsed free from residual reagent before passing on to the next cycle. Thus in the system of *Figure 19*, the activated sample is washed out of the lines and into the recirculating loop with fresh solvent through valves 5, 6, 2b and 3, and the rotary valve and associated tubing washed at a later stage by pumping solvent back into the original sample chamber. Again check valves or additional slider valves are required to minimize or eliminate risk of back flow into the reagent bottles.

With the valving arrangement depicted in *Figure 19*, the various liquid control functions listed in *Table 7* are implemented with the given valve configurations. The fluid paths for the FLOW, RECIRCULATE, FILL, MIX, EMPTY and WASH functions are also shown in *Figure 21*. The manual and automatic control systems are essentially as described for the earlier semi-automatic instrument, with some expansion to accommodate the additional valve switching. Simple toggle switches and indicator lights allow direct manual operation of individual valves. A controlling microcomputer interfaced to relays in parallel with these manual switches provides a higher level of manual control through the keyboard, as well as programmed sequential operation.

In these last modes, valves are operated in combination through software defined functions generally corresponding to those listed in *Table 7*. Software facilities for manual intervention to extend or curtail preset reaction times and for data collection from the uv spectrophotometer and its interpretation are also required.

Figure 20. Laboratory constructed fully automatic-flow synthesizer. From the top, the main unit contains the manual control (toggle switch) box, the computer interface unit, valves and reactor column assembly with the multiple sample chambers to the right, the spectrophotometer and chart recorder. The pump, rotary selection valve and reagent bottles are behind the valve panel.

Table 7. Valve and pump configurations for the various liquid control functions.

	V1	*V2*	*V3*	*V4*	*V5*	*V6*	*V7*	*V8*	*PUMP RV*
Shut down	OFF	OFF	OFF	OFF	OFF	OFF	OFF	OFF	OFF
Recirculate	OFF	OFF	OFF	OFF	OFF	OFF	OFF	OFF	ON
Flow DMF	ON	OFF	OFF	OFF	OFF	OFF	OFF	OFF	ON
Reverse flow DMF	ON	OFF	OFF	ON	OFF	OFF	OFF	OFF	ON
Flow piperidine	ON	OFF	OFF	OFF	OFF	OFF	ON	OFF	ON
Next amino acid	OFF	OFF	OFF	OFF	OFF	OFF	OFF	OFF	ON[a] STEP
Fill chamber	ON	ON	OFF	OFF	ON	OFF	OFF	OFF	ON
Mix	OFF	OFF	OFF	OFF	ON	ON	OFF	OFF	ON[a]
Empty chamber	OFF	OFF	ON	OFF	ON	OFF	OFF	OFF	ON
Rinse sample in	OFF	OFF	ON	OFF	OFF	OFF	OFF	OFF	ON

[a]Optional, but see below.

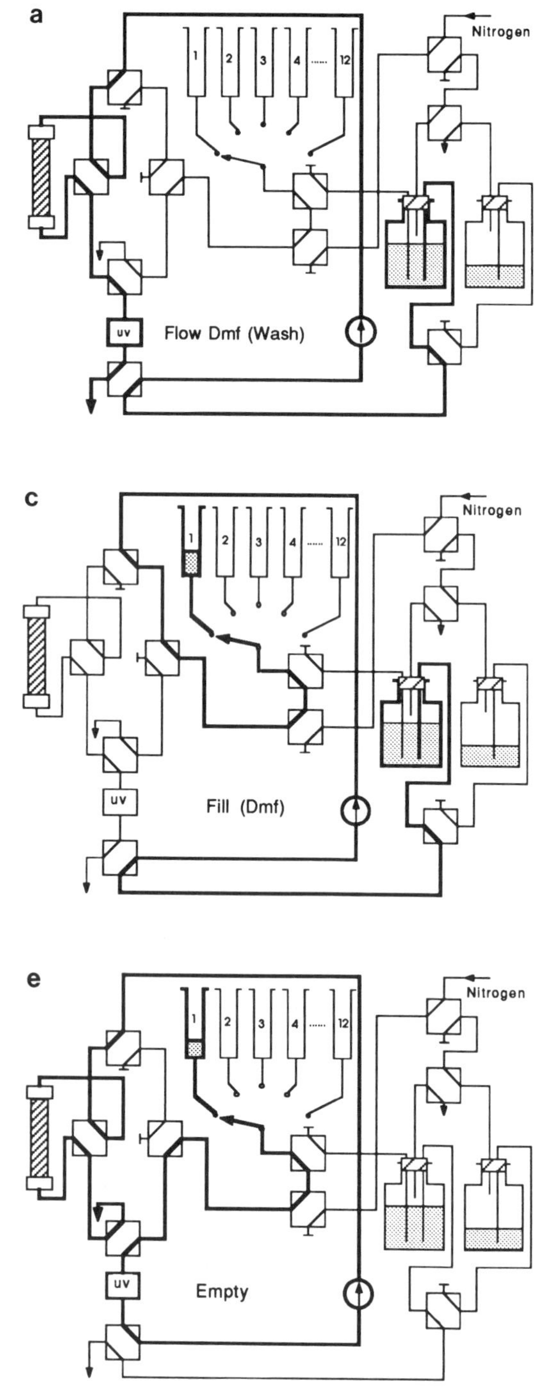

Figure 21. Fluid flow functions.

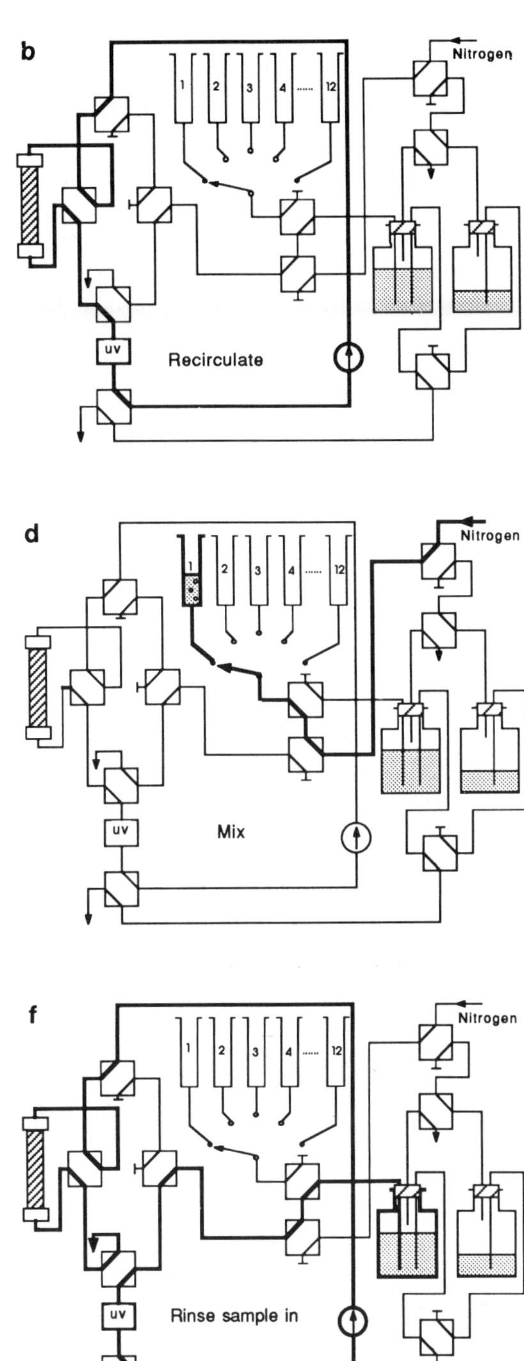
b
Nitrogen
1
2
3
4
12
uv
Recirculate
d
Nitrogen
Mix
f
Nitrogen
Rinse sample in

Further details regarding operation of the synthesizer are given in Chapter 10.

Two fully automatic commercial flow synthesizers have thus far been produced. The first, the Pharmacia-LKB Biochrom Biolynx Model 4170, is illustrated in *Figure 22*. The current version of this instrument has a basic flow system similar to that of *Figure 15*, but with many refinements. A 40-position carousel holds special plastic vials containing preweighed Fmoc-amino acid pentafluorophenyl esters and catalyst hydroxybenzotriazole, or Fmoc-amino acid Dhbt esters. Samples are dissolved by introducing predetermined volumes of solvent into the selected vial with a syringe pump and agitating with nitrogen, and the solution is then transferred to the sample loop. Three columns can be selected automatically, individually or together, enabling simultaneous multiple analogue synthesis. Reactor temperature, flow rates, reaction times and other parameters are all presettable for each amino acid residue. The effluent stream is continuously monitored by an associated uv spectrophotometer, and spot optical density readings and peak areas are automatically checked against preset values. The status of all the valves is also continuously monitored. The synthesizer is normally controlled by an internal microprocessor and IBM-compatible microcomputer, but provision is also made for direct manual operation (in the absence of the external computer) as well as fully automatic and manual keyboard operation.

A more recent introduction is the Milligen automatic synthesizer model 9050 (*Figure 23*). This is similar to the 9020 semi-automatic instrument, with the addition of a 72-vial sample dispensing system which enables fully automatic operation. Fmoc-amino acid

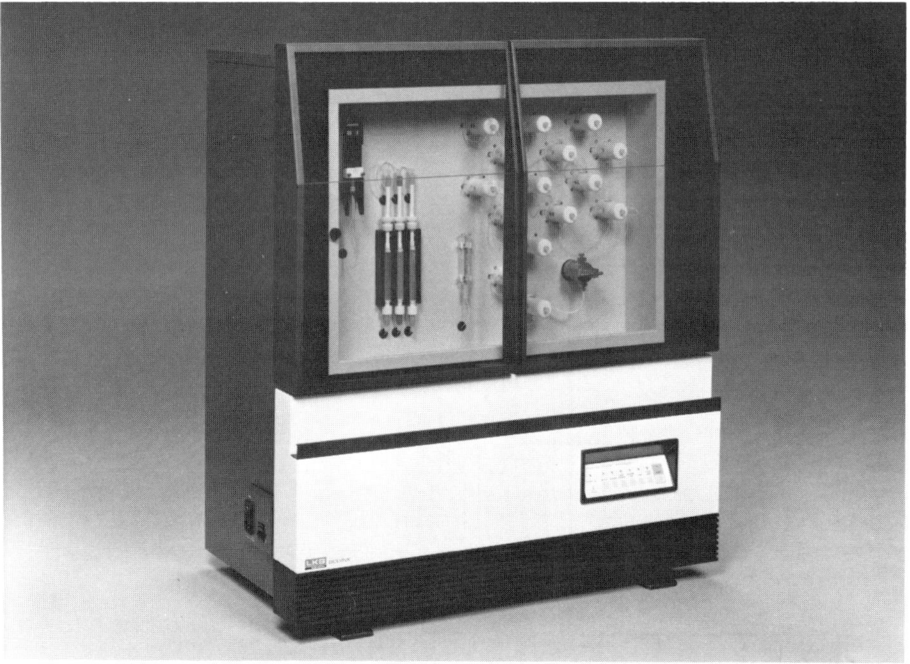

Figure 22. The Pharmacia-LKB Biolynx automatic synthesizer. Operation is normally controlled by an external microcomputer but manual operation through the keypad on the right is also possible.

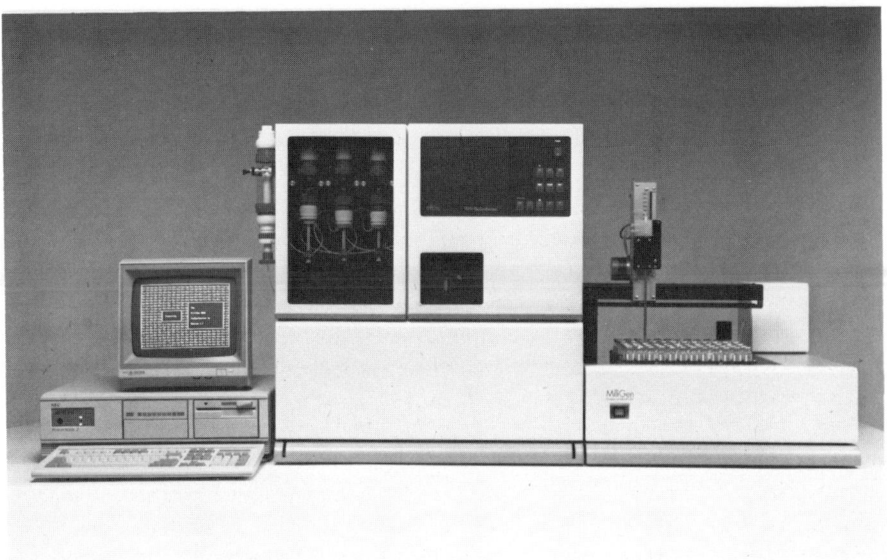

Figure 23. The Milligen Model 9050 automatic peptide synthesizer. The sample changer is on the right of the main synthesizer module and external controlling computer on the left. The semi-automatic instrument, Model 9020, consists essentially of the central synthesizer module alone.

derivatives (usually Pfp or Dhbt esters) are stored in these vials and automatically dissolved in a stock solution of HOBt in DMF, using nitrogen agitation immediately prior to synthesis. A wide-bore probe fitted with a filter at the tip prevents the entry of insolubles and is used to transfer amino acid derivatives into a sample loop. As in the Milligen model 9020, the pump is of a dual-headed hplc type capable of flow rates up to 45 ml min^{-1}, facilitating automatic synthesis of up to 1 mmol of peptide. Provision is made for use of alternative chemistries.

CHAPTER 9

Analytical and monitoring techniques

One of the intrinsic disadvantages of solid phase peptide synthesis is the difficulty of analytical control. Attachment of the growing peptide to an insoluble particle throughout the synthesis means that many of the commonplace analytical and spectroscopic techniques of organic chemistry become of reduced value in assessing the actual peptide bond-forming process (Section 2.2). These traditional techniques are not to be discarded completely, however. They continue to be valuable for the characterization of the basic starting materials of solid phase synthesis. New protected amino acids and activated derivatives still require structural verification, and new preparations or purchases (*caveat emptor*!) of known compounds benefit from confirmation of identity and purity before use. For these purposes the everyday spectroscopic, chromatographic and other analytical techniques of general organic chemistry are essential. For characterization of synthetic peptides, hplc, quantitative amino acid analysis and fast atom bombardment (fab) mass spectrometry provide popular and reassuring if not always compelling evidence for structure and purity. The fastidious would wish to supplement these with other traditional techniques of thin layer chromatography, various forms of electrophoresis, ion-exchange chromatography, sequence analysis, and even high resolution nmr spectroscopy and X-ray crystallography, but the pressures of time, material, and general feasibility commonly prevent this.

In the development of the Fmoc-polyamide technique, particular attention has been paid to the need for analytical control of the peptide bond-forming and deprotection steps, and to the development of new techniques for achieving this. Extensive use has always been made of ninhydrin and other qualitative colour tests to verify completeness of acylation, and of amino acid analysis of peptide resins for confirmation, even though the latter is usually too slow to serve as a controlling function. Additionally, the use of Fmoc derivatives in combination with very acid-labile peptide–resin linkages has permitted easy and rapid detachment and hplc analysis of intermediate peptides with or without prior cleavage of the terminal Fmoc group (*104*). This powerful tool for ensuring that synthesis is proceeding satisfactorily is barely feasible in techniques requiring detachment by liquid hydrogen fluoride. On the other hand, introduction of the acid-labile resin linkage caused us to abandon solid phase Edman degradation for direct sequencing of intermediate and final peptide–resins (*111*), as detachment of the peptide from the solid support occurs during the acid-catalysed cyclization process.

The use of Fmoc derivatives in combination with the development of practical low-pressure continuous-flow technology (*106*) enabled a significant advance in real-time monitoring of both acylation and deprotection reactions (*107*). By passing the flowing reagent stream continuously through appropriate sensor cells, a record is obtained which provides quantitative or semi-quantitative information regarding both Fmoc-amino acid uptake during acylation and protecting group release during deprotection. Perhaps equally importantly, the record also provides continuous and useful verification of correct instrument operation. The more recent introduction of Fmoc-amino acid Dhbt esters has enabled a further advance providing visual (*97,39*) and computer interpretable (*98,99*) data regarding the progress of acylation. It has permitted construction of the first truly automated solid-phase peptide synthesizer in which progression from one amino acid to the next in the target sequence is controlled by quantitative data gathered and processed as the reactions are proceeding.

9.1 **Qualitative colour tests**

The ninhydrin (*108*) and trinitrobenzene sulphonic acid (*109*) colour tests for residual resin-bound amino groups are easy and quick to carry out, and should be used regularly for manual or single-residue automatic synthesis. They provide a seemingly reliable indication of the presence of free primary amino functions on the resin beads, that is, of incomplete acylation. The sensitivity for polydimethyl-acrylamide resins is unknown, but Barany and Merrifield (*16*) state that polystyrene beads give a slight colour with ninhydrin at 5 μmol amino groups g^{-1} resin (99% coupling with an initial loading of 0.5 mmol g^{-1}), and with trinitrobenzene sulphonic acid an orange-red colour with 3 μmol amino groups g^{-1} resin. In our experience, the colour of the beads with ninhydrin varies substantially both in hue and intensity depending on the terminal residue or sequence. Aspartic acid, asparagine and glutamine, sometimes glycine and of course the secondary amino-acid proline may give weaker blue or brownish colours. For peptides with N-terminal proline residues, the colour reaction with isatin is to be preferred. A blank, fully deprotected resin sample withdrawn before acylation is commenced and tested alongside the acylated resin gives an indication of the sensitivity. The fluorescamine reagent appears to be inappropriate in the polydimethylacrylamide series, since some resins tested were themselves fluorescent.

Ninhydrin (Kaiser) colour test (*108*)

Reagents: ninhydrin (1 g) dissolved in ethanol (10 ml); phenol (80 g) dissolved in ethanol (20 ml); potassium cyanide, 2 ml of a stock 0.001 M solution diluted to 100 ml with pyridine.

A small resin sample (5 – 10 mg) is removed at the end of the wash period following deprotection and another 15 – 30 min into the acylation reaction. Both samples are transferred to small sintered glass funnels and washed under suction with DMF, *t*-amyl alcohol (2-methylbutan-2-ol), acetic acid, *t*-amyl alcohol, DMF and ether, the resin being agitated throughout with a small spatula. A few resin beads (10 – 20) from each sample are transferred to small test tubes (*c*. 50 mm × 10 mm diameter) and 2 – 3 drops of each of the above reagents added. The tubes are placed in an oven at *c*. 120°C for 5 min (timed). The blank should be a strong dark blue-purple colour, and the test solution, if negative, a straw-yellow colour with no coloration of the beads. The significance of the result depends upon the colour intensity of the blank, reference sample.

Trinitrobenzene sulphonic acid (*109*)

Reagents: 10% diisopropylethylamine in DMF (prepared daily); trinitrobenzene sulphonic acid (solid).

The same resin samples are used as for the ninhydrin reaction above. A few beads of each are placed in adjacent hollows on a white porcelain test plate. Immediately before carrying out the test, dissolve *c.* 5 mg of trinitrobenzene sulphonic acid in 0.5 ml 10% diisopropylethylamine–DMF, and then add 2–3 drops to each of the samples. The beads should become strongly orange-coloured in the blank and remain colourless in the test sample. Note that the solution surrounding the beads will slowly develop an orange colour and this is not significant. Secondary amino groups (N-terminal proline residues) give no colour in this test.

Isatin test (110)

Reagent: add isatin (2 g) to benzyl alcohol (60 ml) and stir for 2 h; add Boc-Phe-OH (2.5 g) to 50 ml of filtrate.

A few beads of resin in a small test tube are treated with 2–3 drops of the isatin solution, then 2–3 drops of each of the ninhydrin test solutions above, and heated 100°C for 5 min. The mixture is allowed to cool, the deeply-coloured supernatant solution is decanted and the beads washed by decantation with acetone. If the beads are blue/red the test is positive; if colourless, the test is negative.

Although these colour tests are essentially qualitative and somewhat subjective, a negative result for residual amino groups is highly desirable before continuing with the synthesis. The ninhydrin reaction with polystyrene resin samples has been quantitated (*43*) and very high precision claimed, but the significance of the results is somewhat controversial.

9.2 **Quantitative amino acid analysis**

Total acidic hydrolysis and amino acid analysis of resin samples provides reassuring information about the success of coupling reactions, but the method is slow and the accuracy usually barely adequate for the control of solid phase synthesis. It is essential for the final characterization of synthetic peptides. Some amino acid residues may be partly (serine, threonine) or nearly completely (tryptophan) destroyed by hydrolysis in strong mineral acids. Others (methionine, tyrosine, cysteine) may give variable results depending on the total exclusion of oxygen during hydrolysis and the purity of the sample and of the hydrochloric acid used. Sterically hindred residues (isoleucine, valine) may be released incompletely under the usual hydrolysis conditions, especially when two such residues are adjacent. Similar effects are observed when the residue contains a basic centre close to the peptide chain as in histidyl-valine sequences. Thus caution and experience is necessary in interpreting the results of amino acid analysis. Nevertheless, analysis should form part of the characterization of the final free and resin-bound peptide, and preferably of intermediate peptide–resins removed from the reaction vessel before the addition of second, third, etc. residues of the same amino acid type. In general, amino acid analysis is too slow to be used routinely for the analytical control of synthesis while it is progressing, though synthesis may be halted for analysis should an uncertainty arise.

Accelerated hydrolysis conditions have been proposed, for example by use of a microwave oven (*112*) for rapid heating. Prolonged hydrolysis may be necessary for the hindered residues mentioned above, and better results for incompletely stable residues may be obtained from a series of graded hydrolysis and extrapolation.

The value of amino acid analysis is much enhanced if a permanently bound internal reference amino acid has been initially attached to the resin (Chapter 6). This provides a reference point for assessing the efficiency of attachment of the first residue of the sequence proper (for which the above colour tests are inapplicable in the case of hydroxymethyl resins), and for checking for loss of peptide from the resin as the synthesis progresses. It is especially useful for assessing completion of the final peptide cleavage reaction.

Acid hydrolysis and amino acid analysis of peptide resins

A resin sample (*c.* 5 mg) is removed from the reactor vessel or column after the deprotection and final wash stages. A further aliquot of the blank reference resin withdrawn from the above colour tests is commonly used; it should always be taken after deprotection since Fmoc-peptide resins may give low analytical results from the amino terminal residue. The resin is transferred to a small sintered-glass funnel and washed further with DMF and then with ether. The gel resin shrinks dramatically with ether and it is advisable to stir the resin with a small spatula during the washing process to obtain manageable particulate samples. While still in the sintered glass funnel, the resin is transferred to a desiccator and subjected to high vacuum for at least 30 min.

A sample (2–3 mg) of the dried resin is weighed accurately into a dry, acid-washed Pyrex test tube (150 mm × 10 mm diameter is a convenient size), and a solution of 0.1% phenol in redistilled constant boiling hydrochloric acid (1 ml) added. (Alternatively redistilled hydrochloric acid together with a small crystal of phenol may be conveniently used.) The contents of the tube are frozen (acetone–solid carbon dioxide bath) and the tube evacuated using an oil pump and potassium hydroxide trap. The tube is allowed to rewarm until the liquid degasses gently, and the cooling–warming process repeated. The tube is then refrozen, sealed under vacuum in the usual manner, and placed in a covered heating block at 118°C for 18 h. After cooling, the tube is opened and the contents washed with distilled water into a small round-bottomed flask and evaporated *in vacuo* (rotary evaporator). Chloroform (1 ml) and the appropriate quantity (see below) of amino acid analyser loading buffer are added and the mixture shaken gently. A sample for analysis is carefully pipetted from the flask avoiding inclusion of chloroform. The amount of buffer used depends on the peptide loading of the resin. For the Kieselguhr supported resin, *c.* 0.1 mol g^{-1}, a convenient rule of thumb is to use a volume in ml equal to the weight of resin in mg. For gel resins with higher loading, the volume is adjusted appropriately. The weight of peptide covalently linked to the resin should be taken into account when calculating loadings. For the Beckman Amino Acid Analyser Model 119, the volume taken for analysis is 100 μl, for the Beckman System 7300, 50 μl, and for the LKB Alpha plus, 60 μl.

9.3 Hplc examination of partially protected intermediate peptides

Treatment of intermediate peptide resins containing acid-labile linkage agents (**85**, **86**, **92**) with trifluoroacetic acid results in rapid detachment of 90% or more of the assembled peptide. Usually less than one hour is required, and for analytical purposes complete cleavage is unnecessary. Too short a treatment is inadvisable in case an unrepresentative sample of peptide is obtained from only the most reactive sites on the resin. The cleavage reaction may be carried out on the Fmoc or deprotected peptide resin; the former is particularly valuable for short polar peptides which may otherwise emerge very rapidly from reverse-phase hplc columns. Some protecting groups are retained during the acidic cleavage reaction, notably the acetamidomethyl group of cysteine derivatives, and more significantly, some are only partly cleaved. The methoxytrimethylbenzenesulphonyl derivative of arginine is inconvenient in this respect and generates peaks for both the free and protected peptides which may be recognized by carrying out the cleavage reaction for different time periods. Products arising from the protecting group itself may also appear on the hplc trace. These and artefacts derived from scavengers which may be added to the cleavage reaction in the case of tryptophan and methionine-containing peptides (see Section 11.1.2) are usually easily recognized after experience has been gained with the hplc system in use and a variety of peptide sequences.

Hplc analysis of intermediate peptides (104)

Samples (3 – 10 mg) of washed and dried Fmoc or free peptide – resin (not containing tryptophan or methionine) are treated with 95% aqueous trifluoroacetic acid for 1 h (30 min is adequate if the 3-methoxy-4-hydroxymethylphenoxyacetic acid linkage agent is used) and the filtrate evaporated *in vacuo* (rotary evaporator). Ether is added and evaporated twice. The residue is totally dissolved in a suitable solvent (0.5 – 1 ml; methanol, DMF or trifluoroethanol are commonly good solvents;. for larger peptides hplc-grade water is sometimes suitable, and dropwise addition of dilute ammonium hydroxide cautiously from a syringe may aid dissolution of the acidic peptide derivatives). Care should be taken to ensure that the peptide is totally dissolved as otherwise the hplc profile obtained will not be representative of the total cleaved product. Solvents must be hplc pure. Hplc analysis may be carried out by injecting 50 μl samples using a μ-Bondapak C_{18} analytical column and a 0.01 M ammonium acetate/acetonitrile gradient. An alternative system using Aquapore RP300 and 0.1% aqueous trifluoroacetic acid – acetonitrile gradients is also useful; doubtless many others may also be used. The eluant should be monitored at 266 nm (Fmoc-peptides) and at 230 nm or lower. Monitoring at 230 and 248 nm enables arginine and Mtr-arginine peptides to be distinguished.

This technique is not directly applicable to methionine and tryptophan-containing peptides which require more effective scavenging agents for *t*-butyl and other cations to minimize modifications of these residues. Provision to eliminate the scavenger (for example by ether extraction of an aqeous solution) is also necessary in the work-up of the cleavage reaction.

The hplc characterization and purification of free peptides is further discussed in Chapter 11.

9.4 Spectrometric monitoring of the reagent stream in continuous-flow synthesis

Use of the uv-absorbing Fmoc protecting group opened the way to spectrometric monitoring of both acylation and deprotection reactions. In the peptide-bond-forming step, activated Fmoc-amino acid is taken out of solution and transferred to the solid phase. In the deprotection reaction, a fluorenyl derivative is released from the solid phase back into solution. The corresponding changes in absorbance should reflect the efficiencies of the two reactions. In practice it has been found that, although the numerical data are easy to obtain, strictly quantitative interpretation is difficult. There are many pitfalls for the unwary. Nevertheless, continuous monitoring of the reagent stream has proved a most valuable feature of flow synthesis, providing information about both mechanical and chemical functioning of the synthesis. The information is presented to the operator at a time when remedial intervention is possible.

Spectrometric monitoring of reactant concentration in solution is feasible using both conventional (discontinuous) and continuous-flow technology, but is overwhelmingly easier in the latter. Monitoring of discontinuous solid phase synthesis requires that the supernatant liquid be removed from the reaction cell, assayed separately, and then (in the acylation step) returned if reaction is judged incomplete. In continuous-flow techniques, the recirculating or flowing solution is simply passed at all times through an appropriate sensor cell and a continuous record is produced and displayed automatically, and may be computer-interpreted. The sensor cell is usually and most simply a silica flow cuvette placed in a spectrophotometer set to a suitable fixed wavelength. Optical rotation changes have also been measured for the acylation step, but the optical rotations of individual Fmoc-amino acid derivatives vary widely with corresponding changes in sensitivity for individual residues. For glycine derivatives, optical rotation techniques are inapplicable. Measurement of changes in other properties, such as refractive index, can also be envisaged.

Because of the high concentration involved, measurement of optical density at λ_{max} (around 266 nm for fluorene derivatives in DMF) is not normally possible even using the thinnest flow cells available. In our experience, the thinnest practical flow cell for use with DMF solutions has an optical path length of 0.1 mm, permitting measurement at around 304 nm. However, even cells of this thickness may generate undesirably high back-pressure. Positioning of the cell in the optimum position in the flowing stream indicated in *Figures 15* and *19* means that any restricted flow affects the inlet cycle of the reciprocating pump. This may cause entry of air bubbles around the piston seal and into the system. No difficulties of this type are observed with a conventional 1 mm pathlength flow cell. The cell volume is still only about 0.2 ml, and measurements can be made between 310 and 320 nm. Since all measurement wavelengths distant from λ_{max} lie on the falling edge of the fluorenyl absorption spectrum, reproducibility and constancy of spectrometer wavelength setting are important factors for accurate measurements. Insofar as peak areas usually constitute the relevant parameters in continuous-flow monitoring, constancy of pumping rate is also a critical factor.

For other than purely visual qualitative applications, means for digitizing the analogue spectrometric record are required. It is desirable that the spectrometer itself should

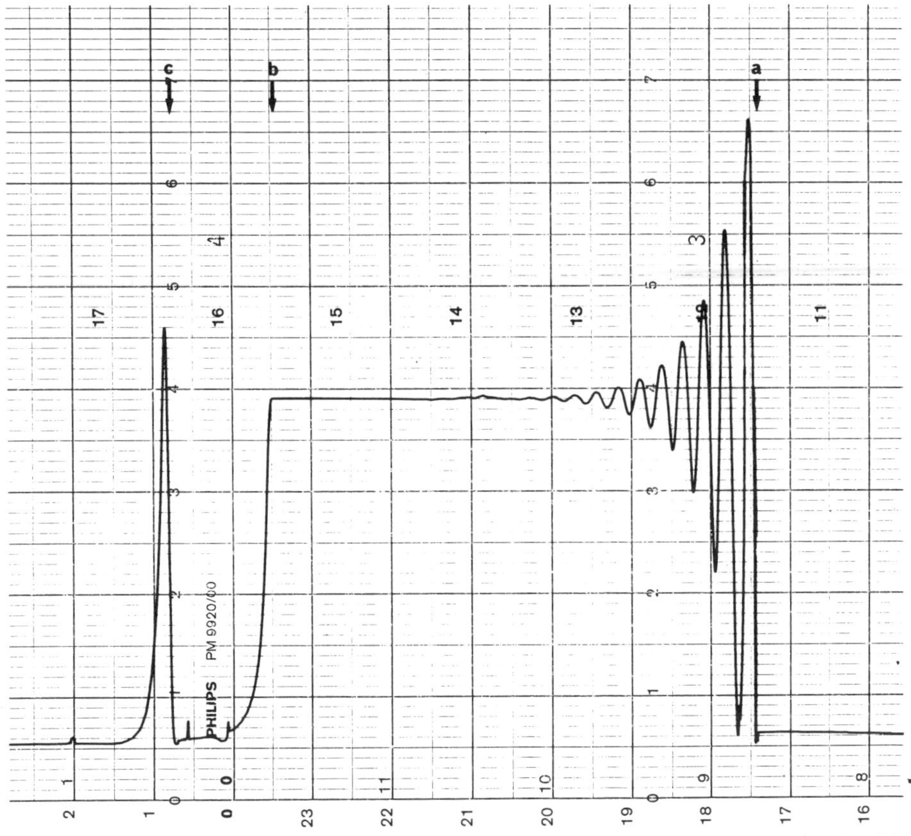

Figure 24. Typical spectrometic record of a complete cycle of acylation and deprotection. The sequence of operations runs from right to left (see text).

also be capable of computer control. In the absence of a digital output connection on the spectrometer, an external 10- or 12-bit analogue-to-digital converter is required with interface appropriate to the controlling computer. The Microlink A-10D and A-12D cards from Biodata Ltd (Appendix) connected to an IEEE 488 (HPIB) interface have proved satisfactory. The LKB Ultrospec spectrophotometer, which provides both analogue and digital outputs, and an RS232 serial input for computer control, is used in the synthesizer illustrated in *Figures 15* and *19*.

A typical spectrometric record for one complete cycle of Fmoc-amino acid addition and deprotection is shown in *Figure 24*.

Although the spectral measurements are easily made, there are substantial problems in translating these accurately into reaction parameters (see below) (*49*). Even in a qualitative sense, however,the spectrometric record provides continuous and reassuring evidence that all is proceeding smoothly, and such evidence is usually completely lacking in other than continuous-flow techniques. This feed-back to the operator has proved to be a significant psychological factor favouring the popularity and success of continuous-flow synthesis.

9.4.1 *The spectrometric record as verification of correct procedures and synthesizer function*

The trace of *Figure 24* provides information relating to most of the synthesizer operations in solid phase synthesis and can be assessed visually by the operator or automatically by a series of spot readings and computer interpretation. Thus introduction of the sample in to the flowing stream produces a sharp rise in absorption which may be checked visually or automatically. The sensing cuvette is usually connected (see *Figures 15* and *19*) so that it receives the incoming sample directly, i.e. before any contact with the resin bed. The height or integrated area of the first peak which is usually well separated from those following is thus a measure of the total sample admitted to the system, and can be checked automatically against preset limits to verify correct sample introduction. Switching of the synthesizer into recirculating mode (in sample loop machines of the type shown in *Figure 15*, sample introduction takes place in recirculating mode) produces the characteristic oscillating pattern of *Figure 24*. Diffusion of the chromophoric reactant into and out of the gel phase results in progressive broadening and lowering of successive peaks, ultimately to a plateau situation when a uniform reactant concentration is present throughout the system. A horizontal trace at this stage is an indication of complete reaction, since no further absorbing material is being taken up from solution, and its height is a measure of the final chromophore concentration. Some trifunctional amino acid derivatives, particularly asparagine and glutamine, may indicate a slight progressive rise in absorption at this stage and long after reaction is judged complete by other means, for example by resin colour tests. This is presumably due to slow decomposition of reactive intermediates initiated by interaction with the amino acid side chains. The plateau height and level may be determined by two or more time-separated measurements, and checked visually or automatically against preset limits.

For acylation reactions using symmetric anhydrides, the relative areas of successive peaks reflects the uptake of Fmoc-amino acid derivative by the resin for each pass through the reactor column. Techniques for area evaluation and their use in assessing reaction completion are discussed in Section 9.4.3.

At completion of the reaction period, switching of the recirculating stream to flow-to-waste results in rapid return to baseline absorption as fluorene derivatives and other reactants or products (for example pentafluorophenol, hydroxybenzotriazole) are washed from the system. Automatic protocols usually include some housekeeping operations, such as valve rinsing during the wash period, and these are reflected by the appearance of small peaks in the trace. At the completion of the wash period and immediately before deprotection, the spectrophotometer baseline is usually readjusted to zero, producing a small change in recorder output. Introduction of the deprotection reagent is followed rapidly by emergence of the cleaved protecting group reaction product. The peak is usually sharp, with return to baseline absorption after a few minutes, though hindered situations result in characteristic broadening and lowering (Section 9.4.2). The last step in the synthetic cycle, washing of reagent piperidine from the resin, is the only one which produces no obvious change in the spectrometric record.

9.4.2 *Spectrometric monitoring of deprotection reactions*

Release of the amino-terminal protecting group into solution when the deprotecting reagent (usually 20% piperidine in DMF) flows through the solution reactor results in a sharp increase in optical density at an accessible wavelength (300–320 nm depending on cell thickness, see Section 9.4). Completion of deprotection is indicated by return to baseline conditions as the fluorene derivative is washed from the system by further reagent. The deprotection reaction results in the initial release of the amine carbamate salt and dibenzofulvene; the latter than reacts further with excess reagent to form the piperidine adduct (*37*).

The details of this process are not clear. It is not known at what rate decarboxylation of the carbamic acid derivative occurs for individual terminal residues or peptide sequences, or indeed whether it occurs at all under the basic conditions of the cleavage reaction. It is conceivable that further elongation of the peptide chain takes place through the carbamate intermediate (*37*). Similarly, the effluent stream passing directly from the column reactor to the spectrometer cuvette may at the time of measurement contain dibenzofulvene (**69**), the piperidine adduct (**71**), or a mixture of both. In the last case, its composition will depend on the time interval since release from the resin support, i.e. on the pumping rate and on the volumes of the reactor, cuvette and intermediate tubing.

These points need to be stressed because they affect the quantitative nature of the spectroscopic data. They imply that equal areas for successsive deprotection peaks will only be obtained if all the conditions, chemical and mechanical, are held constant throughout. Since the deprotection reaction itself will involve successive cleavage of different amino acid residues from different sequences, rates of fluorene release will inevitably vary to some extent.

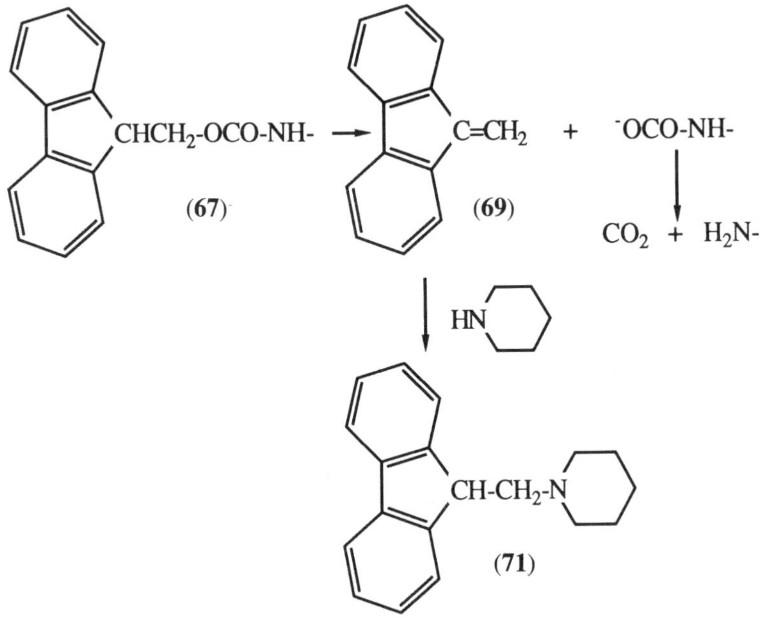

$CHCH_2$-OCO-NH- → C=CH_2 + $^-$OCO-NH-

(**67**) (**69**)

CO_2 + H_2N-

HN

CH-CH_2-N

(**71**)

Table 8. Successive deprotection areas in the synthesis of the decapeptide (**105**) (see text).

	(a)	*(b)*	*(c)*
Leu	15.9	100	103
Gly	16.2	102	105
Leu	15.3	96	99
Glu	15.75	99	102
Asp	15.65	98	101
His	15.0	94	97
Glu	15.1	95	98
Phe	15.4	97	100
Thr	15.3	96	99
Tyr	14.6	92	95

(a) Raw data (arbitary units). (b) Relative to the carboxy-terminal residue = 100%. (c) Relative to the mean = 100%.

Other factors are also important. The Fmoc group cleavage reaction is usually so fast that it is occurring at the leading edge of the piperidine reagent as it passes down the column reactor. The peak is effectively eluted on a gradient of piperidine in DMF, produced not only by mixing at the piperidine–DMF interface but also to some extent by neutralization of the initially formed carbamate salt and by reaction with dibenzofulvene. Thus chromophore from the trailing edge of the deprotection peak is measured under different solvent conditions (higher piperidine concentration) than that of the leading edge. The extinction coefficient of the piperidine adduct is lower at high piperidine concentrations (*49*), and this may reduce substantially the areas of broad or delayed deprotection peaks compared with normal. Finally, the fluorene chromophore is also fluorescent. It is probable that the fluorescence is quenched in the presence of piperidine, and no attempt has been made to apply corrections as has been done in the case of acylation data (see p. 119).

Notwithstanding the cautionary notes above, reasonably consistent deprotection peak areas are commonly obtained in synthesis providing the conditions are kept completely constant and there is no marked slowing of successive reactions. In serious cases this slowing is indicated by lowering and broadening of deprotection peaks (see below). The data of *Table 8* was obtained for the decapeptide sequence (**105**) synthesized by the Dhbt ester technique, and was selected for inclusion here by randomly opening a current laboratory notebook. In this experiment, the final deprotection reaction was carried out after leaving the completed Fmoc-decapeptide resin overnight. Under these circumstances a lower than usual deprotection area for the last residue is normally found, presumably due to slight loss of the Fmoc group on prolonged standing. A small peak usually emerges on washing Fmoc-peptide resin after standing in DMF for some hours. The data of *Table 8* also serve to illustrate a point relating to the use of Fmoc-His(Boc) derivatives in synthesis. Early studies using Fmoc-His(Fmoc)-OH had shown that, as expected, deprotection areas following introduction of the histidine residue were approximately double those preceding it in the peptide chain. This is attributed to incorporation of two Fmoc-amino acid residues at every cycle following complete deprotection of the histidine residue, one on the α-amino group as normal, the other

H-Tyr-Thr-Phe-Glu-His-Asp-Glu-Leu-Gly-Leu-OH (**105**)

H-Lys-Leu-*Ser-Val-Ala*-Thr-Lys-Gly-Pro-Leu-Thr-Val-Ser-Asp-Gly-OH (**106**)

acylating one of the imidazole nitrogen atoms. This did not occur to a significant extent with Fmoc-His(Boc) derivatives, and is confirmed by the near-constancy of the data above.

A substantial fall in peak area occurs when deprotection (and acylation) reactions become particularly sluggish, usually due to the onset of peptide resin aggregation effects. This, and the low, broad appearance of deprotection peaks, provide striking diagnostics for the severely hindered state. Three successive computer-plotted deprotection profiles from the synthesis (*49*) of the pentadecapeptide (**106**, the relevant residues are italicized) are illustrated in *Figure 25*. The first of these (a), alanine, the eleventh amino acid residue in the synthesis, is typical of a normal deprotection reaction with a sharp leading edge and more gently but still rapidly falling tail. The second curve (b) (valine) shows the onset of hindrance with significant lowering and broadening of the peak. The third (c) (O-*t*-butyl serine) shows a fully developed, low broad peak trailing to the extent that release of the chromophore into solution is evidently incomplete at the end of the data collection period (6 min). The integrated peak areas declined by 16% over these three residues; this was not due to incomplete acylation or deprotection (the pentadecapeptide synthesis was completely successful) (*49*) but to the solvent dependence and linearity effects discussed above.

Two effects may contribute to this broadening of the deprotection peak—slow chemical cleavage of the protecting group and slow release of the liberated fluorene derivative from the resin matrix into free solution. It is not possible to separate these effects, but both would be expected to result from internal aggregation effects within the peptide–resin complex which effectively provides additional cross-linking. In discontinuous syntheses using beaded gel resins, physical shrinkage of the resin can sometimes be observed and correlates with reduced reaction rates. Such shrinkage would also be expected if internal aggregation of types (c) or (d) (*Figure 5*, p. 28) was operative. In any event, visual or computer recognition of low, broad deprotection peaks appearing in a synthesis, usually after 8–12 residues have coupled normally, is a strong warning signal for sluggish acylation and deprotection reactions. The controlling computer in the automatic-flow synthesizer illustrated in *Figure 19* has been programmed to recognize this state and calls for operator attention when it occurs. In the synthesis referred to above, deprotection times were increased for the serine and succeeding residues.

This aspect of real-time monitoring of continuous-flow synthesis has proved to be a particulary valuable feature of the technique.

9.4.3 *Spectrometric monitoring of acylation reactions using Fmoc-amino acid anhydrides*

The acylation phase of continuous-flow synthesis gives a characteristic oscillating spectrometric record (*Figure 24*). The sensing cuvette is usually placed so that the incoming Fmoc-amino acid anhydride passes immediately through it without prior contact with the amino resin. Thus it measures in the first instance total sample

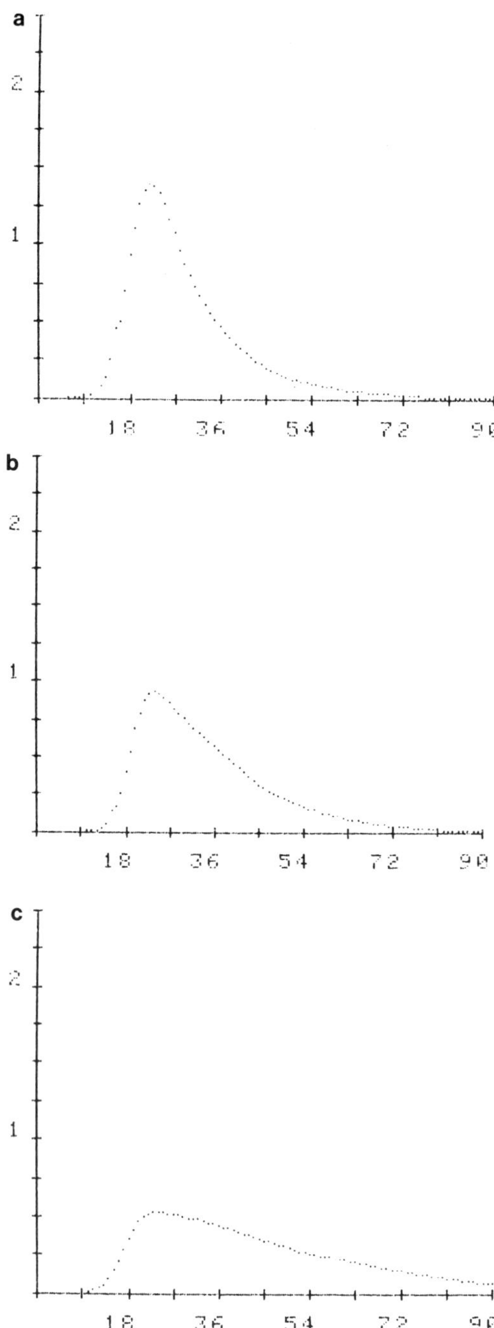

Figure 25. Three successive deprotection profiles showing increasing hindrance in the release of dibenzofulvene or its piperidine adduct.

absorbance (peak area), or, providing the sample volume is large relative to the volume of the cuvette, initial sample concentration (peak height). Area or height may be checked visually or automatically as a test of correct sample dissolution and loading. Successive peaks in the spectrometric record correspond to the combined absorption of residual Fmoc-amino acid anhydride and liberated Fmoc-amino acid after successive passes through the resin bed. Diffusion into and out of the gel phase results in rapid broadening, lowering and overlap of the peaks, ultimately to a straight-line trace when a uniform reactant concentration is present throughout the system.

Some of the caveats discussed in Section 9.4.2 apply in attempting to quantify the spectrometric data for the acylation reaction to a useful degree of accuracy, and there are others. Since measurement of peak areas is most usually involved, constancy of flow rate is crucial. The high reactant concentrations and the fluorescent properties of the fluorene chromophore combine to give a non-linear relationship between absorbance and concentration. Evaluation of areas of peaks of different heights therefore require correction of the absorbance readings using a previously prepared calibration curve (*49*). The Fmoc-amino acid anhydride contains two fluorene chromophores, one of which remains in the reagent stream (as Fmoc-amino acid) after reaction with the resin. This lowers the sensitivity and accuracy of measurement. Using only a two-fold excess of anhydride, complete reaction results in a fall in Fmoc concentration of 25%, one equivalent of anhydride (50% of the total) reacts liberating one equivalent (25% of total fluorene chromophore) of Fmoc-amino acid back into solution. At 95% reaction, the anticipated fall is 23.75%, and the situation worsens with higher initial excesses of anhydride. Other acylating species in which the Fmoc group was the only absorbing constituent would be advantageous in this respect. In choosing acylating species for solid phase synthesis, however, the need for efficient and clean acylation reactions is paramount, and no compromise is acceptable which favours ease of monitoring at the expense of chemical efficiency. Fmoc-amino acid N-hydroxysuccinimide esters which fulfil the uv absorption requirements for effective monitoring were rejected because of side reactions observed during acylation reactions.

The rapid broadening and overlap of the peaks means that simple summation methods for evaluation of peak areas may rapidly become inaccurate. Only in very favourable cases can simple valley-to-valley integration be applied beyond the first three or four peaks. A successful example (*49*) is shown in *Figure 26*. The raw data are computer-plotted in (a) and correspond to 50 measurements at 304 nm taken at 2-sec intervals using a 0.1 mm thick silica flow cell. Integration of the peaks at this stage gives progressively increasing areas as peak heights decline, a consequence of the linearity problems referred to above. In (b) the same data have been corrected for non-linearity in the absorbance–concentration relationship and replotted. Maximum peak height is now set full scale. The solid line corresponds to peak areas obtained by valley-to-valley summation of the readings. The third and fourth peaks (corresponding to two and three passes through the column reactor) have equal areas indicating that reaction is complete. The fall in Fmoc concentration (peak 1 = 100%) is 24%, very close to the theoretical value of 25% for an initial two-fold excess of symmetrical anhydride, and certainly within the limits set by anhydride preparation and introduction.

Similar real-time analytical results have been obtained in very many experiments, but the limited accuracy of the spectrometic measurements, and especially the

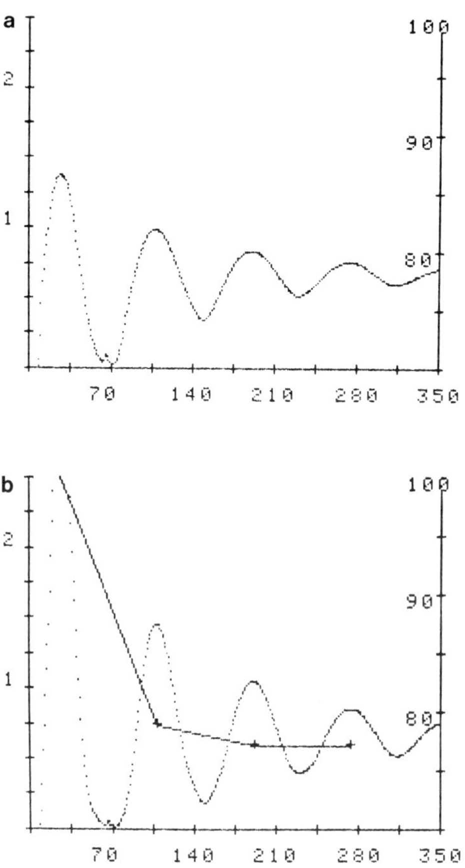

Figure 26. Spectrometric data from a typical acylation reaction. (a) Raw data. 350 measurements were taken at 2-sec intervals. In (b) the same data have been corrected for non-linearity in the concentration–optical density relationship, scaled, and integrated (solid line) by a simple valley-to-valley summation procedure. The small peak at the 69th reading corresponds to switching out of the sample loop in the semi-automatic synthesizer.

over-simple summation technique for overlapping peaks, can lead to marked deviation from ideal behaviour when the chemistry has later been shown to be near-quantitative. Linearized data from two non-ideal examples are illustrated in *Figure 27* (*49*). These deviations are almost certainly due to the integration procedure employed (see below). In general experience, the most significant feature of these results is probably the sharp reduction in area between the first and second peaks, that is, the large fall in Fmoc concentration after a single pass through the reactor column. The good resolution of these peaks means that these data are likely to be the most accurate obtainable and suitable for direct summation. The fall in Fmoc concentration after a single pass shows that the initial acylation rate is high. Solid phase reactions do not necessarily follow the usual kinetic rate equations, and quantitative extrapolation of these initial rate data to the end point is not possible. Thus this simple treatment of the early data indicates only that the acylation reaction is proceeding rapidly towards completion.

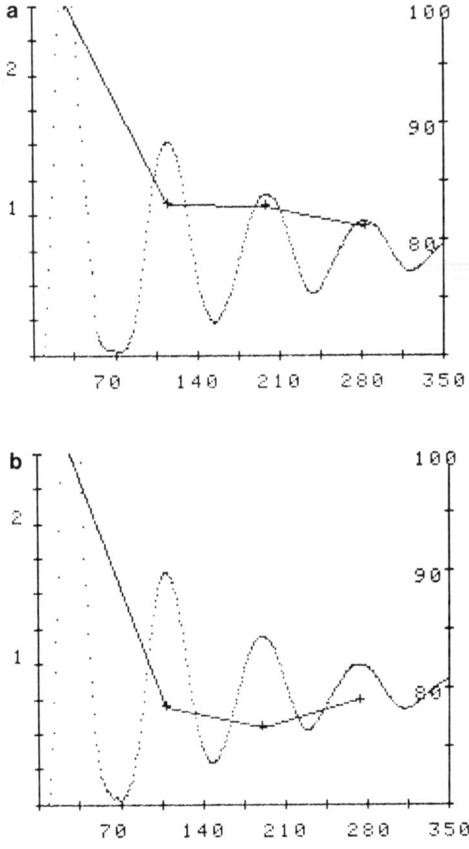

Figure 27. Poor integration of skewed and overlapping peaks in acylation data. A simple valley-to-valley summation was used.

A superior treatment of the acylation has been provided by iterative curve-fitting computer analysis (*113*). The algorithm takes into account skewing evident in the later peaks and provides individual computed curves which sum very closely to the experimental record. The examples illustrated in *Figure 28* are the same data which gave anomalous results on direct integration (*Figure 27*) (*49*). Substantial computing is involved, and on the Hewlett-Packard HP85 controller, each profile may take 20 min or more to complete using the present Basic program.

In summary, photometric monitoring of the reagent stream provides useful and reassuring information about the progress of both deprotection and acylation reactions. The areas and shapes of deprotection profiles are easily determined but cannot be easily corrected for solvent dependence and linearity effects. Reproducibility of peak areas is commonly obtained under closely controlled conditions, but is not an absolute criterion for successful synthesis. Low, broad peaks give much reduced areas. Their appearance is an important diagnostic for serious hindrance and slowing of the deprotection reaction, with the implication of similar hindrance of acylation. The relative areas of early peaks in the acylation profile are readily determined. They require correction for non-linearity

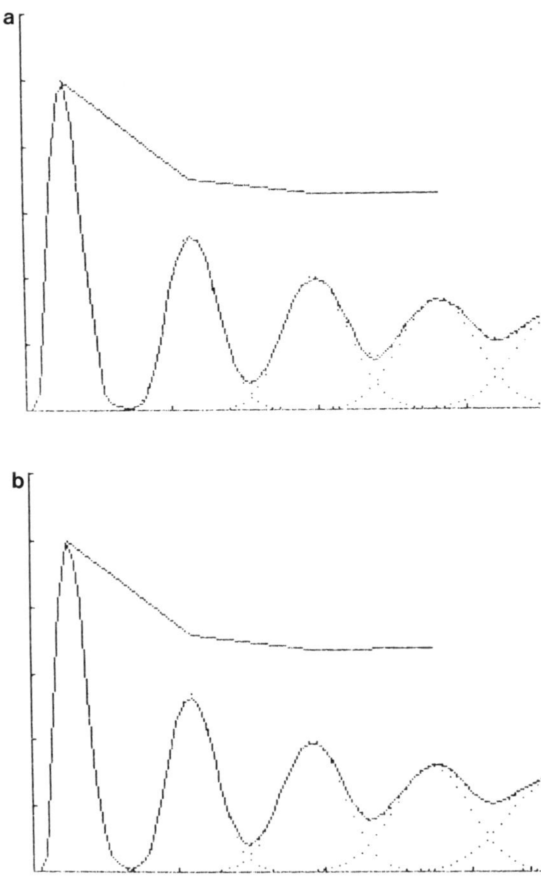

Figure 28. Integration of acylation data by an iterative curve-fitting technique. Computed curves for each peak are plotted (dotted lines) together with their calculated sum. The latter is coincident with the experimental curve (lower solid line). Relative integrated areas of the individual computed peaks are shown in the upper solid line.

by interpolation from a calibration curve. For acylation by Fmoc-amino acid anhydrides, the relative areas of the first two or three corrected peaks provide a useful indication of the initial rate of acylation. For acylation by activated species containing chromophores additional to the Fmoc group, interpretation of the data is much more complicated. For both acylation and deprotection reactions, the accuracy requirements for quantitative interpretation requires optimum performance from the pumping system and spectrophotometer. Qualitatively, the whole spectrometic record is of great value in confirming smooth operation of all the synthesizer functions and general conduct of the synthesis. This information is not easily attainable in other than low-pressure flow systems.

9.5 Spectrometric monitoring of the solid phase using Fmoc-amino acid Dhbt esters

During acylation reactions, spectrometic measurements on the flowing reagent stream are handled subtractively. Reagent is taken up from solution on to the solid phase in amounts related to the difference between initial and subsequent solution values. When large reagent excesses are used, the differences may be small compared with these absolute values, and may be strongly influenced by the accuracy of determination. This is an intrinsic weakness in any solid phase monitoring system which relies upon measurements of reactant uptake.

In principle, a more efficient approach would be to measure the fall to zero of free amino groups on the solid support. The common ninhydrin reaction (Section 9.1), for example, provides a visual estimation of residual amino groups, and it has been quantitated for polystyrene resins (*43*). For several reasons, however, such reactions are generally unsuitable for continuous real-time monitoring of the progress of acylation.

Ideally, continuous monitoring of resin functionality should be entirely non-invasive. There should be no intervention for the removal of resin samples, nor for the addition of analytical reagents to the bulk resin. The efficiency of the synthetic chemistry is the overwhelmingly important factor in solid phase synthesis. There is serious risk that addition of extraneous reagents will be deleterious. Furthermore, residual amino groups remaining on the resin support because they have failed to react with the acylating amino acid derivative are equally likely not to react with added analytical reagent, unless this is a simple protonating species. The analytical process must be quick and the results displayed continuously to the operator. It should preferably be entirely automatic, with the results capable of being computer-processed and checked against acceptable limits as they are obtained. Effectively, this again precludes washing, drying, weighing and analysis of multiple resin samples except as a post-synthesis procedure.

Realization of a near-ideal solid phase monitoring system became possible with the introduction of esters of 3,4-dihydro-3-hydroxy-4-oxobenzotriazine (Section 7.2.2) into continuous-flow solid phase synthesis (*39,97*). It was observed that during acylation of amino resins by Fmoc-amino acid esters (**107**) of this alcohol, a bright yellow coloration appeared on the resin and faded as the reaction proceeded. When acylation was complete, as judged by a negative ninhydrin test for residual amino groups, the resin has returned close to its initial off-white state. There was no coloration of the recirculating liquid. This transient coloration of the amino resin alone was clearly due to formation of the ion pair (**108**), the triazine component being liberated from the active ester as acylation proceeded.

The resin coloration can be used (*39,97*) as a simple visual indication of completion of acylation, and has been judged by experienced users as probably as sensitive as the ninhydrin and trinitrobenzene sulphonic acid colour tests (Section 9.1). The alcohol (**109**) may also be used as an internal indicator in combination with other acylating species (*39*), though caution will be necessary in view of the multiple equilibria which may be involved. Some preliminary tests will be required in each case to ensure that other weakly acidic species which may be formed as co-products of the particular acylation reaction (carboxylic acids, phenols, hydroxybenzotriazole) do not suppress the ionization of (**109**), and thus quench the colour prematurely.

A solid phase photometric device (*Figures 29,30*) has been constructed to measure the intensity of the resin colour, and the data used directly in feedback control of synthesis (*98,99*). Since at the time of writing this device is not commercially available, the laboratory instrument is described in some detail.

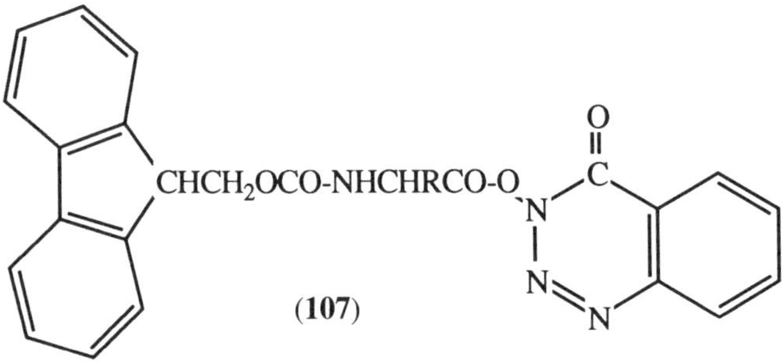

$CHCH_2OCO\text{-}NHCHRCO\text{-}O$

(**107**)

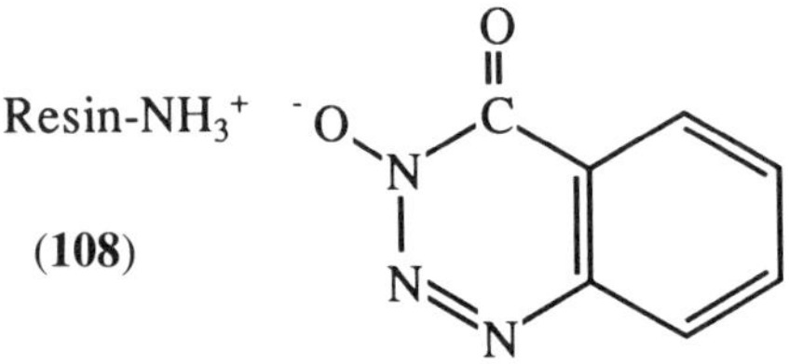

Resin-NH_3^+ ^-O

(**108**)

HO

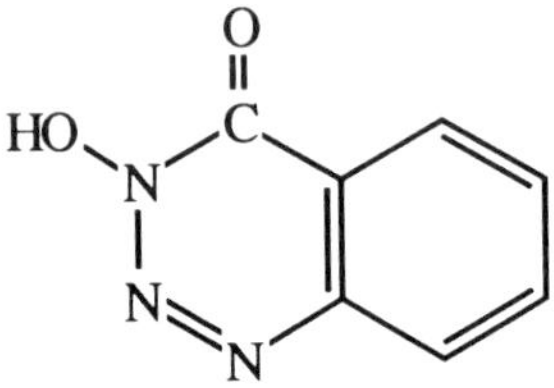

(**109**)

The Kieselguhr-supported resin (*47,49*) presently used in Fmoc-polyamide continuous-flow synthesis is only translucent and, with the limited sensitivity detector initially employed, required a narrow resin bed and a concentrated light source. The resin is contained in a standard chromatographic column (*Figure 29,d*) which has been narrowed and flattened. A resin bed of uniform thickness about 4 mm has proved appropriate. Light from a low-voltage quartz–halogen lamp (a) is focused by lenses (c) on to the surface of the resin, and the diffused, larger light patch on the far side of the resin bed focused again on to the semiconductor photodetector (f). A narrow bandpass filter (e) with maximum transmission at 440 nm is placed immediately in front of the photodetector. The filter, photodetector and integral preamplifier employed in this prototype were originally designed for use in an LKB amino acid analyser.

The detector has maximum sensitivity at much longer wavelength than that employed here, and incident long-wavelength stray light was eliminated by placing the 440 nm filter immediately in front of the detector with a light-tight seal. To minimize exposure of the resin–benzotriazine complex to the high-intensity light source, a mechanical shutter mechanism (b) is interposed between the lamp source and the focusing lens. This is opened automatically for the duration of each reading. Both electromagnetic solenoid and pneumatic actuators have been employed satisfactorily, though the latter is to be preferred, giving a more controlled, less jarring opening and closing action. Use of the shutter enables exposure of the resin bed to be reduced twenty-fold or more.

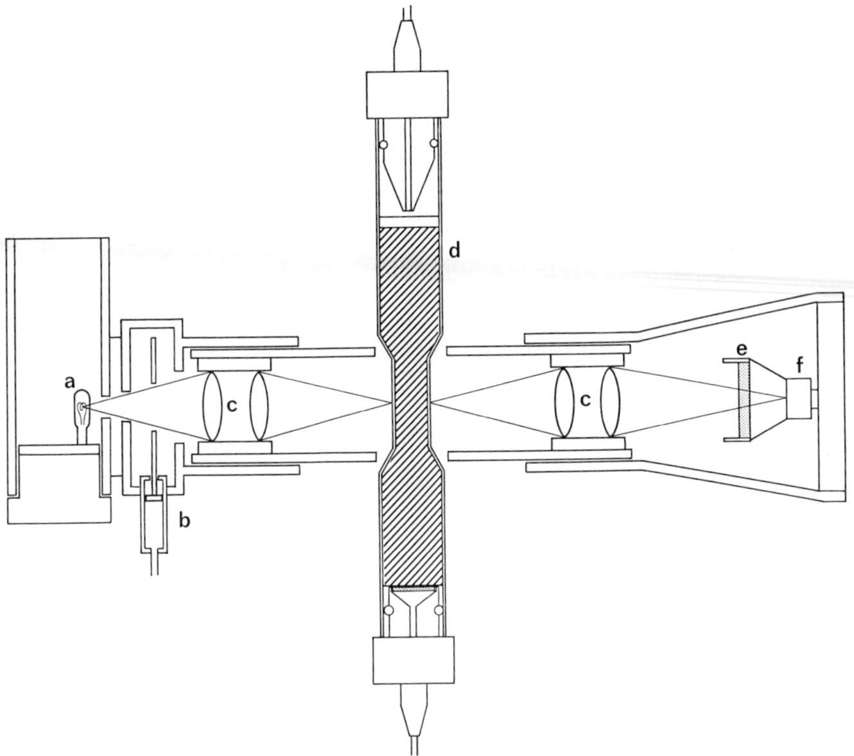

Figure 29. Photometer for measuring colour intenstiy on the solid phase.

Alternatively photodegradation has been eliminated by inserting a second narrow bandpass filter between the first condenser lens and the column reactor (114). A gallium arsenide photodiode detector with enhanced sensitivity at shorter wavelengths has also been employed successfully.

Solid phase photometric system for monitoring acylation reactions

The general layout is illustrated in *Figure 29* and the construction in *Figure 30*. The casing is of turned aluminium in three parts, comprising lamp housing and shutter assembly, optics and column holder, and photodetector and filter assembly. The miniature 12 V, 20 W quartz–halogen lamp is mounted off-centre in a cylindrical holder adjustable for height and rotation. The electrical leads connecting the two-pin lamp socket are firmly tied back to a terminal block mounted on the outside of the holder assembly. A separate 24 V muffin fan directs a cooling airstream through and around the cylindrical housing. The lamp is mounted as close as practicable to a sliding shutter assembly actuated by an internal miniature pneumatic cylinder (Clippard Minimatic type SM-3-3; see Appendix). This is connected through external regulator (45 psi) and needle valves to an electrically switchable nitrogen supply.

Figure 30. Prototype laboratory implementation of the solid phase photometer. See text for details of construction.

The complete lamp and shutter assembly is a sliding fit on to a central column housing turned to size to accommodate focusing lenses (eyepieces from low-power binoculars were found suitable), at each end. The central part is cut away at the front to accommodate the column reactor which is gripped firmly by two Terry clips; a detachable, half-cylindrical plate covers the central part of the column when in use while still leaving the upper and lower parts of the resin bed visible.

The photodetector assembly consists of a small circular printed circuit board with a centrally mounted phototransistor/operational amplifier ic (Radiospares, type RS 308-067; see Appendix) and passive components. The circuit board is adjustable in the plane orthogonal to the light beam, and the entire detector assembly slides on the column holder along the axis of the light beam. The 440 nm narrow bandpass filter (LKB part no. 41440022) is mounted in a light-tight holder fitting directly over the photodetector. The output from the photodetector is connected to a 0.2/2V dual-range digital voltmeter and to analogue input (Biodata Microlink AN1) and 12-bit A/D converter (Biodata Microlink A12D) units. The controlling Hewlett-Packard HP85 computer is connected through an IEEE 488 interface.

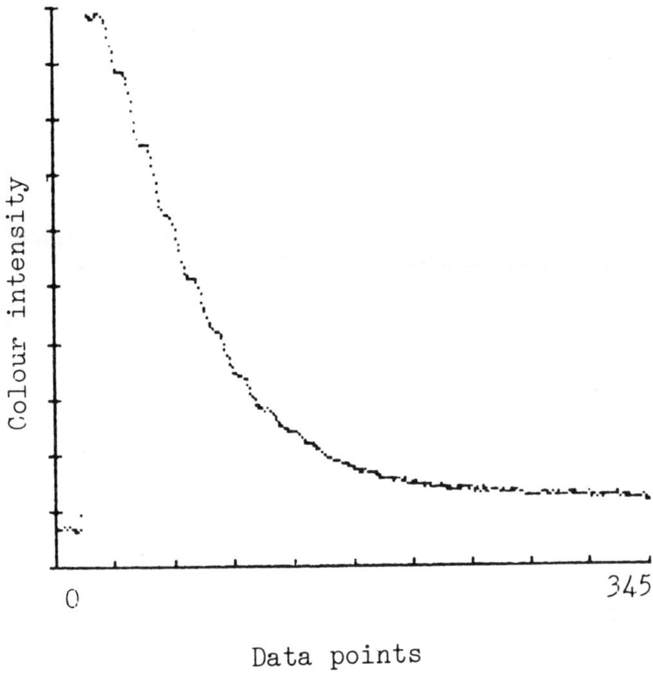

Figure 31. Raw data showing the sharp rise and slower fall in colour of the solid support as the Fmoc-amino acid Dhbt ester contacts the amino resin and acylation proceeds.

Depending on the resin used, the output from the photodetector swings up to about 100 mV when the resin passes from its white to yellow state and vice versa, and is easily measured directly or through a 10- or 12-bit analogue-to-digital converter. The digitized output may be sampled by the controlling microcomputer at regular preset intervals and processed and displayed directly.

The output for an early model coupling reaction, that of Fmoc-valine Dhbt ester to isoleucyl-resin, is illustrated in *Figure 31* (*99*). The controlling system was set to collect 345 readings at 12-sec intervals, giving a total data collection period of 69 min. Plateauing of the colour density indicated that under the particular reaction conditions, this very hindered coupling was complete after about 40 min into this period. The fluctuations in the descending trace of *Figure 31* correspond in position and diminishing relative amplitude to the typical recirculation pattern observed simultaneously for the liquid phase using a flow cell (*Figure 24*). They are thus due to end absorption by the acylating species (**107**) and unionized hydroxy component (**109**) in solution. The normal unsupported polydimethylacrylamide gel swells about 10-fold in DMF, so that after allowing for the inert Kieselguhr element, probably considerably more than half of the column volume is occupied by recirculating liquid. These fluctuations are easily removed or reduced by averaging the data over a time corresponding approximately to the liquid recirculation period.

During peptide synthesis, the photometric data are conveniently presented as shown in *Figure 32*. Introduction of the Dhbt ester is indicated by the near-vertical solid line

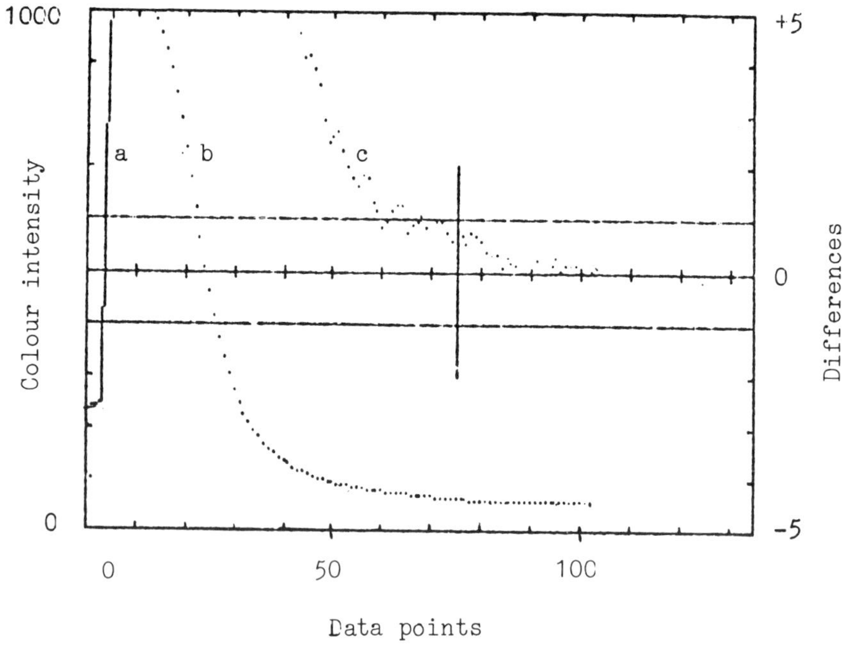

Figure 32. Presentation of the data in an automatic control system. The differences curve (c) is sensed by the computer to determine the acylation end point (see text).

(a) corresponding to the rapid white-to-yellow transition of the resin. Since only the data corresponding to the later stages of the acylation reaction are quantitatively important, the photometer sensitivity is usually adjusted so that the initial colour intensity is substantially over scale in the early stages. The initial rise in photometer output may be sensed by the controlling microprocessor to verify previous deprotection (see below) and correct sample introduction.

During acylation, data averaging commences after sufficient readings have been collected, and the rolling average (b) is plotted on a vertical scale of 0 − 1000.* It falls smoothly with little contribution from the recirculating liquid. To detect the plateau point, the differences between successive data readings are evaluated and are also displayed on the screen (c) at the much enhanced sensitivity of −5 to +5 units full scale. The arbitrary criterion that five successive difference points should lie between the +1 and −1 delimiters shown has been adopted as an indicator for completion of the reaction. Additionally, the colour intensity plot should have fallen below the 400 ordinate but not below zero. This prevents premature termination if the density readings are over- or under-range (when the differences between successive digitized values become zero), and helps to ensure that extremely slow reactions do not cause false termination by nearly plateauing at an early stage. There is in our view no great merit in striving to achieve maximum speed in the conduct of solid phase peptide synthesis

*Resolution in the figures is limited by the visual display unit to 192 (vertical) × 256 points.

at the expense of product purity, and our current controlling program therefore allows an additional arbitrarily fixed safety period after the above termination criteria have been met. Currently this is 10 min in the laboratory prototype, but more logically it should be a fixed fraction of the reaction time already elapsed. If automatic termination does not occur within the preset data collection period, acylation continues for a maximum of 999 minutes before proceeding automatically to the next step. This allows ample time for operator intervention if desired. It is of course a simple matter to program the controller to carry out alternative automatic actions, including safe shut-down or alarm signals if preferred.

More sophisticated software has also been written (*114*) which allows continuous data collection until termination. The fixed-length data array is compacted when full by discarding alternate data points and continuing data collection at double the previous time interval. Data presentation then becomes similar for both fast and slow reactions with differing time-scaling along the horizontal axis.

Operation of the prototype system in actual synthesis has been extremely encouraging. The upper and lower parts of the resin bed remain exposed for visual checking of reaction progress. It is essential to maintain an undisturbed, uniformly packed resin bed as far as possible; only the top of the resin bed clear of the light path should be disturbed for the removal of samples for amino acid analysis or for any confirmatory colour tests thought necessary, and the downwards direction of liquid flow should not be reversed. The baseline position is altered if the recirculating solution becomes yellow. This is usually due to incomplete washing of all traces of piperidine from the system after the deprotection step. The column end-piece (*Figure 29*) should be designed so that liquid does not become trapped around the sealing O-ring. The liquid level is set initially below the orifice of this end-piece, and in the laboratory instrument depicted in *Figures 15* and *19* is stable under low-pressure conditions. The lower column fitting appears to be relatively unimportant.

Solid phase monitoring of acylation reactions by this method is at a relatively early stage in development. A number of enhancements can be envisaged, particularly development of more transparent supports and of more sensitive detector systems.

Use of the automated solid phase monitoring system has been described for synthesis of the difficult acyl carrier protein decapeptide sequence residues 65–74 (**110**) (*98*) and for a nonadecapeptide sequence (**111**) (*99*). Slowing of coupling reactions at sterically hindered residues was easily detected, as was the extreme hindrance due to the previously recognized internal aggregation effect in the acyl carrier protein synthesis.

The possible extension of solid phase monitoring to deprotection reactions has been discussed (*99*). In principle, the colour produced by reaction of the deprotected resin with the triazine (**107**) should be a measure of amino group concentration, and hence of deprotection efficiency. This technique has been investigated briefly (*Figure 33*)

H-Val-Gln-Ala-Ala-Ile-Asp-Tyr-Ile-Asn-Gly-OH (**110**)

H-Asp-Asp-Glu-Val-Asp-Val-Asp-Gly-Thr-Val-Glu-Glu-Asp-Leu-Gly-Lys-Ser-Tyr-Gly-OH (**111**)

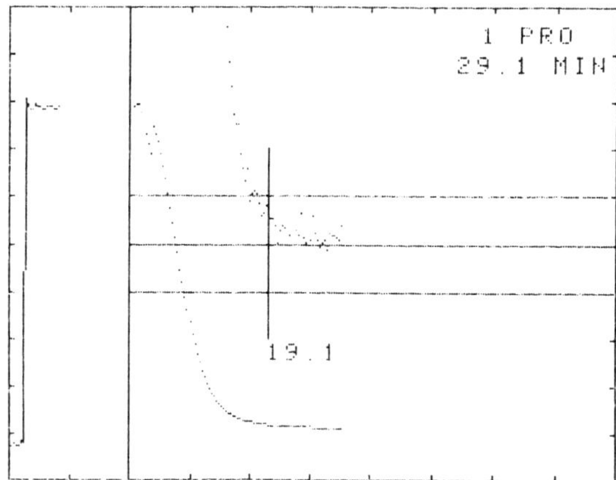

Figure 33. Extension of the solid phase monitoring system to include assessment of deprotection efficiency. The trace is produced by flowing Dhbt-OH through the amino resin, followed by the Fmoc-amino acid Dhbt ester.

but there are problems of linearity and calibration yet to be studied. A more interesting approach may be to use a coloured amino-protecting group, cleavage of which generates a falling solid phase spectrometic deprotection record analogous to *Figure 31*. Clearly such a new protecting group will need to absorb at a very different wavelength in the visible spectrum to that of resin–triazine complex (**108**). All this is for the future!

CHAPTER 10

Reaction procedures and operating techniques

Peptide synthesis using the Fmoc-polyamide technique may be broken down into four stages.

(1) The polyamide resin (beaded gel or physically supported) is functionalized, usually complete with an internal reference amino acid and an appropriate linkage agent.
(2) The first Fmoc-amino acid is attached (esterified) to the resin-bound linkage agent and the Fmoc protecting group removed.
(3) The peptide chain is assembled through successive deprotection and acylation reactions.
(4) The peptide–resin linkage is cleaved (usually with simultaneous removal of all or most of the side-chain-protecting groups) and the free peptide is isolated and purified.

Conditions for peptide cleavage and purification vary depending upon the amino acid composition and overall properties of the peptide and are discussed separately in Chapter 11. In the following discussion, reaction protocols are presented for steps 1–3 for both beaded gel (discontinuous, shaking technique) and Kieselguhr-supported resin (continuous-flow technique).

These protocols have been developed over a number of years. Those for the beaded gel resin considerably antedate those for the more modern continuous-flow technique. Advancing knowledge and increased confidence has led to changes in technique, particularly, for example, in the use of smaller excesses of acylating species as experience has grown and the efficiency of the system has been recognized. The procedures described may therefore differ in detail from those published in the earlier literature, but represent current laboratory practice.

The precise details of technique to be employed will vary depending upon the instrumentation in use as well as on the sequence to be synthesized. In the following, two generalized techniques are described, suitable respectively for beaded gel resins using simple shaken or nitrogen-agitated equipment and for physically supported gels using pumped-flow instruments. The beaded gel resin should be suspended in DMF and allowed to swell for at least 30 min before use. The Kieselguhr-supported resin may be packed in the reactor column as a slurry in DMF or by adding the dry resin slowly through a small glass funnel to the DMF-filled column. Solvent is removed by pumping under manual control as the column is filled with resin. If problems with high pressure are encountered, these are usually due to the presence of fine particles in the resin which may be removed by repeatedly swirling the resin in DMF, decanting, and repacking the column directly with the slurry. The porous ptfe supporting filters in the column reactor should be changed at the start of each synthesis.

Most users of the Fmoc-polyamide technique will purchase commercially available polydimethylacrylamide resins (Pepsyn, Macrosorb SPR, Pepsyn K, Ultrasyn). For others, preparative details have been given in Chapter 4. The commercial resin is available both in the simple methyl ester form, and also fully functionalized with an internal reference norleucine residue and acid- or base-labile linkage agents. Users of these functionalized resins require only to esterify the first amino acid residue (Section 10.2) before commencing peptide synthesis proper. Very recently a range of 20 Kieselguhr resins with individual Fmoc-amino acids attached through the usual acid-labile linkage agent have been catalogued by Milligen and by Pharmacia-LKB (see Appendix). Users of these supports proceed directly with elaboration of the peptide chain (Section 10.3).

10.1 **Resin functionalization**

The beaded gel and Kieselguhr-supported methyl ester resins (**66b**) require treatment with ethylene diamine to generate the aminoethyl resin (**66c**). Neat diamine is used to minimize the cross linking side reactions. Methanolic ethylene diamine is unsatisfactory. The conversion is often carried out on a small scale immediately before use. Large quantitites of resin can be handled; the amino-polymer is not usually stored as such, but a protected internal reference amino-acid (usually norleucine) is added immediately (Chapter 6).

Aminoethyl functionalized polydimethylacrylamide resin (41,49)

The beaded resin is covered with redistilled ethylene diamine in a round-bottom flask and the flask stoppered firmly and shaken gently overnight using a wrist-action shaker. Next morning the ethylene diamine is removed by decantation and the resin washed with DMF first by decantation and then on a sintered glass funnel or in the peptide synthesizer reaction vessel until the fitrate gives a negative test with ninhydrin.*

The physically supported resin may be converted with ethylene diamine similarly, but extra caution should be taken to avoid over-vigorous agitation and the generation of fine particles. Continuous agitation is unnecessary, and a suitable timing mechanism may be used to switch the wrist shaker on for 0.5 min, off for 10 min for about 100 cycles or overnight. Stirring, especially with a magnetic bar which has a strong grinding effect, should not be used. After the initial washing by decantation, the DMF-wet resin may be packed in the reaction column and DMF pumped through until the effluent gives a negative colour test with ninhydrin.*

Addition of a permanently bound internal reference amino acid is not essential but is a useful adjunct to amino acid analysis in following the course of peptide synthesis (Section 9.2). An amino acid residue not present in the peptide sequence to be assembled, commonly a readily available non-protein amino acid such as norleucine, is usually chosen. Acylation of the resin-bound aminoethyl group may be carried out using symmetrical anhydride or pentafluorophenyl ester intermediates, and is usually completely straightforward.

*Some users prefer to carry out a standard Fmoc-deprotection cycle here to ensure complete removal of ethylene diamine.

Fmoc-norleucyl-polydimethylacrylamide resin

This simple coupling reaction can be carried out in the synthesizer reaction vessel or column reactor in the usual manner (Section 10.3), or on a large scale more conveniently in a round-bottomed flask. Typically, the well-washed and drained aminoethyl resin is treated with freshly prepared (Section 7.1) Fmoc-norleucine anhydride (2 eq) or pentafluorophenyl ester (2 eq) and hydroxybenzotriazole catalyst (2 eq) in the minimum volume of DMF to make a mobile slurry. The mixture is swirled gently at frequent intervals for 1 h. The ninhydrin reaction (Section 9.1) should be negative after 15–25 min. The mixture is then washed well with DMF on a sintered glass filter funnel or in the synthesizer reaction vessel. Ten DMF washes should be used for the beaded gel resin; Kieselguhr resin is washed in the column reactor until there is no further fall in UV absorption at 304 nm (0.1 mm flow cell) or 312 nm (1 mm flow cell). A sample of the resin (10–20 mg) is washed further with ether, dried in a vacuum desiccator and subjected to quantitative amino acid analysis after removal of the Fmoc group (Section 9.2) to determine the loading.

The bulk resin may be dried and stored at this stage, but it is usually more convenient to convert it to a directly useful state by addition of the appropriate linkage agent.

Hydroxymethylphenoxyacetyl-norleucyl-polydimethylacrylamide resin (Hmpa-Nle-resin)

(1) *Beaded gel resin.* The foregoing Fmoc-norleucyl-resin is subjected to a typical cycle of deprotection and acylation. The resin is placed in the reaction vessel and washed (5 × 1 min) with DMF (typically 15 ml g^{-1} resin–the minimum volume required to produce a mobile slurry varies slightly with different batches of resin), and then twice with 20% piperidine in DMF (15 ml g^{-1}, 3 min and 7 min). The drained resin is washed (10 × 1 min) with DMF, hydroxybenzotriazole (3 eq dissolved in DMF, 7.5 ml g^{-1} resin) added and shaken for 1 min, followed without draining by 2,4,5-trichlorophenyl 4-hydroxymethylphenoxyacetate (3 eq dissolved in DMF 7.5 ml g^{-1}). The mixture is shaken for 1 h; the ninhydrin test should be negative after about 30 min. It is unusual to obtain positive colour reactions in this and the foregoing acylations. If the reaction is not complete after 1 h this is an indication of system-associated problems, and the coupling should be repeated after investigation. After completion of each acylation, excess reagents are removed with 5 × 1 min DMF washes (15 ml g^{-1} resin).

(2) *Kieselguhr-supported resin.* Addition of the linkage agent is conveniently carried out using the normal deprotection–acylation steps of continuous-flow synthesis. The sequence of operations given in *Table 11* (Section 10.3.2.1) (*49*) is typical. The washed resin is deprotected by flowing 20% piperidine in DMF for 10 min, washed with DMF for a total of 25 min, and a mixture of 2,4,5-trichlorophenyl 4-hydroxymethylphenoxyacetate (2 eq) and hydroxybenzotriazole (2 eq) dissolved in DMF (*c.* 4 ml $mmol^{-1}$) introduced through a sample loop (automatic synthesizer) or through a manual loading port or directly on to the column (manual

instrument). The solution is rinsed on to the column with further DMF (*c*. 2 ml $mmol^{-1}$) in the case of manual loading. Recirculation is continued for about 40 min. A negative ninhydrin test should be obtained after 25 min. Excess reagent is removed by washing for 12 min.

On a large scale, these reactions can be conveniently carried out in a round-bottomed flask.

The commercially available pentafluorophenyl ester may be used equally satisfactorily, as may symmetrical anhydride freshly prepared in dichloromethane in the same manner as for Fmoc-amino acids (Section 7.1). Self-acylation does not appear to be a significant side reaction in the absence of basic catalysts. Other linkage agents can be added similarly; 2,4,5-trichlorophenyl 4-hydroxymethylbenzoate appears to react more slowly.

10.2 **Attachment of the first amino acid**

In most Fmoc-polyamide (and Fmoc-polystyrene) peptide synthesis, the first amino acid is attached to the resin through an ester bond. The ester has the lability associated with the particular linkage agent previously attached to the resin, which provides the hydroxy component of the ester group. Exceptionally, for linkage agents of the benzhydrylamine type (Chapter 6) which are cleaved by acids to generate peptide amides directly, the first amino acid is attached through an amide bond. This presents no special problems and may be carried out as the first of the normal peptide coupling reactions (Section 10.3).

Formation of ester bonds is usually considerably more difficult than that of amide bonds, and special care needs to be taken if complete coverage of resin hydroxyl groups is to be obtained. Maximum concentration of a larger excess than normal of activated Fmoc-amino acid is used, and an esterification catalyst, usually 4-dimethylamino-pyridine, is required. This catalyst is able to promote hydrolysis of the activated Fmoc-amino acid as well as reaction with resin-bound hydroxyl groups, so scrupulously dry resin and solvent are necessary. Resin which has been prepared beforehand and stored as a dry powder should be redried in a vacuum desiccator over phosphorus pentoxide. Resins stored wet with DMF should be well washed with freshly distilled, dry DMF before reaction. Dimethylaminopyridine also significantly promotes the racemization of activated urethane-protected amino acids (*132*). In practice it is found that esterification with a large excess (5 eq) of Fmoc-amino acid anhydride and 1 eq or less of dimethylaminopyridine (relative to resin functionality) is usually complete or nearly complete (>90% of norleucine content) within 45–60 min as determined by amino acid analysis. In case of difficulty, it is better to repeat the esterification with fresh reagents than to prolong the reaction unduly. Residual hydroxyl groups may be masked by acetylation (see p. 136), but in the absence of basic catalysts they do not seem to act as growth points for the gradual development of new peptide chains during synthesis. A possibly exceptional situation is in the synthesis of histidine-containing peptides, where any free imidazole group may catalyse further esterification. For synthesis of histidyl peptides, acetylation of residual hydroxyl groups is recommended.

Possible racemization during attachment of the first residue is an important consideration. This was first encountered during syntheses in the gastrin series which has phenylalanine amide as the carboxy-terminal residue (*128*). A study of the esterification to the resin of Fmoc-isoleucine and separation of resulting diastereoisomers showed that racemization is low (<2% D-isomer) providing low concentrations of catalyst dimethylaminopyridine are used, and prior contact of the activated amino acid and the basic catalyst is strictly avoided (*132*). A more general method for monitoring racemization of carboxy terminal residues is to couple a small amount of deprotected resin with a second, racemization-proof optically pure amino acid derivative and to separate any diastereoisomeric dipeptide (by ion-exchange chromatography on an amino acid analyser or by hplc) after cleavage (*115*). Authentic diasteromer pairs may be generated by coupling the corresponding DL-amino acid. Boc-L-leucine *p*-nitrophenyl ester and its DL counterpart have been used successfully in our laboratory (*115*) but the full range of amino acids and linkage agents have not yet been examined. Early results suggest that amino acids bearing electronegative substituents (hetero-atoms, carbonyl groups) on the β-carbon atom may be most at risk (*115*).

Pentafluorophenyl esters may often be used in place of anhydrides, but their reactivity appears to be appreciably smaller.

Esterification of the first Fmoc-amino acid residue using anhydrides.

(1) *Beaded gel resin.* The hydroxymethylphenoxyacetylnorleucyl resin is washed with DMF (*c.* 15 ml g^{-1}; 5 × 1 min). Freshly prepared Fmoc-amino acid anhydride (Section 7.1) (5 eq dissolved in *c.* 14 ml DMF g^{-1} resin) is added and the mixture agitated for 1 min, followed by 4-dimethylaminopyridine (1 eq dissolved in *c.* 1 ml DMF g^{-1} resin). Agitation is continued for 1 h. Excess reagents are then removed by thorough washing with DMF (10 × 1 min).

(2) *Kieselguhr-supported resin* (*49*). The Fmoc-amino acid anhydride (5 eq) dissolved in the minimum volume of DMF is loaded manually or automatically on to the reactor column containing the hydroxymethylphenoxyacetylnorleucyl resin and washed on with further DMF (0.5–1 ml). 4-Dimethylaminopyridine (1 eq) is similarly dissolved in the minimum volume of DMF, applied to the column and rinsed on. The instrument is set in recirculation mode and acylation allowed to proceed for 45 min to 1 h. Excess reagents are removed by washing with DMF for 10 min. The reaction may also be carried out in a gently agitated round-bottomed flask using the same proportions of reagents and the minimum volume of DMF to make a mobile slurry. Excess reagents are removed by filtration and thorough washing on the filter.

The same techniques are used for 4-hydroxymethylbenzoyl resin. The 3-methoxy-4-hydroxymethylphenoxyacetyl resin reacts more slowly, and repeated acylation after washing is recommended. In general, anhydrides are recommended for the more sterically hindered residues (valine, isoleucine, O-*t*-butyl-threonine) or otherwise difficult (arginine) residues. Two acylations, each of 45–60 min, are recommended for pentafluorophenyl esters of amino acids other than glycine. Exceptionally for glycine where there is no potential racemization problem, an amount of dimethylaminopyridine equivalent to the Fmoc-glycine anhydride or pentafluorophenyl ester may be used. Some commercial resin samples have been reported to react more slowly in the esterification step than others.

A new method of esterification (*101*) of considerable promise involves the use of thiophene dioxide esters (**101**) (Section 7.2.3). These undergo base-catalysed trans-esterification with resin-bound hydroxyl groups without the need for dimethylamino-pyridine, and appear to be correspondingly free from racemization. They react more rapidly than do pentafluorophenyl esters in the presence of dimethylaminopyridine. In the cases thus far studied, the yields have been good.

Attachment of Fmoc-alanine TDO ester to Pepsyn gel resin (101)

A suspension of the dry functionalized gel resin (0.2 meq norleucine) in DMF (15 ml) was shaken gently with Fmoc-alanine TDO ester (0.356 g, 0.6 mmol) and diisopropylethylamine (0.102 ml, 0.6 mmol) for 2 h at room temperature. The red solution was filtered and the resin washed thoroughly with DMF. Amino acid analysis showed that the incorporation of alanine was quantitative.

No colour tests are presently available to test for completion of the esterification reaction, though the procedure using TDO esters has potential for spectroscopic monitoring (*101*). Amino acid incorporation relative to the internal reference amino acid is usually determined by acidic hydrolysis and amino acid analysis (Section 9.2). The Fmoc-protecting group must be removed from the analytical sample before hydrolysis. If incorporation of the first amino acid is unsatisfactory, that is, its ratio to the internal reference amino acid is less than say 0.9:1, then the esterification may be repeated. Alternatively, the residual hydroxyl groups may be masked by acetylation and the synthesis continued.

Low concentrations of residual hydroxyl groups on the resin do not usually interfere with subsequent peptide synthesis. The risk of their acting as growth points for new peptide chains is slight, though some users make a general practice of blocking residual hydroxyl groups by acetylation after addition of the first amino acid residue. This is to be commended for synthesis of histidine-containing peptides, where any free imidazole groups that might arise during the synthesis through partial deprotection of the histidine residue could catalyse further esterification.

Acetylation after addition of the first Fmoc-amino acid

The esterification procedure described above for Fmoc-amino acid anhydrides (or pentafluorophenyl esters) is repeated on the washed (DMF) resin using acetic anhydride (2 eq) in place of the amino acid derivative, together with dimethyl-aminopyridine (1 eq). Excess reagents are removed by thorough washing as before.

Before proceeding to the peptide-bond-forming steps, the terminal Fmoc protecting group of the first amino acid is removed. This follows the standard deprotection procedures given in the sections following (for example *Table 9*, step 7; *Table 11*, step 9), and is not described separately here. The acylation and deprotection cycle is merely started at the appropriate point depending on whether the resin is currently in its free amino or Fmoc-protected form.

10.3 **Assembly of the peptide chain**

Addition of each successive amino acid residue involves a reaction and washing cycle containing the following steps.

(1) Preliminary washing of the polymer support bearing the first or previous deprotected amino acids.
(2) Dissolution of the activated Fmoc-amino acid and addition to the washed polymer support.
(3) Gentle agitation of the resin slurry or continuous circulation of the solution through the resin bed during the reaction period.
(4) Removal of co-products and excess reagents by thorough washing.
(5) Cleavage of the new terminal Fmoc-protecting group by treatment with 20% piperidine.
(6) Washing of the protecting group reaction product from the resin together with excess cleavage reagent.

DMF is used as the sole solvent and washing agent in all the steps.

Additional operations are required for analytical control. In the absence of instrumentation for continuous monitoring of acylation reactions (Sections 9.4, 9.5), determination of completion of acylation by colour reactions (Section 9.1) on withdrawn resin samples is strongly recommended. Only when familiar sequences are being assembled or when overnight or unattended synthesis (of straightforward sequences) is positively required should these simple tests be dispensed with. Resin samples should also be removed from time to time for later hydrolysis and amino acid analysis (Section 9.2).

Peptide bond formation may be carried out using Fmoc-amino acid anhydrides, pentafluorophenyl esters (with or without addition of catalyst 1-hydroxy-benzotriazole), or 3,4-dihydro-4-oxobenzotriazin-3-yl esters. Illustrative protocols are provided below for these procedures using both beaded gel and physically supported gel resins. Other activated intermediates have been used from time to time (for example *p*-nitrophenyl and trichlorophenyl esters) but these have been essentially superseded by the above. Doubtless other activation procedures can also be used, but are not recommended here because they have not been tested in our laboratory. Some have been tested and found unsatisfactory, for example esters of N-hydroxysuccinimide.

10.3.1 *Synthesis using beaded gel polydimethylacrylamide resin*

The manual systems required to handle beaded gel resins conveniently are the shaken Merrifield-type cell (*Figure 9*) or the bubbler (*Figure 11*) (Section 8.1). Most commercial instruments designed for polystyrene gel can probably also be used. Essentially the same reaction protocol is used in both systems. Reagents DMF and 20% piperidine in DMF may be introduced manually using a Zippette (Jencons Scientific; see Appendix) or other automatic pipette. Connection of the Merrifield reaction cell to the simple two-valve system of *Figure 10* greatly increases the convenience of reagent addition. A simple

Table 9. Typical reaction protocol for peptide assembly on beaded gel resins. The volumes given are for 1 g of resin and for the acylation step should correspond to the minimum required to make a mobile slurry.

		Volume (ml)	*Time (min)*	*Repeat*
Prewash	1. Wash DMF.	15	1	5
Acylation	2. Preformed Fmoc-amino acid anhydride or Pfp ester and HOBt, or Dhbt ester (2–3 eq[a]) dissolved in DMF and added to the drained resin.	10–15		
	3. Agitate gently.		30	
Test	4. Remove resin sample for colour test.			
	5. Continue agitation.	Variable		
Wash	6. Wash DMF.	15	1	10
Deprotect	7. Add 20% piperidine in DMF.	15	3	
	8. Drain and repeat.	15	7	
Wash	9. Wash DMF.	15	1	5
Test	10. Remove resin sample for colour test.			

[a]This may be increased as the synthesis proceeds if the acylation steps show signs of slowing.

timer is necessary to signal the end of each operation and *each completed step must be recorded immediately in a laboratory notebook if confusion is to be avoided.* A typical notebook record for the assembly of a pentapeptide using anhydride coupling of the first amino acid and Dhbt and pentafluorophenyl esters thereafter is shown later (*Table 10*).

The dry resin with the C-terminal residue added is transferred to the reaction vessel or bubbler, and enough DMF added to form a mobile slurry. After 30 min gentle agitation the gel will be fully swollen and ready for the first step of the cycle of amino acid addition. A typical protocol for handling 1 g of the beaded gel (1 meq g^{-1}) is shown in *Table 9*. Exceptionally, at the start of a new synthesis or when an ongoing synthesis has been interrupted and the peptide resin stored with its Fmoc-protecting group attached, the protocol is begun by preliminary washing (step 1) followed by deprotection (steps 7–10).

After each step the resin is drained by the application of nitrogen pressure in the case of the shaker and by suction in the bubbling system. The first step, 5 × 1 min washes of the resin with DMF, is followed by acylation with either the preformed symmetrical anhydride of the appropriate activated ester derivative (2–3 eqs) dissolved (usually with hydroxybenzotriazole in the case of pentafluorophenyl esters) in the appropriate volume of DMF. This is the minimum volume to give a mobile resin slurry which can be agitated easily. There should be only a thin layer (*c.* 2 mm) of clear liquid over the settled resin. The symmetrical anhydride is prepared immediately before use (Section 7.1) and is freshly dissolved in the DMF just prior to addition to the resin. The concentration of the activated derivative in the DMF solution should preferably be greater than about 0.13 M. After 30 min agitation a sample of the resin is removed, washed in a small sintered glass funnel and subjected to the colour tests for free amino groups (Section 9.1). It is advisable to test the reference sample taken as step 10 in

Table 10. Typical laboratory record for the synthesis of a pentapeptide

11/8/88 Synthesis of laminin pentapeptide Tyr-Ile-Gly-Ser-Arg
1.0 g HMPA-Nle-Pepsyn[a] 1.1 mequiv/g^{-1}
5.5 mmol Fmoc-Arg(Mtr)-OH (5-fold excess), 2.70 mmol DCCI (form anhydride)
1.1 mmol DMAP
2.75 mmol Fmoc-AA-OPFp/Dhbt (2.5-fold excess).

	Weight (g)	*Reacn time*	*DMF × 10*	*Nin. test*	*20% Pip. 3+7 min*	*DMF × 10*	*Nin. test*
Fmoc-Arg(Mtr)-OH[c]	3.21	1155–	/ / / / /	+ + +[b]	/ /	/ / / / /	+ + +
DCCI	0.56	1255	/ / / / /			/ / / / /	blue
DMAP	0.134						
Fmoc-Ser(Bu^t)-ODhbt	1.45	0920–	/ / / / /	– – –	/ /	/ / / / /	+ + +
		1020	/ / / / /			/ / / / /	blue
Fmoc-Gly-OPfp	1.27	1440–	/ / / / /	– – –	/ /	/ / / / /	+ + +
HOBt	0.37	1540	/ / / / /			/ / / / /	blue
Fmoc-Ile-OPfp	1.43	1645–	/ / / / /	– – –	/ /	/ / / / /	+ + +
HOBt	0.37	1745	/ / / / /			/ / / / /	blue
Fmoc-Tyr(Bu^t)-OPfp	1.72	0930–	/ / / / /	– – –	/ /	/ / / / /	+ + +
HOBt	0.37	1030	/ / / / /			/ / / / /	blue

[a]HMPA = hydroxymethylphenoxyacetyl (linkage agent).
[b]After a trial deprotection of a small resin sample to verify satisfactory esterification of the first residue.
[c]Preformed symmetrical anhydride (Section 7.1). Note that in this assembly, ninhydrin colour tests were carried out at 30 min into the acylation period and negative results were obtained in every case, but the operator preferred to allow acylation to proceed routinely for 1 h.

the previous cycle at the same time, since colours of amino peptide resins on polydimethylacrylamide tend to vary in intensity and hue, and a direct comparison is essential when determining completeness of reaction.

If the colour test is negative after 30 min reaction (as is commonly the case) then step 5 can be terminated and the cycle continued. Many operators, however, prefer to allow acylation to continue for the full 1 h period. If the test indicates incomplete acylation after 30 min, agitation is continued for a further 30 min and the procedure repeated. If after this time a positive colour test is still obtained, it is advisable to wash out the acylation mixture (5 × 1 min DMF) and repeat the acylation step with fresh activated derivative.

After the acylation is complete the resin is washed with DMF (step 6) and then deprotected with 20% piperidine in DMF (steps 7 and 8). This is carried out in two stages to allow for dilution by DMF contained in the swollen gel. The piperidine is largely removed by five more 1 min DMF washes (step 9), a fully deprotected reference resin sample is taken, washed (Section 9.1) and used for the colour test during the next acylation and for hydrolysis and amino acid analysis if required. After step 10 the cycle is complete and the resin is ready for step 1 of the next cycle. If the synthesis is to be halted at this stage, then further washing (step 1) should be carried out to remove all traces of piperidine.

10.3.2 *Continuous-flow synthesis using polydimethylacrylamide gel supported in macroporous Kieselguhr*

10.3.2.1 *Synthesis under manual control*

Instrumentation similar to that outlined in *Figure 12* (Section 8.3) is required. A flow cell and UV monitor are not absolutely necessary, but provide valuable confirmation that the various operations are proceeding normally. A simple clock or timer is also required, and a notebook in which the steps to be carried out are recorded in advance, and are checked off as they are completed. Freshly distilled DMF (Section 3.4) and freshly prepared 20% piperidine in DMF are placed in the two reservoirs. The physically supported resin, on which the internal reference amino acid, linkage agent, and first (carboxy-terminal) amino acid residue have usually already been assembled, is packed in the reaction column, either by pouring as a slurry or by tapping the dry resin into the column partially filled with DMF. Excess DMF is removed by pumping or with a Pasteur pipette as required. Space for a small (*c*. 5 mm) liquid layer and similar air-space should be left in the column above the resin. The column is then washed by pumping DMF for at least 5 min. The column should be free-flowing (removal of the top and bottom end connections allows DMF to drain freely under gravity), and negligible back pressure is generated during normal operation. If back pressure is experienced, it is almost invariably due to the presence of fines in the original resin and consequent blockage of the lower filter. It is good practice to replace the lower filter before each synthesis, and to fine commercial resin by slurrying and decantation with DMF if necessary.

A typical protocol for manually controlled synthesis is given in *Table 11*. Exceptionally, at the start of a new synthesis or when an ongoing synthesis has been interrupted and the peptide resin stored with its Fmoc-protecting group attached, the

Table 11. Typical protocol for manual continuous-flow synthesis.

		Time (min)
Prewash	1. Flow DMF	Variable[b]
Acylation	2. Apply preformed Fmoc-amino acid anhydride or activated ester solution (2–3 eq[a]) to the reactor column and rinse on.	
	3. Recirculate.	20–30
	4. Pause. Remove resin sample.	
	5. Recirculate.	Variable[b]
Wash	6. Flow DMF.	7
	7. Recirculate.	0.5
	8. Flow DMF.	5
Deprotect	9. Flow 20% piperidine–DMF.	10
Wash	10. Flow DMF	8
	11. Pause. Remove resin sample.	
	12. Flow DMF.	10

[a]This may be increased as the synthesis proceeds if the acylation steps show signs of slowing.
[b]See text.

protocol is begun by preliminary washing (step 1) followed by deprotection (steps 9–12).

The times given for each operation are not rigidly fixed. Thus after the first residue has been added, the final wash (step 12) is followed immediately by the prewash (step 1) for the following residue, and the latter is usually omitted. On the other hand, the prewash is valuable at the start of the synthesis and after any substantial (such as overnight) pause, when on restart a small amount of UV-absorbing material is sometimes washed from the column. Our practice is to remove the reactor column at the end of each day's synthesis and to store it, capped at both ends, in a refrigerator or freezer. At least 5 min should be allowed for the prewash after an overnight halt, and 30 min for a start from dry resin. The freshly prepared symmetrical anhydride or activated ester derivative should be dissolved in the minimum amount of DMF (typically 1–2 ml/ 0.2 meq. of resin) before addition, in order to achieve a high initial concentration. It is applied either directly to the top of the reactor column, pumped into the resin bed and rinsed on with DMF (0.5–1 ml), or through a sample chamber as shown in *Figure 12*. The sample chamber should be rinsed with sufficient DMF to clear the line to the flow recirculate valve. Catalyst hydroxybenzotriazole if used may be dissolved along with the activated ester, or added separately if preferred. The total volume introduced through the sample chamber must not exceed that of the recirculation loop. This is ensured if no increase in UV absorption is indicated by the spectrometer during sample addition.

At step 4, recirculation is halted while a small resin sample is removed for ninhydrin or other colour tests (Section 9.1). Recirculation is continued (step 5) while the colour test is being carried out, and if a clearly negative result is obtained, step 5 is then terminated. If a positive colour test is obtained, this second recirculation period is extended to 20–30 min and a second test carried out. Synthesis should not be continued to the deprotection stage and addition of the next residue until the result of the colour test is satisfactory. Addition of fresh activated amino acid may very occasionally be necessary, especially for residues with functional side chains (asparagine, glutamine, arginine) which may slowly interact with the activating group.

At the completion of the acylation reaction, excess reactants and co-products are washed from the resin in two stages. The first wash period (step 6) should be of sufficient duration to bring the optical density at 304 nm (0.1 mm flow cell) or 312 nm (1 mm flow cell) of the reactor effluent down to the baseline. Step 7 then purges the internal channels of the flow/recirculate valve with DMF. Opportunity is usually taken at this time to detach and rinse the sample chamber thoroughly with DMF, replace it, and wash the connecting line and valve by pumping fresh DMF from the chamber into the system. The resin wash phase (step 8) is then completed. Deprotection is initiated by flowing 20% piperidine through the system (step 9). The reaction may be followed by UV monitoring of the flowing stream (Section 9.4.2). The 10 min reaction period indicated is usually more than adequate, and the flow may be terminated when the UV trace has clearly returned to a steady baseline state. Alternatively, the reaction may be extended if UV-absorbing product continues to elute after 10 min. A long, low profile for the UV deprotection peak is usually indicative of the onset of internal aggregation with steric hindrance of both acylation and deprotection reactions, and special care should be taken when this is observed. At completion of the deprotection step, the piperidine is washed from the reactor in two stages (steps 10 and 12). The intervening pause (step 11) is for removal of a resin sample for amino acid analysis or colour reaction blank. It also serves the function, useful with some column headpieces, of allowing any trapped piperidine to escape when the headpiece is removed from the top of the column. After completion of step 12, the resin is ready for addition of the next amino acid.

10.3.2.2 *Semi-automatic (single-residue addition) synthesis*

Simple electronically controlled equipment for carrying out automatically all the operations required for single-residue addition is easily constructed and is available commercially (Section 8.4). Operation of the laboratory instrument (*49*) illustrated in *Figures 15* and *16* is described. Procedures for the various commercial instruments available are similar and are given in the appropriate technical manuals. Semi-automatic equipment is particularly appropriate for synthesis using Fmoc-amino acid anhydrides as acylating agents (*49*). These need to be prepared immediately before each acylation reaction. Equipment has been constructed for the automatic preparation of anhydrides of Boc-amino acids, but the Fmoc series presents much greater solubility problems, and comparable equipment for the preparation of Fmoc-amino acid anhydrides has not been described. Thus the anhydride method requires manual intervention at each stage for anhydride preparation. Of course the same semi-automatic peptide-synthesizing system can also be used with pentafluorophenyl (*94*) and Dhbt ester (*99*) activated intermediates.

The instrument illustrated in *Figure 15* is basically similar to the manual synthesizer referred to above. The essential differences are that the activated Fmoc-amino acid is introduced into the recirculating stream through a sample loop rather than a sample chamber, and the valving is operated pneumatically or electrically rather than manually. This enables the various valve configurations required for the flow, recirculate and sample introduction functions to be selected automatically in sequence. The original instrument was controlled by a dedicated electronic controller constructed from discrete logic elements, but microprocessor technology now offers a much simpler and cheaper solution. Only a very simple microcomputer is required to control the synthesizer, and with appropriate interfaces this can simultaneously gather and process spectrometric data from the UV monitor.

The instrument of *Figure 15* also contains an additional valve for reversing the flow direction through the column reactor. This is convenient during the column packing process and to aid removal of any air bubbles which become trapped in the resin, but is usually not necessary for semi-automatic peptide synthesis. Reverse flow should not be employed if the upper column endpiece does not contain an efficient filter.

The column reactor is packed with resin as described in Section 10.3.2.1. A typical protocol for peptide synthesis using computer-controlled semi-automatic instrumentation is given in *Table 12* (*49*).

The cycle starts with the usual prewash (step 1). While this is under way, the final stages of the preparation of the Fmoc-amino acid symmetric anhydride (2−3 eq) (Section 7.1) are carried out, and the product (or the alternative pentafluorophenyl or other activated ester and catalyst) dissolved in the minimum amount of DMF (usually 1−2 ml g^{-1} of resin and at least 1 ml less than the volume of the sample loop), and introduced manually into the loop from the sample chamber by suction with a second

Table 12. Typical operating protocol for semi-automatic peptide synthesis.

		Time (min)
Prewash	1. Flow DMF (Load activated Fmoc-amino acid manually into sample loop).	5
Monitor	2. Set wavelength, 304–312 nm Data points, 350 Time interval, 2 sec.	
Acylation	3. Recirculate DMF.	
	4. Sample loop in.	1.74
	5. Sample loop out.	
	6. Set reaction time.	25
	7. Pause. Remove resin sample.	
	8. Continue recirculation.	10
Wash	9. Flow DMF.	6.5
	10. Recirculate.	0.5
	11. Flow DMF.	
	12. Sample loop in.	5
	13. Sample loop out.	
	14. Pause–proceed to deprotection?	
Deprotect	15. Flow 20% piperidine–DMF.	1
Monitor	16. Set wavelength, 304–312 nm Data points, 90 Time interval, 4 sec.	
	17. Set reaction time.	9
Wash	18. Flow DMF	8
	19. Pause. Remove resin sample.	
	20. Flow DMF.	2
Reset	21. Halt and reset.	

syringe. The loop itself should have been washed in the previous cycle and left filled with DMF, but care should be taken to avoid contamination from residual previous amino acid derivative in the connecting tubes (see below). The sample is rinsed into the loop with a small volume of DMF. When sample introduction is complete, the prewash is usually terminated manually and the program advanced to the next step manually; it may similarly be extended manually if sample introduction is delayed for any reason. It is important that the controlling software has these facilities for manual HOLD, RESUME, and ADVANCE interventions. The remaining operations for the complete cycle of acylation and deprotection may be carried out fully automatically, although manual intervention for colour tests is advised. If a UV flow cell and monitor is included in the synthesizer, this is set (step 2) manually or by the controlling computer to the appropriate wavelength depending on the cell pathlength. Data is either collected continuously and displayed directly on an analogue recorder, or collected by the computer at preset time intervals and displayed numerically or graphically on the screen. The valving is switched into recirculate mode (step 3) and the sample loop then introduced into the recirculating stream (step 4). Entry of the sample is indicated by a steep rise in output of the UV monitor (see *Figure 24*). While the loop is switched into the recirculating stream, it is convenient to rinse the sample chamber and connecting tubes by passing fresh DMF directly through to the suction syringe (see *Figure 15*). The emptied sample loop is switched from the system (step 5) either automatically at a time depending on the loop volume and pumping rate, or automatically or manually when the UV absorption (*Figure 24*) reaches it first minimum. It should not be left switched into the recirculating stream during the recirculation period, as its dead volume contributes only to the eventual dilution of the acylating agent.

The remaining operations listed in *Table 12* are largely self-explanatory. The pauses indicated are optional, and provide opportunity for resin removal for colour tests or amino acid analysis (steps 7 and 19), or for operator decision before proceeding irrevocably to the deprotection reaction (step 14). They usually activate a warning tone to call the operator. The main acylation period is divided into two parts in the protocol given. This is a convenient arrangement in combination with the pause at step 7; acylation is continued (step 8) while the colour test is being carried out, and is then terminated or extended manually depending upon the result obtained.

The first wash period (step 9) includes 'housekeeping' operations to rinse the channels of the flow/recirculate valve (step 10) and the sample loop (steps 12 and 13). Note that the tubes connecting the syringe and sample chamber to the loop are not rinsed in this step. This can be done manually later by passing DMF from the syringe to the chamber, which should then be removed for cleaning.

Deprotection follows a similar regime. The flow of piperidine–DMF through the resin bed (step 15) is usually commenced before initialization and collection of spectroscopic data commences (step 16). Flow is terminated either automatically after a preset time, or manually or automatically when the UV trace indicates that elution of the cleaved protecting group derivative is complete. The wash operation is again carried out in two stages, permitting removal of a deprotected resin sample as well as freezing any traces of piperidine trapped in the column upper endpiece. Manual preparation of the symmetrical anhydride of the following residue is usually started during the deprotection wash period. At the end of the cycle the pump is switched off and all the valves are reset to their resting state (recirculation mode), ready for completion of manual anhydride formation and commencement of the next cycle.

10.3.2.3 *Automatic (multiple residue addition) continuous-flow synthesis*

The development of efficient synthesis techniques based on preformed Fmoc-amino acid pentafluorophenyl esters (*93,94*) and more recently on 3,4-dihydro-4-oxo- benzotriazin-3-yl esters (*39,99*) made the design of fully automatic continuous-flow synthesizers particularly simple. An easily constructed laboratory instrument (*94*) is illustrated in *Figures 19* and *20*. Commercial machines manufactured by Pharmacia-LKB (*Figure 22*) and Milligen (*Figure 23*) have since appeared on the market. Peptide synthesis using the laboratory synthesizer is described below; operation of the commercial instruments is similar and is detailed in the appropriate manuals.

The standard controlling protocol for automatic peptide synthesis using Fmoc-amino acid pentafluorophenyl or Dhbt esters is given in *Table 13* (*94*). This is presented in the form of a series of DATA statements from the original Basic software program which are read in turn and acted upon by the controlling microcomputer. Valve configurations corresponding to the various commands are listed in *Table 7*. Numerical values following

Table 13. Standard controlling protocol for sequential addition of Fmoc-amino acid activated esters and deprotection.

```
100 DATA #01 FLOW, 1
105 DATA #02 TIME, 2
110 DATA #03 SAMPLE
115 DATA #04 FILL, 1
120 DATA #05 MIX, 1
125 DATA #06 FILL, .13
(130 DATA #07 MONITOR)
135 DATA #08 EMPTY, 1.3
140 DATA #09 WASH, .5
150 DATA #11 RECIRCULATE, 1
155 DATA #12 TIME, 30
156 DATA #XX PAUSE
160 DATA #13 TIME, 30
165 DATA #14 FLOW, 1
170 DATA #25 TIME, 6.5
175 DATA #16 RECIRCULATE, 1
180 DATA #17 TIME, .5
185 DATA #18 FLOW, 1
190 DATA #19 TIME, 5
195 DATA #20 FILL, .5
200 DATA #21 MIX, .2
205 DATA #22 REAGENT, 2
210 DATA #23 FLOW, 1
215 DATA #24 TIME, .5
220 DATA #25 MONITOR, 90, 4, 312
225 DATA #26 TIME, 9
230 DATA #27 REAGENT, 1
235 DATA #28 FLOW, 1
240 DATA #29 TIME, 10
241 DATA #XX PAUSE
245 DATA #30 TIME, 10
250 DATA #31 CYCLE
255 DATA #32 HALT
260 DATA #33 END
```

some of the commands are parameters relevant to that command. Thus after FLOW and RECIRCULATE, the constant 1 selects a corresponding pump speed, presently 3 ml min^{-1}. After other liquid or gas transfer functions (FILL, MIX, EMPTY, and WASH) relating to the sampling system, the numerical value determines the time duration (in min) for each operation. Exceptionally for FLOW and RECIRCULATE, these times are set in separate TIME statements. Other parameters control reagent selection and data collection. REAGENT,1 is DMF; REAGENT,2 is piperidine/DMF. MONITOR,90,4,312 sets the spectrometer to a wavelength of 312 μm, zeros the baseline, and collects 90 optical-density readings at 4-sec intervals.

The resin to which the first Fmoc-amino acid, appropriate linkage agent, and internal reference amino acid have already been attached is packed into the column reactor as described above. Synthesis is initiated by removing the Fmoc-protecting group by starting the program at line 205 (select reagent 2). While this is proceeding, individual clean sample chambers (see below for cleaning the lines connecting the sample chambers) are loaded in turn with the solid Fmoc-amino acid activated esters (2–3-fold excess; this may be increased if there is evidence for slowing of acylation reactions), beginning with the penultimate carboxy-terminal residue. For pentafluorophenyl esters, an equivalent amount of solid 1-hydroxybenzotriazole is usually placed in the same sample chamber. This speeds the reaction markedly and seems to be completely without any deleterious effect. It is not required with Dhbt esters. When deprotection and the following wash is complete, the program halts and is restarted for the first complete cycle of Fmoc-amino acid addition and deprotection.

After the usual prewash with DMF for 2 min, the first sample chamber is selected by the rotary valve (line 110) and is filled with DMF for a time set by the parameter in line 115. '1 Minute' corresponds to a normal 3 ml at the usual flow rate, though since the lines to the sample chambers are usually left empty after cleaning, an amount smaller than this enters the sample chamber at this stage. The sample is dissolved by bubbling nitrogen through the mixture (line 120) and a second brief FILL operation (line 125) displaces nitrogen from the sample chamber connecting tubing. Because of the multiple chromophores present in the Fmoc-amino acid pentafluorophenyl ester–hydroxybenzotriazole reaction system, quantitative interpretation of UV data from the flowing stream is not easily possible. The usual monitor statement (line 130) may therefore be omitted unless the controlling software detects the first UV-absorbing peak as a check on correct sample entry. The spectrometer continues to measure optical density of the recirculating stream, and this is presented to the operator continuously on an analogue chart recorder. In instruments equipped with the solid phase monitoring (*99*) (Section 9.5) and utilizing Dhbt esters, it is replaced with a command initiating data collection from the resin (see below). The sample is then pumped onto the reaction column (EMPTY) and rinsed on briefly with DMF (WASH) (lines 135, 140). The various time parameters are dependent on the instrument volumes.

The first recirculation period of 30 min is followed by the optional PAUSE command. This stops further reading of the programme data statements, and sounds an alarm calling the operator to remove a sample of resin for qualitative ninhydrin or other colour tests. This and the second PAUSE command (line 241; at this point a resin sample is often removed for quantitative amino acid analysis) are deleted for unattended overnight operation. An additional PAUSE is sometimes inserted as line 201. This prevents automatic (and irrevocable) progression to the deprotection cycle without positive action by the operator. Operation of the synthesizer is resumed after the PAUSE (at line 156) has been cancelled from the keyboard, and acylation allowed to continue for a second 30-min recirculation period. Generally, ninhydrin tests indicate complete reaction after the first 30-min period. The excess pentafluorophenyl ester and liberated pentafluorophenol are washed from the column in two stages by FLOW (DMF) for a total of 11.5 min. The brief intermediate RECIRCULATE (lines 175/180) is used to rinse the flow/recirculate valve V1, and the final FILL and MIX operations (lines 195/200) flush and empty the lines to the sample chamber. The acylation step is now complete.

In the absence of an inserted PAUSE command or manual intervention, deprotection follows immediately. Reagent 2 is selected and flowed through the column. This continues while the monitor command is issued to the spectrometer. The optical-density readings are immediately displayed on the computer screen (Section 9.4.2). The flow of deprotecting reagent (20% piperidine) is terminated after a total of about 10 min, or earlier, either by manual intervention or automatically by computer interpretation of the UV data. Some experienced operators reduce deprotection times to 3 min or less. Under these circumstances, the deprotection product continues to emerge from the column during the following DMF wash (lines 230–240). As indicated above, the optional PAUSE at line 241 enables a resin sample to be removed for analysis. The wash is then continued (total 20 min) before the cycle command restores the reading of DATA statements to line 100 and synthesis continues with the next programmed amino acid residue.

At the completion of the synthesis or when all the sample chambers have been used, the HALT command stops the pump and resets all the valves to their resting state. The END statement terminates reading of the data statements. It is convenient to run a subsidiary program at this stage which further washes the sampling system by filling each chamber in turn with DMF and then empties the lines by blowing nitrogen using the MIX command.

10.3.2.4 *Automated synthesis using 3,4-dihydro-4-oxobenzotriazine (Dhbt) esters and solid phase monitoring*

The new principle (*98,99,114*) of continuous solid phase monitoring using Dhbt esters (**107**) has been described in Section 9.5, together with details of the photometer (*99*) required. It enables acylation reactions to be monitored for completion and terminated automatically. Deprotection reactions could already be monitored continuously by following release of the cleaved fluorene derivative from the solid phase into solution (Section 9.4.2), and the absorption data also provided a number of computer-readable checks on correct instrument operation. Thus the construction and operation of automated (as opposed to automatic) (*107*) peptide synthesizers has now become possible (*99*).

Two laboratory instruments have thus far been built and their use described (*99*). The chemical procedures for peptide synthesis using Dhbt esters do not differ substantially from those using pentafluorophenyl esters. Catalyst 1-hydroxybenzotriazole (optional with pentafluorophenyl esters) is not required. The reaction protocol of *Table 13* with an appropriate command and software (*99*) for solid phase monitoring replacing line 130 is appropriate. The recirculation period (line 155) depends upon the form of the controlling software. In the laboratory instrument described (Sections 8.4 and 9.5), it is set arbitrarily at 999 min with automatic termination when the criteria for reaction completion are met. If these criteria are not met, that is, autotermination does not occur for any reason, recirculation continues until time-out or operator intervention. The long preset time provides ample opportunity for the latter, even if the problem arises during the night. The second recirculation period (line 160) may be used to provide a safety margin, or this may be included in the monitoring software. The various pause commands are not required in the automated system. In the absence of solid phase monitoring instrumentation the bright yellow colour developed on the resin when the acylation reaction begins and its rapid fading provides a useful visual indicator of completion (*39*).

10.3.2.5 *Automated synthesis using alternative chemistries*

With flexible sample dissolution and reagent dispensing systems, alternative chemistries may often be implemented without difficulty. Both of the commercial continuous-flow synthesizers presently available (Chapter 8) contain one or more reagent bottles additional to those required for the simple preformed activated ester chemistry described. Additional reagents may also be placed in successive sample chambers in the Fmoc-amino acid sample dispensing system, or two solid reagents may be placed together in the same chamber. The main user limitation with commercial automatic machines may be the availability of appropriate controlling software. Both Pharmacia-LKB and Milligen instruments currently use compiled software not easily amenable to user modification. Esters of hydroxybenzotriazole (analogous to Dhbt esters but without the monitoring potential) formed *in situ* through the 'BOP' reagent or the uronium derivative

(Section 7.3) or by use of a carbodiimide have already been used in the Milligen synthesizer. Diisopropylcarbodiimide, which gives the relatively soluble diisopropylurea on reaction with carboxylic acids (cf. Section 1.2.3), is preferred to dicyclohexylcarbodiimide for this and similar applications, since it avoids problems of filtration.

CHAPTER 11

Resin cleavage and purification

These two final aspects of solid phase peptide synthesis are of great importance. The Fmoc-polyamide method encourages use of a range of peptide–resin linkage agents, each cleavable under mild reaction conditions to give free or side-chain-protected peptides, or various derivatives modified at the carboxy terminus. The optimum reaction conditions for cleaving each linkage may vary depending on the composition of the peptide. For most applications, peptides prepared by solid phase synthesis will require purification. Continuing improvements in separation procedures, particularly in reverse-phase and ion-exchange chromatography, have provided the techniques necessary for solid phase synthesis to achieve its present wide acceptance.

11.1 Cleavage of the peptide from the solid support

One of the most crucial steps in solid phase peptide synthesis is the cleavage of the peptide from the solid support. Usually this step is combined with removal of most side-chain-protecting groups. Solid phase synthesis requires that the linkage between the peptide being assembled and the support remains intact throughout many reaction cycles and is then cleaved selectively in the final step. Unlike more conventional solid phase procedures, the Fmoc-polyamide technique does not usually rely upon differential lability of protecting groups to the same reagent type, and allows considerable flexibility in the choice of peptide resin linkages. The linkage agents (**84–86**) mostly commonly used in the past have been described earlier (Chapter 6). When incorporated into the peptide–resin assembly they constitute the benzyl ester structures (**112–114**), and are usually used to produce respectively peptides amides or substituted amides, peptide free acids, and side-chain-protected peptide acids. Use of linkage (**112**) to produce simple peptide amides is now recognized as somewhat cumbersome. It requires pretreatment of the resin with trifluoroacetic acid to remove *t*-butyl groups, particularly side chain esters of aspartic and glutamic acids, before cleavage by methanolic ammonia. This ammonolysis reaction may be slow with hindered residues (valine and isoleucine), and contaminating methyl esters can be generated. For the production of simple peptide amides, the newer acid-sensitive, amide-producing linkage agent (**92**) is now recommended as in the benzhydrylamide (**115**). However, (**112**) is still a useful and versatile linkage, being completely resistant to acids (even to liquid hydrogen fluoride) and yet is cleaved very readily by a variety of nucleophilic reagents. In appropriate circumstances it can be used for preparing a wide range of modified amides (including hydrazides), esters, and even free acids.

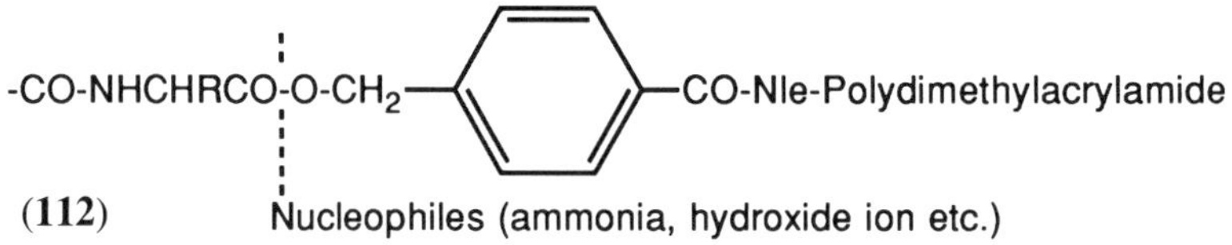

-CO-NHCHRCO-O-CH_2-C_6H_4-CO-Nle-Polydimethylacrylamide

(**112**) Nucleophiles (ammonia, hydroxide ion etc.)

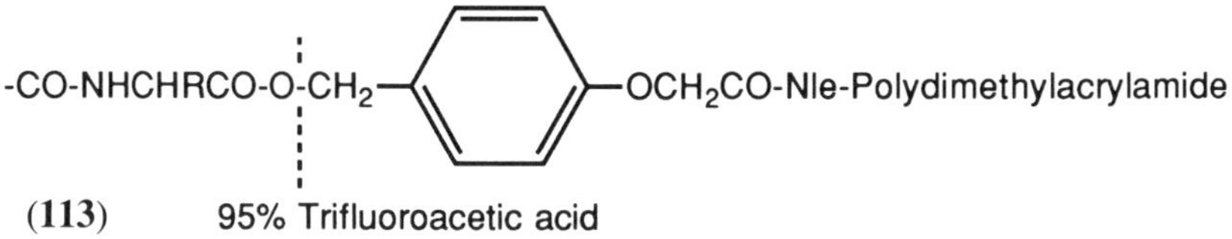

-CO-NHCHRCO-O-CH_2-C_6H_4-OCH_2CO-Nle-Polydimethylacrylamide

(**113**) 95% Trifluoroacetic acid

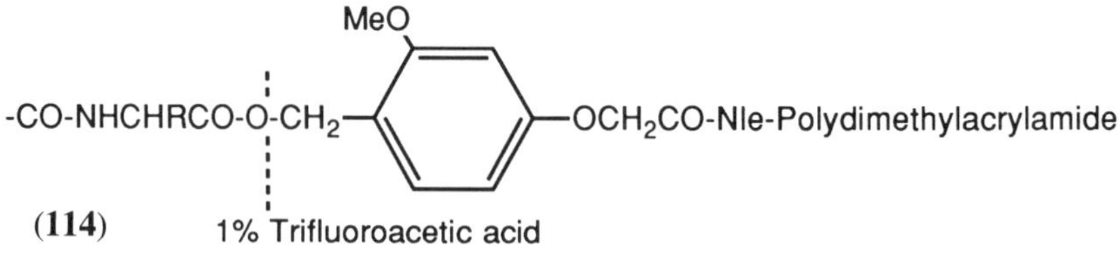

MeO

-CO-NHCHRCO-O-CH_2-C_6H_3-OCH_2CO-Nle-Polydimethylacrylamide

(**114**) 1% Trifluoroacetic acid

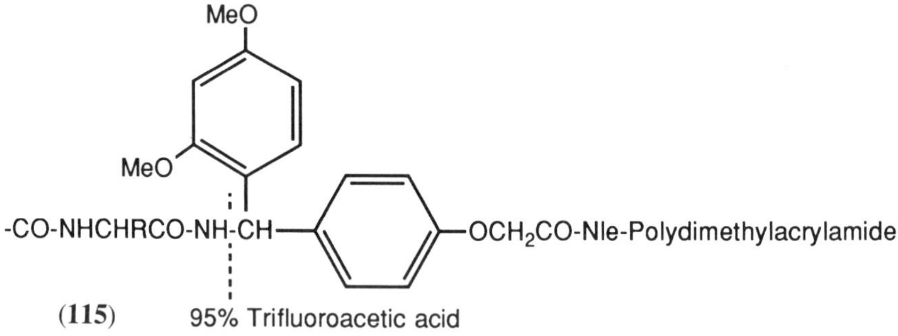

MeO

MeO

-CO-NHCHRCO-NH-CH-C_6H_4-OCH_2CO-Nle-Polydimethylacrylamide

(**115**) 95% Trifluoroacetic acid

Benzyl esters in the linkages (**113**) and (**114**) are readily cleaved by trifluoroacetic acid. For (**113**) the reaction conditions required, typically 95% trifluoroacetic acid for 0.5–2 h, cause simultaneous cleavage of all O-*t*-butyl side-chain-protecting groups. The additional alkoxy substituent in (**114**) confers much greater acid lability, and such dialkoxybenzyl esters can be cleaved under exceptionally mild conditions by 1% trifluoroacetic acid in dichloromethane (*84,87*). This linkage has been used extensively to produce fully protected peptide fragments which can be further utilized in fragment condensation procedures (*87*). To keep the loss of side-chain protecting groups to the absolute minimum, this procedure is best carried out by flowing the cleavage reagent through the resin, the effluent (containing the detached peptide) being immediately neutralized.

Acidic cleavage of the benzyl esters (**113** and **114**), and the benzhydrylamide (**115**) generate resin-bound cations. The more acid-sensitive the ester, the more stable the cation formed and hence the greater opportunity for reaction with electron-rich amino

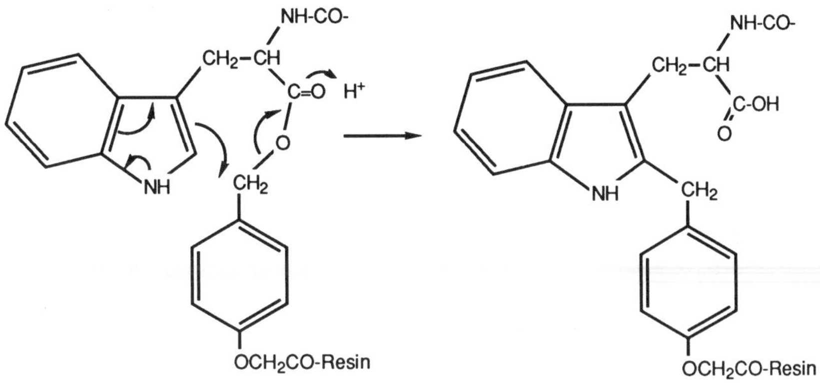

(**116**) (**117**)

acid side chains. Amino acids containing divalent sulphur (methionine and cysteine) and the aromatic amino acids tryptophan and possibly tyrosine, appear to be most at risk, and require addition of carbonium ion scavengers to the cleavage reagent. In the absence of these particularly susceptible residues, water is usually the only quenching agent required, and ester bonds in (**113**) or (**114**) can be cleaved cleanly with aqueous trifluoroacetic which also scavenges *t*-butyl carbonium ions. For peptides containing sensitive amino acid residues, it is usually best to carry out some preliminary small-scale studies to determine the best combination of additives for a particular peptide sequence. The cleavage reagent mixtures given below are to be regarded as suggestions to be further optimized as experience grows.

Attention is drawn to two new cleavage reagents, trimethylsilyl trifluoromethane sulphonate (*71*) and trimethylsilyl bromide in the presence of trifluoroacetic acid (*123*) which may have potential in the Fmoc-polyamide series, especially for peptides containing Mtr-arginine.

Reaction of resin-bound benzylic cations with peptide side chains results in reattachment of the peptide to the resin. This phenomenon is sometimes wrongly interpreted as lack of initial peptide–resin cleavage. Even in the presence of scavengers, reattachment may not be totally suppressed. For peptides containing C-terminal tryptophan, a low cleavage yield has been observed (*93*,*129*) probably because reaction with the resin-bound cation occurs intramolecularly (**116**→**117**). Under these circumstances, added scavengers are unlikely to be completely successful in eliminating the side reaction.

Carboxy-terminal methionine residues appear to behave similarly. When the methionine is present within the peptide chain (**118**), however, reaction with carbonium ions can lead to fragmentation. Presumably the cation acts in the same way as cyanogen bromide, causing chain cleavage and giving one or more peptide fragments, each terminating in a homoserine lactone residue (**119**). Thus far this has been observed only when cleaving linkage (**114**).

The peptide resin should be washed and dried thoroughly before cleavage. This is especially important with acidic cleavage reagents, as residual basic DMF has a marked

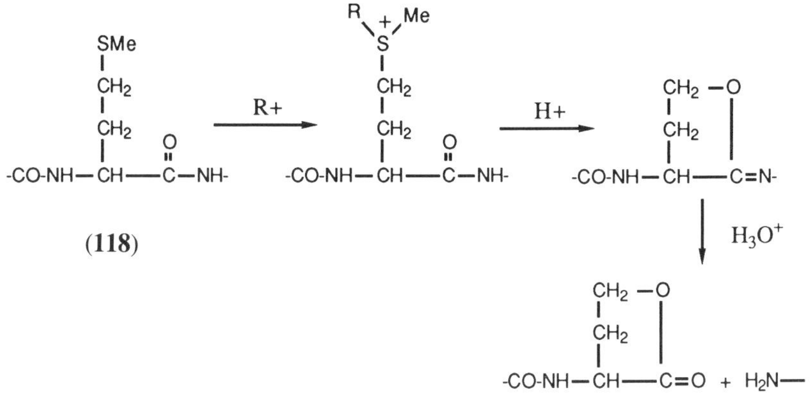

(118) $\xrightarrow{R+}$ $\xrightarrow{H+}$ $\xrightarrow{H_3O^+}$ (119)

inhibitory effect on acidolysis. Since the polydimethylacrylamide resin itself is structurally similar to DMF, washing with a mildly acidic reagent (acetic acid) that does not effect release of the peptide is desirable. A washing procedure is included in the cleavage methods described for each particular linkage agent. It is assumed that the amino terminal Fmoc-group has already been removed except when fully protected peptides are required, that is, with linkage (**114**).

In the following experimental procedures, the weights of resin given refer to Pepsyn gel. For Kieselguhr-supported resin (Pepsyn K, Ultrasyn), these may be increaed three-fold.

11.1.1 *Cleavage from linkage (**112**) by nucleophiles*

All cleavage reactions involving attack by strong nucleophiles on the resin benzyl ester (**112**) (or of other ester linkages) must usually be preceded by removal of the amino terminal Fmoc group, and by acidic cleavage of side chain *t*-butyl derivatives. Fmoc groups are liable to be at least partly removed by the nucleophilic reagent. In some cases, it may be appropriate to complete the chain assembly using a Boc-amino acid derivative. This allows hydrazinolysis to produce a terminally protected hydrazide. *t*-Butyl esters of aspartyl and glutamyl residues may undergo transpeptidation reactions ($\alpha \rightarrow \beta$ and $\alpha \rightarrow \gamma$ shifts of the peptide chain). Strongly basic reagents may induce β-elimination of S-protected cysteine residues when they are C-terminal. On the other hand, free thiol groups arising, for example, through acidic cleavage of S-trityl derivatives, may undergo base-catalysed oxidation reactions. A more stable thiol protecting group such as S-acetamidomethyl is preferred, but in general, caution is required in the use of this peptide–resin linkage for the synthesis of cysteine peptides.

---

(1) *Formation of peptide amides by ammonolysis: (a) by methanolic ammonia.*

The DMF-wet peptide resin from the reaction vessel is washed successively with *t*-amyl alcohol, acetic acid, *t*-amyl alcohol and ether and dried in high vacuum. *t*-Butyl derivatives, especially side-chain esters of aspartic and glutamic acids, must be cleaved beforehand. Typically, peptide gel resin (0.4 g) is treated with trifluoroacetic acid (15 ml) containing water (5%) or other scavenger (see below) for 1 h and then washed successively with *t*-amyl alcohol, DMF, 10% diisopropylethylamine in DMF, DMF, *t*-amyl alcohol, DMF, and ether. The resin is then dried by placing the funnel in a vacuum desiccator over phosphorus pentoxide for at least 1 h. Failure to dry the resin at this stage can lead to the formation of contaminating peptide acids (*128*). The resin is reswollen in DMF, excess DMF removed by suction, and the resin is transferred to a round-bottomed flask or small pressure bottle containing ice-cold methanolic ammonia, approximately 50 ml (see note below) and a magnetic bead. The flask stopper is tightly wired on and the resin stirred gently overnight at room temperature.

Next morning the flask is cooled again, opened, and the resin filtered and washed with methanol. The filtrate and washings are evaporated and the residual peptide amide dried before characterization and purification.

Some peptide amides are not completely soluble in methanol and a more polar solvent may be necessary to separate them from the resin. If aqueous extraction of the resin is required then the resin should be thoroughly freed from ammonia beforehand to avoid excessive alkalinity. Instead of using methanolic ammonia, peptide resins may be cleaved with anhydrous liquid ammonia in a sealed pressure bottle in the presence of a catalytic amount of acetic acid (*130*). This eliminates the possibility of contaminating methyl ester formation.

---

(2) *Formation of peptide amides by ammonolysis: (b) Cleavage with liquid ammonia* (*130*)

Glacial acetic acid (0.4 ml) is added to the peptide resin (1 g) prepared as in (a) above, contained in a pressure bottle which is then cooled in an acetone–solid carbon dioxide bath and dry liquid ammonia (15–20 ml) added. The bottle is sealed, allowed to warm to room temperature and kept overnight. The bottle is then re-cooled, opened, and the ammonia allowed to evaporate. The peptide amide is separated from the resin using methanol as above.

(3) *Formation of free peptide acids: cleavage with hydroxide ion*

Before cleavage the peptide resin is washed, treated with trifluoroacetic acid and then washed again as in (a) above. The peptide resin is then treated with aqueous sodium hydroxide—typically, ice-cold 1 M sodium hydroxide (5 ml) is added to the peptide resin (1 g) cooled in an ice-bath. After 15 min the mixture is filtered into a cooled flask containing 10% aqueous acetic acid (5 ml). The resin is washed further with water and the filtrate collected in the same flask. Further acetic acid is added if necessary to bring the pH below 7. The peptide solution should now be desalted either by gel filtration before further purification, or purified directly by preparative-scale reverse-phase chromatography.

NOTE. Saturated ammonia in methanol can be prepared by passing ammonia into ice-cold Analar methanol, taking precautions to avoid ingress of moisture. A steady stream of ammonia will saturate cold methanol (100–150 ml) in approximately 30 min.

Racemization studies have not been carried out using the above strongly basic cleavage agent. However, no racemization was detected when the dipeptide leucylalanine was cleaved from the same linkage by 66% aqueous methanol containing diisopropylethylamine (10 eq., 0.4 M) (*131*).

---

(4) *Formation of substituted amides: example of cleavage with ethanolamine*

The resin is washed and treated with trifluoroacetic acid as in (a) above. Sufficient DMF is added to swell the peptide resin fully, and then ethanolamine (approximately 5 ml for 2 g of resin) is added to give a mobile slurry. After 18–20 h, methanol (50 ml) is added and the resin removed by filtration. Evaporation of the filtrate results in an oily slurry containing ethanolamine which can be removed by gel filtration or reverse-phase chromatography.

(5) *Formation of esters: example of cleavage with methanol*

After washing the peptide resin and treatment with trifluoroacetic acid as above, the peptide resin is swollen as in (1) above and treated with a 10% solution of triethylamine in methanol (sufficient to produce a mobile slurry) overnight. The methyl ester is recovered by filtration and evaporation.

11.1.2 *Cleavage from the alkoxybenzyl ester linkage (***113***) by acids. Formation of free peptides*

The alkoxybenzyl linkage (**113**) is most commonly used in the Fmoc-polyamide technique. It is cleaved by acids under conditions (e.g. trifluoroacetic acid, room temperature, 0.5–2 h) very similar to those required for removal of *t*-butyl-based protecting groups, and in the majority of cases leads directly to free peptide acids. Only cysteine (but not S-trityl cysteine) and sometimes arginine residues [Arg(Mtr) but not Arg(Pmc)] commonly bear protecting groups resistant to these conditions. Special scavengers for the alkoxybenzyl cation are required in the presence of methionine, cysteine, and tryptophan, and possibly tyrosine. Arginine residues protected with Mtr and Pmc protecting groups require the presence of scavengers, due not to the arginine side chain but to the reactive arylsulphonyl cleavage products. In other cases a small proportion of water appears adequate to quench both *t*-butyl and benzyl cations.

Detachment of alkoxybenzyl-linked peptides

After washing the peptide resin on a sintered glass funnel with *t*-amyl alcohol, glacial acetic acid, *t*-amyl alcohol and ether it is dried in high vacuum.

(1) *Cleavage in the absence of Trp, Arg(Mtr), Arg(Pmc), Cys(X) and Met.* Typically, the peptide-resin (0.1–0.5 g of gel, up to 2 g of Kieselguhr resin) is treated with 95% aqueous trifluoroacetic acid (30–40 ml) for 1–1.5 h in a 100 ml round-bottomed flask. For gel supports, gentle stirring of the reaction mixture is ap-

propriate. With Pepsyn K, periodic hand-swirling is sufficient, since stirring will cause fragmention and produce filtering problems. The resin is filtered through a sintered glass funnel and washed 3 or 4 times with trifluoroacetic acid.

Evaporation of the filtrate under high vacuum gives the cleaved peptide. Residual acid should be removed as much as possible by repeatedly washing the residue with ether and evaporation before drying in a desiccator over potassium hydroxide pellets and phosphorus pentoxide. The purity of the peptide should be established by hplc at this stage, and then purified as necessary, depending upon the application.

The above conditions are also commonly satisfactory for tyrosine-containing peptides, though cleavage by trifluoroacetic acid–phenol mixture [see (2) below] is also to be recommended.

(2) *Cleavage of peptides containing Arg(Mtr) or Arg(Pmc).* The peptide resin is treated as above but then cleaved using a mixture of trifluoroacetic acid and phenol (95:5, v/w). The time of cleavage is dependent upon the number of Mtr-arginine residues present; for peptides containing 3 or 4 arginines, overnight treatment may be necessary. It is advisable to monitor the cleavage reaction by removing small samples of the trifluoroacetic acid–phenol mixture (50–100 μl), blowing off the trifluoroacetic acid in a nitrogen stream, partitioning the resultant product between water (100–150 ml) and ether, extracting with ether several times to remove the phenol, and then examining the aqueous phase by hplc. When the Mtr groups are completely removed, the resin is filtered and washed with trifluoroacetic acid as above, and after evaporation, the peptide is triturated with ether to remove residual phenol and finally isolated as above.

Cleavage is considerably faster with peptides containing Pmc-arginine and is likely to be complete within 2 h, that is, within the normal time span for *t*-butyl based protecting groups.

(3) *Cleavage of peptides containing Arg(Mtr) (or Arg/Pmc), and Met, Cys(X) or Trp.* The procedure is essential as in (2) above, using a mixture of trifluoroacetic acid–phenol–anisole–ethanedithiol (94:2:2:2; v/w/v/v).

(4) *Cleavage of peptides containing Met, Cys(X) and Trp.* The procedures is as in (2) above, using the mixture trifluoroacetic acid–anisole–ethanedithiol (95:2.5:2.5; v/v/v).

(5) *Cleavage of peptides containing Met and Cys.* The procedures is as in (2) above, using trifluoroacetic acid–ethanedithiol (95:5; v/v).

Other combinations of scavenging agents may be suitable for particular peptides, and it is recommended that small-scale trial cleavage experiments are carried out to determine the most efficient mixture.

11.1.3 *Cleavage from linkage (**115**) by acids. Formation of peptide amides*

Exactly the same considerations apply when cleaving from this linkage to produce peptide amides directly as for linkage (**113**) (see Section 11.1.2).

11.1.4 *Cleavage from linkage* (**114**) *by dilute acids. Formation of fully protected peptide fragments*

This cleavage reaction is carried out with minimum exposure of the peptide derivative (resin-bound or in solution) to the acidic reagent to minimize loss of acid-sensitive side-chain-protecting groups (*87*). The currently preferred procedure is to flow a very dilute solution of trifluoroacetic acid in dichloromethane slowly through the dried peptide resin contained in a sintered glass funnel. The effluent, containing detached protected peptide, is immediately quenched by allowing it to fall directly into a cooled, weakly basic reagent. DMF itself is satisfactory, with subsequent removal of DMF-trifluoroacetic acid complex by gel filtration on Sephadex LH-20.

Cleavage of protected peptides

The final Fmoc-peptide resin is washed with *t*-amyl alcohol, acetic acid, *t*-amyl alcohol and ether and dried in high vacuum. Typically the peptide resin (0.3–0.5 g) is transferred to a sintered funnel and treated with 1% trifluoroacetic acid in dichloromethane (100–140 ml). The reagent is allowed to flow continuously through the resin bed into a cooled (0°C) flask containing DMF (2 ml). This reduces the contact time of the cleaved protected peptide with the acid reagent and materially reduces loss of side-chain *t*-butyl groups (*87*). During the cleavage process the resin gradually acquires a pink coloration, presumably due to the resin dialkoxybenzylic cation. The total filtrate is evaporated and then purified by gel filtration, usually on Sephadex LH-20 using DMF as elutant. This procedure is the best of a number investigated for separation of the protected peptide from the DMF–trifluoroacetic acid complex. For use in peptide fragment condensation reactions, protected peptide fragments should be thoroughly freed of trifluoroacetic acid. Peptides containing methionine, cysteine, and/or tryptophan require the addition of scavengers to the cleavage reagent. The mixture trifluoroacetic acid–dichloromethane–anisole–ethanedithiol (1.5:95:3.2:0.95, v/v/v/v) has been applied successfully to a peptide containing these sensitive residues.

11.2 **Peptide purification**

It is inevitable that the products of solid phase synthesis will be initially impure. For bimolecular and higher-order coupling reactions, strictly quantitative yields are not attainable within a finite reaction time and in practice yields significantly less than 100% are frequently obtained. There may also be significant side reactions. It is in the nature of solid phase synthesis that the products of incomplete and aberrant reaction must accumulate and contaminate the desired product.* In this respect solid phase peptide synthesis is no different from any other technique where multiple chemical reactions are performed without rigorous purification of intermediates. Chain assembly is followed

*A peptide 15 residues long usually requires 30 successive chemical steps in its solid phase assembly. It is a salutary thought that 99% yield in every one of these steps will theoretically lead to a product containing only 74% of the desired sequence. More importantly, *the crude peptide will contain 26% of very closely related impurities.*

by at least one further step to remove the peptide from the resin and to cleave side-chain-protecting groups. This multiple reaction at many sites in the protected peptide is also subject to possible incompleteness and to side reactions.* Regrettably, side-chain protection of some common residues remains one of the weaker aspects of current solid phase synthesis.

If these by-products are not separated from the target sequence, they could have a major influence on its biological properties. However, because deletion peptides and modified derivatives may differ only slightly in structure from the target sequence, they may exhibit such similar physicochemical characteristics as to present major problems of removal, or even of detection.

Purification becomes disproportionately more difficult as the crude product becomes more impure. Early experience showed that the highly heterogeneous solid phase products obtained in inadequately controlled or over-ambitious syntheses may be particularly intractable and defy purification. They tend to be difficult to dissolve and hence not amenable to any chromatographic technique. Optimization of the chain assembly and, particularly, when the assembly is complete, of the final cleavage procedure, will pay dividends when the purification stage is reached.

Conventional separation procedures based on molecular size and charge differences continue to be of great value in peptide purification. These are now complemented most powerfully by the more recent developments in reverse-phase chromatography which depend largely on hydrophobicity differences. Other techniques such as affinity chromatography and countercurrent distribution are also often applicable, and every peptide laboratory has its own favourite procedures. Some are very specialized or may require cumbersome or costly equipment, or may not lie within the experience of the authors. These are not discussed here. Nor are simple gel-filtration procedures which are routine to most laboratories. Discussed below are the systems for anion- and cation-exchange chromatography and for high-performance reverse-phase liquid chromatography (hplc) which are important as both characterization and purification tools, and which have proved of value in our laboratory.

Analytical hplc systems have been in regular use since the mid-1970s. Equipment is now available (at a cost!) to extend hplc to modest preparative and even process scales. This is capable of high solvent flow rates (180 ml min^{-1} or more) through large stainless-steel columns. For smaller or less-well endowed laboratories, a simple low-pressure system using glass columns and often capable of handling 300–500 mg of crude synthetic peptide is described below. These inexpensive glass column systems appear to work well providing the silica support does not generate excessive back-pressure. For this reason, a larger particle size than the analytical grade is essential. In our experience, a suitable reverse phase silica is Vydac C_{18}, 300 Å pore size, 15–20 μm particle size (see Appendix).

*Again it is worth noting that 90% efficient removal of individual side-chain-protecting groups is of little value in solid phase synthesis. If there are 10 such groups in the chain, only 35% of fully deprotected product is obtained and there will be 65% of contaminating, largely singly-protected side products. If the yield is a disastrous 80% for cleavage of each protecting group, there will be 90% of impurities arising from this cause alone.

11.2.1 *Ion-exchange chromatography*

---

(1) *Cation-exchange chromatography on carboxymethyl cellulose*

Whatman CM52 ion-exchange cellullose is stirred gently with 0.5 N aqueous sodium hydroxide (10–15 vols), allowed to settle, and the supernatant decanted. A further equal volume of sodium hydroxide solution is added, the suspension stirred gently for approximately 15 min, and the resin collected on a sintered glass funnel and washed thoroughly with water until the washings have pH 7–8. The support is then stirred twice with 0.5 N aqueous hydrochloric acid. In a similar manner, filtered, and excess acid removed by washing with water until the filtrate has pH 4–5. The resin is finally washed with the starting buffer which is to be used in the actual chromatography, suspended in this buffer and packed as a slurry, pouring as much as possible into the column. If more than one pouring is required, the top of the support bed should not be allowed to settle before further amounts of support are added, thus avoiding joins in the column which could affect the chromatography.

Residual unused ion-exchanger can be stored in the cold room under the starting buffer containing a little sodium azide.

Several column volumes of the low-ionic-strength starting buffer (see below) are then pumped through the column at the flow rate at which the chromatography is to be operated. Before starting the column, the pH and ionic strength of the eluate are checked to establish that the support is fully equilibrated with starting buffer.

Typical conditions for chromatography of an overall monobasic peptide of unit positive charge at pH 6 are:

Column 15–36 cm × 1 cm diameter
Whatman CM52 cation-exchange resin
Linear gradient, 0.01 M–0.15 M ammonium acetate, pH 6.0
Two-chamber gradient maker, 250 ml of buffer in each chamber
Flow rate 0.5 ml/min (peristaltic pump)
Fraction size 3 ml (6 min fractions)
Effluent absorbance monitored at 230 nm (or 278 nm for tryptophan- or tyrosine-containing peptides)
Flow cell path length 0.5 or 1 cm
Recorder chart speed 0.05 cm min^{-1}
Sample size up to 500 mg or more in favourable cases.

The starting low-ionic-strength buffer is made from the stronger buffer by dilution and pH adjustment with dilute acetic acid or ammonia if necessary. The crude peptide mixture is dissolved in water, the solution adjusted to pH 6, and the ionic strength checked against the starting buffer using a conductivity meter. If the solution has a higher conductivity it should be diluted so that it is equal to or lower than that of the starting buffer. The peptide solution can then be applied to the column through the peristaltic pump and the gradient elution started.

More basic peptides require the use of higher ionic strength buffers for elution.

For an overall tribasic peptide, a gradient of 0.015 M to 0.25 M ammonium acetate, pH 6.0, may be suitable.

The above system can have quite remarkable resolving power. On occasions, a peptide containing a single arginine residue has been separated from the analogue containing ornithine. Factors other than net charge at the pH of the buffer system are evidently also important.

---

(2) *Anion-exchange chromatography on diethylaminoethyl cellulose*

The preliminary treatment of the Whatman DE52 cellulose ion-exchanger is similar to that described above for CM52 but the washing order is reversed. 0.5 N Aqueous hydrochloric acid is used first, followed by 0.5 N sodium hydroxide. The support is further washed with water to pH 7–8 and then with the initial buffer which is to be used in the chromatography. A slurry of the washed support in the starting buffer is packed into the column as described above.

Typical chromatography conditions for an overall mono-acidic peptide are:

Column 15–36 cm × 1 cm diameter
Whatman DE-52 anion-exchange resin
Linear gradient, 0.01 M–0.5 M ammonium bicarbonate, pH 8.1
Two-chamber gradient-maker, 250 ml of buffer in each chamber
Flow rate 0.5 ml min^{-1} (peristaltic pump)
Fraction size 3 ml (6-min fractions)
Effluent absorbance monitored at 230 nm (or 278 nm for tryptophan- or tyrosine-containing peptides)
Flow cell pathlength 0.5 or 1 cm
Recorder chart speed 0.05 cm min^{-1}
Sample size up to 500 mg or more in favourable cases

Precautions regarding buffer and sample preparation for DE52 chromatography are similar to those for CM52 chromatography above. pH adjustment of diluted buffer and of peptide solution can be made by cautious addition of ammonium hydroxide or by bubbing carbon dioxide gas through the solution. More strongly acidic peptides require buffers of higher ionic strength. A linear gradient, 0.01–0.80 M ammonium bicarbonate, pH 8.1, has proved suitable for chromatography of a peptide bearing six negative charges at pH 8. Degassing of ammonium bicarbonate often occurs at room temperature and this system is best operated in a cold-room.

Many other suitable ion-exchange materials are also available, notably the various modified Sephadexes and similar products, which may be advantageous in particular cases. More strongly acidic ion exchangers, such as phosphoethyl cellulose, are sometimes useful for purification of neutral peptides.

11.2.2 *Preparative reverse-phase high-performance liquid chromatography*

The techniques of analytical hplc are essential adjuncts to solid phase peptide synthesis, and access to hplc equipment is required in any peptide synthesis laboratory. Its operation depends on the particular system available and is not discussed here. Octyl (Aquapore RP300) and octadecyl (μBondapac, Vydac) silica of particle size 5 – 10 μm, in columns of 4.6 mm diameter eluted by linear gradients of acetonitrile in 0.1% trifluoroacetic acid or 0.01 M ammonium acetate, pH 4.5, have proved useful in analytical applications.

The same hplc equipment is usually able to accommodate commercial semi-preparative steel columns of up to about 1 cm diameter. Such columns can be used to separate modest amounts depending on the separation involved, and repeated applications enable larger quantities to be purified, albeit tediously. For larger separations, large stainless-steel columns and specialized equipment become necessary if the very high resolutions obtained under analytical conditions are to be approached. The following simple and inexpensive low-pressure system presents a reasonable compromise between cost and efficiency.

Low-pressure reverse-phase preparative chromatography

Typically a thick-walled glass column, 50 cm × 1 cm diameter, equipped with screw-on solvent-resistant plastic end fittings (Omnifit, see Appendix) is dry-packed with the reverse-phase silica support (Vydac C_{18}, 300 Å pore size, 15 – 20 μm particle size, see Appendix). This packing is carried out carefully, ensuring that the support is fully settled by tapping the column as it is slowly poured. There should be minimum dead space between the top of the column bed and the upper endpiece.

Several column volumes of methanol are pumped through the support at a flow rate of 5 ml min^{-1}, followed by acetonitrile. It is useful at this stage to monitor the efflucent by uv absorption to determine when the support is equilibrated with the mobile phase (steady baseline); the column is then equilibrated with the starting elutant (see below).

Such columns can be attached to most analytical hplc machines, and the ability to program flow rates and gradients is a distinct advantage. When using an analytical hplc instrument, provision for injecting larger volumes of solution is necessary. This can be achieved either by fitting a larger loop into the existing injector or by introducing a new injector valve and loop (Anachem, Omnifit and other suppliers) between the gradient-maker and the column. Alternatively and more simply, these columns can be operated independently using a single solvent-resistant pump capable of flow rates of at least 5 ml min^{-1} (for example, LDC/Milton Roy Mini Pump, see Appendix), a two-chamber gradient-making system and a suitable injector valve and loop.

The volatile solvent system, (A) 0.1% trifluoroacetic acid in water, (B) 0.1% trifluoroacetic acid in acetonitrile, is generally suitable. The concentration of organic phase in the initial elutant is most easily determined by prior analytical hplc of the crude peptide mixture using a 5 or 10 μm C_{18} Vydac column. This establishes the concentration of organic phase at which the component of interest emerges from the analytical column. Preparation gradients are then generally run over a period of about 100 min up to this concentration. A typical program for a two-pump gradient-maker system would be 100% A, 5 min (isocratic) followed by $0-x\%$ B linear gradient over 95 min where x is the analytical elution concentration of the component to be isolated.

In a single-pump system, chamber A contains 0.1% trifluoroacetic acid in water, and B, 0.1% trifluoroacetic acid in $x\%$ acetonitrile-water mixture, 250–500 ml in each chamber.

The peptide mixture (usually up to about 0.3 g; up to 0.5 g may be fractionated in favourable circumstances) is dissolved in water for applying to the column. If the peptide is highly acidic, the minimum amount of dilute ammonium hydroxide may be added to effect solution. Some peptides may require the addition of an organic solvent to dissolve them. This should be kept to an absolute minimum, as too much may cause immediate partial elution or seriously reduce resolution. Injection volumes should be also be kept to a minimum to maximize the efficiency of separation.

The eluate is monitored at 230 or 278 nm in the usual manner, and 2 ml fractions are collected. When the separation is completed, the column is washed with pure acetonitrile, then methanol in which the column can be stored until further use.

Caution should be exercised regarding operating pressures within the glass column. The pump should preferably be fitted with a pressure limiter gauge, and pressures should not be allowed to exceed recommendations for the column. Cracking of columns, although not dangerous, has occurred. As a precautionary measure, plastic tape should be wrapped around the column or a suitable safety net fitted.

CHAPTER 12

Illustrative syntheses

In this chapter, a number of actual syntheses are described in detail, some of which have not been reported previously. They have been chosen from among the many hundreds carried out in the MRC Laboratory of Molecular Biology and at Cambridge Research Biochemicals Ltd to illustrate a number of facets of Fmoc-polyamide synthesis. They are deliberately not just routine or 'best' syntheses, but often have particular sequence features which caused concern and received special attention in the design and conduct of the synthesis. Most utilize the current continuous-flow technique with the composite Kieselguhr–polydimethylacrylamide support, though we have also included older syntheses using the beaded gel resin. A range of linkage agents, activated amino acid derivatives, amino acid compositions, and other features are covered. The chapter concludes with a straightforward synthesis using a modern commercial flow synthesizer. We hope the descriptions may serve as models for successful syntheses elsewhere and help to draw attention to possible problems before they occur.

12.1 Synthesis of a dodecapeptide containing carboxy-terminal tryptophan (*93,129*)

H-Leu-Ala-Glu-Leu-Gly-Ala-Ser-Leu-Leu-Lys-His-Trp-OH (**120**)

The dodecapeptide (**120**) is an analogue of the carboxy terminus of penicillinase. Most of the sequence is entirely straightforward and assembled well using continuous-flow techniques. Pentafluorophenyl ester derivatives were used at every stage, including the linkage agent and the carboxy-terminal amino acid. This was a relatively early exploratory synthesis using these activated esters. Tryptophan had not previously been encountered at the carboxy terminus of a synthetic objective, and was recognized as a potential cause of difficulty, both during its introduction and final cleavage of the peptide. Special steps were taken to establish its integrity and these are described in some detail.

The composite Kieselguhr–polydimethylacrylamide resin was pepared using pentafluorophenyl esters for the introduction of the internal reference norleucine residue and for the normal hydroxymethylphenoxyacetic acid linkage agent. Both reactions were carried out in the laboratory semi-automatic flow synthesizer. Details are given below. Transesterification of the carboxy-terminal amino acid (tryptophan) of the sequence to this linkage agent also used the pentafluorophenyl ester. In the presence of catalyst 4-dimethylaminopyridine, attachment was 75% complete after 1 h, and 92% complete after overnight reaction. Incorporation of the first amino acid is usually determined by acidic hydrolysis and amino acid analysis relative to the internal reference norleucine residue. Because of the instability of tryptophan to acids, its incorporation was determined for the first (1 h) sample by reaction of a small amount of deprotected resin with excess Boc-L-leucine *p*-nitrophenyl ester until a negative colour reaction for residual amino groups was obtained, acidic hydrolysis, and analysis for leucine and norleucine content. The coupling with leucine also enabled the optical purity of the tryptophan residue to be assessed (see below). The second (overnight) transesterification sample was analysed after addition of the second residue of the sequence proper (histidine), and determination of the histidine–norleucine ratio.

Opportunity was also taken to determine the dipeptide (Trp–Trp) content of the resin, since this might have been considerable after the prolonged base-catalysed transesterification reaction. A small sample of the deprotected tryptophyl resin was coupled with Boc-Trp *p*-nitrophenyl ester (the pentafluorophenyl ester would of course have been equally suitable) to generate an authentic sample of Boc-dipeptidyl resin. This and the initial tryptophyl-resin were cleaved in the presence of an ethane dithiol–anisole scavenger mixture and the products examined by hplc. The tryptophyl resin gave a peak coincident with that from the dipeptide, indicating the presence of up to 1.2% of the latter in the overnight transesterification product.

The optical purity of the tryptophan residue was checked by conversion to diasteroisomeric leucyltryptophan dipeptides (Section 10.2). The Boc-L-leucyltryptophyl resin referred to above, together with another prepared using a Boc-DL-leucine *p*-nitrophenyl ester were cleaved as for the tryptophyltryptophanyl resin. Separation of the diasteroisomeric dipeptides by hplc gave only a very small peak in the L-leucyl-L-tryptophan preparation coincident with D-leucyl-L-tryptophan which could not easily be quantified. Thus racemization in the base-catalysed transesterification was probably not significant*. Three equivalents of Fmoc-amino acid pentafluorophenyl ester derivatives were used in the chain extensions. Up to residue 8 (glycine), all acylations were complete at the time of the first colour test (20 min) apart from serine-6 (60 min). A non-crystalline sample of this Fmoc pentafluorophenyl ester was used in this early experiment and the more easily purified Dhbt ester would now be preferred. After glycine-8, acylation reactions became noticeably slower and catalyst hydroxybenzotriazole was added. Coupling of the last residue was repeated for safety, since a marginally positive colour test was initially obtained. The slowing of acylation reactions was mirrored in broadening and trailing of deprotection peaks (Section 9.4.2).

The crude peptide was detached from the resin with trifluoroacetic acid in the presence of ethane dithiol *t*-butyl cation-scavenger. Only 42% of the peptide was cleaved from the resin and 37% of crude peptide obtained, although this was of good quality (*Figure 34*) for a sequence containing both tryptophan and histidine. It seems probable that this low yield was due not to incomplete cleavage of the *p*-alkoxybenzyl ester bond, but to readdition of the intermediate benzyl cation to the indole nucleus (Section 11.1). In agreement, no further peptide was released from the resin on repeated treatment with trifluoroacetic acid, although analysis showed that about half remained resin-bound. The C-terminal position of the tryptophan residue could favour the intramolecular process (**116**→**117**). The free peptide was purified by ion-exchange chromatography; 72% of

*This simple procedure for determination of optical purity of the C-terminal amino acid in solid phase synthesis was developed in our laboratory by Dr P.Goddard (*115*).

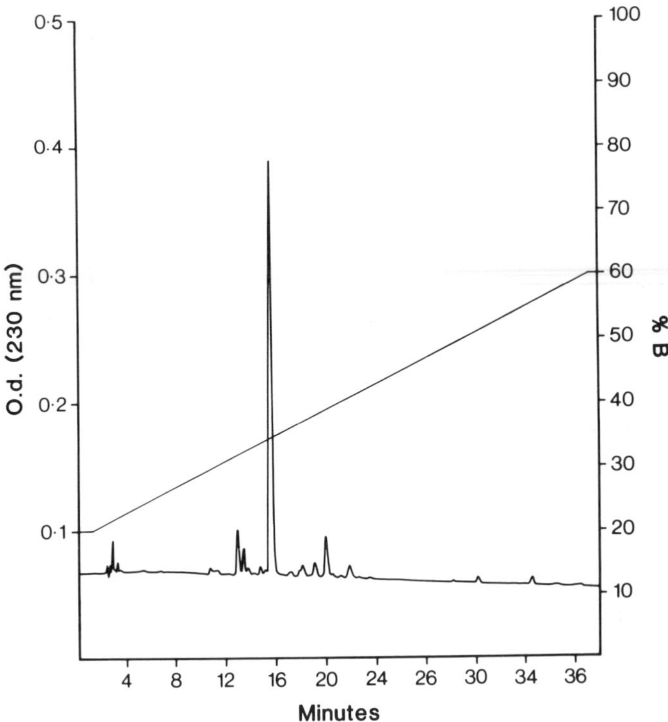

Figure 34. Analytical hplc of total crude dodecapeptide (**120**). Conditions, Aquapore RP-300 column Reservoir A contained 0.1% aqueous trifluoroacetic acid; reservoir B contained 90% acetonitrile, 10% A. After 2 min elution with 5% B, a linear gradient of 20–60% B was developed over 36 min.

the material applied to the column was recovered in the main peak and characterized by hplc (*Figure 35*) and amino acid analysis.

Synthesis of H-Leu-Ala-Glu-Leu-Gly-Ala-Ser-Leu-Leu-Lys-His-Trp-OH

(1) *Resin preparation and esterification of the first residue.* The Kieselguhr-supported polydimethylacrylamide resin (2.5 g, nominal sarcosine content 0.11 mmol g^{-1}) was treated with ethylene, amine (15 ml) overnight with gentle shaking for 30 sec every 10 min and then filtered and washed with DMF. The resin was poured into the reaction column as a slurry and washed thoroughly by flowing DMF (3 ml min^{-1}) for 60 min. Fmoc-Nle-OPfp (0.39 g, 0.75 mmol in DMF, 2.5 ml) was added automatically and recirculated for 37 min. A resin sample gave negative ninhydrin and trinitrobenzene sulphonic acid colour tests at this stage. After 47 min the resin was washed (DMF, 6.5 min) and then deprotected with 20% piperidine in DMF (9 min). After further washing (DMF, 12 min), the pentafluorophenyl ester of 4-hydroxymethylphenoxyacetic acid (0.26 g, 0.75 mmol in DMF, 2.5 ml) was added and recirculated for 20 min (negative colour tests). After 40 min the resin was washed (DMF, 13 min) and Fmoc-Trp-OPfp (0.74 g, 1.25 mmol in DMF, 2.5 ml) added as above. After brief recirculation, 4-dimethyl-

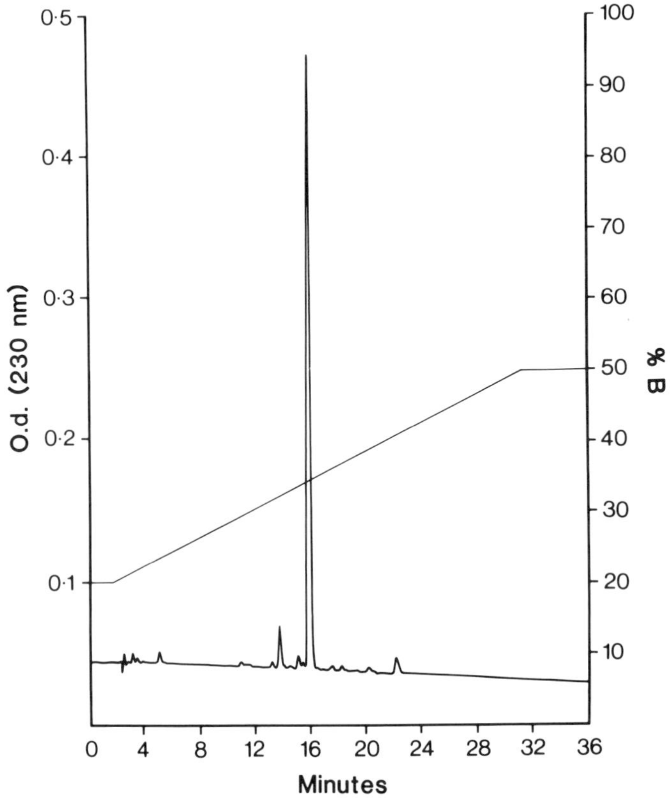

Figure 35. Analytical hplc of dodecapeptide (**120**) after ion-exchange chromatography. Conditions as **Figure 34** except that a linear gradient of 20–50% B was developed over 30 min.

aminopyridine (31 mg, 0.25 mmol) dissolved in the minimum volume of DMF was added manually to the top of the column and recirculation continued for 60 min. After removal of a resin sample, the mixture was left recirculating overnight (16.5 h), and a second sample removed. The resin was washed (DMF, 6.5 min), deprotected (20% piperidine, 9 min), and then acylated by recirculating acetic anhydride (0.75 mmol) in the presence of 4-dimethylaminopyridine (31 mg, 0.25 mmol) for 15 min. The resin samples removed after 60 min and 16.5 h reaction were separately washed on a sintered funnel with DMF and 20% piperidine in DMF, and then treated with 20% piperidine in DMF (1 × 3 min and 1 × 7 min periods) followed by washing with DMF, *t*-amyl alcohol, acetic acid, *t*-amyl alcohol, DMF, 10% diisopropylethylamine in DMF, DMF, ether and dried in high vacuum.

(2) *Rate of ester bond formation*. The resin sample taken after 60 min acylation (90 mg) was treated with a solution of Boc-Leu-ONp (13.8 mg, 39 μmol) in DMF (0.3 ml) for 90 min (negative colour tests). The resin was then washed with DMF,

t-amyl alcohol, acetic acid, *t*-amyl alcohol, DMF, 10% diisopropylethylamine in DMF, DMF, ether, and dried in a high vacuum. (Found: Leu/Nle 0.75.) This is to be compared with a resin sample taken after addition of the histidine residue to the main bulk of resin (see later). (Found: His/Nle 0.92.)

(3) *Degree of dipeptide formation during esterification.* The bulk Fmoc-tryptophyl-resin was deprotected and washed in the usual manner. A sample (15 mg) was acylated with Boc-Trp-ONp (16.6 mg, 39 μmol) in DMF (0.3 ml) in the presence of 1-hydroxybenzotriazole (5.8 mg, 39 μmol) to obtain authentic tryptophyl-tryptophan standard. After 60 min (negative colour tests), the resin was washed, deprotected, washed, and dried as above. A portion of this resin (13.5 mg) and a sample of the precursor H-Trp-resin (13.5 m) were then treated separately with a mixture of trifluoroacetic acid, anisole, ethanedithiol (30:1:0.3 v/v/v) for 90 min. The resin samples were then filtered and washed with the same mixture. The total filtrate was evaporated at reduced pressure, the residue triturated several times with ether, dissolved in water (0.5 ml) and this solution washed several times with ether. Hplc (Aquapore 300 C_{18} column, pump A 0.1% trifluoroacetic acid in water; pump B 90% acetonitrile in 10%, linear gradient 10 to 50% B over 20 min) of both samples together with a tryptophan standard showed the presence of 1.2% dipeptide in the 16.5 h esterification resin.

(4) *Degree of racemization.* A sample (20 mg) of the foregoing deprotected tryptophyl resin (16.5 h esterification) was reacted with Boc-Leu-ONp (13.8 mg, 39 μmol) in DMF (0.3 ml). Aftr 1.75 h (negative colour tests) the resin was washed and the dipeptide leucyltryptophan cleaved as described above for tryptophyl-tryptophan. A separate sample of tryptophyl resin (20 mg) was acylated in DMF (0.5 ml) with the symmetrical anhydride prepared from Boc-DL-leucine (36.2 mg, 156 μmol) and dicyclohexylcarbodiimide (16.0 mg, 78 μmol) in dichloromethane. After 60 min (negative colour tests) the resin was washed and cleaved as above. The peptides were triturated several times with ether, dissolved in water (0.5 ml) and washed with ether. Both samples were examined by hplc under the foregoing conditions. The L–L dipeptide (eluting at 29% solvent B) showed only trace contamination with L–D dipeptide (eluting at 35.5% B) which could not be quantified.

(5) *Completion of the dodecapeptide assembly.* The remaining amino acids were added to the tryptophyl resin by the following general procedure. Flow DMF (2 min), Fmoc-amino-acid-OPfp ester (0.75 mmol) applied automatically in DMF (2.5 ml) and recirculated, flow DMF (6.5 min), flow 20% piperidine in DMF (9 min), flow DMF (22 min). O-*t*-Butyl or N-Boc derivatives were used for side-chain protection where required, including the histidine residue. Apart from Ser(Bu^t)-6, negative colour tests were obtained after 20 min in the first eight cycles, and these reactions were terminated after 40 min. Fmoc-Ser(Bu^t)-OPfp was reacted for 60 min. 1-Hydroxybenzotriazole (0.75 mmol) was added to all subsequent couplings. A slightly positive ninhydrin test was obtained after 120 min reaction for the final leucine. The column was washed and the acylation repeated

for 36 min. The final peptide resin was deprotected and washed as above, transferred to a sintered funnel and further washed with DMF, *t*-amyl alcohol, acetic acid, *t*-amyl alcohol, ether, and dried in high vacuum. Yield 2.65 g. Found: 0.058 mmol Gly g^{-1}; Nle 1.11 (1); His, 0.97 (1); Lys 1.04 (1); Leu 4.02 (4); Ser, 0.78 (1); Ala, 1.97 (2); Gly, 1.00 (1); Glu, 0.94 (1).

(6) *Cleavage and isolation.* The deprotected peptide resin (0.654 g, 37.93 μmol) was treated with trifluoroacetic acid–anisole–ethanedithiol (15 ml, 0.5 ml, 0.15 ml) for 90 min at room temperature. The resin was filtered, washed thoroughly with trifluoroacetic acid and the total filtrate evaporated under reduced pressure. The peptide was dissolved in water (30 ml) and washed three times with ether. The ether layer was back-extracted with water (20 ml) and the combined aqueous phases freeze-dried to yield 13.9 μmol, 36.6% of peptide. Found: His, 1.00 (1); Lys, 1.07 (1); Leu, 4.04 (4); Ser, 0.80 (1); Ala, 1.98 (2); Gly, 1.00 (1); Glu, 1.00 (1). Reverse-phase hplc gave the profile shown in *Figure 34*. The residual resin was washed with *t*-amyl alcohol, DMF, 10% diisopropylethylamine DMF, DMF, ether and dried in high vacuum (found: Gly/Nle, 0.53). Retreatment of this peptide resin with trifluoroacetic acid containing scavengers failed to release more peptide.

(7) *Purification.* The crude dodecapeptide (13.5 μmol) was chromatographed on a freshly poured column (14 × 1 cm diameter) of Whatman CM-52 ion-exchange resin which was eluted with a linear gradient of 0.01–0.05 M ammonium acetate, pH 4.25–6.25. The resevoirs contained 240 ml of each buffer. The eluent was monitored at 278 nm and fractions (4 ml) collected every 6 min. The major peak, comprising fractions 72–78, was collected and freeze-dried, yield 9.75 μmol, 72% recovery. Found: His 0.99 (1); Lys 0.98 (1); Leu 3.99 (4); Ser 0.79 (1); Ala 1.94 (2), Gly 1.00 (1); Glu 1.04 (1). The hplc profile is shown in *Figure 35*.

12.2 Synthesis of a heptadecapeptide amide containing an amino-terminal pyroglutamyl residue (*128*)

Glp-Gly-Pro-Trp-Leu-Glu-Glu-Glu-Glu-Glu-Ala-
Tyr-Gly-Trp-Leu-Asp-Phe-NH_2 **(121)**

The gastrins are a family of natural hormones which stimulate gastric acid secretion in mammals. The so-called 'little gastrin' is a heptadecapeptide amide formed biosynthetically by cleavage from a larger protein precursor. During this post-synthesis processing, an amino-terminal glutamine residue is transformed into a pyroglutamyl (pyrrolid-2-one carbonyl) derivative, and the C-terminal amide function is formed oxidatively from a glycine residue. In the chemical synthesis of the human little gastrin analogue (**121**) described, the base-labile 4-hydroxymethyl benzoic acid linkage agent (**112**) was used, enabling the amide function to be formed by ammonolysis of the peptide–resin ester bond. The pyroglutamyl residue was generated by cyclization of N-terminal glutamine (**122→123**). Direct addition of an activated pyroglutamic acid derivative is a perfectly feasible alternative. The cyclization route was chosen because

$$\begin{array}{ccc} H_2N\text{-}CO\text{-}CH_2\text{-}CH_2 & & OC\text{-}CH_2\text{-}CH_2 \\ H_2N\text{———}CH\text{-}CO\text{-} & \longrightarrow & HN\text{———}CH\text{-}CO\text{-} \\ \textbf{(122)} & & \textbf{(123)} \end{array}$$

it permitted possible extension of the synthesis to longer gastrins. Assembly of the peptide chain up to the penultimate residue was a straightforward example of symmetrical anhydride chemistry using the beaded gel polydimethylacrylamide resin.

The carboxy-terminal phenylalanine residue was esterified to the functionalized resin as its *t*-butoxycarbonyl derivative. This is a sometimes useful procedure for use with the acid-stable, base-labile hydroxymethylbenzoyl linkage for amino acids which do not bear acid-labile side-chain-protecting groups. It avoids any risk of partial removal of Fmoc groups by 4-dimethylaminopyridine. This synthesis was carried out before racemization of carboxy-terminal residues was recognized as a potential danger in dimethylaminopyridine-catalysed esterifications, and the larger amount than usual of this reagent used (equivalent to that of symmetrical anhydride) resulted in the eventual separation of a few percent of C-terminal diastereosiomer. After cleavage of the *t*-butoxycarbonyl group with hydrogen chloride in acetic acid and neutralization, the following 15 residues were all added by the standard Fmoc-symmetric anhydride procedure. Colour tests were negative after 10–15 min and excellent incorporations were achieved (*Table 14*). The final glutamine residue was added as its *p*-nitrophenyl ester catalysed by 1-hydroxybenzotriazole.

All the protecting groups (Fmoc and side-chain *t*-butyl esters and ethers) were removed from the completed heptadecapeptide resin prior to ammonolysis. This is important because of the serious risk of $\alpha \rightarrow \beta$ or $\alpha \rightarrow \gamma$ shift on exposure of aspartyl and glutamyl peptide esters to the strongly basic conditions of ammonolysis. In this respect, the complete acid-stability of the hydroxymethylbenzoyl linkage has been an important factor favouring its use. Removal of *t*-butyl groups while the peptide is still attached to the resin also minimizes attack of *t*-butyl cations on tryptophan residues, and no scavenger other than water was required. In a later synthesis of the analogous octadecapeptide *acid* terminating in phenylalanylglycine using the standard acid-labile linkage (**113**),

Table 14. Amino acid composition of resin-bound peptides referred to Phe = 1.00. The norleucine (Nle) residue is the internal reference amino acid directly attached to the polydimethylacrylamide resin.

Residue	*17*	*10–17*	*9–17*	*8–17*	*7–17*	*6–17*	*1–17*
Nle	1.07	1.09	1.10	1.11	1.08	1.13	1.07
Phe	1.00	1.00	1.00	1.00	1.00	1.00	1.00
Asp		1.01	1.02	1.02	1.01	1.00	0.94
Leu		0.99	1.01	1.00	1.00	2.02	1.99
Gly		1.00	1.01	1.00	1.01	1.01	1.97
Tyr		1.00	1.00	1.01	1.00	1.00	1.00
Ala		1.01	1.01	1.01	1.02	1.01	1.06
Glu		1.19	2.11	3.14	4.18	5.27	6.18
Pro							1.02

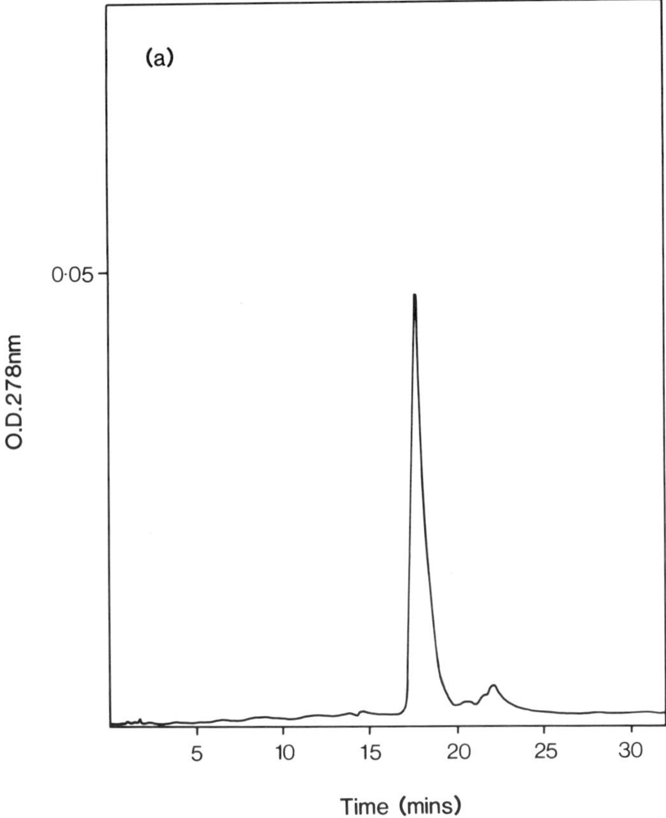

Figure 36. Hplc on μ-Bondapak C_{18} at pH 4.5 of total crude heptadecapeptide amide. Linear gradient of 20–50% MeCN in 0.1 M aqueous ammonium acetate, pH 4.5 over 30 min.

substantially increased *t*-butylation of tryptophan residues occurred when the peptide–resin bond and side-chain-protecting groups were cleaved in the same reaction. Ammonolysis of the deprotected heptadecapeptide resin using methanolic ammonia was more than 90% complete after overnight reaction.

The detailed description of the characterization of the cleavage product has been published elsewhere (*128*), and only the important points will be discussed here. The hplc chromatogram of the crude amide was encouraging and revealed (*Figure 36*) a single main peak with very minor, later-eluting impurities. Previous experience (*133*) strongly suggested that these more lipophilic impurities were likely to be *t*-butylated tryptophan artefacts. The hplc profile was unchanged after purification by ion-exchange chromatography [Section 11.2.1, procedure (2)]. On the other hand, at least partial conversion of the terminal glutamine residue to the cyclized pyroglutamyl form (**122**→**123**) was to be expected under the ammonolysis conditions. Simple changing of the pH of the hplc eluting buffer revealed that this was indeed the case (*Figure 37*). The two principal components were identified as the pyroglutamyl and glutaminyl heptadecapeptides, and nearly complete conversion of the latter and purification of the

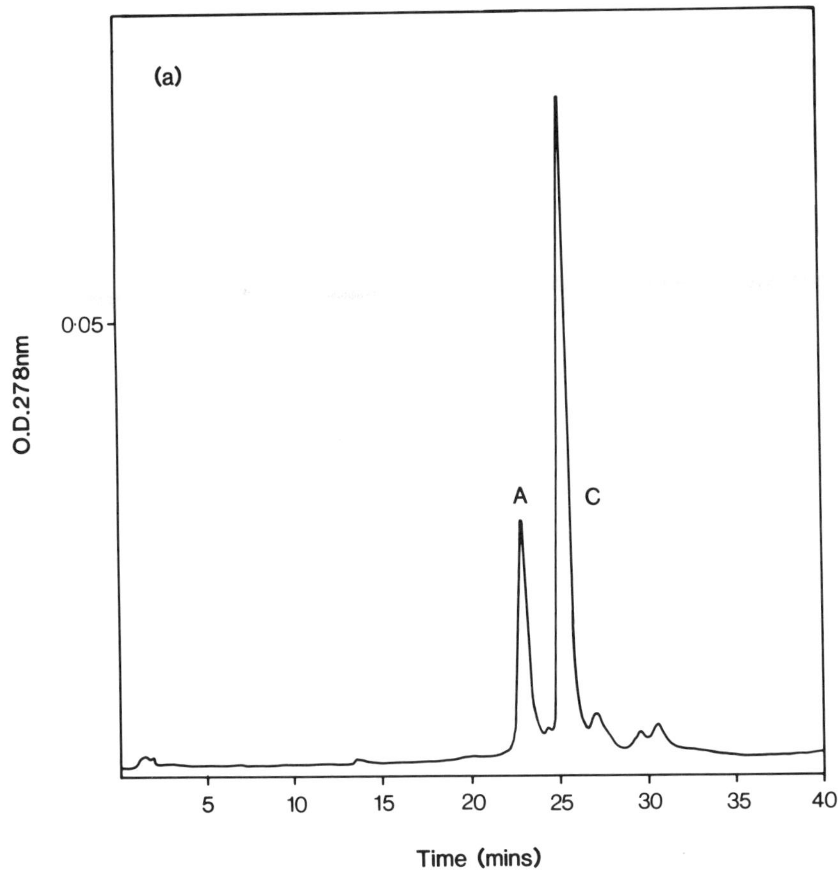

Figure 37. Hplc at pH 3.5 of principal peak from anion-exchange chromatography of crude heptadecapeptide amide. Conditions as *Figure 36*, except that the pH of the aqueous buffer was readjusted.

gastrin analogue (**121**) was readily achieved (*Figure 38*). Minor impurities were identified as the D-phenylalanine diastereosiomer and a *t*-butylated heptadecapeptide.

The implications regarding use of a single analytical hplc for characterization of synthetic products are clear.

Solid-phase synthesis of [*15-leucine*]-*human little gastrin* (**123**)

The beaded polydimethylacrylamide gel resin (0.254 g, containing 0.10 mmol of sarcosine) was treated with 1,2-diaminoethane (*c*. 10 ml) for 20 h, and after thorough washing was acylated with preformed Fmoc-norleucine anhydride (0.59 mmol) in dimethylacetamide (DMA, 5 ml) for 1 h. The incorporation of norleucine was 0.25 meq g^{-1}. 2,4,5-Trichlorophenyl 4-hydroxymethylbenzoate (0.60 mmol) was coupled in the presence of 1-hydroxybenzotriazole (0.59 mmol) in DMA (5 ml) for 20 h. To the washed resin, solutions of Boc-Phe anhydride (0.59 mmol), DMA (1.25 ml), and 4-dimethylaminopyridine (0.59 mmol), in DMA

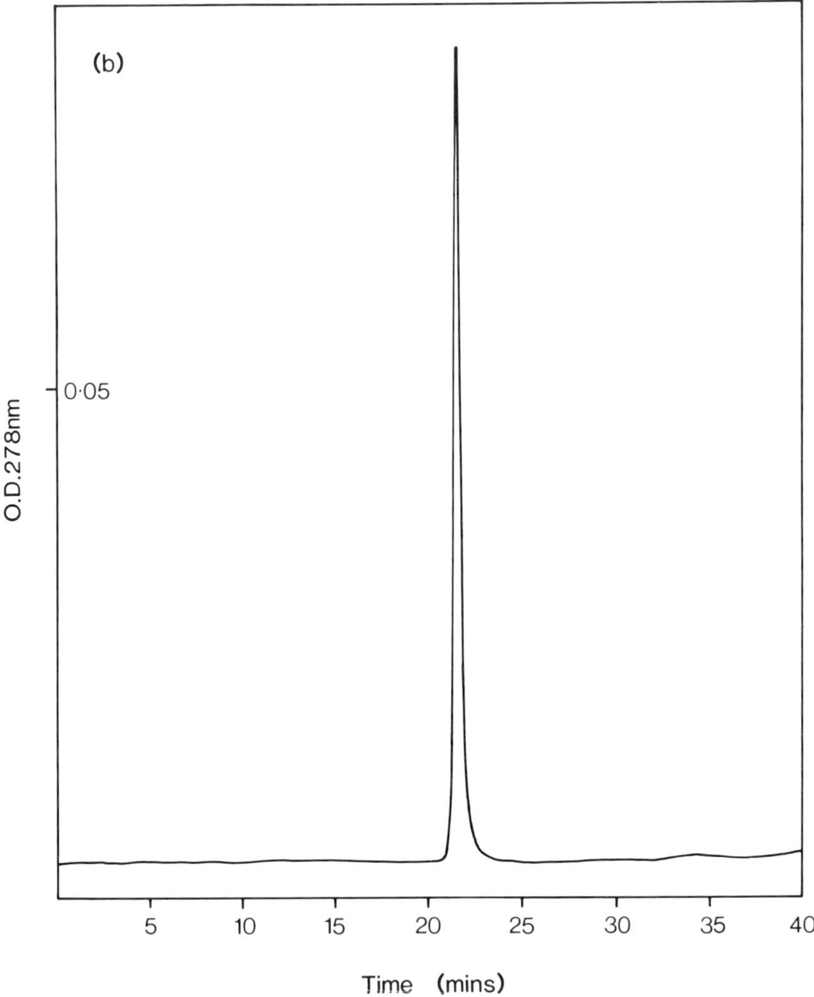

Figure 38. Hplc of purified heptadecapeptide (see text). Conditions as *Figure 37*.

(1.25 ml were added). After 2 h the resin was washed, deprotected with 1.5 N-HCl-AcOH, and neutralized. The following procedure was used to avoid direct contact of DMA with acids (acetic acid, hydrogen chloride) which is strongly exothermic: *t*-amyl alcohol (*t*-AmOH), 5 × 2 min; acetic acid, 5 × 2 min; 1.5 M HCl−acetic acid, 5 + 25 min; acetic acid, 5 × 2 min, *t*-AmOH, 5 × 2 min; DMA, 10 × 2 min; 10% diisopropylethylamine−DMA, 3 × 2 min; DMA, 5 × 2 min. The following 12 Fmoc-amino acid anhydrides (0.59 mmol) were added in DMA (5 ml) and shaken for the times given before washing with DMA (5 × 1 min), deprotection (20% piperidine−DMA, 3 + 7 min), and further washing (DMA, 10 × 1 min); Fmoc-Asp(OBu^t)-OH, 17.5 h (overnight); Fmoc-

Leu-OH, 60 min; Fmoc-Trp-OH, 72 min; Fmoc-Gly-OH, 108 min; Fmoc-Tyr-(Bu^t)-OH, 60 min; Fmoc-Ala-OH, 140 min; Fmoc-Glu(OBu^t)-OH, 60 min; Fmoc-Glu(OBu^t)-OH, 65 min; Fmoc-Glu(OBu^t)-OH, 110 min; Fmoc-Glu(OBu^t)-OH, 60 min; Fmoc-Glu(OBu^t)-OH, 16 h; Fmoc-Leu-OH, 75 min. A sample of resin (*c*. 35 mg) was removed for comparison with tridecapeptide amide prepared earlier (*133*). The loading of phenylalanine on the resin at the tridecapeptide stage was 0.154 meq g^{-1}. For amino acid analysis data of selected intermediate peptide resins, see *Table 14*.

The remaining resin was deprotected and acylated with the amino acid anhydrides (0.59 mmol) of Fmoc-Trp-OH, 60 min; Fmoc-Pro-OH, 90 min; and Fmoc-Gly-OH, 60 min. The final residue was added by the active ester procedure with Fmoc-Gln-ONp (0.59 mmol) in the presence of 1-hydroxybenzotriazole (0.59 mmol) in DMA (7 ml) for 60 min. The washed resin was stored at 5°C under nitrogen until required. Samples of resin were removed for qualitative ninhydrin tests after every amino acid addition and deprotection step. The final loading of phenylalanine on the resin was 0.135 meq g^{-1}.

A sample of heptadecapeptide resin was deprotected with 20% piperidine in DMA as during the assembly, washed with dichloromethane and diethyl ether and then kept *in vacuo* for 1 h. The dried resin (20.1 mg, 2.71 μmol) was side-chain deprotected under nitrogen as follows: 90% aqueous trifluoroacetic acid, 1 × 5 min and 1 × 25; acetic acid, 5 × 1 min; *t*-AmOH, 5 × 1 min; DMA, 5 × 1 min; dichloromethane, 2 × 1 min; diethyl ether, 2 × 1 min; DMA, 5 × 1 min, dichloromethane, 2 × 1 min; diethyl ether, 2 × 1 min. The resin was dried *in vacuo* for 2 h, and after re-swelling in DMA (15 min) it was washed with DMA, 5 × 1 min; 10% diisopropylethylamine-DMA, 3 × 1 min; DMA, 5 × 1 min.

The swollen resin was treated with methanolic ammonia (*c*. 12 ml, saturated at 0°C) in a sealed flask for 17 h. The suspension was filtered and the resin washed with methanol. (Found: Asp, 0.08; Nle, 1.00; 9% residual peptide.) The filtrate and methanol washings were combined and evaporated to dryness to yield peptide (2.42 μmol, 89.3%). (Found: Phe, 1.04; Asp, 1.00; Leu, 2.01; Gly, 1.93; Tyr, 0.98; Ala, 1.04; Glu, 6.32; Pro, 0.95.) This product (2.27 μmol, hplc *Figure 36*, see text) was applied to a column of diethylaminoethyl cellulose (Whatman DE52, 10.2 × 1 cm diameter) and eluted with a linear gradient of 0.01–0.8 M aqueous ammonium hydrogen carbonate, pH 8.1 at a flow rate of 1 ml min^{-1}. The product emerged as a single peak at 198–270 ml (1.77 μmol; 78.0% recovery). (Found: Phe, 1.01; Asp, 1.00; Leu, 2.03; Gly, 1.89; Tyr, 0.97; Ala, 1.06; Glu, 6.09; Pro, 0.94.) Analytical hplc (*Figure 37*) indicated that this product contained a mixture of pyroglutamyl peptide amide (25%) and glutaminyl peptide amide (75%) (see ref. *128* for enzymic characterization of this material). The product (1.6 μmol) was dissolved in 20% aqueous acetic acid (20 ml), kept at 30°C for 64 h under argon, and then evaporated. This product (1.58 μmol) was applied to a column of diethylaminoethyl cellulose (Whatman DE52, 12.5 × 1 cm) and eluted with a linear gradient of 0.01–1.0 M ammonium acetate, pH 6.5 at 1 ml min^{-1}. The glutaminyl heptadecapeptide eluted between 285 and 315 ml, and the pyroglutamyl heptadecapeptide eluted between 330 and 381 ml (1.03 μmol, 65% recovery; there was some physical loss at this stage) (found: Phe, 1.00; Asp, 0.97; Leu, 2.02;

Gly, 2.03; Tyr, 1.00; Ala, 1.05; Glu, 6.40; Pro, 1.07). Part (0.613 μmol) of this product was further purified by μ-Bondapak C_{18} using a convex gradient of 0–35% B during 25 min followed by a linear gradient of 35–100% during 10 min at 2 ml min^{-1} (solvent A = 0.01 M-ammonium acetate, pH 4.5; solvent B = 90% acetonitrile and 10% solvent A). The heptadecapeptide amide (0.43 μmol, 70% recovery, overall yield 32.3%) was obtained. (Found: Phe, 1.00; Asp, 0.96; Leu, 2.03; Gly, 2.03; Tyr, 1.00; Ala, 1.06; Glu, 6.34; Pro, 1.04.) This product was identical with authentic heptadecapeptide amide (**121**) on tlc (butanol–acetic acid–pyridine–water, 60:6:20:24), R_f 0.23; analytical hplc on μ-Bondapak C_{18}, 20–50% acetonitrile during 30 min at 2 ml min^{-1} in 0.01 M ammonium acetate, pH 4.5 (retention time, 16.4 min) and 0.01 M-ammonium acetate, pH 3.5 (retention time, 21.5 min) (*Figure 38*). Analytical hplc 'fingerprint' analysis after limited proteolysis with α-chymotrypsin, *S.aureus* protease V8, and thermolysin was used to compare this product with authentic 15-leucine little gastrin (*128*).

12.3 Synthesis of a peptide amide using a benzhydrylamine linkage

H-Trp-Asp-Asn-Gln-OH (**124**)

This short synthesis illustrates the use of the acid-cleavable amide-producing linkage agent (**115**) for the synthesis of the C-terminal tetrapeptide sequence of the opiate dynorphin. It highlights the particular value of this linkage agent for the formation of the side-chain amides of C-terminal glutamine and asparagine peptides. In this synthesis, the terminal glutamine residue was generated by coupling the α-*t*-butyl ester of Fmoc-*glutamic acid* to the benzhydrylamine linkage agent through its side-chain carboxyl group. At the end of the assembly cleavage with trifluoroacetic acid gave the glutamine-containing peptide. This procedure may become generally preferable for the synthesis of terminal asparagine and glutamine peptides, since direct esterification of these residues to the resin linkage agent is sometimes troublesome and may require use of side-chain-protecting groups.

The assembly was carried out on a high-loading Pepsyn K with a nominal sarcosine content of 0.25 mmol g^{-1}. The ethylene diamine derivatized resin was stored as its hydrochloride salt, and the free base liberated in the column reactor of a CRB PEPSYNthesiser II by piperidine as in a normal Fmoc-deprotection cycle. The linkage agent (**92**) was incorporated using a 2.5-fold excess of the pentafluorophenyl ester catalysed by 1-hydroxybenzotriazole (1 eq). Since the γ-pentafluorophenyl ester of Fmoc-α-*t*-butyl glutamate was not available, opportunity was taken to couple the side-chain carboxyl group directly using the hydroxybenzotriazolyl-tetramethyluronium reagent (**104**, Section 7.3) in the presence of diisopropylethylamine. This reagent is particularly suitable for direct coupling of Fmoc-amino acids in flow synthesis, as no precipitation occurs and there is no risk of blockage. Pentafluorophenyl esters were used for all other couplings. All acylations gave negative colour tests after a 30 min recirculating period.

After removal of the terminal Fmoc group, the resin was washed and dried in the usual manner and the peptide cleaved from part of the resin with trifluoroacetic acid containing ethanedithiol, anisole and phenol. On analytical hplc, the product gave the

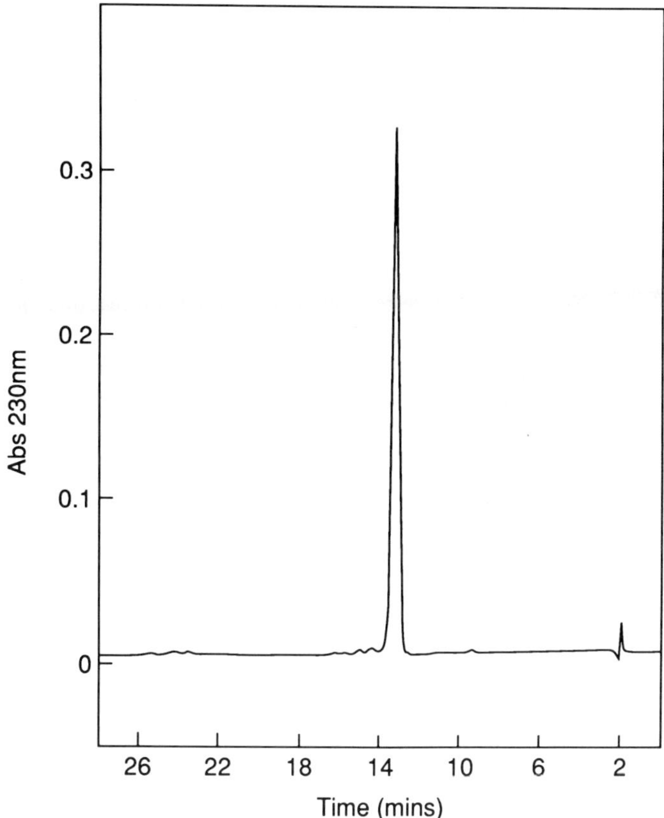

Figure 39. Analytical hplc of total crude tetrapeptide H-Asp-Asn-Gln-OH on a Vydac C_{18} 10 μM 300 Å column (0.46 × 25 cm). Reservoir A contained 0.1% trifluoroacetic acid in water; reservoir B contained 0.1% trifluoroacetic acid in acetonitrile. A linear gradient of 0–30% was run over 30 min; flow rate 1.5 ml min^{-1}, absorbance measured at 230 nm, scale 0.4, chart 0.5 cm min^{-1}.

profile shown in *Figure 39*. The synthesis of **124** was also carried out using the standard acid cleavable linkage agent (**85**) and the side-chain-protected glutamine derivative Fmoc-Gln(Mbh)-OH. The product from this assembly gave a main peak which co-eluted on hplc with the product obtained from the above synthesis.

Synthesis of H-Trp-Asp-Asn-Gln-OH

(1) *Resin preparation*. The Kieselguhr-supported polydimethylacrylamide resin (2 g, nominal sarcosine content 0.25 mmol g^{-1}) was treated with ethylene diamine (20 ml) overnight. The support was then washed with DMF, 0.1 N aqueous HCl, water (until the filtrate was neutral), methanol, and ether, and then dried in high vacuum.

(2) *Assembly*. The resin hydrochloride (0.5 g) was transferred to a reactor column as a slurry in DMF, washed with DMF at a flow rate of 3 ml min^{-1} (10 min)

followed by 20% piperidine in DMF (10 min) and then DMF (10 min). Fmoc-Nle-OPfp (0.16 g, 0.31 mmol) was dissolved together with 1-hydroxybenzotriazole (42 mg, 0.31 mmol) in DMF (1 ml) and the mixture recirculated for 45 min. After 30 min, negative colour tests for residual amine (Section 9.1) were obtained. The resin was washed with DMF for 10 min. Subsequent residues were added using the wash and reaction cycle, DMF (15 min), 20% piperidine DMF (10 min), DMF (15 min) acylation with 2.5-fold excess of acylating derivative, recirculation (45 min), DMF (10 min). The linkage agent (**92**) was added as its pentafluorophenyl ester derivative (0.22 g, 0.31 mmol) in the presence of 1-hydroxybenzotriazole (42 mg). Negative colour tests were obtained after 30 min, and the acylation mixture was washed out after 45 min. The coupling to the amino group of the linkage agent was accomplished using Fmoc-Glu-OBu^t (0.13 g, 0.31 mmol) with O-(1-hydroxybenzotriazolyl)tetramethyluronium hexafluorophosphate (**104**) (0.12 g; 0.31 mmol) as the coupling agent in the presence of diisopropylethylamine (0.053 ml, 0.31 mmol). This mixture was dissolved in the minimum volume of DMF, added directly to the column reactor and recirculated for 45 min. Negative colour tests were obtained after 30 min. Fmoc-Asn-OPfp (0.16 g, 0.31 mmol), Fmoc-Asp(OBu^t).OPfp (0.18 g 0.31 mmol), and Fmoc-Trp-OPfp (0.18 g, 0.31 mmol) were all added as described above for the norleucine residue. All gave negative colour tests after 30 min acylation, and were washed out after 45 min. The Fmoc group was removed from the completed peptide resin using the above wash cycle, the resin transferred to a sintered glass funnel and washed with DMF, *t*-amyl alcohol, acetic acid, *t*-amyl alcohol, and ether, and dried in high vacuum (0.54 g). [Found: Nle, 1.0 (1); Asp, 1.82 (2); Glu, 1.07 (1); Trp, nd (1).]

(3) *Cleavage and isolation.* A sample of the Fmoc deprotected peptide resin (50 mg) was treated with a trifluoroacetic acid–ethanedithiol–anisole–phenol mixture (94:2:2:2; v/v/v/w) for 1.5 h. The resin generated a bright orange-yellow colour immediately on addition of the acid which faded after 1 h. The resin was filtered (found: Glu, 0.06; Nle, 1.00; 95% cleavage), washed with trifluoroacetic acid, and the filtrate and washings evaporated. The residue was triturated with ether several times, followed by evaporation, and the residue was dissolved in water (*c*. 2 ml) and ether. The ether was removed using a pipette and the aqueous phase extracted three more times with ether. The residual ether was evaporated and the aqueous solution applied to hplc to give the profile shown in *Figure 39*. [Found: Asp, 1.82 (2); Glu, 1.12 (1); Trp, nd (1).]

12.4 Synthesis of a complex natural peptide containing a difficult combination of amino acids (*73*)

H-Asp-Thr-Met-Arg-Cys-Met-Val-Gly-Arg-Val-Tyr-Arg-
Pro-Cys-Trp-Glu-Val-OH (**125**)

Perhaps the least satisfactory aspect of current solid phase peptide synthesis concerns side-chain protection. Most trifunctional amino acids are adequately protected in Nα-Fmoc synthesis as *t*-butyl ether, ester, or urethane derivatives, but for others, equally satisfactory groups do not exist. Current protection strategies may be particularly weak for certain *combinations* of amino acids. The success of this present synthesis depended largely on the effectiveness of the purification methods employed.

Melanin-concentrating hormone (MCH) (**125**) is a natural 17-residue peptide liberated from the hypothalamus of teleost fishes. Its amino acid composition includes three arginine residues, two methionines, two cysteines forming a disulphide bridge, and a single tryptophan. No side-chain protection is normally required for tryptophan or methionine under the non-acidic conditions of the Fmoc-polyamide method, though both are susceptible to electrophilic attack, including oxidation. Experience with the natural peptide suggests that both methionine residues may be particularly susceptible to sulphoxide formation (*73*). In this synthesis the arginine residues were protected as the usual methoxytrimethylbenzene sulphonyl (Mtr) derivatives. A significant by-product was formed by the previously unknown reaction of the cleaved Mtr protecting group with the indole ring of tryptophan. Other impurities may have been formed through similar attack on methionine residues, or by oxidation. Acetamidomethyl groups were used for the protection of thiol groups of the two cysteine residues. The disulphide bond was formed by direct iodine oxidation of the acetamidomethyl cysteines; again, impurities were introduced, probably through oxidation elsewhere in the molecule.

The synthesis used symmetrical anhydrides in the continuous-flow technique. The sterically hindered C-terminal residue (valine) esterified smoothly (94%) to the linkage agent in 1 h. Assembly of the peptide chain was not completely straightforward, with slowing of the acylation reactions soon evident. The excess of anhydride was increased from 2- to 4-fold at step 4. Several acylations were repeated, notably tryptophan when the anhydride precipitated during preparation, two arginines (steps 9 and 14), and cysteine (step 13). Probably the anhydrides of these last two amino acids are incompletely stable and do not persist long enough in the reaction mixture in particularly slow couplings. Under these circumstances, repetition with fresh reagent is clearly better than prolonging coupling times. Amino acid analysis carried out after the assembly had been completed suggested that the incorporation of the first arginine may nevertheless have been incomplete, though no substantial proportion of truncated or failure peptide was detected in the careful purification studies.

The best conditions found for cleavage of protecting groups (except the acetamidomethyl groups on cysteine) and detachment from the resin used ethane dithiol and anisole as scavengers. Extended (5 h) treatment was required for complete deprotection of the multiple Mtr–arginine residues.

The hplc profile at this stage (*Figure 40*) indicated a major impurity (B) now known to be a product of substitution of a cleaved Mtr group into the indole ring. Its high uv absorption exaggerates the amount present; the peptide content was actually about 25% of that of the main peak (A). There are in addition a large number of minor impurities grouped around the principal components. A remarkable purification (*Figure 41*) was achieved by ion-exchange chromatography, which separated peaks A and B from each other and all the contaminants. The main component (peak E, corresponding to Peak A in *Figure 41*) was oxidized with iodine in acetic acid to give the cyclic disulphide, accompanied by a number of minor products of over-oxidation. Again, ion-exchange chromatography was effective in separating the mixture (*Figure 42*), yielding highly purified MCH. An alternative procedure also described

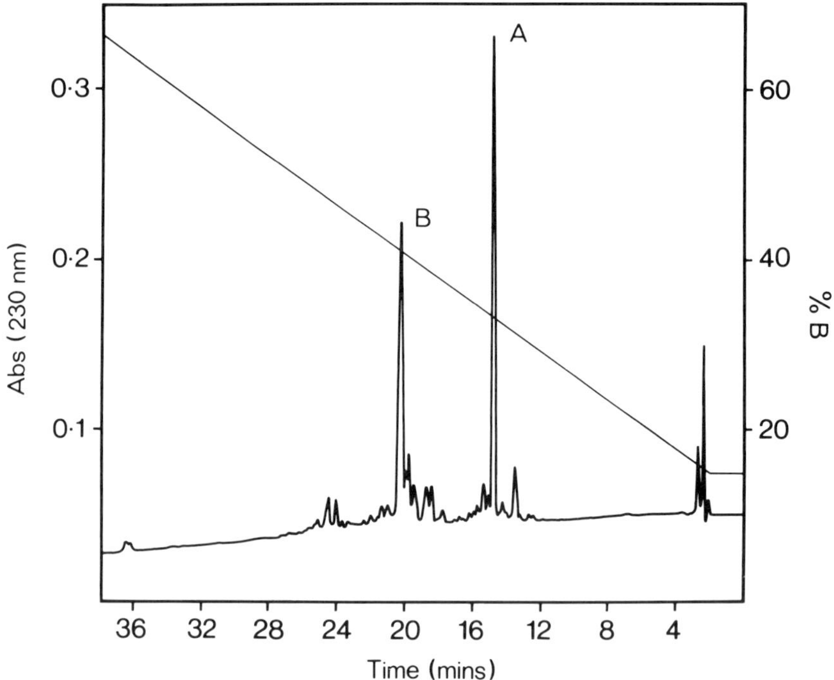

Figure 40. Hplc of total crude resin cleavage product. Conditions: analytical Aquapore RP 300 column; eluent A, 0.1% aqueous trifluoroacetic acid; B, 90% acetonitrile, 10% A. The column was eluted isocratically for 2 min with 15% B and then with a gradient of 15–100% B over 60 min. Flow rate 1.5 ml min^{-1}; chart speed 0.5 cm min^{-1}. Optical density was monitored at 230 nm, absorbance range 0.5, cell thickness 1 cm.

below used gel filtration and then hplc to isolate the nearly pure hormone.

Further discussion of this difficult synthesis may be found in the original publication (*73*).

Solid-phase synthesis of melanin-concentrating hormone

Kieselguhr-supported polydimethylacrylamide resin (*c.* 2.5 g, 0.11 meq sarcosine g^{-1}) was treated overnight with an excess of ethylene diamine (30 ml), washed briefly with DMF by swirling and decantation, and most transferred to a glass column reactor (*c.* 44 mm × 15 mm i.d.). The column was attached to the semi-automatic synthesizer and washing with DMF continued until the effluent gave no colour with ninhydrin. Fmoc-norleucine anhydride (0.5 mmol), and *p*-hydroxy-methylphenoxyacetic acid trichlorophenyl ester (0.5 mmol) in the presence of hydroxybenzotriazole (0.5 mmol) were coupled successively to the resin in the usual manner, the intermediate Fmoc derivative being cleaved with 20% piperidine-DMF. Both acylation reactions were complete within 25 min as judged by ninhydrin and trinitrobenzenesulphonic acid and colour tests. 4-Dimethylaminopyridine (0.25 mmol) dissolved in DMF (0.5 ml) was added to the top of resin bed, rinsed on with DMF (0.5 ml), and then a solution of Fmoc-valine anhydride (1.25 mmol)

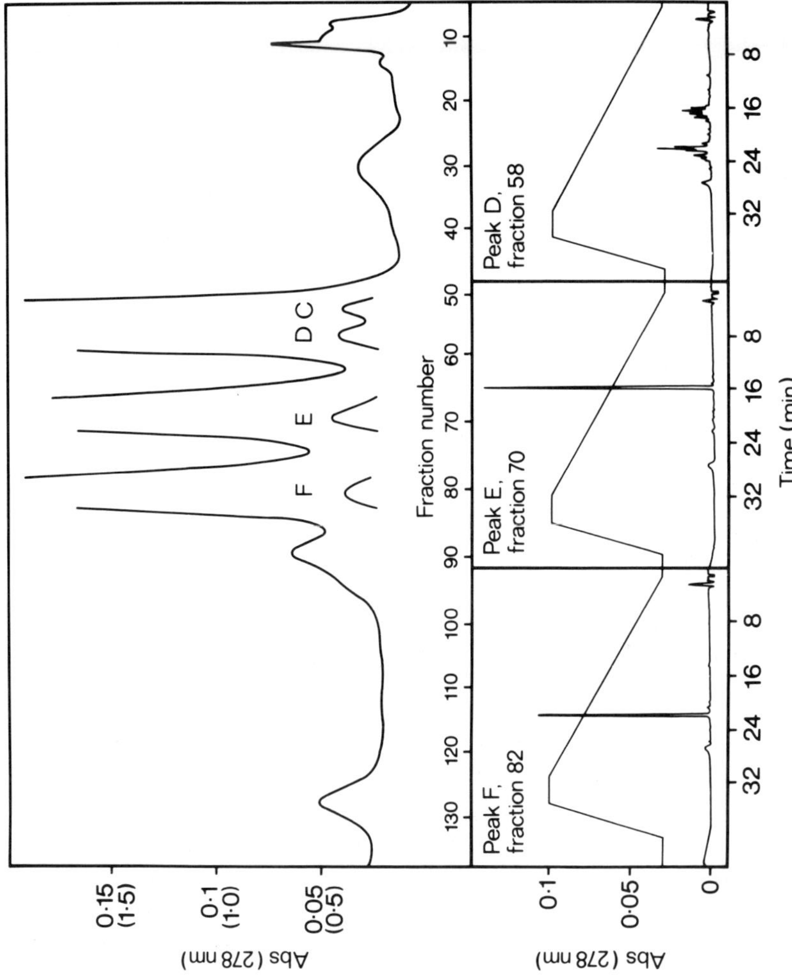

Figure 41. Column chromatography of crude cleavage product on carboxymethylcellulose. For conditions see text. Insets: hplc profiles of peak fractions indicated. Hplc conditions as in *Figure 40*, except that the gradient was from 15 to 50% B over 30 min. Optical density was measured at 278 nm, absorbance range 0.2.

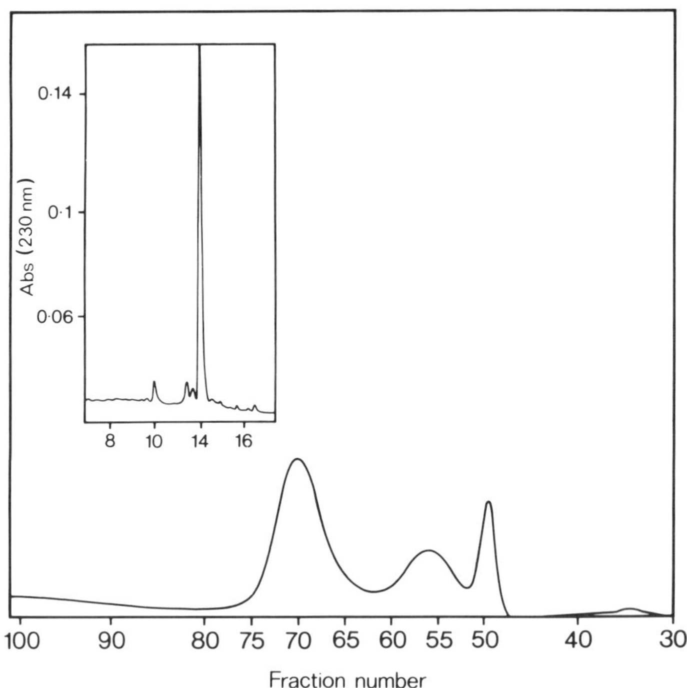

Figure 42. Column chromatography of crude MCH on carboxymethylcellulose. For conditions see text. Inset: hplc of combined fractions 65–77. Conditions as *Figure 40*, except that the absorbance was measured at 230 nm.

in DMF (3 ml) added. The synthesizer was put into recirculation mode and the esterification reaction allowed to proceed for 1 h. Excess of reagents was then washed out with DMF (12 min). The Fmoc group was cleaved with 20% piperidine-DMF (11 min) (this time was used throughout) and washed with DMF (24 min). The following 16 Fmoc-amino-acids were coupled and deprotected using the amounts of anhydride and the coupling time indicated in parentheses: Fmoc-Glu(OBu^t) (0.5 mmol, 50 min); Fmoc-Trp (0.5 mmol, 50 min; 0.5 mmol, 50 min); Fmoc-Cys(Acm) (0.5 mmol, 60 min); Fmoc-Pro (1 mmol, 50 min); Fmoc-Arg(Mtr) (1 mmol, 60 min); Fmoc-Tyr(Bu^t) (1 mmol, 50 min); Fmoc-Val (1 mmol, 50 min); Fmoc-Arg(Mtr) (1 mmol, 90 min; 0.5 mmol added directly, 110 min); Fmoc-Gly (1 mmol, 80 min); Fmoc-Val (1 mmol, 80 min); Fmoc-Met (1 mmol, 60 min); Fmoc-Cys(Acm) (1 mmol, 90 min; 0.5 mmol, 60 min); Fmoc-Arg(Mtr) (1 mmol, 50 min; 0.5 mmol added directly, 120 min); Fmoc-Met (1 mmol, 90 min); Fmoc-Thr(Bu^t) (1.5 mmol, 90 min); Fmoc-Asp(OBu^t) (1 mmol, 110 min; 0.5 mmol, 75 min). Samples were removed for colour tests after each acylation and deprotection reaction, and for amino acid analysis after the addition of Val-17, Pro-13, Val-10, Cys-5, and Asp-1 (*Table 15*).

After the completion of the synthesis, the resin was removed from the column, washed thoroughly with DMF *t*-AmOH, acetic acid, *t*-AmOH, DMF, and ether, and dried *in vacuo* (2.12 g).

Table 15. Amino acid analysis of intermediate peptide resins.

	17	*13–17*	*10–17*	*5–17*	*1–17*
Nle	1.07	1.20	1.20	1.22	1.19
Val	1.00[a]	0.93	1.77	2.86	2.61
Glu		1.00[a]	1.00[a]	1.00[a]	1.00[a]
Pro		1.01	1.07	1.05	1.00
Arg			0.88	1.75	2.51
Tyr			0.81	0.84	0.80
Gly				0.90	0.86
Met				0.82	1.58
Thr					0.79
Asp					0.77

[a]Values are relative to the amino acid marked set equal to 1.00. Cysteine and tryptophan were not determined.

Table 16. Amino acid analysis of intermediate fractions in the purification of bisacetamidomethyl-MCH and MCH. Columns: (1) crude cleavage product; (2) 1st carboxymethylcellulose chromatography, fractions 56–60 (*Figure 41*, peak D); (3) fractions 62–72 (*Figure 41*, peak E, bisacetamido-methyl-MHC); (4) fractions 76–84 (*Figure 41*, peak F); (5) crude oxidation product after G15 chromatography; (6) 2nd carboxymethyl cellulose chromatography, fractions 65–77 (MCH) (*Figure 42*). All values are based on Glu = 1.00.

	(1)	*(2)*	*(3)*	*(4)*	*(5)*	*(6)*
Val	2.57	2.69	3.06	2.95	2.27	2.83
Glu	1.00	1.00	1.00	1.00	1.00	1.00
Pro	1.08	0.93	1.15	1.11	nd	0.77
Arg	2.47	2.14	2.85	2.74	2.54	2.86
Tyr	0.74	0.76	0.77	0.95	0.76	0.87
Gly	0.83	1.00	1.00	1.00	0.89	1.09
Met	1.58	2.77	1.83	1.75	2.27	0.59
Thr	0.91	0.72	0.96	0.95	0.79	0.99
Asp	0.82	0.78	0.96	0.95	0.93	1.02
Met(O)						0.98[a]

[a]The colour constant of aspartic acid was used. The very high proportion of sulphoxide and the general difficulty in obtaining acceptable analyses for methionine may be due to metal ion contamination. Tryptophan and cysteine were not determined.

A sample of the dried peptide resin (0.202 g) was treated with a mixture of trifluoroacetic acid, anisole, and ethane dithiol (30:1:0.3) for 350 min at room temperature. The filtered resin was washed with trifluoroacetic acid, and the filtrate and washings evaporated under reduced pressure. The residue was partitioned between water (60 ml) and ether (60 ml), the aqueous layer washed further with ether (4 × 60 ml), the ether extracts back-washed once with water and the combined aqueous solution lyophilized. The residual resin was washed thoroughly as above, and a sample taken for amino acid analysis (found: Glu, 0.08; Nle, 1.00; 91% cleavage). The crude, freeze-dried peptide was dissolved in water (5 ml). Samples (0.1 ml) were withdrawn for amino acid analysis (*Table 16*) and hplc (*Figure 40*). The residual solution was adjusted to pH 6.0 with dilute ammonium hydroxide and the ionic strength checked to be below that of the starting buffer (0.01 M ammonium acetate, pH 6.0). The solution was centrifuged from some insoluble material and applied to a freshly prepared column of carboxymethylcellulose CM52 (36 cm × 1 cm diameter) which had been equilibrated with 0.01 M ammonium acetate, pH 6.0, at 5°C. The column was developed with a linear gradient of the starting buffer to 0.15 M ammonium acetate, pH 6.0 (260 ml in each reservoir) at 5°C. Fractions (2.9 ml) were collected every 6 min. The effluent was monitored continuously at 278 nm using a 5 mm silica flow cell and dual absorbance ranges of 0.2 and 2 max. The chart speed was 0.05 cm/min (*Figure 41*). Fractions from the four peaks were examined by hplc (*Figure 41*, insets).

Fractions 62–72, 76–84, 49–54 and 56–60 were separately combined and freeze-dried; for amino acid analysis, see *Table 16*.

Material (1.22 μmol from fractions 62–72 was dissolved in glacial acetic acid (4.35 ml), a sample (0.05 ml) removed for hplc, and the remainder added dropwise over 1 min at room temperature to a briskly stirred solution of iodine (0.1 M in acetic acid, 1.94 ml, diluted with further acetic acid, 2.52 ml). The mixture was stirred for a further 10 min and then quenched with M aqueous sodium thiosulphate. The mixture was concentrated under reduced pressure to *c*. 3 ml and then diluted to *c*. 5 ml with acetic acid to dissolve the prcipitate which had formed. The solution was applied to a column of Sephadex G15 (25 cm × 2.5 cm diameter) (some further precipitation occurred at this stage and addition of further acetic acid was necessary). The column was developed with 2 M aqueous acetic acid, fractions (3.6 ml) being collected every 6 min. The effluent was monitored at 230 nm with dual absorbance ranges (0.2 and 2 O.D. units maximum). The first peak (fractions 19–27) was collected and freeze-dried (for amino acid analysis, see *Table 16*) and then chromatographed on a freshly prepared column (33 cm × 1 cm diameter) of carboxymethylcellulose CM52 under the same conditions as previously. The effluent was monitored at 278 nm (*Figure 42*). Fractions 65–77 were combined and freeze-dried. Amino acid analysis, *Table 16*; hplc, *Figure 42* (inset).

The foregoing isolation and oxidation experiments were repeated using the same peptide resin as starting material. Two batches of resin (0.5 g each) were treated with a mixture of trifluoroacetic acid (60 ml), anisole (2 ml), and ethanedithiol (0.6 ml) for 1 h at room temperature with gentle agitation every 3 min. The solutions were filtered and the filtrate evaporated under reduced pressure and the residues re-exposed to a mixture of trifluoroacetic acid (45 ml), anisole (1.5 ml), and ethanedithiol (0.45 ml) for 6, 6.5 h. The solutions were evaporated, re-evaporated with methanol until a dry residue was obtained, dissolved in water (50 ml), and extracted with ether (40 ml), one sample twice and the other five times. Lyophilization of the aqueous solutions gave 75 mg and 63 mg of crude product respectively. Both preparations gave hplc profiles very similar to that of the crude bis(acetamidomethyl) linear heptadecapeptide shown in *Figure 40*. For amino acid analysis, see *Table 17*.

The two samples were chromatographed individually on columns (35 cm × 1 cm diameter) of carboxymethylcellulose CM52, using the same gradient of aqueous ammonium acetate as before. The elution profiles were very similar to that of *Figure 41*. The appropriate peaks were collected and lyophilized, yielding 20.5 mg

Table 17. Amino acid analysis of intermediate fractions in the larger scale purification of bisacetamidomethyl-MCH and MCH. Columns: A, crude cleavage product; B, bisacetamidomethyl-MCH after carboxymethylcellulose chromatography; C, MCH after chromatography on LH-20; D, hplc-purified MCH.

	A	*B*	*C*	*D*
Val	2.86, 2.56	2.58	2.31, 2.73	2.60
Glu	1.00, 1.00	1.00, 1.00	1.00, 1.00	1.00
Pro	0.91	0.99	0.91, 0.99	0.99
Arg	2.68, 2.51	3.17, 2.82	2.26, 2.77	2.55
Tyr	0.84, 0.84	0.88, 0.96	0.80, 0.97	0.84
Gly	1.02, 0.95	1.04, 1.08	1.00, 1.10	0.99
Met	0.18, 0.19	1.94, 1.78	1.51, 1.55	0.77
Thr	0.82, 0.79	0.95, 0.72	0.86, 0.73	0.98
Asp	1.03, 0.81	1.00, 0.93	0.83, 0.83	0.93
Met(O)*	1.66, 1.25	– –	0.10 –	1.08

[a]The colour constant for aspartic acid was used; see footnote to *Table 16*. All values are based on Glu = 1.00. Tryptophan and cysteine were not determined.

and 19.5 mg of purified heptadecapeptide derivative; for amino acid analysis, see *Table 17*.

After a number of small-scale preliminary experiments, the following procedure was adopted for oxidative closure of the disulphide ring. A solution of the linear heptadecapeptide (4.9 mg, 2 μmol) in glacial acetic acid (2 ml) containing L-methionine (1.49 mg, 10 μmol) was added dropwise over 5 min under a nitrogen atmosphere to a vigorously stirred solution of iodine (101.6 mg, 400 μmol) in acetic acid (20 ml). The mixture was stirred for a further 25 min and concentrated aqueous ascorbic acid solution added until colourless (*c*. 6 ml). The solution was evaporated under reduced pressure to less than 5 ml and applied directly to a column of Sephadex LH-20 (140 cm × 3.5 cm diameter) packed in 1% acetic acid and eluted with the same solvent. The effluent was monitored at 280 nm. Fractions (10 ml) were collected every 10 min. Selected individual fractions were examined by hplc before being combined and lyophilized. Fractions 53–57 furnished 2.95 mg; for amino acid analysis, see *Table 17*. Fractions 51, 52 and 58–62 were pooled, lyophilized, and further purified by hplc to give a further 0.95 mg. The total yield was thus 3.9 mg (80%). A second similar experiment gave 3.8 mg. The synthetic MCH gave single spots on tlc, developed with ninhydrin and the Reindel–Hoppe reagent, in *n*-butanol–acetic acid–pyridine–water (50:12.5:12.5:25), R_f 0.35, and butan-1-ol–acetic acid–pyridine–water (42:4:24:30), R_f 0.27.

12.5 Synthesis of an N-terminal and side-chain-protected octapeptide

Fmoc-Thr(Bu^t)-Lys(Boc)-Thr(Bu^t)-Ala-
Lys(Boc)-Asp(OBu^t)-Leu-Gly-OH **(126)**

The bacteriophage λ-Cro repressor is a small regulatory protein which binds specifically with DNA. The octapeptide derivative (**126**) is one of a series of protected fragments spanning the entire sequence of Cro which were prepared during exploratory studies on solid phase fragment condensation synthesis (*134*). The very acid labile linkage

Table 18. Amino acid analysis of peptide resins and free peptide. All ratios are expressed relative to Gly = 1.00.

Step	1	5	6	7	8	Peptide
Nle	1.23	1.27	1.27	1.25	1.24	
Gly	1.00	1.00	1.00	1.00	1.00	1.00
Leu		1.00	1.00	0.98	0.97	0.98
Asp		1.01	1.01	1.00	0.99	0.99
Lys		0.99	0.99	1.92	1.91	2.08
Ala		1.00	0.99	0.98	0.97	1.04
Thr			0.98	0.98	1.96	1.96

(**114**) cleavable in the presence of side chain *t*-butyl derivatives was specially developed for these studies. Its use and cleavage under very mild conditions is illustrated in this synthesis.

The assembly of the octapeptide sequence was carried out on a high-loading beaded gel polydimethylacrylamide using symmetrical anhydrides for all the amino acids except lysine (*p*-nitrophenyl ester). The symmetrical anhydride was also used for the hydroxymethyl linkage agent itself. No evidence of self-acylation was obtained using the unprotected anhydride, but current practice now utilizes the pentafluorophenyl ester for this acylation. The dimethylaminopyridine-catalysed esterification of the first amino acid (glycine) on to the rather hindered linkage proceeded in lower (87%) yield than usual. However the residual unacylated hydroxyl groups did not act as growth points for new peptide chains during the assemby, and no capping off (acetylation) reaction was necessary. Assembly of the peptide chain was smooth, with excellent amino acid incorporation at every stage (*Table 18*).

The peptide–resin linkage was cleaved in the presence of four *t*-butyl-protected side chains under conditions designed to minimize contact with the acidic reagent. The reaction was carried out by flowing dilute trifluoroacetic acid through the resin and immediately quenching the effluent with DMF. The TFA–DMF complex was conveniently removed by chromatography on Sephadex LH-20. The protected peptide had an excellent amino acid analysis (*Table 18*) and hplc profile (*Figure 43*).

Assembly and cleavage of the protected Cro octapeptide

Pepsyn gel (3 g, nominal sarcosine content of 1.18 mmol g^{-1}) was reacted with ethylene diamine, Fmoc-norleucine anhydride (8.9 mmol) (Section 10.1.2), and then with the freshly prepared anhydride of 3-methoxy-4-hydroxymethylphenoxyacetic acid (8.9 mmol, reaction time 65 min). The resin (4.03 g) had a norleucine content of 0.606 mmol g^{-1}. This resin (2.8 g) was acylated with Fmoc-glycine anhydride (0.5 mmol) (the anhydride precipitated during its preparation in dichloromethane–see Section 7.1) in the presence of 4-dimethylaminopyridine (3.4 mmol) in a total volume of 37 ml of DMF for 15 min (Section 10.2). After thorough washing with DMF, dichloromethane, and then ether, the dried resin had amino acid analysis, Gly, 0.87; Nle, 1.00 (87% incorporation of the C-terminal residue).

This resin (0.5 g, 0.303 mmol) was deprotected and the peptide chain assembled

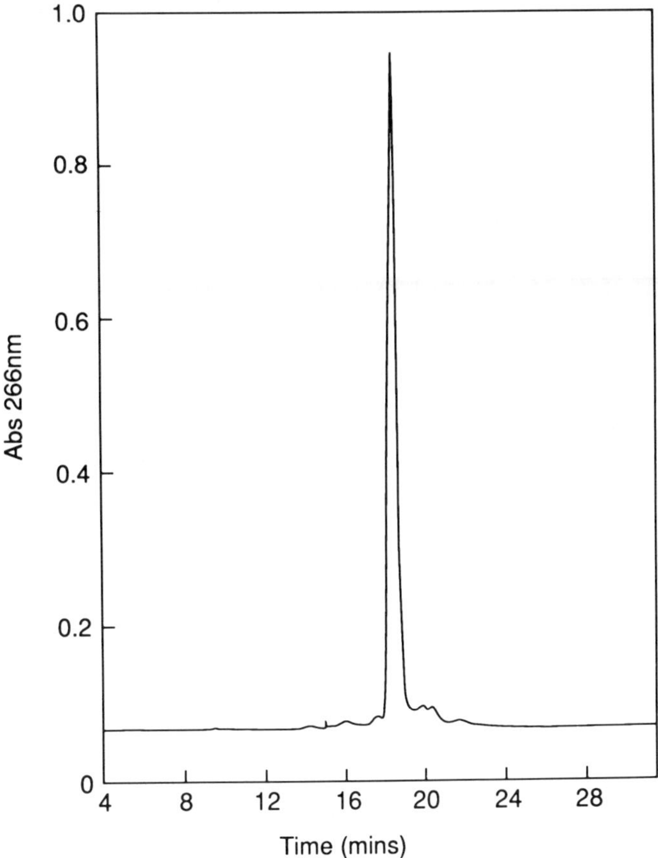

Figure 43. Hplc of protected octapeptide after chromatography on Sephadex LH-20. Conditions, μ-Bondapak C_{18} column. Linear gradient of 40 to 100% acetonitrile in 0.01 M aqueous ammonium acetate, pH 4.5.

(Section 10.3.1). The general procedure was DMF (5 × 1 min); 20% piperidine in DMF (3 + 7 min); Dmf (10 × 1 min); acylation reaction in the minimum volume of DMF; DMF (5 × 1 min). Preformed symmetrical anhydrides (2.5 eq) were used for Fmoc-Leu, Fmoc-Asp(OBu^t), Fmoc-Ala and Fmoc-Thr(Bu^t); the *p*-nitrophenyl ester (2.5 eq) in the presence of HOBt (2.5 eq) was used for Fmoc-Lys(Boc) (see Section 5.1.3.1). In all cases, negative colour tests were obtained within the 60 min acylation period. Resin samples were removed for amino acid analysis after the 5th, 6th, 7th and 8th residues (*Table 18*). The final resin loading was 0.314 mmol g^{-1}.

The washed and dried peptide resin (0.414 g) was placed in a sintered glass funnel and a solution of 1% trifluoroacetic acid in dichloromethane (75 ml) allowed to flow slowly through over a period of 40 min (Section 11.1.4). The effluent was quenched by allowing it to drop directly into DMF (1.5 ml) cooled in an ice-bath. The residual resin was subjected to amino acid analysis (found: Gly, 0.063; Nle, 1.00), corresponding to 92% detachment of peptide.

The dichloromethane solution was concentrated *in vacuo*, and the residual oil (protected peptide and trifluoroacetic acid–DMF complex) dissolved in a small volume of DMF and applied to a column (83 cm × 2.5 cm diameter) of Sephadex LH-20 packed in DMF. The column was eluted with DMF at a flow rate of 0.5 ml min^{-1} and the effluent monitored at 270 nm using a 0.2 cm flow cell. The peptide peak eluted between 156 and 189 ml. Amino acid analysis (*Table 18*) indicated a yield of 113 μmol. For hplc profile, see *Figure 43*.

12.6 Synthesis of 9-, 16-, 23- and 30-residue peptides using pentafluorophenyl and Dhbt esters in a commercial continuous-flow synthesizer *(137)*

The carboxy-terminal region of the largest subunit of eukaryotic RNA polymerase II, contains a heptapeptide sequence which is repeated many times and is required for optimal function *in vivo*. Model peptides (**127**, $n = 1-4$) containing this subunit were required for studying steps in the transcription process.

$$\text{H-(Pro-Thr-Ser-Pro-Ser-Tyr-Ser)}_n\text{-Pro-Gly-OH} \qquad \textbf{(127)}$$

The assembly was carried out in a Pharmacia-LKB Biolynx automatic synthesizer and was very straightforward. The sequence is uncomplicated and all reactions proceeded rapidly and evidently to completion. It is possible that the high proline content contributed to the smooth assembly by inhibiting regular secondary structure and internal aggregation.

The starting Fmoc-glycine resin bearing the usual acid-labile hydroxymethylphenoxy-acetyl linkage agent and norleucine internal reference amino acid was a commercial

Table 19. Reaction and instrument parameters for one cycle of Fmoc-amino acid addition and deprotection using the Biolynx continuous-flow synthesizer (see text).

Amino Acid	**Pro-05**
Active species	**PFPE**
Column	**A**
Isomer	**L**
Temperature	**22°C**
Column load	**2.0**
Load repeat	**No**
Agitation time	**04:00**

Side-chain protecting group	**None**
Load amino acid manually	**No**
Third reagent for deprotection	**No**

	Flow	*Time*	*Repeat*	*Pause*	*Wave*	*Min.*	*Max.*	*Time*	*Area*
Prewash	**4.00**	**0:05:00**	**No**						
Recirculation	**4.00**	**0:45:00**		**No**	**304**	**1.5**	**3.00**	**0:00:32**	**15%**
						0.50	**3.00**	**0:40:00**	
Flush	**4.00**	**0:05:00**	**No**	**No**					
Acetylation	**0.00**	**0:00:00**							
Deprotection	**4.00**	**0:10:00**		**No**	**304**	**0.00**	**0.05**	**0:09:30**	**15%**

preparation. One gram (*c.* 0.1 mmol) of the resin in reaction column A was used. A facsimile of the Biolynx synthesis file for addition of the first proline residue (formation of the first peptide bond) is shown in *Table 19*. A separate synthesis file presets the instrument, spectrophotometer, and reaction parameters individually for each residue in the sequence. Default files for each amino acid type are stored in memory and are modified as necessary for each residue in the sequence. Reading from the top, the amino acid reagent is identified as (Fmoc)-proline Pfp ester in a vial containing 0.5 mmol (5 eq; only 0.5 mmol and 1.25 mmol vials are available from the instrument makers), and is to be added to reaction column A. (The synthesizer contains three reaction columns which may be selected individually or connected in series.) The amino acid is designated as the L-enantiomer. The column temperature control is set at 22 °C, and the sample is to be dissolved in 2 ml of DMF by agitation with nitrogen for 4 min.

The reaction parameters are indicated in the lower left-hand area of *Table 19*. The resin is subjected to a prewash for 5 min (this effectively is an extension of the similar wash period after the previous deprotection cycle), and the acylation (Recirculation) time is 45 min. Excess reagent is washed out (Flush) for 5 min, there is no acetylation (capping) step, and deprotection proceeds immediately for 10 min. Deprotection is followed by a mandatory 5 min wash (not shown).

There are no repeat operations or pauses inserted for manual intervention.

The photometric monitoring parameters are given in the lower right-hand part of *Table 19*. For the acylation (Recirculation) step, the UV spectrophotometer is set at 304 nm, and an absorbance of the flowing stream of between 1.5 and 3 optical density units is expected 32 sec into the acylation period. This corresponds to the first pass of the dissolved Fmoc-amino acid derivative through the flow cell and is a check for correct sample dissolution and transfer from the vial. If this absorbance is not achieved, a warning is displayed and the synthesizer shuts down safely. The area of this first peak in the acylation profile (see *Figure 24*) is also checked against that of the preceding residue and must not deviate from it by more than 15%. Another optical density check is to be made after 40 min near the end of the reaction period, when an absorbance between 0.5 and 3 units is expected. (These limits could have been set much closer.) This is in the plateau region of the acylation profile. Deprotection is similarly checked, with a near-zero absorbance (return to baseline) required after 9.5 min at the end of the reaction and a peak area not deviating from that of the previous residue by more than 15%. The synthesis file for each of the succeeding amino acids is generally similar. For DHbt esters (O-*t*-butylserine and threonine) the spectrophotometer is set at 320 nm

Table 20. Amino acid analysis for the crude synthetic peptides (**127**, $n = 1-4$). All figures are referred to the C-terminal glycine residue = 1.00. Theoretical integer values are in parentheses.

Residue	*Peptide length*			
	9 (n = 1)	16 (n = 2)	23 (n = 3)	30 (n = 4)
Gly	1.00 (1)	1.00 (1)	1.00 (1)	1.00 (1)
Pro	2.80 (3)	4.54 (5)	6.76 (7)	8.38 (9)
Ser	2.72 (3)	5.25 (6)	8.09 (9)	10.34 (12)
Thr	0.96 (1)	1.83 (2)	2.81 (3)	3.64 (4)
Tyr	0.95 (1)	1.84 (2)	2.87 (3)	3.68 (4)

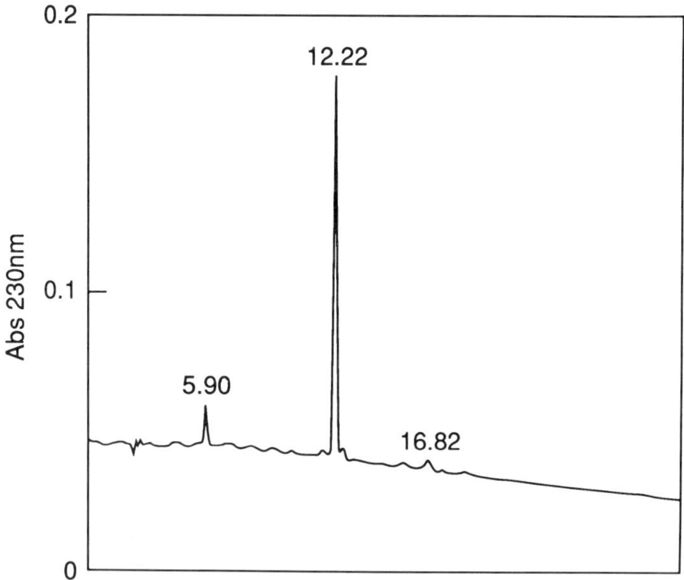

Figure 44. Hplc profile for total crude 16-residue peptide (**127**, $n = 2$). Conditions, Aquapore RP 300 column. Reservoir A contained 0.1% aqueous trifluoroacetic acid; reservoir B contained 90% acetonitrile, 10% A. After 2 min elution with 5% B, a linear gradient of 10–40% B over was developed over 25 min. The effluent was monitored at 230 nm.

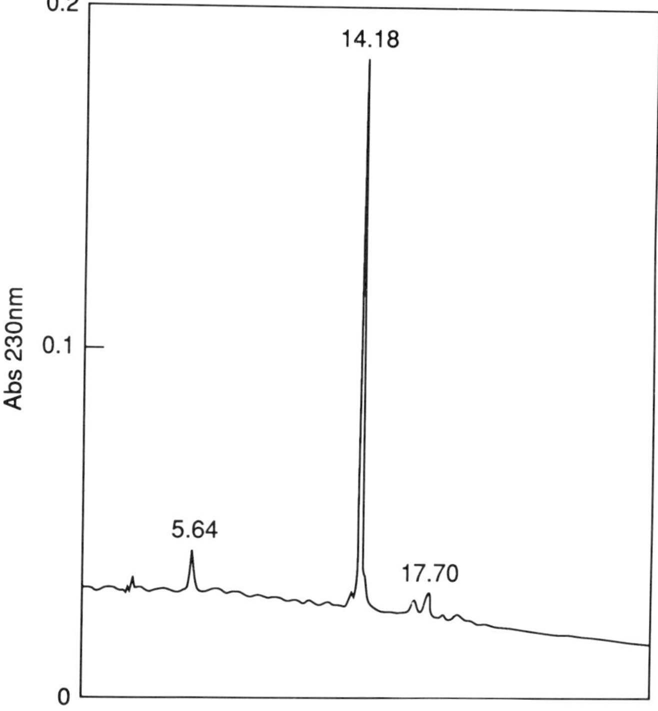

Figure 45. Hplc profile for total crude 23-residue peptide (**127**, $n = 3$). Conditions as above.

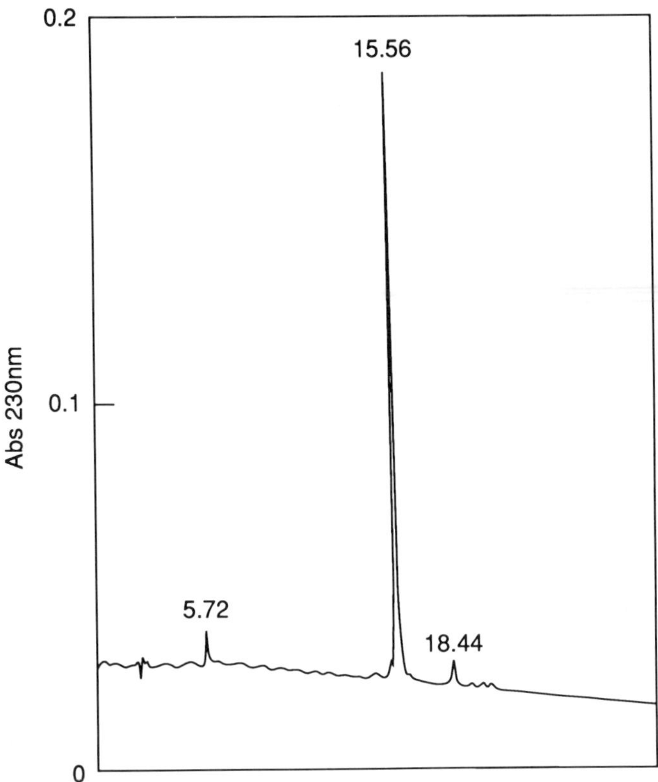

Figure 46. Hplc profile for total crude 3-residue peptide (**127**, $n = 4$). conditions as above.

during the acylation period, and for these more soluble residues the dissolution time is also reduced to 3 min.

Conduct of the synthesis was straightforward, with all the synthesis and extensive housekeeping operations (instrument wash) performed sequentially under computer control. Small samples of resin were removed after 9, 16, 23, 30 residues, washed, dried and cleaved with 95% trifluoroacetic acid for 70–75 min, and the crude peptide characterized by amino acid analysis (*Table 20*) and analytical hplc (*Figures 44–46*).

Amino acid analysis of the crude peptides was good, though complicated by the unfavourable composition (Section 9.2). Serine and threonine, and sometimes also tyrosine, may be partly destroyed during acidic hydrolysis, and proline gives a low colour yield with the ninhydrin reagent. Recoveries of 86–91% for serine and 91–96% for threonine were obtained, in agreement with expectation. In conjunction with the excellent hplc traces (*Figures 44–46*), this data provides very good indication of efficient synthesis. It is being further extended and all the products examined closely to determine to what extent peptide purity can be established with increasing chain length (*135*).

References

1. Goddard,P., McMurray,J.S., Sheppard,R.C. and Emson,P. (1988) *J. Chem. Soc. Chem. Commun.*, 1025.
2. For a review of the early history of peptide synthesis, see Fruton,J.S. (1987) in *Peptides 1986,* Theodoropoulos,D. (ed.), Walter de Gruyter, Berlin, p. 25.
3. du Vigenaud,V., Ressler,C., Swann,J.M., Roberts,C.W. and Katsoyannis,P.G. (1954) *J. Amer. Chem. Soc.*, **76**, 3115.
4. *The Peptides, Analysis, Synthesis, Biology,* Gross,E. and Meienhofer,J. (eds), Academic Press, New York, 1979–, Vols 1–9. Bodanszky,M., Klausner,Y.S. and Ondetti,M.A. (1976) *Peptide Synthesis,* Wiley, New York, 2nd edn; Bodanszky,M. (1984) *Principles of Peptide Synthesis,* Springer-Verlag, Berlin; Bodanszky,M. (1984) *The Practice of Peptide Synthesis,* Springer-Verlag, Berlin; Wunsch,E. (1974) *Methoden der Organischen Chemie (Houben Weyl),* Vol. XXV/1,2, '*Synthesen von Peptiden*', Georg Thieme Verlag, Stuttgart; Sheppard,R.C. (1979) in *Comprehensive Organic Chemistry,* Barton,D.H.R. and Ollis,W.D. (eds), Pergamon Press, Oxford.
5. Bergmann,M. and Zervas,L. (1932) *Chem. Berichte,* **65**, 1192.
6. McKay,F.C. and Albertson,N.F. (1957) *J. Amer. Chem. Soc.*, **79**, 4686.
7. Carpino,L.A. and Han,G.Y. (1972) *J. Org. Chem.*, **37**, 3404.
8. Kisfaludy,L. and Schon,I. (1983) *Synthesis,* 325; Schon,I. and Kisfaludy,L. (1986) *Synthesis,* 303.
9. Konig,W. and Geiger,R. (1970) *Chem. Berichte,* **103**, 2024.
10. Konig,W. and Geiger,R. (1973) *Chem. Berichte,* **106**, 3626.
11. Sheehan,J.C. and Hess,G.P. (1955) *J. Amer. Chem. Soc.*, **77**, 1067.
12. Merrifield,R.B. (1962) *Fed. Proc. Fed. Amer. Soc. Exp. Biol.*, **21**, 412.
13. Merrifield,R.B. (1963) *J. Amer. Chem. Soc.*, **85**, 2149.
14. Merrifield,R.B. (1964) *Biochemistry,* **3**, 1385.
15. Erickson,B.W. and Merrifield,R.B. (1976) In *The Proteins.* Neurath,H. and Hill,R.L. (eds), Vol. 2, 3rd edn, Academic Press, New York, pp. 255–527.
16. Barany,G. and Merrifield,R.B. (1979) In *The Peptides.* Gross,E. and Meienhofer,J. (eds), Vol. 2, Academic Press, New York, pp. 3–285.
17. Meienhofer,H. (1973) *Hormonal Proteins and Peptides,* **2**, 46; Stewart,J.M. and Young,J.D. (1969) *Solid Phase Peptide Synthesis,* Freeman, San Francisco; Birr,Chr. (1978) *Aspects of the Merrifield Peptide Synthesis,* Springer-Verlag, Berlin.
18. Gait,M.J. (ed.) (1984) *Oligonucleotide Synthesis: A Practical Approach.* IRL Press, Oxford.
19. Birr,Chr. and Lochinger,W. (1971) *Synthesis,* 319; Birr,Chr., Flor,F., Fleckenstein,P., Lochinger,W. and Wieland,T. (1973) in *The Peptides 1971,* Nesvadba,H. (ed.), North-Holland, Amsterdam, p. 175.
20. Wang,S.S. (1973) *J. Amer. Chem. Soc.*, **95**, 1328.
21. Tamm,J.P. (1987) *Int. J. Peptide Prot. Res.*, **29**, 421.
22. Sheppard,R.C. (1973) In *Peptides 1971.* Nesvadba,H. (ed.), North Holland, Amsterdam, p. 111.
23. Atherton,E., Gait,M.J., Sheppard,R.C. and Williams,B.J. (1979) *Bioorg. Chem.*, **8**, 351. Sheppard,R.C. (1986) *Science Tools,* **33**, 9–16.
24. Atherton,E. and Sheppard,R.C. (1981) In *Perspectives in Peptide Chemistry.* Eberle,A., Geiger,R. and Wieland,Th (eds), Karger, Basle, p. 101.
25. Kent,S.B.H. (1985) *Proc. 9th Amer. Peptide Symp.*, Toronto 1985, Deber,V., Hruby,V. and Kopple,K. (eds), Pierce Chemical Co., Rockford, Illinois, p. 407; Atherton,E. and Sheppard,R.C., *ibid.*, p. 415.
26. Merrett,F.M. (1957) *J. Polym. Sci.*, **24**, 467.
27. Chou,F.C.H., Chawla,R.K., Kibler,R.F. and Shapira,R. (1971) *J. Amer. Chem. Soc.*, **93**, 267.
28. Hagenmeier,H. (1974) *Tetrahedron Lett.*, 283.
29. Hancock,W.S., Prescott,D.J., Vagelos,P.R. and Marshall,G.R. (1973) *J. Org. Chem.*, **38**, 774.
30. Westall,F.C. and Robinson,A.B. (1970) *J. Org. Chem.*, **35**, 2842.
31. Kemp,D.S. (1973) In *Peptides 1971.* Nesvadba,H. (ed.), North Holland, Amsterdam, p. 1.
32. Kemp,D.S., Choong,S.L.H. and Pekaar,L. (1974) *J. Org. Chem.*, **39**, 3841.
33. Pepper,K.W., Paisley,H.M. and Young,M.A. (1953) *J. Chem. Soc.*, 4097.
34. Merrifield,R.B. and Kent,S.B.H. (1981) In *Peptides 1980.* Brunfeldt,K. (ed.), Scriptor, Copenhagen, p. 328.
35. Inman,J.K. and Dintzis,H.M. (1969) *Biochemistry,* **8**, 4074.
36. Atherton,E. and Sheppard,R.C. (1974) In *Peptides 1974.* Wolmer,W. (ed.), Wiley, New York, p. 123.
37. Atherton,E., Logan,C.J. and Sheppard,R.C. (1981) *J. Chem. Soc., Perkin Trans. 1,* 538.
38. Florr,F., Birr,Chr. and Wieland,Th. (1973) *Annalen,* 1601.
39. Atherton,E., Holder,J., Meldal,M., Sheppard,R.C. and Valerio,R.M. (1988) *J. Chem. Soc., Perkin Trans. 1,* 2887.

40. Atherton,E., Clive,D.L.J. and Sheppard,R.C. (1975) *J. Amer. Chem. Soc.*, **97**, 6585.
41. Arshady,R., Atherton,E., Clive,D.L.J. and Sheppard,R.C. (1981) *J. Chem. Soc., Perkin Trans. 1,* 529.
42. Kaiser,E., Colescott,R.L. Bossinger,C.D. and Cook,P.I. (1970) *Analyt. Biochem.*, **34**, 595.
43. Sarin,V.K., Kent,S.B.H., Tam,J.P. and Merrifield,R.B. (1981) *Analyt. Biochem.*, **117**, 147.
44. Lukas,T.J., Prystowsky,M.B. and Erickson,B.W. (1981) *Proc. Natl. Acad. Sci. USA,* **78**, 2791.
45. Chaturvedi,N., Sigler,G., Fuller,W., Verlander,M. and Goodman,M. (1981) In *Chemical Synthesis and Sequencing of Peptides and Proteins.* Lynn, Schechter, Henrikson and Canoliffe (eds), Elsevier-North Holland, Amsterdam, p. 169.
46. Jonczwk,A. and Meienhofer,J. (1983) In *Proc. 8th Amer. Peptide Symp.*, Tucson, 1983, Hruby,V. and Rich,D. (eds), Pierce Chemical Co., Rockford, Illinois, p. 73.
47. Atherton,E., Brown,E., Sheppard,R.C. and Rosevear,A. (1981) *J. Chem. Soc., Chem. Comm.*, 1151.
48. Sheppard,R.C. (1983) *Chem. Brit.*, 402.
49. Dryland,A. and Sheppard,R.C. (1986) *J. Chem. Soc., Perkin Trans. 1,* 125.
50. Smith,C.W., Stahl,G.L. and Walter,R. (1979) *Int. J. Peptide Prot. Res.*, **13**, 109.
51. Epton,R., Goddard,P., Marr,G., McLaren,J.V. and Morgan,G.J. (1979) *Polymer,* **20**, 1444.
52. Arshady,R., Kenner,G.W. and Ledwith,A. (1974) *J. Polym. Sci.*, **12**, 2017.
53. Stewart,J.M. and Young,J.D. (1969) *Solid Phase Peptide Synthesis.* Freeman, San Francisco.
54. Miles,B.J., *Brit. Pat.* 1586364 (1976); Thompson,A.R. and Miles,B.J., *Brit. Pat.* 1421531 (1971).
55. Sheppard,P.W., Cambridge Research Biochemicals Ltd, personal communication.
56. Chang,C.D. and Meienhofer (1978) *Int. J. Peptide Prot. Res.*, **11**, 246.
57. Atherton,E. and Sheppard,R.C. (1987) In *The Peptides, Analysis, Synthesis, Biology,* Gross,E. and Meienhofer,J. (eds), Academic Press, New York, Vol. 9, p. 1.
58. Atherton,E., Fox,H., Harkiss,D., Logan,C.J., Sheppard,R.C. and Williams,B.J. (1978) *J. Chem. Soc., Chem. Comm.*, 537.
59. Sigler,G.F., Fuller,W.D., Chaturvedi,N.C., Goodman,M. and Verlander,M. (1983) *Biopolymers,* **22**, 2157.
60. Lapatsanis,L., Milias,G., Proussios,K. and Kolovos,M. (1983) *Synthesis,* 671.
61. Paquet,A. (1982) *Can. J. Chem.*, **60**, 976.
62. Atherton,E., Bury,C., Sheppard,R.C. and Williams,B.J. (1979) *Tetrahedron Lett.*, 3041.
63. Chang,C.D., Waki,M., Ahmad,M., Meienhofer,J., Lundell,E.O. and Haug,J.D. (1980) *Int. J. Peptide Prot. Res.*, **15**, 59.
64. Martinez,J., Tolle,J.C. and Bodanszky,M. (1979) *J. Org. Chem.*, **44**, 3596.
65. Atherton,E., Logan,C.J. and Sheppard,R.C. (1981) *J. Chem. Soc., Perkin Trans. 1,* 538.
66. Richards,J.D., unpublished results.
67. Colombo,R., Colombo,F. and Jones,J.H. (1984) *J. Chem. Soc., Chem. Comm.*, 292.
68. Sieber,P. and Riniker,B. (1987) *Tetrahedron Lett.*, **28**, 48.
69. Atherton,E., Cammish,L.E., Goddard,P. Richards,J.D. and Sheppard,R.C. (1984) In *Peptides 1984,* Ragnarsson, Almquist and Wiksell (eds), Stockholm, p. 153.
70. Atherton,E., Sheppard,R.C. and Wade,J.D. (1983) *J. Chem. Soc., Chem. Comm.*, 1060.
71. Fujii,N., Otaka,A., Ikemura,O., Akaji,K., Funakoshi,Y., Hayashi,Y., Kuroda,Y and Yajima,H. (1987) *J. Chem. Soc., Chem. Comm.*, 274.
72. Ramage,R. and Green,J. (1987) *Tetrahedron Lett.*, **28**, 2287.
73. Eberle,A.N., Atherton,E., Dryland,A. and Sheppard,R.C. (1986) *J. Chem. Soc., Perkin Trans. 1,* 361.
74. Sieber,P. (1987) *Tetrahedron Lett.*, **28**, 1637.
75. Cammish,L.E. (1987) *PhD Thesis,* University of Cambridge, unpublished.
76. Atherton,E., Pinori,M. and Sheppard,R.C. (1985) *J. Chem. Soc., Perkin Trans. 1,* 2057.
77. Wade,W., Cambridge Research Biochemicals Ltd, unpublished.
78. Veber,D.F., Milkowski,J.D., Vargas,S.L., Denkewalter,R.G. and Hirschmann,R. (1972) *J. Amer. Chem. Soc.*, **94**, 5456.
79. Fontana,A. (1975) *J. Chem. Soc., Chem. Comm.*, 976.
80. Kamber,B. (1971) *Helv. Chim. Acta,* **54**, 927.
81. Chimiak,A. (1963) In *Peptides 1962,* Young,G.T. (ed.), Pergamon Press, Oxford, p. 37; Beyerman, H.C. (1963) In *Peptides 1962,* Young,G.T. (ed.), Pergamon Press, Oxford, p. 53.
82. Weber,U. and Hartter,P. (1970) *Z. Physiol. Chem.*, **351**, 1384; Ruegg,U.T. and Gattner,H.G. (1975) *Z. Physiol. Chem.*, **356**, 1527.
83. Atherton,E., Sheppard,R.C. and Ward,P. (1985) *J. Chem. Soc., Perkin Trans. 1,* 2065.
84. Sheppard,R.C. and Williams,B.J. (1982) *Int. J. Peptide Prot. Res.*, **20**, 451.
85. Galpin,I.J., Hardy,P.M., Kenner,G.W., McDermott,J.R., Ramage,R., Seeley,J. and Tyson,R.G. (1979) *Tetrahedron,* **35**, 2577.
86. Priestley,G., Cambridge Research Biochemicals Ltd, unpublished results.
87. Atherton,E., Brown,E., Priestley,G., Sheppard,R.C. and Williams,B.J. (1981) *Proc. 7th Amer. Peptide*

Symp., Rich,D.H. and Gross,E. (eds), Pierce Chem. Co., Rockford, Illinois, p. 163; Sheppard,R.C. and Williams,B.J. (1982) *J. Chem. Soc., Chem. Comm.*, 587.
88. Colombo,R., Atherton,E., Sheppard,R.C. and Woolley,V. (1983) *Int. J. Peptide Prot. Res.*, **21**, 118.
89. Pedroso,E., Grandas,A., de las Heras,X., Eritja,R. and Giralt,E. (1986) *Tetrahedron, Lett.*, **27**, 243.
90. Rink,H. (1987) *Tetrahedron Lett.*, **28**, 3787.
91. Atherton,E. and Woodhouse,D., Cambridge Research Biochemicals Ltd, unpublished results.
92. Atherton,E. and Sheppard,R.C. (1985) *J. Chem. Soc., Chem. Comm.*, 165.
93. Atherton,E., Cameron,L.R. and Sheppard,R.C. (1988) *Tetrahedron,* **44**, 843.
94. Dryland,A. and Sheppard,R.C. (1988) *Tetrahedron,* **44**, 859.
95. Atherton,E., Glass,J.C., Matthews,B.H., Priestley,G.P., Richards,J.D., Sheppard,P.W. and Wade,W.A. (1988) *Proc. 10th Amer. Peptide Symp.*, Marshall,G.R. (ed.), ESCOM, Leiden, p. 267.
96. Heimer,E.P., Chang,C.D., Lambros,T. and Meienhofer,J. (1981) *Int. J. Peptide Prot. Res.*, **18**, 237.
97. Atherton,E., Cameron,L.R., Meldal,M. and Sheppard,R.C. (1986) *J. Chem. Soc., Chem. Comm.*, 1764.
98. Cameron,L.R., Meldal,M. and Sheppard,R.C. (1987) *J. Chem. Soc., Chem. Comm.*, 270.
99. Cameron,L.R., Holder,J.L., Meldal,M. and Sheppard,R.C. (1988) *J. Chem. Soc., Perkin Trans. 1,* 2895.
100. Kirstgen,R., Olbrich,A., Rehwinkel,R. and Steglich,W. (1988) *Annalen,* 437.
101. Kirstgen,R., Sheppard,R.C. and Steglich,W. (1987) *J. Chem. Soc., Chem. Comm.*, 1870.
102. Merrifield,R.B. (1969) *Adv. Enzymol.*, **32**, 221.
103. Loffet,A. and Close,J. (1968) In *Peptides 1968.* Bricas,E. (ed.), North Holland, Amsterdam, p. 189; Gut,V. and Rudinger,J. (1968) in *Peptides 1968*, Bricas,E. (ed.), North Holland, Amsterdam, p. 185.
104. Atherton,E., Hubscher,W., Sheppard,R.C. and Woolley,V. (1981) *Z. Physiol. Chem.*, **362**, 833.
105. Atherton,E., Caviezel,M., Fox,H., Harkiss,D., Over,H. and Sheppard,R.C. (1983) *J. Chem. Soc., Perkin Trans. 1,* 65; Barany,G. and Merrifield,R.B. in *The Peptides,* Gross,E. and Meienhofer,J. (eds), Academic Press, New York, Vol. 2, p. 156.
106. Sheppard,R.C. (1983) *Chem. Brit.*, 402.
107. Sheppard,R.C. (1988) *Chem. Brit.*, 557.
108. Kaiser,E., Colescott,R.L., Bossinger,C.D. and Cook,P.I. (1970) *Analyt. Biochem.*, **84**, 595.
109. Hancock,W.S. and Battersby,J.E. (1976) *Analyt. Biochem.*, **71**, 261.
110. Fischer,W. and Richards,J.D., personal communication; Kaiser,E., Bossinger,C.D., Colescott,R.L. and Olser,D.D. (1980) *Analyt. Chemica Acta,* **118**, 149.
111. Atherton,E., Bridger,J. and Sheppard,R.C. (1976) *FEBS Lett.*, **64**, 173.
112. Chen,S.-T., Chiou,S.-H., Chu,Y.-H., and Wang,K.-T. (1987) *Int. J. Peptide Prot. Res.*, **30**, 572.
113. Diamond,R. (1986) *J. Chem. Soc., Perkin Trans. 1,* 139.
114. Meldal,M., personal communication.
115. Goddard,P., unpublished.
116. Rule,W.K., Shen,J.H., Tregear,G.W. and Wade,J.D. (1988) *Proc. 20th European Peptide Symp.*, Tubingen, in press.
117. Knorr,R., Trzeciak,A., Bannwarth,W. and Gillessen,D. *Proc. 20th European Peptide Symp.*, Tubingen, 1988, in press.
118. Schallzenberg,E.E. and Calvin,M. (1955) *J. Amer. Chem. Soc.*, **77**, 2779.
119. Penke,B. and Rivier,J. (1987) *J. Org. Chem.*, **52**, 1197.
120. Albericio,F. and Barany,G. (1987), *Int. J. Peptide Prot. Chem.*, **30**, 206.
121. Sieber,P. (1987) *Tetrahedron Lett.*, **28**, 2107.
122. Dreipol,G., Knolle,J. and Stuber,W. (1987) *Tetrahedron Lett.*, **28**, 5651.
123. Funakoshi,S., Murayama,E., Guo,L., Fujii,N. and Yajima,H. (1988) *J. Chem. Soc., Chem. Comm.*, 382.
124. Hudson,D. (1988) *J. Org. Chem.*, **53**, 617.
125. Castro,B., Domoy,J.R., Evin,G. and Selve,C. (1975) *Tetrahedron Lett.*, **14**, 1219.
126. Dourtoglou,V., Zigler,J.C. and Gross,B. (1978) *Tetrahedron Lett.*, **15**, 1269.
127. Dourtoglou,V., Gross,B., Lambropoulou,V. and Ziodrou,C. (1984) *Synthesis,* 572.
128. Brown,E., Sheppard,R.C. and Williams,B.J. (1983) *J. Chem. Soc. Perkin 1,* 1161.
129. Atherton,E. and Sheppard,R.C., *Proc. 9th Amer. Peptide Symp.* Deber,C.M., Hruby,V.J. and Kopple,K.D. (eds), Pierce Chemical Co., Rockford, p. 249.
130. Ewan,G.B., Glaxo Research, personal communication.
131. Kitchen,J. and Seale,P., Glaxo Research, personal communication.
132. Atherton,E., Benoiton,N.L., Sheppard,R.C. and Williams,B.J. (1981) *J. Chem. Soc., Chem. Comm.*, 336.
133. Brown,E., Sheppard,R.C. and Williams,B.J. (1983) *J. Chem. Soc. Perkin 1,* 75.

134. Atherton,E., Cammish,L.E., Dryland,A., Goddard,P., Richards,J.D., Sheppard,R.C. and Wade,J.D., unpublished.
135. Marfey,P. (1984) *Carlsberg Res. Comm.*, **29**, 591.
136. Fujino,M., Wakimasu,M. and Kitada,E. (1981) *Chem. Pharm. Bull. Jap.*, **29**, 2825.
137. Johnson,T. and Nguyen,O.T., unpublished.

Appendix

1. *Abbreviations and nomenclature*

The use of three-letter amino acid symbols follows IUPAC practice, for example

	Gly	$H_2N\text{-}CH_2\text{-}CO_2H$
	-Gly-	$\text{-}NH\text{-}CH_2\text{-}CO\text{-}$
and hence	Ac-Gly-OMe	$CH_3CO\text{-}NHCH_2CO\text{-}OCH_3$

Side-chain substituents replace -H or -OH as appropriate, and are placed above the amino acid symbol or following it in parenthesis, for example

$$\overset{\displaystyle Bu^t}{\overset{|}{\text{Ser}}} \text{ or Ser}(Bu^t) \qquad\qquad H_2N\text{-}\overset{\displaystyle CH_2\text{-}OBu^t}{\overset{|}{C}}H\text{-}CO_2H$$

Protecting and activating groups are represented as radicals compatible with amino acid symbols.

Amino-protecting groups

Adoc-	Adamantyloxycarbonyl
Boc-	*t*-Butoxycarbonyl, $Me_3C\text{-}OCO\text{-}$
Bpoc	Biphenylisopropoxycarbonyl
Fmoc-	9-Fluorenylmethoxycarbonyl
Nps-	*o*-Nitrophenylsulphenyl
Phth>	Phthaloyl
Z-	Benzyloxycarbonyl, $C_6H_5CH_2\text{-}OCO\text{-}$
Tfa-	Trifluoroacetyl, $CF_3CO\text{-}$
Tos-	Toluene sulphonyl, $CH_3\text{-}C_6H_4\text{-}SO_2\text{-}$
Trt-	Triphenylmethyl, $(C_6H_5)_3C\text{-}$

Carboxy-protecting groups

$\text{-}OBu^t\text{-}$	*t*-Butoxy-, $\text{-}OCMe_3$
-OBzl	Benzyloxy-, $\text{-}OCH_2C_6H_5$
-OMe	Methoxy-, $\text{-}OCH_3$
-OEt	Ethoxy-, $\text{-}OC_2H_5$

Other side-chain-protecting groups

Acm-	Acetamidomethyl, $CH_3CO\text{-}NHCH_2\text{-}$
Bom-	Benzyloxymethyl, $C_6H_5CH_2OCH_2\text{-}$
Bum-	*t*-Butoxymethyl-, $Me_3COCH_2\text{-}$
$Bu^t\text{-}$	*t*-Butyl-, $Me_3C\text{-}$
Bzl-	Benzyl, $C_6H_5CH_2\text{-}$
Dnp-	2,4-Dinitrophenyl-
Mbh-	4,4-Dimethoxybenzhydryl-
Mbs-	4-Methoxybenzene sulphonyl-
Mds-	4-Methoxy-2,6-dimethylbenzene sulphonyl-
Mtr	4-Methoxy-2,3,6-trimethylbenzene sulphonyl-
Pmc	Pentamethylchroman sulphonyl-

Carboxyl activating groups are also abbreviated as radicals; the corresponding reagent is usually formed by appending a single hydrogen atom to the abbreviated radical. In the text, abbreviations are sometimes used informally, with the hyphens and linking atoms (-O- or -OH) omitted, for example 'Pfp esters', 'Dhbt esters' etc.

-OPfp	Pentafluorophenoxy- (pentafluorophenyl ester from HOPfp or PfpOH)
-OTcp	2,4,5-Trichlorophenoxy-
-OPcp	Pentachlorophenoxy-
-ONp	*p*-Nitrophenoxy-
-OBt	1-Benzotriazoleoxy- (from HOBt)
-ODhbt	3,4-Dihydro-4-oxo-benzotriazine-3-oxy- (from HODhbt or DhbtOH)
-OSu	Succinimidoxy-
-OTDO	2,3-Dihydro-2,5-diphenyl-3-oxo-thiophen-1,1-dioxide-4-oxy-

Miscellaneous reagents

AcOH	Acetic acid
t-AmOH	*t*-Amyl alcohol
BOP	Benzotriazolyloxy-trisdimethylaminophosphonium hexafluorophosphate
CHA	Cyclohexylamine
DCHA	Dicyclohexylamine
DCCI	Dicyclohexylcarbodiimide
DCM	Dichloromethane
DIEA	Diisopropylethylamine
DIPC	Diisopropylcarbodiimide
DMAP	4-Dimethylaminopyridine
DMA	Dimethylacetamide
DMF	Dimethylformamide
HBTU	Benzotriazolyloxytetramethyluronium hexafluorophosphate
HMPA	4-Hydroxymethylphenoxyacetic acid
HMBA	4-Hydroxymethylbenzoic acid
HMMPA	4-Hydroxymethyl-3-methoxyphenoxyacetic acid
TEA	Triethylamine
TFA	Trifluoroacetic acid

Miscellaneous

hplc	High-performance liquid chromatography
fab-ms	Fast atom bombardment mass spectroscopy
ptfe	Polytetrafluoroethylene
tlc	Thin-layer chromatography

2. *Molecular weights*

2.1 *Amino acid derivatives*

	Fmoc amino acid	*Pfp ester*	*Dhbt ester*
Ala	311.3	477.4	456.5
Arg	396.4	562.5	541.6
Arg(Mtr)	608.7	774.8	753.8
Asn	354.4	520.4	499.6
Asn(Mbh)	580.6	746.7	725.8
Asp(OBu^t)	411.5	577.5	556.7
Cys(Acm)	414.4	580.5	559.6
Cys(But)	399.5	565.6	544.7
Cys(Trt)	585.7	751.8	730.9
Gln	368.4	534.4	513.6
Gln(Mbh)	594.4	760.5	739.6
Glu(OBu^t)	425.5	591.5	570.7
Gly	297.3	463.4	442.5
His(Fmoc)	599.6	765.7	744.8
His(Boc)	477.5	643.6	622.7
Ile	353.4	519.5	498.6
Leu	353.4	519.5	498.6
Lys(Boc)	468.6	634.6	613.8
Met	371.5	537.5	516.7
Nle	353.4	519.5	498.6
Orn(Boc)	454.5	620.6	599.7
Phe	387.4	553.5	532.6
Pro	337.4	503.4	482.6
Ser(Bu^t)	383.4	549.5	528.6
Thr(Bu^t)	397.5	563.6	542.6
Trp	426.5	592.5	571.7
Tyr(Bu^t)	459.5	625.6	604.7
Val	339.4	505.4	484.6

2.2 *Reagents*

4-(α-Fmoc-amino-2′,4′-dimethoxybenzyl)phenoxyacetic acid	539.6
4-Hydroxymethylphenoxyacetic acid	182.2
4-hydroxymethylbenzoic acid	152.2
4-Hydroxymethyl-3-methoxyphenoxyacetic acid	212.2
4-Hydroxymethylphenoxyacetic acid pentafluorophenyl ester	348.3
4-hydroxymethylbenzoic acid pentafluorophenyl ester	318.3
4-Hydroxymethyl-3-methoxyphenoxyacetic acid pentafluorophenyl ester	378.3
9-Fluorenylmethoxycarbonyl-succinimide	337.3
1-Hydroxybenzotriazole monohydrate	153.1
3,4-Dihydro-3-hydroxy-4-oxobenzotriazine	163.2
Dicyclohexylcarbodiimide	206.3
Diisopropylcarbodiimide	126.2
4-Dimethylaminopyridine	122.2

3. *Equipment and chemical suppliers*

Anachem Ltd Anachem House 20 Charles Street Luton Beds LU2 0EB UK	Ptfe valves, tubing, and connectors
Bachem Feinchemikalien AG Haupstrasse 144 CH-4416 Bubendorf-Schweiz Switzerland	Protected amino acids
Bachem Inc 3132 Kashiwa Street Torrance Ca 90505 USA	Protected amino acids
Beckman Instruments (UK) Ltd Progress Road Sands Industrial Estate High Wycombe Bucks HP12 4JL UK	Ptfe valves
Biodata Lower Ormond Street Manchester M1 5QF UK	Computer control interfaces
Cambridge Research Biochemicals Ltd Button End Industrial Estate Harston Cambridge UK	Custom peptide synthesis
Dosapro Milton Roy 27360 Pont-Saint-Pierre Boite Postale No. 5 France	Pumps
Fluka AG Chemische Fabrik 9470 Buchs SG Switzerland	Chemical reagents
Milligen Biosearch 11–15 Peterborough Road Harrow Middlesex HA1 2YH UK	Peptide synthesizers and reagents

Milton Roy-LDC Milton Roy House 52 High Street Stone Staffordshire ST15 8AR UK	Pumps
Novabiochem (UK) Ltd Heathcoat Buildings Highfields Science Park University Boulevard Nottingham NG7 3TT UK	Protected and activated amino acids, resins, and other reagents
Omnifit Ltd 51 Norfolk Street Cambridge CB1 2LD UK	Ptfe valves, tubing, connectors, and reactor columns
Pharmacia LKB Biochrom Ltd Cambridge Science Park Milton Road Cambridge CB4 4FJ UK	Peptide synthesizers and reagents
RS Components Ltd (Radiospares) PO Box 99 Corby Northants NN17 9RS UK	Electronic components
Sterling Organics Ltd Hadrian House Fawdon Newcastle upon Tyne NE3 3TT UK	Macrosorb SPR resins
Technicol Ltd Brook Street Higher Hillgate Stockport Cheshire SK1 3HS UK	Vydac hplc resin
Valeader Engineering Ltd Pneumatic Equipment Distributors Unit 19 Coral Park Estate Henley Road Cambridge UK	Pneumatic pistons, etc.

INDEX

S-Acetamidomethyl-cysteine, 7, 60
Acetylation, 136
Acryloylsarcosine methyl ester, 39, 41
Activated esters, 9
  preparation of 10, 76
Activation of Fmoc-amino acids, 75
Adamantyloxycarbonyl, 3
Aggregation effects, 28, 117, 141
p-Alkoxybenzyl alcohol polystyrene, 19
Amino acid analysis, 109
Amino-protecting groups, 3
Aminoethyl polydimethylacrylamide, 132
Ammonolysis of peptide–resin linkage, 149, 152
Analogue to digital conversion, 113
Analytical control, 107
Anhydrides, 9
Anion-exchange chromatography, 159, 168, 173, 177, 182
Area integration of deprotection peaks, 119
Arginine, side-chain protection, 7
Arginine lactam, 7
Arginine(Mtr), interaction with tryptophan residues, 177
Attachment of the first amino acid using TDO esters, 136
Attachment of the first amino acid, 134

Beaded gel resins, reaction protocol for use of, 138
Benzhydrylamine linkage, 66, 72, 174
Benzotriazolyloxytetramethyluronium hexafluorophosphate, 85, 174, 176
Benzotriazolyloxytrisdimethylaminophosphonium hexafluorophosphate, 84
S-Benzlcysteine, 19
Benzyloxycarbonyl derivatives, 3, 13
Biolynx, 41, 70, 75, 92, 104, 186
Biphenylisopropoxycarbonyl, 3
Bis-Fmoc-histidine, 55
Bisacryloylethylene diamine, 40
Boc-Alanyloxymethylphenylpropionic acid 2,4,5-trichlorophenyl ester, 72
Boc-γ-Benzyl-glutamyloxymethylphenylpropionic acid 2,4,5-trichlorophenyl ester, 72
Boc-Glycyloxymethylphenylpropionic acid 2,4,5-trichlorophenyl ester, 71
Boc-Phenylalanyloxymethylphenylpropionic acid 2,4,5-trichlorophenyl ester, 72
BOP reagent, 84
'Bubbler' system for solid phase synthesis, 88
Bradykinin, solid phase synthesis, 13
2-Bromobenzyl-tyrosine, 19
4-Bromomethylbenzoic acid, 70
t-Butoxycarbonyl derivatives, 3, 13, 16, 17
S-*t*-Butyl-cysteine, 7
t-Butyl-cysteine, 7, 60
S-*t*-Butylsulphenyl-cysteine, 7, 60

Capping of unreacted hydroxyl groups, 136
Carbodiimides, 9, 21
  water-soluble, 11
Carboxymethyl cellulose, 158
Carboxy-protecting groups, 4
Cation-exchange chromatography, 158
Chiral amino acids, 11
Chloromethylation (of polystyrene), 17
3-(4-Chloromethylphenyl)propionic acid, 60
Cleavage of Fmoc groups,
  mechanism of, 115
Cleavage of peptide from support, 22, 149
Colour tests (for residual amino groups), 108
Continuous-flow protocols, 140
Continuous-flow synthesis,
  automatic system, 93
  manual system, 90, 91
Cro repressor protein, 183
Curve fitting of acylation profiles, 121
β-Cyanoalanine, 21
Cysteine, side-chain protection, 7, 60

Deprotection reactions, spectrometric monitoring of, 115
Dhbt esters, 9, 78, 123
2,6-Dichlorobenzyloxycarbonyl-lysine, 19
Dichloromethane, purification of, 35
Dicyclohexylcarbodiimide, 9, 20, 75
  purification of, 37
Dicyclohexylurea, 20
Diethylaminoethyl cellulose, 159
3,4-Dihydro-3-hydroxy-4-oxo-1,2,3-benzotriazine, 9
3,4-Dihydro-4-oxo-1,2,3-benzotriazinyl esters, 9
Diisopropylcarbodiimide, 20
Diisopropylethylamine, purification of, 37
Dimethylacrylamide, 40
Dimethylaminopyridine, purification of, 37
α, α-Dimethyl-3,5-dimethoxybenzyloxycarbonyl carbonyl derivatives, 16
Dimethylformamide, purification of, 35
3,5-Dimethoxyphenylisopropoxycarbonyl derivatives, 17, 71
Dipeptide formation in esterification, 164, 167
Dipolar character of amino acids, 2
Disulphide bond formation, 182

Esterification of the first amino acid to the resin, 134
Ethylene diamine, purification of, 37

Fining of resins, 140
Flow cell thickness, 92, 112
Fluorenylmethoxycarbonyl-protecting group, 3, 31, 47
Fluorenylmethoxycarbonyl-amino acid anhydrides, 75, 117

Fluorenylmethoxycarbonyl-amino acid
Dhbt esters, 78, 123
Fluorenylmethoxycarbonyl-amino acid
pentafluorophenyl esters, 50, 76
Fluorenylmethoxycarbonyl-amino acid
TDO esters, 82, 136
Fluorenylmethoxycarbonyl-amino acids, 50
Fmoc-S-acetamidomethyl-cysteine, 60
Fmoc-S-acetamidomethyl-cysteine Dhbt ester, 82
4-(α-Fmoc-amino-2′,4′-dimethoxybenzyl) phenoxyacetic acid, 73
Fmoc-arginine derivatives, 56
Fmoc-asparagine, 49
Fmoc-asparagine Dhbt ester, 81
Fmoc-N_{im}-Boc-histidine, 56
stability of Boc group in, 116
Fmoc-N_{im}-Boc-histidine Dhbt ester, 82
Fmoc-N_{ϵ}-Boc-lysine Dhbt ester, 80
Fmoc-S-*t*-butyl-cysteine, 61
Fmoc-γ-*t*-butyl-glutamate, 52
Fmoc-γ-*t*-butyl-glutamate TDO ester, 84
Fmoc-S-*t*-butylsulphenyl-cysteine, 60
Fmoc-O-*t*-butyl threonine, 52
Fmoc-cysteine derivatives, 59
Fmoc-glycine Dhbt ester, 80
Fmoc-histidine derivatives, 54
Fmoc-isoleucine, 51
Fmoc-leucine pentafluorophenyl ester, 78
Fmoc-lysine derivatives, 53
Fmoc-methionine, 51
Fmoc-N_G-Mtr-arginine, 57
Fmoc-N_G-Mtr-arginine Dhbt ester, 81
Fmoc-N_G-Mtr-arginine pentafluorophenyl ester, 78
Fmoc-norleucyl-polydimethylacrylamide resin, 133
Fmoc-polyamide synthesis, 25
Fmoc-N_{ϵ}-trifluoroacetyl-lysine, 53
Fmoc-S-trityl-cysteine, 60
Fmoc-valine, 49
Formation of the peptide bond, 8, 20
4-Formylphenoxyacetic acid, 67

Gastrin, 168
Glutamine residues, cyclization of, 168
Glutamine, as carboxy-terminal residue, 174
Guanidino group, pK_a, 7

Histidine, side-chain protection, 7, 54
Hplc analysis of intermediate peptides, 111
Hydrolysis (of samples for
amino acid analysis), 110
Hydrazinolysis of peptide–resin linkage, 149, 152
Hydrogen fluoride, 22
Hydroxyamino acids, side-chain protection, 7
Hydroxybenzotriazole, 8
purification of, 37
Hydroxybenzotriazolyl esters, 9
4-Hydroxymethylbenzoic acid, 70
4-Hydroxymethylbenzoic acid 2,4,5-
trichlorophenyl ester, 70
3-(4-Hydroxymethylphenyl)propionic acid, 67
3-(4-Hydroxymethylphenyl)propionic acid 2,4,5-
trichlorophenyl ester, 67
4-Hydroxymethylphenoxyacetic acid, 68
4-Hydroxymethylphenoxyacetic acid
Dhbt ester, 68
4-Hydroxymethylphenoxyacetic acid
pentafluorophenyl ester, 68
4-Hydroxymethylphenoxyacetic acid 2,4,5-
trichlorophenyl ester, 68
p-Hydroxyphenylacetic acid, 18
Hydroxysuccinimide esters, 9, 32

Instrumentation, 87
Internal reference amino acid, 132
Ion-exchange chromatography, 158
Isatin colour test, 109

Kaiser reaction, 33, 108
Kieselguhr-supported resins, reaction protocols
for use of, 140

Linearity correction, 119
Linkage agents, 18, 63
addition of to resin, 133
Low–high HF cleavage, 22

Macroporous Kieselguhr, 44
Macrosorb, 44
Macrosorb SPR, 45
MCH, 177
Melanin concentrating hormone, 177
Merrifield reaction vessel, 89
Merrifield technique, 13, 22
Methanolysis of peptide–resin linkage, 154
Methionine residues, fragmentation of
during cleavage, 151
S-*p*-Methoxybenzyl-cysteine, 19
S-*p*-Methylbenzyl-cysteine, 19
3-Methoxy-4-formylphenoxyacetic acid, 69, 184
3-Methoxy-4-hydroxymethylphenoxyacetic acid, 69
3-Methoxy-4-hydroxymethylphenoxyacetic acid
pentafluorophenyl ester, 70
Methoxytrimethylbenzene sulphonyl, 7, 57
Milligen 9020 synthesiser, 99
Milligen 9050 synthesiser, 105
Mtr-protecting group, 7, 57

Ninhydrin colour test, 33, 108
Nitro-arginine, 20
Nitrobenzyl ester linkage, 13
3-Nitro-4-bromomethylbenzoic acid, 71
3-Nitro-4-hydroxymethylbenzoic acid, 71
3-Nitro-4-hydroxymethylbenzoic acid
2,4,5-trichlorophenyl ester, 71
Nucleophilic cleavage of peptide–resin linkage, 152

Overactivation, 8
Oxazolones, 11
4-(α-Oximino-2′,4′-dimethoxybenzyl)
phenoxyacetic acid, 73
4-(α-Oxo-2′,4′-dimethoxybenzyl)phenol, 72
4-(α-Oxo-2′,4′-dimethoxybenzyl)
phenoxyacetic acid, 73

PAM–resin, 17
Penicillinase, C-terminal dodecapeptide
analogue of, 163
Pentafluorophenyl esters, 32
Pepsyn, 39
Pepsyn K, 45
PEPSYNthesiser, 92
PEPSYNthesiser II, 98
Peptide cleavage, 149
Peptide purification, 149
Physically supported resins, 44
Piperidine, purification of, 37
Polydimethylacrylamide, 39, 43
Polystyrene, 16
Preparative reverse-phase chromatography, 160
Protected peptide, synthesis of, 183
Protecting groups, 2
permanent, 2
temporary, 2
Protocols, 131
Pumps, 92
Purification of reagents, 34
Purification of synthetic peptides, 156
Pyroglutamyl derivatives 6, 168
Pyrrolidonecarbonyl derivatives, 6, 168

Racemization, 11, 134, 164, 167
during attachment of the first amino acid, 134
Rates of acylation, 29
Reaction procedures, 131
for beaded gel resins, 138
for continuous-flow synthesis, 140, 143, 145
Reaction vessel, 88
Reactor columns, 92
packing of, 140, 142
Reagent purification, 34
Resins,
fining of, 131, 140
packing of, 140
preliminary swelling of, 131
reaction of with ethylene diamine, 110, 132

Sarcosine methyl ester hydrochloride, 41
Scavenging agents in cleavage reactions,
17, 151, 154
Segment condensation, 1
Side-chain protecting groups, 5
Solid phase monitoring, 122
Solid phase photometer, 125
Solid phase principle, 14
Solid supports, 16, 39
Solvation (of polymer supports), 28
Solvent effects in acylation, 29
Spectrometric monitoring, 107, 112, 117
Spectrometric record, 113
Succinimide derivatives, 6
Symmetrical anhydrides, 9, 20, 32
preparation of, 10, 75

TDO esters of Fmoc-amino acids, 82, 136
p-Toluene sulphonyl, 4
p-Toluene sulphonyl-arginine, 20
Trifluoroacetic acid,
purification of, 37
use of in cleavage of peptide–resin linkage,
150, 154
Trifluoromethane sulphonic acid, 23
Trimethylsilyl bromide, 151
Trimethylsilyl trifluoromethane sulphonate, 151
Trinitrobenzene sulphonic acid colour test, 108
Triphenylmethyl, 4
Trityl, 4
Tryptophan, as carboxy-terminal residue, 163
Tryptophan peptides, reattachment of
during cleavage, 151

Urethanes, 3

Wang resin, 19

Zwitterions, 2